Standardized Service Contract
"Services within the same service inventory are in compliance with the same contract design standards."

Service Loose Coupling
"Service contracts impose low consumer coupling requirements and are themselves decoupled from their surrounding environment."

Service Abstraction
"Service contracts only contain essential information and information about services is limited to what is published in service contracts."

Service Reusability
"Services contain and express agnostic logic and can be positioned as reusable enterprise resources."

Service Autonomy
"Services exercise a high level of control over their underlying runtime execution environment."

Service Statelessness
"Services minimize resource consumption by deferring the management of state information when necessary."

Service Discoverability
"Services are supplemented with communicative meta data by which they can be effectively discovered and interpreted."

Service Composability
"Services are effective composition participants, regardless of the size and complexity of the composition."

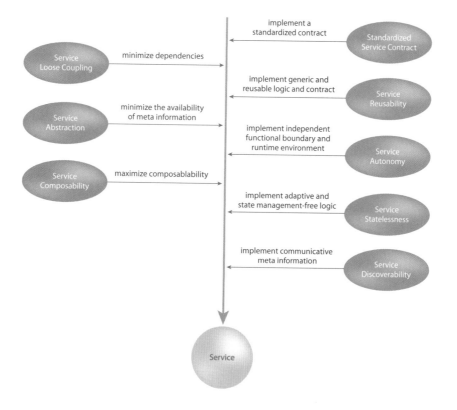

Praise for This Book

"An absolute pleasure to read…the best SOA book I've read.

A book I would recommend to all of my colleagues; it provides much insight to the topics often overlooked by most books in this genre…the visuals were fantastic."

—*Brandon Bohling, SOA Architecture and Strategy, Intel Corporation*

"I recommend this book to any SOA practitioner who wishes to empower themselves in making service design real…gives readers the 360° view into service design [and] gives SOA practitioners the depth and understanding needed into the principles of SOA to assist in the design of a mature and successful SOA program."

—*Stephen G. Bennett, Americas SOA Practice Lead, BEA Systems*

"There are few references for SOA that give you the nuts and bolts and this one is at the top of the list. Well written and valuable as a reference book to any SOA practitioner."

—*Dr. Mohamad Afshar, Director of Product Management,*
Oracle Fusion Middleware, Oracle Corporation

"A very clear discussion of the subject matter. Provides a good structure that facilitates understanding and readily highlights key points."

—*Kareem Yusuf, Director of SOA Strategy and Planning, IBM Software Group*

"This book does a great job laying out benefits, key ideas and design principles behind successfully adopting service-oriented computing. At the same time, the book openly addresses challenges, risks and trade-offs that are in the way of adopting SOA in the real-world today. It moves away from ivory-tower views of service orientation, but still lays out a strong vision for SOA and outlines the changes necessary to realize the full potential."

—*Christoph Schittko, Senior Architect, Microsoft*

"This book strikes a healthy balance between theory and practice. It is a perfect complement to the SOA series by the author."

—*Prakash Narayan, Sun Microsystems*

"This book could be described as an encyclopedia of service design—Erl leaves nothing to chance. Indispensable."

—*Steve Birkel, Chief IT Technical Architect, Intel Corp.*

"I liked this book. It contains extremely important material for those who need to design services."

—*Farzin Yashar, IBM SOA Advanced Technologies*

"Thomas Erl's books are always densely filled with information that's well structured. This book is especially insightful for Enterprise Architects because it provide s great context and practical examples. Part 1 of the book alone is worth getting the book for."

—*Markus Zirn, Senior Director, Product Management,*
Oracle Fusion Middleware, Oracle Corporation

"This book is a milestone in SOA literature. For the first time we are provided with a practical guide on defining service characteristics and service design principles for SOA from a vendor-agnostic viewpoint. It's a great reference for SOA discovery, adoptions, and implementation projects."

—*Canyang Kevin Liu, Principal Enterprise Architect, SAP Americas, Inc.*

"There are very few who understand SOA like Thomas Erl does! The principle centric description of service orientation from Thomas canonizes the underpinnings of this important paradigm shift in creating agile and reusable software capabilities. The principles, so eloquently explained, leave little room for any ambiguity attached to the greater purpose of SOA. Most organizations today are creating services in a bottoms-up approach, realizing composition and reuse organically. The time is ripe for a book like this that prepares architects for a principle centric approach to SOA."

—*Hanu Kommalapati, Architect, Microsoft Corporation*

"If you are going to be designing, developing, or implementing SOA, this is a must have book."

—*Jason "AJ" Comfort Sr., Booz Allen Hamilton*

"An excellent book for anyone who wants to understand service-orientation and the principles involved in designing services…a clear, concise and articulate exploration of the eight design principles involved in analyzing, designing, implementing, and maintaining services…"

—Anish Karmarkar, Oracle Corporation

"Very well written, succinct, and easy to understand."

—Raj Balasubramanian, IBM Software Group

"A thorough examination of the considerations of service design. Both seasoned SOA practitioners and those endeavoring to realize services can benefit from reading this book."

—Bill Draven, Enterprise Architect, Intel Corporation

"I am very impressed. Comprehensive. Educative. This book helped me to step back and look at the SOA principles from broader perspective. I'd say this is a must-read book for SOA stakeholders."

—Radovan Janecek, Director R&D, SOA Center, Hewlett-Packard

"A comprehensive exploration of the issues of service design which has the potential to become the definitive work in this area."

—James Pasley, Chief Technology Officer, Cape Clear Software

"SOA projects are most successful when they are based on a solid technical foundation. Well accepted and established design principles are part of this foundation. This book takes a very structured approach at defining the core design principles for SOA, thus allowing the reader to immediately applying them to a project. Each principle is formally introduced and explained, and examples are given for how to apply it to a real design problem. A 'must read' for any architect, designer or developer of service oriented solutions".

—Andre Tost, Senior Technical Staff Member, IBM Software Group

"This is the book for the large organization trying to rationalize its IT assets and establish an agile platform for the future. By highlighting risk and rewards, Thomas Erl brings clarity to how Service Orientation can be applied to ensure a responsive IT organization. This book finally brings software engineering principles to address the real world development challenges being faced.

To effectively serve the business, let alone embrace SOA, everyone involved should be familiar with the concepts investigated here. Thomas Erl thoroughly clarifies the nuances and defines the practice of service design.

We expect that this will become a classic text in software engineering, corporate training and colleges."

—Cory Isaacson, President, Rogue Wave Software and Ravi Palepu,
SOA Author and Speaker

"Thomas Erl does a great job...an easy read."

—Michael H. Sor, Booz Allen Hamilton

"...a must read for SOA Architects to develop a firm foundation and understanding of the principles (and trade-offs) that make up a good SOA service.

After reading this book, it finally 'clicked' as to why a properly designed SOA system is different (and better) than a system based on previous enterprise architectures."

—Fred Ingham, Platinum Solutions Inc.

"Lays a tremendous foundation for business and technical workers to come to common terms and expectations...incredibly enlightening to see the details associated with achieving the SOA vision."

—Wayne P. Ariola, Vice President of Strategy, Parasoft

"[Erl does] and excellent job of addressing the breadth of [his] audience to present to those new to SOA and weaved in enough detail to assist those who are already actively involved in SOA development."

—R. Perry Smith, Application Program Manager, EDS/OnStar

"It is easy to miss the big picture of what SOA means for the design of larger scale systems amidst the details of WS technologies. Erl helps provide a broader perspective, surveying the landscape from a design standpoint."

—*Jim Clune, Chief Architect, Parasoft*

"Lays a firm foundation for the underlying principles of good service design. Cuts through the hype and provides a cogent resource for improving architectural judgment on SOA projects."

—*Jim Murphy, Vice President of Product Management, Mindreef, Inc.*

"The first book to concisely, gradually and comprehensively explain how to apply SOA principles into enterprise-level software design. It is an excellent book."

—*Robin G. Qiu, Ph.D., Division of Engineering and Information Science, Pennsylvania State University*

"I really think that this is a very useful book that a lot of people really need out there in the industry."

—*Dr. Arnaud Simon, Principal Software Engineer, Red Hat*

"…indispensable companion to designing and implementing a service-oriented architecture. It condenses all information necessary to design services and is the most relevant source I know if in the field."

"[This book is] not only helpful, but fundamental to successfully designing an SOA."

—*Phillipp Offermann, Research Analyst, University of Berlin*

"Service-Oriented Architecture is an important topic in IT today. Its vast scope could span an organization's enterprise. Designing it properly is a major undertaking. This book provides timely, expert and comprehensive discussions on the principles of service design. Thomas has a keen sense in identifying the subtle points of various subjects and explains them in an easy-to-understand way. The book is a valuable resource for IT professionals working in SOA."

—*Peter H. Chang, PhD, Associate Professor of Information Systems, Lawrence Technological University*

SOA: Principles of Service Design

The Prentice Hall Service-Oriented Computing Series from Thomas Erl aims to provide the IT industry with a consistent level of unbiased, practical, and comprehensive guidance and instruction in the areas of service-oriented architecture, service-orientation, and the expanding landscape that is shaping the real-world service-oriented computing platform.

For more information, visit www.soabooks.com.

SOA
Principles of Service Design

Thomas Erl

PRENTICE HALL

UPPER SADDLE RIVER, NJ • BOSTON • INDIANAPOLIS • SAN FRANCISCO

NEW YORK • TORONTO • MONTREAL • LONDON • MUNICH • PARIS • MADRID

CAPETOWN • SYDNEY • TOKYO • SINGAPORE • MEXICO CITY

Many of the designations used by manufacturers and sellers to distinguish their products are claimed as trademarks. Where those designations appear in this book, and the publisher was aware of a trademark claim, the designations have been printed with initial capital letters or in all capitals.

The author and publisher have taken care in the preparation of this book, but make no expressed or implied warranty of any kind and assume no responsibility for errors or omissions. No liability is assumed for incidental or consequential damages in connection with or arising out of the use of the information or programs contained herein.

The publisher offers excellent discounts on this book when ordered in quantity for bulk purchases or special sales, which may include electronic versions and/or custom covers and content particular to your business, training goals, marketing focus, and branding interests. For more information, please contact:

> U.S. Corporate and Government Sales
> (800) 382-3419
> corpsales@pearsontechgroup.com

For sales outside the United States please contact:

> International Sales
> international@pearsoned.com

This Book Is Safari Enabled

The Safari® Enabled icon on the cover of your favorite technology book means the book is available through Safari Bookshelf. When you buy this book, you get free access to the online edition for 45 days.

Safari Bookshelf is an electronic reference library that lets you easily search thousands of technical books, find code samples, download chapters, and access technical information whenever and wherever you need it.

To gain 45-day Safari Enabled access to this book:

- Go to http://www.prenhallprofessional.com/safarienabled
- Complete the brief registration form
- Enter the coupon code ERHG-JTFH-BJHN-RFHR-4I87

If you have difficulty registering on Safari Bookshelf or accessing the online edition, please e-mail customer-service@safaribooksonline.com.

Visit us on the Web: www.prenhallprofessional.com

Library of Congress Cataloging-in-Publication Data

Erl, Thomas.
  SOA: principles of service design / Thomas Erl.
      p. cm.
  ISBN 0-13-234482-3 (hardback : alk. paper) 1. Web services. 2. Computer architecture. 3. System analysis. 4. System design. I. Title.
  TK5105.88813.E75 2008
  004.2'2—dc22

ISBN-13: 9780132344821
ISBN-10: 0132344823
Text printed in the United States on recycled paper at R.R. Donnelley in Crawfordsville, Indiana.
Second printing November, 2007

Editor-in-Chief
Mark L. Taub

Managing Editor
Gina Kanouse

Senior Project Editor
Kristy Hart

Copy Editor
Language Logistics, LLC

Senior Indexer
Cheryl Lenser

Proofreader
Williams Woods Publishing

Publishing Coordinator
Noreen Regina

Compositor
Jake McFarland

Cover Designer
Thomas Erl

Graphics
Zuzana Cappova
Spencer Fruhling

Photos
Thomas Erl

To my wife and family for their support.

Contents

Chapter 2: Case Study 19

PART I: FUNDAMENTALS

Chapter 3: Service-Oriented Computing and SOA 25

PART II: DESIGN PRINCIPLES

PART III: SUPPLEMENTAL

Chapter 14: Service-Orientation and Object-Orientation: A Comparison of Principles and Concepts 445

Chapter 16: Mapping Service-Orientation Principles to Strategic Goals. 497

PART IV: APPENDICES

Appendix A: Case Study Conclusion. 513

Appendix B: Process Descriptions 517

Preface

Over the past few years I've been exposed to many different IT environments as part of a wide range of SOA initiatives for clients in both private and public sectors. While doing some work on a project for a client in the defense industry, I had an opportunity to learn more about not just their technical landscape, but also the various policies and procedures that are specific to the defense culture. During this time I came across the DoD Standardization Program, an initiative comprised of documents and specifications that establish guiding principles and standards for various aspects of the military, including the design of weapons and military equipment, as well as the definition of methods and processes used by military personnel.

While reading about this program, I learned that several other standardization programs have been in existence for some time, facilitating standardization within public sector organizations (such as the Coast Guard and NASA), as well as numerous private sector industries. The goals of these programs tend to revolve around the establishment of industry standards to enhance interoperability with the ultimate objective of reducing operational overhead, reducing risk, and increasing the organization's overall effectiveness.

In the case of the aforementioned public sector-related standards, interoperability may refer to the exchange of equipment or weapons or the exchange and collaboration of personnel from different locations.

For example, an ammunition clip manufactured in Iowa, stored in Virginia, and delivered to and used by someone at a training base in Texas will work perfectly with a gun manufactured in Kansas because both of these products were built according to the same set of specifications. Similarly, in response to a natural disaster a rescue team may need to be quickly assembled from individuals based out of different cities and who have never previously worked together. This team can still function effectively because all team members were trained as per the same procedures and processes, using the same vocabulary and conventions.

These standardization programs have much in common with the rationale and objectives behind SOA and service-orientation. The fundamental goal is to produce something with repeatable value, long-term benefit, and inherent flexibility, all for the strategic good of the organization. The greatest obstacle to achieving this goal in the world of SOA has been a lack of understanding as to what service-orientation, as an industry paradigm, really is. It is my hope that this book will help rectify this situation by providing some clarity for what it means for something to be "service-oriented."

Acknowledgments

To ensure the accuracy and legitimacy of the content in this book, I decided early on to subject it to a rigorous quality assurance process that involved technical reviews by over 60 industry professionals. I am deeply grateful for the time and effort these individuals dedicated to these reviews. Specifically, I would like to thank Kevin Davis, PhD, Ronald Bourret, Robert Schneider, Ravi Palepu, Wes McGregor, Judith Myerson, and Cyrille Thilloy for their early feedback, and the following technical reviewers that participated in the full manuscript review (in alphabetical order by last name):

Dr. Mohamad Afshar, Oracle Corporation

Wayne Ariola, Parasoft

Raj Balasubramanian, IBM Software Group

Stephen Bennett, BEA Systems, Inc.

Steve Birkel, Intel Corporation

Brandon Bohling, Intel Corporation

Peter Chang, PhD, Lawrence Technological University

Robin Chen, PhD, Google, Inc.

Jim Clune, Parasoft

Jason "AJ" Comfort Sr., Booz Allen Hamilton, Inc.

Bill Draven, Intel Corporation

Darryl Hogan, Microsoft Corporation

Continues

Fred Ingham, Platinum Solutions Inc.

Cory Isaacson, Rogue Wave Software

Radovan Janecek, Hewlett-Packard

Anish Karmarkar, Oracle Corporation

Hanu Kommalapati, Microsoft Corporation

Robert Laird, IBM EAI/SOA Advanced Technologies Group

Dr. Mark Little, Redhat

Canyang Kevin Liu, SAP Americas, Inc.

David Michalowicz, MITRE Corporation

Jim Murphy, Mindreef, Inc.

Prakash Narayan, Sun Microsystems

Philipp Offermann, University of Berlin

James Pasley, Cape Clear Software

Robin G. Qiu, PhD, Pennsylvania State University

Christoph Schittko, Microsoft Corporation

Dr. Arnaud Simon, Redhat

R. Perry Smith, EDS/OnStar

Michael H. Sor, Booz Allen Hamilton, Inc.

Philip Thomas, IBM United Kingdom Limited

Andre Tost, IBM Software Group

Sameer Tyagi, Fidelity Investments

Umit Yalcinalp, SAP

Farzin Yashar, IBM SOA Advanced Technologies

Kareem Yusuf, IBM Software Group

Markus Zirn, Oracle Corporation

Chapter 1

Introduction

L earning from one's mistakes is one of the most essential principles of life. As the old saying goes, "One cannot achieve success without failure." When I hear that saying I sometimes mentally append it with "…unless one happens to be lucky." While there may be some truth to this, the fact is that luck is not something we want to ever have to depend on when building service-oriented architecture (SOA). Optimistic project plans or risk assessments qualified with "…as long as we get lucky" won't have much success instilling confidence (or receiving funding).

A personal mantra of mine that has emerged from involvement in numerous SOA projects preaches that "the key to successfully doing something is in successfully understanding what you're doing." Again, disregarding the luck factor, this philosophy is very relevant to service-oriented computing and forms the basis and purpose of this book.

The content provided in the upcoming chapters is intended to help you become a "true" SOA professional. By that I mean someone who has a clear vision of what it means for a software program to be "service-oriented," who can speak about service-oriented computing from a real-world perspective, and who approaches the design of services with a deep insight into the dynamics behind service-orientation.

Furthermore, such an individual requires the ability to assess options in technology, design, development, delivery, and governance—all important success factors in SOA initiatives. What this translates into for the SOA professional is a need for an increased level of judgment.

Judgment can be seen as a combination of common sense plus a sound knowledge of whatever is being judged. In the world of SOA projects, this points to two specific areas: a need to understand service-oriented computing with absolute clarity and a need to understand your own environments, constraints, and strategic goals just as well. With this range of knowledge, you can leverage what the service-oriented computing platform has to offer in order to fulfill your strategic goals within whatever boundaries you are required to operate.

In theory this makes sense, but there is still something important missing from this formula. Nothing helps raise the level of one's judgment more than actual experience. There's no better way to truly appreciate the strategic potential of service-oriented

computing and the spectrum of challenges that come with its adoption, than to person-
ally go through the motions of a typical enterprise SOA project. This book can't replace
real-world experience, but it strives to be the next best thing.

1.1 Objectives of this Book

The focus of this book is first and foremost on the design of services for SOA. There is a
constant emphasis on how and where design principles can and should be applied with
the ultimate goal of producing high quality services.

Specifically, this book has the following objectives:

- to clearly establish the criteria for solution logic to be classified as
  "service-oriented"

- to provide complete coverage of the service-orientation design paradigm

- to document specific design characteristics realized by the application of
  individual design principles

- to describe how the application of each principle affects others

- to explain the link between the design characteristics realized by service-
  orientation and the strategic goals associated with SOA and service-oriented
  computing

- to establish the origins of service-orientation and identify how this paradigm
  differs from other design approaches

Essentially, this guide intends to provide practical, comprehensive, and in-depth coverage of the service-orientation design paradigm, which encompasses the official definition and detailed explanation of eight key principles, each of which is explored in a
separate chapter.

1.2 Who this Book Is For

As a guide dedicated to service design, this book will be useful to IT professionals interested in or involved with technology architecture, systems analysis, and solution design.

Specifically, this book will be helpful to developers, analysts, and architects who:

- want to know how to design services for SOA so that they fully support the goals
  and benefits of service-oriented computing

- want to understand the service-orientation design paradigm

- want to learn about how SOA and service-orientation relate to and can be implemented through Web services

- want in-depth guidance for designing different types of services

- want an understanding of how services need to be designed in support of complex service aggregation and composition

- want to learn about design considerations that apply not just to the entire service, but also to individual service capabilities

- want to better comprehend how services can and should relate to each other

- want deep insight into how service contracts should be shaped in support of service-orientation

- want to know how to determine the appropriate levels of service, capability, data, and constraint granularity

- want an awareness of how WSDL, XML schema, and WS-Policy definitions are best positioned within service designs

- want to understand the origins of service-orientation and how specifically it differs from object-orientation

- will be involved with creating design standards for SOA-based solutions

1.3 What this Book Does Not Cover

SOA and service-oriented computing represent broad subject matters. Many books can be written to explore various aspects of technology, architecture, analysis, and design. This book is focused solely on service engineering and the science of service design.

Topics Covered by Other Books

A primary objective of the *Prentice Hall Service-Oriented Computing Series from Thomas Erl* is to establish a library of complementary books dedicated to service-oriented computing. To accomplish this, an effort has been made to minimize overlap between this title and others in the series.

For example, even though service design touches upon numerous architectural issues, it is important to acknowledge that this is a book about designing services for SOA, not about designing SOA itself. The companion title, *SOA: Design Patterns*, provides a catalog of patterns, many of which deal directly with architectural design.

Furthermore, this book is not a tutorial about Web services or SOA fundamentals. Several books have already covered this ground sufficiently. Although some chapters provide introductory coverage of service-oriented computing, they do not go into detail. A number of sections also assume some knowledge of WSDL, XML schema, and WS-Policy. Basic tutorials for these technologies and structured "how-to" content for SOA is provided in *Service-Oriented Architecture: Concepts, Technology, and Design,* another official companion guide also part of this book series.

Finally, although this book includes a number of case study examples, it does not provide full code samples of implemented services or service contracts. The book *Web Service Contract Design for SOA* is wholly dedicated to the design of Web service contracts and provides both basic and advanced tutorials for WSDL, XML schema, WS-Policy, SOAP, and WS-Addressing. Additionally, several other series titles in development are dedicated to supplying comprehensive coverage of how to build services using different development platforms, such as .NET and Java.

> **NOTE**
>
> There are references to other series titles throughout this book. These references were not added for promotional reasons. In order to establish a well-structured library of complementary books, cross-title references are necessary. They are included for the benefit of the reader to indicate the location of additional relevant resources.

SOA Standardization Efforts

There are several efforts underway by different standards and research organizations to produce abstract definitions, architectural models, and vocabularies for SOA. These projects are in various stages of maturity, and some overlap in scope.

The mandate of this book series is to provide the IT community with current, real-world insight into the most important aspects of service-oriented computing, SOA, and service-orientation. A great deal of research goes into each and every title to follow through on this commitment. This research includes the detailed review of existing and upcoming technologies and platforms, relevant technology products and technology standards, architectural standards and specifications, as well as interviews conducted with key members of leading organizations in the SOA community.

As of the writing of this book, there has been no indication that the deliverables produced by the aforementioned independent efforts will be adopted as industry-wide SOA standards. In order to maintain an accurate, real-world perspective, these models and vocabularies can therefore not be covered or referenced in this book.

However, given the unpredictable nature of the IT industry, there is always an on-going possibility that one or more of these deliverables will attain industry standard status at some point in time. Should this occur, this book will be supplemented with online content that describes the relationship of the standards to the content of this text and further maps the concepts, terms, and models documented in this book to whatever conventions are established by the standards. This information would be published on the corresponding update page, as described in *Updates, Errata, and Resources* section later in this chapter. If you'd like to be automatically notified of these types of updates, see the *Notification Service* section at the end of the chapter for more information.

> **NOTE**
>
> This comment regarding standardization refers to SOA-related specifications only. There are numerous standards initiatives that have and continue to produce highly relevant technology specifications (primarily focused on XML and Web services). These are referenced, explained, and otherwise documented wherever appropriate in all series titles.

1.4 How this Book Is Organized

The organization of content is very straight forward. Chapters 1 and 2 provide background information for the book and its case study, respectively. All subsequent chapters have been grouped into the following primary parts:

- Part I: Fundamentals
- Part II: Design Principles
- Part III: Supplemental

Part I consists of three introductory chapters that set the stage for the detailed exploration of service-orientation design principles provided in Part II. All chapters within these parts communicate primary topics with the assistance of visual style elements and conventions. Diagrams, color, and shading are important style characteristics that have been incorporated to maximize content clarity.

Another means by which additional perspectives are provided is through the use of case study examples. Chapter 2 (which precedes Part I) establishes a case study background from which multiple examples are drawn to supplement the content in subsequent chapters. This supplies a common, real-world context to many of the topics explained in abstract. Up next are brief descriptions of what is covered in subsequent chapters.

Part I: Fundamentals

Although this book is more about applying and realizing service-orientation than it is about understanding SOA basics, we do need to take the time to establish and define key concepts and fundamental terms. These concepts and terms are used throughout the guide, and it is important that their meaning is always clear and consistent. The initial three chapters fulfill this requirement by providing concise introductory coverage.

How these chapters are organized is illustrated in Figure 1.1 and further explained in the upcoming sections.

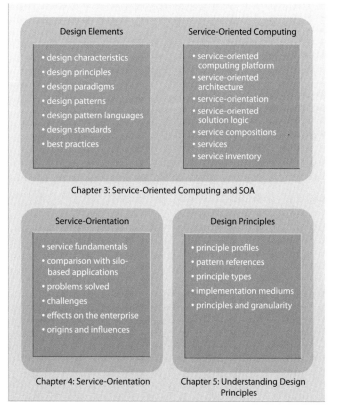

Figure 1.1
The three chapters in Part I deal with the ambiguity surrounding many of the terms and concepts associated with service-oriented computing.

Chapter 3: Service-Oriented Computing and SOA

We begin Part I by establishing the key goals and benefits associated with service-oriented computing. Collectively these goals provide strategic context for all chapters in Part II that document design principles.

This chapter furthermore establishes the service-oriented computing platform by providing definitions for the following terms:

- Service-Oriented Computing

- Service-Oriented Architecture

- Service-Orientation

- Service-Orientation Design Principles

- Service-Oriented Solution Logic

- Services

- Service Compositions

- Service Inventory

In addition to being explained conceptually, the physical relationships of each of these architectural components are also described. The chapter concludes with brief supplemental coverage of additional SOA-related terms, concepts, and processes.

Chapter 4: Service-Orientation

This next chapter zooms in on the design paradigm that underlies service-oriented computing. It begins with an overview of service-orientation by establishing its purpose and goals and then moves on to introduce its eight key design principles. How these principles specifically relate to and support service-oriented architecture is also discussed.

The manner in which the application of service-orientation changes the way solutions are delivered is explored next. Pros and cons of previous approaches are documented and contrasted with the potential for service-orientation to improve upon them. Also explained are the challenges and impositions made by a transition toward this paradigm.

We move on to cover how the adoption of service-orientation transforms not only the technology and the design of an enterprise, but also the mindset and perception of solution logic. Traditional terms, such as "application" and "integration," for example, can be challenged by the fluid nature of service and composition-based automation.

Finally, this introduction ends with a look at some of the key influences of service-orientation. Because this paradigm is very much an evolutionary representation of IT, it is important to acknowledge its roots in past platforms and technology trends.

Chapter 5: Understanding Design Principles

In preparation for Part II, this chapter provides a clear explanation of how subsequent chapters describe service-orientation principles within the context of SOA and service design, and how these principles may relate to design patterns. Different types of principles are categorized, including a study of those that result in implemented design characteristics compared to those that tend to shape and moderate how others are applied. Additionally, four specific forms of contract granularity are established; subsequent chapters then cover how principles affect these granularity types.

Chapter 5 concludes with a case study section that documents a business process for which services will be designed in subsequent chapters.

Part II: Design Principles

Service-orientation is a multi-dimensional subject matter. It is through the application of its design principles that its benefits are realized and that we can build solution logic that can be classified as being truly "service-oriented." This results in an automation environment with unique dynamics and characteristics, all of which need to be understood and planned for.

For example, there are guiding principles that each address a narrow aspect of service design and foster the creation of specific design characteristics. Then there are the issues that arise from combining principles and seeking the right balance for each to be implemented to an appropriate extent.

Part II consists of eight chapters—one for each service-orientation principle, as shown in Figure 1.2. The chapters are structured with a baseline set of sections that are detailed in the *Principle Profiles* section of Chapter 5. Each chapter is further supplemented with a case study example that demonstrates the application of a principle within scenarios drawn from the background established in Chapter 2.

Part II: Design Principles

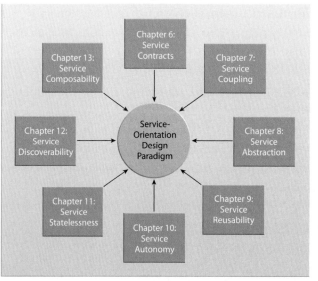

Figure 1.2

A separate chapter is dedicated to exploring each of the eight service-orientation principles. Collectively, these chapters provide a comprehensive documentation of the service-orientation paradigm.

The following sections briefly introduce each chapter:

Chapter 6: Service Contracts (Standardization and Design)

The service contract represents a core part of a service's architecture and is a focal point during the service design process to the extent that a principle is dedicated to its customization. This chapter explains different types of required contract standardization and establishes common levels at which contracts can be harmonized. Issues implicitly introduced by the use of service contracts, such as data models and policies, are discussed, and contracts are further architecturally positioned with an emphasis on Web services.

Chapter 7: Service Coupling (Intra-Service and Consumer Dependencies)

Numerous types of coupling are explored, including the coupling of the service contract to underlying technology and implementation characteristics, as well as the coupling of the service consumers to the contract. This chapter explores levels of attainable coupling and the implications of implementing more or less inter-service dependency. Additionally, the concept of design centralization is introduced as a means of supporting the realization of loose coupling in coordination with other principles.

Chapter 8: Service Abstraction (Information Hiding and Meta Abstraction Types)

The application of this principle determines how much of a service is revealed to the outside world. Achieving a balanced level of abstraction can be one of the most difficult parts of service design. Subsequent to describing the various forms and levels of abstraction, this chapter discusses several associated design risks and the influence abstraction, as a design consideration, has on other principles.

Chapter 9: Service Reusability (Commercial and Agnostic Design)

Increasing the value of solution logic by positioning services as reusable IT assets is a fundamental characteristic and objective of service-orientation. This chapter provides a comprehensive profile of Service Reusability and its implications and extends into an exploration of service reuse levels and the specific influences raised by commercial design considerations. Planned versus actual reuse measuring is discussed, along with the risks and enterprise-wide effects of building and exposing agnostic service logic.

Chapter 10: Service Autonomy (Processing Boundaries and Control)

The ability for a service to have control and governance over its execution environment is key for it to provide reliable, predictable runtime performance, a consideration especially important to the design of service compositions. This chapter explores both runtime and design-time autonomy and provides measurable levels that define an extent of autonomy based on degrees of normalization and functional isolation.

Chapter 11: Service Statelessness (State Management Deferral and Stateless Design)

Service designs capable of deferring state data and state management-related processing enable the implemented service to maximize its availability, an important quality especially in highly concurrent usage environments. Provided in Chapter 11 is a detailed explanation of different types of state information and state management functions followed by levels of attainable service statelessness.

Chapter 12: Service Discoverability (Interpretability and Communication)

The opportunity for services to be utilized to their full potential can only be realized if their existence, purpose, and capabilities are either known or easily located and understood. This chapter focuses on design characteristics associated with the discoverability and interpretability of services as they relate to the overall discovery aspect of service-oriented architecture. A checklist for measuring discoverability is provided, along with sections that document the risks and impacts of discoverability on service models and other principles.

Chapter 13: Service Composability (Composition Member Design and Complex Compositions)

Service composition is a fundamental, yet potentially complex aspect of service-oriented design. This principle deals with it head-on by establishing design requirements to ensure that services can effectively participate in larger composition configurations. A study of how compositions tend to evolve and grow within an enterprise is also provided, along with a series of evaluation criteria to assist in the measuring of a service composition's effectiveness potential.

Part III: Supplemental

Chapter 14: Service-Orientation and Object-Orientation: A Comparison of Principles and Concepts

Object-oriented analysis and design (OOAD) is an established modeling and design paradigm that has influenced numerous aspects of service-orientation. This supplemental comparison is focused on concepts and principles only and is intended for those with an OOAD background.

Chapter 15: Supporting Practices

This next chapter provides a set of supplementary practices and techniques for successfully incorporating and applying service-orientation principles within the common IT enterprise. Specifically, it discusses the use of service profile documents and associated vocabularies, along with common organizational roles.

Chapter 16: Mapping Service-Orientation Principles to Strategic Goals

The book concludes with an exploration of how the eight service-orientation design principles individually relate to and support the strategic goals established in Chapter 3. The content of this final chapter essentially establishes the strategic significance of each design principle.

Appendices

Appendix A: Case Study Conclusion

The case study storyline is concluded here, as the original goals established in Chapter 2 are revisited and assessed against all that transpired in the subsequent case study examples.

Appendix B: Process Descriptions

Service-oriented analysis and design processes are illustrated and briefly described for reference purposes. These processes are explained in detail in the book, *Service-Oriented Architecture: Concepts, Technology, and Design.*

Appendix C: Principles and Patterns Cross-Reference

This last appendix is comprised of a list of design patterns referenced in this book. These patterns are documented separately in the book *SOA: Design Patterns.*

1.5 Symbols, Figures, and Style Conventions

Symbol Legend

This book contains over 240 diagrams, which are referred to as "figures." The primary symbols used throughout all figures are individually described in the symbol legend located on the inside of the front cover.

How Color Is Used

Symbols have distinct colors associated with them so that they are easily recognized within the different figures. The one exception to this convention is when portions of a figure need to be highlighted for a particular reason. In this case, symbols may be colored red. The conflict symbol (which looks like a lightning bolt) is always red because we usually need to highlight points of conflict.

The Service Symbol

When this book series began, I had already been part of numerous service modeling and design projects during which various tools were (often awkwardly) used to define services and inter-service relationships. I found that it can be beneficial to visually distinguish a technical service contract from other components and systems that also need to be modeled either as parts of the service or as parts of an enterprise environment that need to co-exist with services.

The base symbol I introduced to represent a service throughout the books in this series is a circle divided into two areas (Figure 1.3). This symbol is by no means an industry standard convention. It is only an alternative notation—a means of stating, "This represents something to which we have or intend to apply service-orientation." The remainder of this section provides some background as to how the use of this symbol came about, followed by guidelines.

Figure 1.3

Inspired by the UML class symbol, the service symbol is comprised of two areas wherein the service's name and capabilities are expressed.

Background

In plane geometry, a circle is a highly self-contained form. The use of this shape is appropriate in that it reflects the levels of autonomy, independence, and individuality we seek to establish in every unit of logic we call a service.

This service symbol was recently given an official name: the *chorded circle*, a term coined by Paul Zablosky from the University of British Columbia. This term is also inspired by plane geometry and provides an appropriate metaphor. In the 16th century, mathematician Robert Recorde (also the inventor of the equals "=" sign) wrote, *"If the line goe crosse the circle, and passe beside the centre, then is it called a corde…"* Circles with chords look very much like the symbols in Figure 1.4.

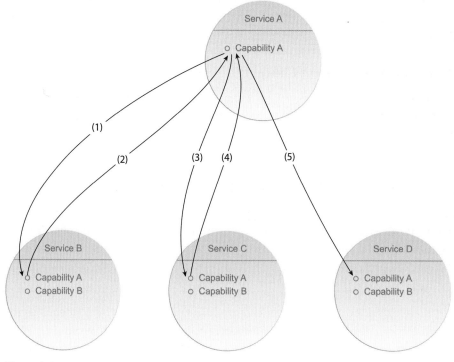

Figure 1.4

A service composition expressed using the chorded circle notation.

When using the chorded circle (or any supplemtary notation you may decide on), the following guidelines are recommended:

The Chorded Circle is an Abstract and Implementation-Neutral Expression of a Service

This symbol does not imply that a service exists as a component or Web service. The symbol simply abstracts the official public technical contract details to establish an official service endpoint definition and to also represent interface details made available to the outside world.

Throughout this book, chorded circles express services with no hint of how the services are actually implemented. Different symbols are used to illustrate physical implementation details of services as components and Web services. (These symbols are explained in the symbol legend mentioned previously.)

The Chorded Circle Is Complementary to UML

As explained in Chapter 14, this symbol can be used on its own to represent abstract technical service contracts, it can be used in conjunction with traditional UML notation, or it does not need to be used at all. Portions of UML can be adapted and used instead to express technical service contract details.

The Chorded Circle Represents a Member of a Service Inventory

What is most important about what this symbol visually communicates is that it represents a unit of logic designed as a service. In other words, it is not used to represent just a Web service or a component, but an actual service shaped by service-orientation and part of a larger collective known as a service inventory (as explained in Chapter 3).

The Basic Chorded Circle Is Most Useful for Modeling Purposes

The base version of this symbol does not provide a great deal of detail about the service contract. It will therefore get you only so far within a service delivery lifecycle. Its primary usage is during the service-oriented analysis process during which service modeling is carried out and service candidates are collaboratively defined and repeatedly refined by business and technology experts as part of a service inventory blueprint.

The Chorded Circle Notation Is Extensible

While the base version of this symbol provides only a simple, abstract expression of a service, extended versions can be created with more detail. Additional labels and qualifiers are available to express further service characteristics, such as message exchange patterns, policy assertions, service models, implementation and encapsulation characteristics, and lifecycle status. However, to keep things simple, these extensions are not used in this book.

1.6 Additional Information

The following sections provide supplementary information and resources for the *Prentice Hall Service-Oriented Computing Series from Thomas Erl*.

Updates, Errata, and Resources (www.soabooks.com)

Information about other series titles and various supporting resources can be found at www.soabooks.com. I would encourage you to visit the update page for this book regularly to check for content changes and corrections. I periodically review and revise book content to reflect industry developments.

Master Glossary (www.soaglossary.com)

To avoid content overlap and to ensure constant content currency, the books in this series do not contain glossaries. Instead, a dedicated Web site at www.soaglossary.com provides a master glossary for all series titles. This site continues to grow and expand with new glossary definitions as new series titles are developed and released.

Referenced Specifications (www.soaspecs.com)

Various series titles reference or provide tutorials and examples of open XML and Web services specifications and standards. The www.soaspecs.com Web site provides a central portal to the original specification documents created and maintained by the primary standards organizations.

Service-Oriented Computing Poster (www.soaposters.com)

The inside of the front cover contains a collection of diagrams for quick reference purposes. A separate color reference poster including these and additional illustrations and content is also available. Visit www.soaposters.com for more information.

The SOA Magazine (www.soamag.com)

The SOA Magazine is a regular publication provided by SOA Systems Inc. and Prentice Hall/PearsonPTR and is officially associated with the *Prentice Hall Service-Oriented Computing Series from Thomas Erl.* The SOA Magazine is dedicated to publishing specialized SOA articles, case studies, and papers by industry experts and professionals. The common criteria for contributions is that each explores a distinct aspect of service-oriented computing.

Notification Service

If you'd like to be automatically notified of new book releases in this series, new supplementary content for this title, or key changes to the previously listed Web sites, send a blank e-mail to `notify@soabooks.com`.

Contact the Author

To contact me directly, visit my bio site at `www.thomaserl.com`.

Chapter 2

Case Study

2.1 Case Study Background: Cutit Saws Ltd.

This background description establishes the starting point for a storyline that carries on throughout this book and then concludes with results documented in Appendix A. The chapters in Part I supplement this chapter with more background details in preparation for the case study examples provided at the end of each chapter in Part II. The purpose of these examples is to supply real-world context for many of the key topics described in abstract. No new topics are introduced in case study sections; reading them is therefore optional.

To make navigation easier, a special style element has been incorporated. Light gray shading has been applied to all case study content in subsequent chapters.

2.1 Case Study Background: Cutit Saws Ltd.

In a crowded marketplace of power tool vendors, Cutit Saws has positioned itself as a boutique manufacturer and reseller of hydraulic diamond chainsaws. It has established its models as distinct, high-end saws with chains crafted from a unique, patented blade design capable of cutting through concrete as easily as wood.

History

Several years ago, a team of university graduates invented a type of blade that was surprisingly effective at penetrating dense matter. The design was based on the cut of the blade and a special formula of materials applied to the blade's surface. Subsequent to being issued a patent and receiving venture capital support, the team started up Cutit Saws Ltd.

Initially, business was slow. The financing they had to work with allowed for a very limited marketing budget, and it took longer than expected to raise an awareness of their product. Eventually, though, they established a solid clientele consisting of construction firms and lumber companies who appreciated the unique qualities of their blade design. While part of the founding team took on the managerial responsibilities of running the company, the others continued to work in Cutit's private development lab.

Six months ago they developed a new variation of their diamond blade that increased penetration effectiveness by an additional 25%. Cutit subsequently released a new chain model (the "Ripit 5000") that caught the eye of their business community. Once its claims were proven and documented, orders for the new chain began arriving from everywhere. Because the manufacturing process for this new model is more time consuming, Cutit has not been able to keep up with the demand, and backorders are mounting.

Technical Infrastructure and Automation Environment

Cutit's IT environment is a hodge podge of servers and workstations. Hardware and software is purchased on an "as-needed" basis by different departments. The lab, for example, has an array of servers used for chemical analysis and technical blueprints, while the rest of the staff use a variety of workstations and laptops that connect to a central LAN. The IT department employs a full-time staff of 12, two of whom are dedicated development resources.

One of Cutit's principals and original founders has a computer science background and put his knowledge to good use for the company. He developed a simple accounting and inventory management system that processes standard paperwork and keeps track of materials and product stock. This system has since been extended many times and has established itself as somewhat of an integration hub. Other products have been purchased and, to various extents, integrated with the core system.

Business Goals and Obstacles

Although the founding team cannot complain about the success of their venture and the wide acceptance of their latest product release, they are overwhelmed by the current demand. While orders continue to pour in, they have been limited in their ability to expand their manufacturing staff. Some of the skills required are so specialized that they are finding it difficult to locate qualified personnel, and those that they do hire require significant up-front training.

Rumors have already begun circulating that a competing chainsaw manufacturer is attempting to re-engineer Cutit's new blade design into a similar product. This competitor is larger and has more resources already in place. Cutit knows it must expand soon, or it will lose out on a chance for significant growth. After the competitor releases its product, their window of opportunity to establish new clients will rapidly shrink.

One of the biggest challenges to expanding the company is its current automation environment. The home grown system that has served them for so long is simply not scalable anymore. There have already been numerous performance and concurrent usage problems that the on-staff developers have tried to address. The team has been in agreement for some time that a new enterprise solution needs to be introduced.

During a strategy meeting it is decided that this new enterprise be based, from the ground up, on SOA. This decision was reached for two primary reasons:

1. The success of the latest chain model caught the team by surprise and made them realize that they cannot anticipate what will be in store for the duration of their tenure as owners. Therefore, simply replacing the existing system with one that is suitable for their immediate expansion plans is risky and expensive. If they were to expand again, they may have to undergo the same type of overhaul. They conclude that a service-based approach will allow them to continue to grow and scale as required.

2. The owners' plan is to sell the company within the next five years. To maximize its value, they don't want to jeopardize future opportunities for growth and expansion. As a result, it is critical that their automation environment be contemporized. Furthermore, they are hoping that by investing into an SOA model, their company will be a more attractive acquisition target; by modularizing their enterprise into services, foreign integration and reorganization will be easier and more cost-effective.

Despite the rationale, the path ahead still poses some significant challenges. For example, their immediate need for an expanded system may compromise some of the upfront effort generally required to properly model and design services.

NOTE
Additional background information is provided at the end of Chapters 3, 4, and 5. Case study examples are then supplied at the end of subsequent chapters in Part II. Appendix A concludes the case study storyline.

Part I

Fundamentals

To fully understand service-oriented architecture you need to become familiar with what constitutes the service-oriented computing platform. To fully understand service-oriented computing, you need to comprehend the meaning and significance of its most fundamental building block: the service. And, in order to gain that comprehension, you need to know how a unit of solution logic can be shaped into something that can legitimately be called "service-oriented."

That knowledge lies within the service-orientation paradigm, a subject covered in much detail throughout Part II. These initial introductory chapters provide a starting point for this exploration by establishing high-level concepts and associated terminology.

Chapter 3

Service-Oriented Computing and SOA

One of the most challenging aspects of writing about or discussing technology is using industry terminology. Many IT terms suffer from wide-spread ambiguity, which sometimes makes having even the simplest conversation difficult. Take IT professionals from different organizations, put them in the same room, and you'll very likely hear questions like, "What exactly do you mean by component?" or "What is your definition of service?" or, my personal favorite, "What kind of SOA are you referring to?"

Fortunately, the primary subject matter of this book is very clear. We describe a distinct approach to designing solution logic. To ensure that the descriptions of associated topics are easily understood, a communications framework needs to be established, comprised of a collection of terms with very explicit definitions. That is what this chapter is dedicated to providing.

3.1 Design Fundamentals

Before we can begin exploring the details of service-oriented computing, we first need to establish some basic design terminology. The books in this series use a common vocabulary comprised of the following design-related terms:

- Design Characteristic
- Design Principle
- Design Paradigm
- Design Pattern
- Design Pattern Language
- Design Standard
- Best Practice

Depending on your sources, you will find differing definitions for these terms. More often than not, though, you will notice that they all are somewhat intertwined. The following sections explain each term and conclude with a section that illustrates how they form a common, fundamental design framework.

Design Characteristic

A characteristic of something is simply an attribute or quality. An automated business solution will have numerous unique characteristics that were established during its initial design (Figure 3.1). Hence, the type of *design characteristic* we are interested in is a specific attribute or quality of a body of solution logic that we document in a design specification and plan to realize in development.

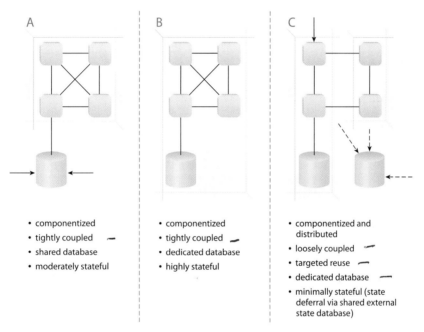

Figure 3.1

In this simple example, three distinct application designs (A, B, C) are established, each with its own list of design characteristics. We will continue to reference these applications in the upcoming sections. (Note that the small squares represent units of solution logic, solid arrows represent reuse or shared access, and dashed arrows represent state data transfer.)

Service-orientation emphasizes the creation of very specific design characteristics, while also *de*-emphasizing others. It is important to note that almost every design characteristic we explore is attainable to a certain *measure*. This means that it is generally not about whether solution logic does or does not have a certain characteristic; it is almost always about the extent to which a characteristic can or should be realized.

Although each system can have its own unique characteristics, we are primarily interested in establishing *common* design characteristics. Increased commonality ensures an increased degree of consistency, making different kinds of solution logic more alike. When things are more alike they become more predictable. In the world of distributed, shareable logic, predictability is a good thing. Predictable design characteristics lead to predictable behavior. This, in turn, leads to increased reliability and the opportunity to leverage solution logic in many different ways.

Much of this book is dedicated to providing a means of establishing a specific collection of design characteristics that spread consistency, predictability, and reliability on many levels and for different purposes.

Design Principle

A principle is a generalized, accepted industry practice. In other words, it's something others are doing or promoting in association with a common objective. You can compare a principle with a best practice in that both propose a means of accomplishing something based on past experience or industry-wide acceptance.

When it comes to building solutions, a *design principle* represents a highly recommended guideline for shaping solution logic in a certain way and with certain goals in mind (Figure 3.2). These goals are usually associated with establishing one or more specific design characteristics (as a result of applying the principle).

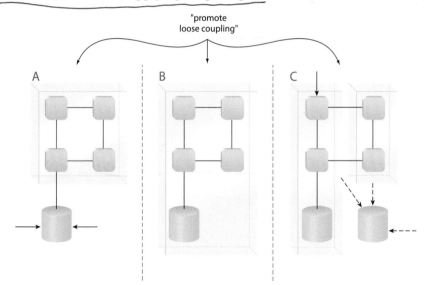

Figure 3.2

The repeated application of design principles increases the amount of common design characteristics. In this case, the coupling between solution logic units A and B has been loosened (as indicated by a reduction of connection points).

For example, we can have a principle as fundamental as one that states that solution logic should be distributable. Applying this principle results in the solution logic being partitioned into individually distributable units. This then establishes the distinct design characteristic of the solution logic becoming componentized. This is not only an example of a very broad design principle, but it is also the starting point for service-orientation.

The eight design principles documented in this book provide rules and guidelines that help determine exactly how solution logic should be decomposed and shaped into distributable units. A study of these principles further reveals what design characteristics these units should have to be classified as "quality" services capable of fulfilling the vision and goals associated with SOA and service-oriented computing.

Design Paradigm

There are many meanings associated with the term "paradigm." It can be an approach to something, a school of thought regarding something, or a combined set of rules that are applied within a predefined boundary.

A *design paradigm* within the context of business automation is generally considered a governing approach to designing solution logic. It normally consists of a set of complementary rules or principles that collectively define the overarching approach represented by the paradigm (Figure 3.3).

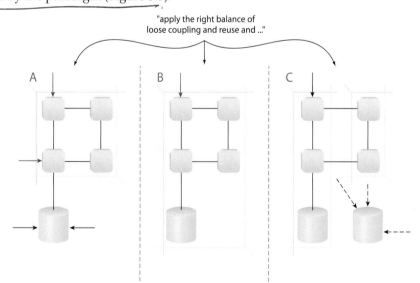

"apply the right balance of loose coupling and reuse and ..."

A   B   C

Figure 3.3

Because a design paradigm represents a collection of design principles, it further increases the degree of commonality across different bodies of solution logic. In the example, the amount of reuse in A and B has increased.

Object-orientation (or object-oriented design) is a classic example of an accepted design paradigm. It provides a set of principles that shape componentized solution logic in certain ways so as to fulfill a specific set of goals.

Along those very same lines, service-orientation represents its own distinct design paradigm. Like object-orientation, it is a paradigm that applies to distributed solution logic. However, because some of its principles differ from those associated with object-orientation (as explained in Chapter 14), it can result in the creation of different types of design characteristics.

Design Pattern

We've established that service-orientation is a design paradigm comprised of a set of design principles, each of which provides a generalized rule or guideline for realizing certain design characteristics. The paradigm itself sounds pretty complete, and it actually is. However, to successfully apply it in the real world requires more than just a theoretical understanding of its principles.

Service designers will be regularly faced with obstacles and challenges when attempting to apply a design paradigm because the realization of desired design characteristics is frequently complicated by various factors, including:

- Constraints imposed by the technology being used to build and/or host the units of solution logic.

- Constraints imposed by technology or systems that reside alongside the deployed units of solution logic.

- Constraints imposed by the requirements and priorities of the project delivering the units of solution logic.

A *design pattern* describes a common problem and provides a corresponding solution (Figure 3.4). It essentially documents the solution in a generic template format so that it can be repeatedly applied. Knowledge of design patterns not only arms you with an understanding of the potential problems designs may be subjected to, it provides answers as to how these problems are best dealt with.

Figure 3.4

Patterns provide recommended solutions for common design problems. In this simplified example, a
pattern suggests we reduce external access to a
database to increase application autonomy.

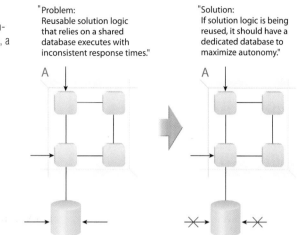

"Problem:
Reusable solution logic
that relies on a shared
database executes with
inconsistent response times."

"Solution:
If solution logic is being
reused, it should have a
dedicated database to
maximize autonomy."

Design patterns are born out of experience. Pioneers in any field had to undergo cycles
of trial and error and by learning from what didn't work, approaches that finally did
achieve their goals were developed. When a problem and its corresponding solution
were identified as sufficiently common, the basis of a design pattern was formed. Design
patterns can be further combined into compound patterns that solve larger problems
and a series of patterns can form the basis of a pattern language, as explained next.

> **NOTE**
>
> Appendix C provides cross-references of design principles and associ-
> ated design patterns documented as part of the pattern catalog
> published in *SOA: Design Patterns*.

Design Pattern Language

The application of one design pattern can raise new issues or problems for which
another pattern may be required. A collection of related patterns can establish a formalized expression of a design process whereby each addresses a primary decision point.
Combining patterns in this manner forms the basis of a *pattern language*.

A pattern language is essentially comprised of a chain of related design patterns that establish a configurable sequence in which the patterns can be applied (Figure 3.5). Such a language provides a highly effective means of communicating fundamental aspects of a given design approach because it supplies detailed documentation of each major step in a design process that shapes the design characteristics of solution logic.

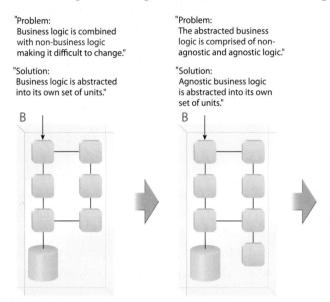

"Problem:
Business logic is combined with non-business logic making it difficult to change."

"Solution:
Business logic is abstracted into its own set of units."

"Problem:
The abstracted business logic is comprised of non-agnostic and agnostic logic."

"Solution:
Agnostic business logic is abstracted into its own set of units."

Figure 3.5
A sequence of related design patterns formalize the primary decision points of a design paradigm. In this example, the logic in application design B is decomposed as a result of one pattern, and then further decomposed as a result of another. Subsequent fundamental patterns continue to shape the logic.

> **NOTE**
>
> The fundamental paradigm and underlying philosophies of service-orientation and SOA are expressed through a basic pattern language as part of *SOA: Design Patterns*.

Design Standard

For an organization to successfully apply a design paradigm, it will require more than an adherence to the associated design principles and a knowledge of supporting design patterns. Every organization will have unique strategic goals and unique enterprise environments. These form a distinct set of requirements and constraints that need to be accommodated within solution designs.

Design standards are (usually mandatory) design conventions customized to consistently pre-determine solution design characteristics in support of organizational goals and optimized for specific enterprise environments. It is through the use of internal design standards that organizations can consistently deliver solutions tailored to their environments, resources, goals, and priorities (Figure 3.6).

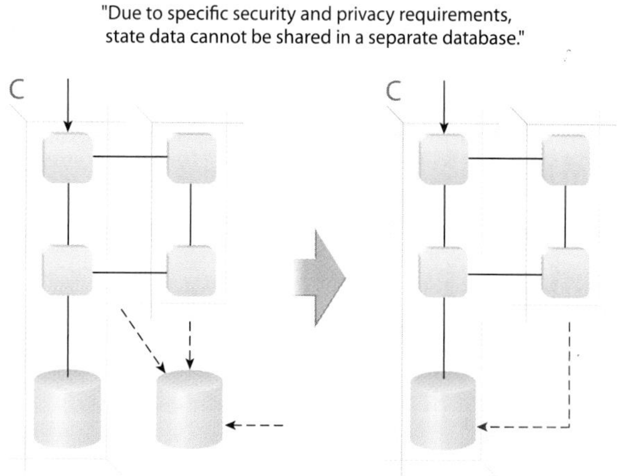

Figure 3.6

In this case, a design standard requires that C's original design be altered to remove access to a shared, external state database.

"Due to specific security and privacy requirements, state data cannot be shared in a separate database."

As with design principles, the application of design standards results in the creation of specific design characteristics. As with design patterns, design standards foster and refine these characteristics to avoid potential problems and to strengthen the overall solution design. In fact, it is recommended for design standards to be based upon or even derived from industry design principles and patterns.

Can you have design standards without design principles? Yes, it is actually common to have many design standards. Only some may need to relate back to principles in order to see through the application of the overall design paradigm. Different design standards may also be created to simply support other goals or compensate for constraints imposed by specific environmental, cultural, or technology-related factors. Although some standards may have no direct association with accepted design principles, there should always be an effort to keep all standards in relative alignment.

Can you have design principles without design standards? It usually depends on how committed an organization is to the governing design paradigm. If it sees potential in only using a subset of the paradigm's principles, then some principles may not be supported by corresponding design standards. However, this approach is not common.

Essentially, as with design principles, through standardization we want to build consistency into specific design characteristics—consistency in the quality of the characteristics and in how frequently they are implemented.

One point of clarification often worth making when discussing standards is the difference between design standards and *industry standards*. The former, as we just described, refers to internal or custom standards that apply to the design of solution logic and systems for a particular enterprise. The latter generally represents open technology standards, such as those that comprise the XML and Web services platforms.

Sometimes organizations assume that if they use industry standards, they will end up with a standardized IT enterprise. While those XML and Web services specifications that have become ratified and accepted industry standards do establish a level of technology standardization, it is still up to an organization to consistently position and apply these technologies. Without design standards, industry standards can easily fail in achieving their potential.

Best Practice

A *best practice* is generally considered a technique or approach to solving or preventing certain problems (Figure 3.7). It is usually a practice that has industry recognition and has emerged from past industry experience.

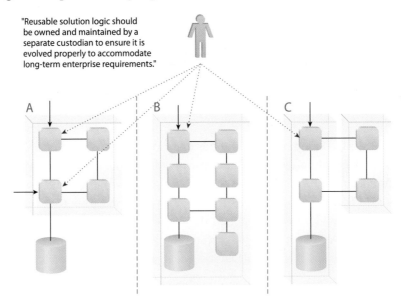

Figure 3.7

Best practices provide guidance in the form of general "lessons learned." In the example, it is suggested that the on-going maintenance of reusable solution logic units from all applications fall under a single custodian.

How then is a best practice differentiated from a design principle? In this book we make a clear distinction in that a design principle is limited to design only. A best practice can relate to anything from project delivery to organizational issues, governance, or process. A design principle could be considered a best practice associated only with solution design.

Note that several best practices are provided throughout this book in support of applying design principles. An additional set of more detailed practices is located in Chapter 15.

A Fundamental Design Framework

Each of the previous sections described a piece of intelligence that can act as input into an overall design process. When designing service-oriented solutions it is practically inevitable that some or all of these pieces be used together. It is therefore important to understand how they relate to each other so that we can gain a foreknowledge of how and where they are best utilized.

Figure 3.8 shows how some of the more common parts of a design framework typically inter-relate and highlights how central the use of design principles can be. Figure 3.9 expands on this perspective by illustrating how the use of design patterns can further support and extend a basic design framework. Finally, Figure 3.10 shows how the parts of a design framework can ultimately help realize the application of the overarching design paradigm.

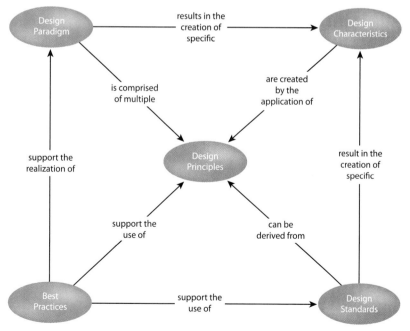

Figure 3.8

Fundamental design terms establish a basic taxonomy used throughout the upcoming chapters. This diagram hints at how some parts of a basic design framework can relate to each other.

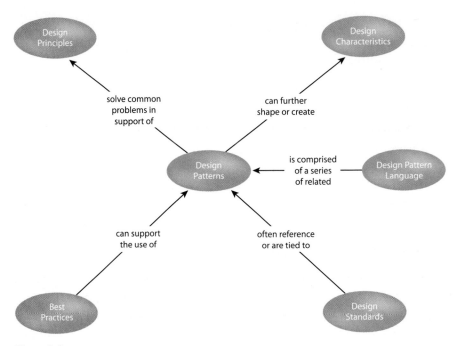

Figure 3.9
Design patterns provide additional intelligence that can enrich a design framework with a collection of proven solutions to common problems.

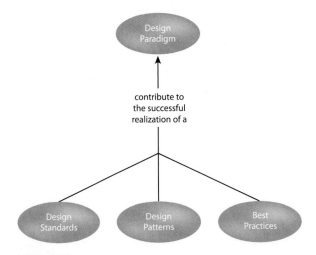

Figure 3.10
The purpose of applying a design paradigm is the achievement of certain goals. It is important to emphasize how design standards, design patterns, and best practices can all support the successful application of a design paradigm and, as a result, the attainment of its goals.

SUMMARY OF KEY POINTS

- A design principle is an accepted design guideline or practice that, when applied, results in the realization of specific design characteristics.

- A design paradigm represents a set of complementary design principles that are collectively applied in support of common goals.

- A design pattern identifies a common problem and provides a recommended solution.

- A design standard is a convention internal and specific to an enterprise that may or may not be derived from a design principle or pattern.

3.2 Introduction to Service-Oriented Computing

Service-oriented computing represents a new generation distributed computing platform. As such, it encompasses many things, including its own design paradigm and design principles, design pattern catalogs, pattern languages, a distinct architectural model, and related concepts, technologies, and frameworks.

It sounds like a pretty big umbrella, and it is. Service-oriented computing builds upon past distributed computing platforms and adds new design layers, governance considerations, and a vast set of preferred implementation technologies. That's why taking the time to understand its underlying mechanics *before* proceeding to the actual design and construction phases of a delivery project is time well spent.

To better appreciate the fundamental complexion of a typical service-oriented computing platform we need to describe each of its primary parts, which we'll refer to as *elements*:

- Service-Oriented Architecture

- Service-Orientation

- Service-Oriented Solution Logic

- Services

- Service Compositions

- Service Inventory

The following sections define each of these elements and conclude with a section that explains how they can inter-relate conceptually and physically. The basic symbols introduced in these sections are used repeatedly within subsequent parts of this book.

Service-Oriented Architecture

SOA establishes an architectural model that aims to enhance the efficiency, agility, and productivity of an enterprise by positioning services as the primary means through which solution logic is represented in support of the realization of strategic goals associated with service-oriented computing.

On a fundamental basis, the service-oriented computing platform revolves around the service-orientation design paradigm and its relationship with service-oriented architecture. In fact, the term "service-oriented architecture" and its associated acronym have been used so broadly by the media and within vendor marketing literature that it has almost become synonymous with service-oriented computing itself. It is therefore very important to make a clear distinction between what SOA actually is and how it relates to other service-oriented computing elements.

As a form of technology architecture, an SOA implementation can consist of a combination of technologies, products, APIs, supporting infrastructure extensions, and various other parts (Figure 3.11). The actual face of a deployed service-oriented architecture is unique within each enterprise; however it is typified by the introduction of new technologies and platforms that specifically support the creation, execution, and evolution of service-oriented solutions. As a result, building a technology architecture around the service-oriented architectural model establishes an environment suitable for solution logic that has been designed in compliance with service-orientation design principles.

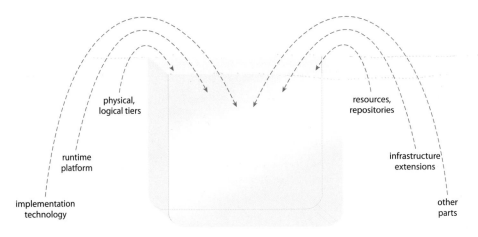

Figure 3.11

Container symbols are used to represent architectural implementation environments.

Service-Orientation, Services, and Service-Oriented Solution Logic

Service-orientation is a design paradigm comprised of a specific set of design principles. The application of these principles to the design of solution logic results in *service-oriented solution logic*. The most fundamental unit of service-oriented solution logic is the *service*.

Services exist as physically independent software programs with distinct design characteristics that support the attainment of the strategic goals associated with service-oriented computing. Each service is assigned its own distinct functional context and is comprised of a set of capabilities related to this context. Those capabilities suitable for invocation by external consumer programs are commonly expressed via a published service contract (much like a traditional API).

Figure 3.12 introduces the symbol used in this book to represent a service from an endpoint perspective. See the *SOA and Web Services* section for an introduction to the symbols used to illustrate a physical design perspective of services implemented as Web services. Note also that services and service-orientation are explored in detail in Chapter 4.

Figure 3.12

The yellow sphere symbol is used to represent a service. Alternatively, the chorded circle symbol introduced in Chapter 1 can also be used.

Service Compositions

A *service composition* is a coordinated aggregate of services. As explained in the *Effects of Service-Orientation on the Enterprise* section in Chapter 4, a composition of services (Figure 3.13) is comparable to a traditional application in that its functional scope is usually associated with the automation of a parent business process.

Figure 3.13

The symbol comprised of three connected spheres represents a service composition. Other, more detailed representations are based on the use of chorded circle symbols to illustrate which service capabilities are actually being composed.

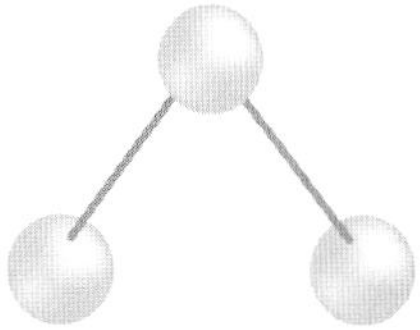

The consistent application of service-orientation design principles leads to the creation of services with functional contexts that are agnostic to any one business process. These agnostic services are therefore capable of participating in multiple service compositions.

As further discussed in Chapters 13 and 16, the ability for a service to be naturally and repeatedly composable is fundamental to attaining several of the key strategic goals of service-oriented computing. Therefore, many of the design characteristics that distinguish a service enable it to effectively participate in service compositions.

Service Inventory

A *service inventory* is an independently standardized and governed collection of complementary services within a boundary that represents an enterprise or a meaningful segment of an enterprise. Figure 3.14 establishes the symbol used to represent a service inventory in this book.

An IT enterprise may include a service inventory that represents the extent to which SOA has been adopted. Larger initiatives may even result in the enterprise in its entirety being comprised of an enterprise-wide service inventory. Alternatively, an enterprise environment can contain multiple service inventories, each of which can be individually standardized, governed, and supported by its own service-oriented technology architecture.

Figure 3.14

The service inventory symbol is comprised of yellow spheres within a blue container.

Service inventories are typically created through top-down delivery processes that result in the definition of service inventory blueprints. The subsequent application of service-orientation design principles and custom design standards throughout a service inventory is of paramount importance so as to establish a high degree of native inter-service interoperability. This supports the repeated, agile creation of effective service compositions. (Note that service inventory blueprints are explained later in this chapter.)

Understanding Service-Oriented Computing Elements

We'll be making reference to the previously defined elements throughout this book. Understanding them individually is just as important as understanding how they can relate to each other because these relationships establish some of the most fundamental dynamics of service-oriented computing.

Let's therefore revisit these elements with an emphasis on how each ties into others:

- *Service-oriented architecture* represents a distinct form of technology architecture designed in support of *service-oriented solution logic* which is comprised of *services* and *service compositions* shaped by and designed in accordance with *service-orientation*.

- *Service-orientation* is a design paradigm comprised of *service-orientation design principles*. When applied to units of solution logic, these principles create *services* with distinct design characteristics that support the overall goals and vision of *service-oriented computing*.

- *Service-oriented computing* represents a new generation computing platform that encompasses the *service-orientation paradigm* and *service-oriented architecture* with the ultimate goal of creating and assembling one or more *service inventories*.

These relationships are further illustrated in Figure 3.15.

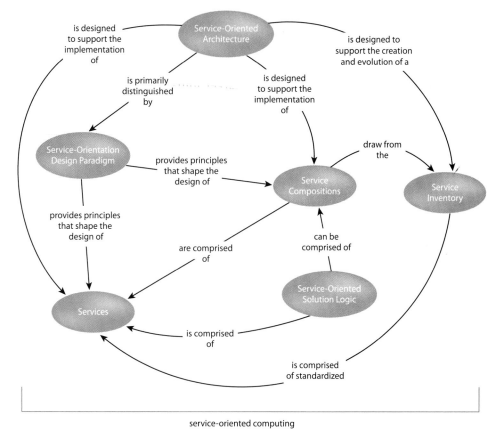

Figure 3.15

A conceptual view of how the elements of service-oriented computing can inter-relate.

To fully appreciate how these elements are ultimately used we need to explore how they translate into the real world. To do so, we need to clearly distinguish the role and position of each element within a physical implementation perspective, as follows:

- *Service-oriented solution logic* is implemented as *services* and *service compositions* designed in accordance with *service-orientation design principles*.

- A *service composition* is comprised of *services* that have been assembled to provide the functionality required to automate a specific business task or process.

- Because *service-orientation* shapes many *services* as agnostic enterprise resources, one *service* may be invoked by multiple consumer programs, each of which can involve that same *service* in a different *service composition*.

- A collection of standardized *services* can form the basis of a *service inventory* that can be independently administered within its own physical deployment environment.

- Multiple business processes can be automated by the creation of *service compositions* that draw from a pool of existing agnostic *services* that reside within a *service inventory*.

- *Service-oriented architecture* is a form of technology architecture optimized in support of *services*, *service compositions*, and *service inventories*.

This implementation-centric view brings to light how service-oriented computing can change the overall complexion of an enterprise. Because the majority of services delivered are positioned as reusable resources agnostic to business processes, they do not belong to any one application silo. By dissolving boundaries between applications, the enterprise is increasingly represented by a growing body of services that exist within an expanding service inventory (Figure 3.16).

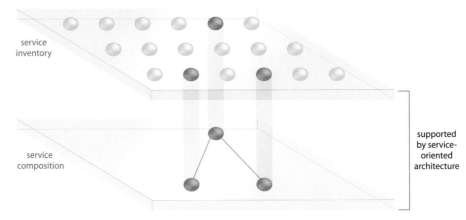

service inventory

service composition

supported by service-oriented architecture

Figure 3.16

A service inventory establishes a pool of services, many of which will be deliberately designed to be reused within multiple service compositions.

> **NOTE**
>
> So far, an introductory perspective of service-oriented computing and its key elements has been established. However, when making reference to the service-oriented computing platform, we need to acknowledge the vast amounts of vendor development and runtime technologies that comprise its technology landscape. It is the makeup of these platforms and their combined technology innovations that have helped drive the evolution of service-oriented computing in the mainstream IT industry.

Service Models

When building various types of services, it becomes evident that they can be categorized depending on:

- the type of logic they encapsulate
- the extent of reuse potential this logic has
- how this logic relates to existing domains within the enterprise

As a result, there are three common classifications that represent the primary *service models* referenced throughout this book:

- Entity Services
- Task Services
- Utility Services

The use of these service models results in the creation of logical service abstraction layers, as shown in Figure 3.17.

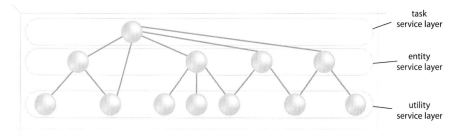

Figure 3.17

Common service abstraction layers established by service models, each of which is comprised of services shaped through the application of the service-orientation paradigm. Though these layers tend to form a natural composition hierarchy, there are no rules as to how services can be assembled.

Each of these three service models is further explained in the following sections.

Entity Services

In just about every enterprise, there will be business model documents that define the organization's relevant business entities. Examples of business entities include customer, employee, invoice, and claim. The *entity service* model (Figure 3.18) represents a business-centric service that bases its functional boundary and context on one or more related business entities. It is considered a highly reusable service because it is agnostic to most parent business processes. As a result, a single entity service can be leveraged to automate multiple parent business processes.

Entity services are also known as *entity-centric business services* or *business entity services*.

○ GetWeeklyHoursLimit
○ UpdateWeeklyHoursLimit
○ GetHistory
○ UpdateHistory
○ DeleteHistory
○ AddProfile
○ GetProfile
○ UpdateProfile
○ DeleteProfile

Employee

Figure 3.18

An example of an entity service. Several of its capabilities are reminiscent of traditional CRUD (create, read, update, delete) methods.

Task Services

A business service with a functional boundary directly associated with a specific parent business task or process is based on the *task service* model (Figure 3.19). This type of service tends to have less reuse potential and is generally positioned as the controller of a composition responsible for composing other, more process-agnostic services.

When discussing task services, one point of clarification often required is in relation to entity service capabilities. Each

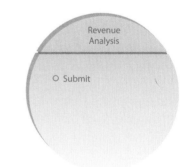

Revenue Analysis

○ Submit

Figure 3.19

An example of a task service with a sole exposed capability required to initiate its encapsulated parent business process.

capability essentially encapsulates business process logic in that it carries out a sequence of steps to complete a specific task. An entity Invoice service, for example, may have an Add capability that contains process logic associated with creating a new invoice record.

How then is what a task service encapsulates different from what an entity service's capabilities contain? The primary distinction has to do with the functional scope of the capability. The Invoice service's Add capability is focused solely on the processing of an invoice document. To carry out this process may require that the capability logic interact with other services representing different business entities, but the functional scope of the capability is clearly associated with the functional context of the Invoice service.

If, however, we had a billing consolidation process that retrieved numerous invoice and PO records, performed various calculations, and further validated consolidation results against client history billing records, we would have process logic that *spans* multiple entity domains and does not fit cleanly within a functional context associated with a business entity. This would typically constitute a "parent" process in that it consists of processing logic that needs to coordinate the involvement of multiple services.

Services with a functional context defined by a parent business process or task can be developed as standalone Web services or components—or—they may represent a business process definition hosted within an orchestration platform. In the latter case, the design characteristics of the service are somewhat distinct due to the specific nature of the underlying technology. In this case, it may be preferable to qualify the service model label accordingly. This type of service is referred to as the *orchestrated task service*.

Task services are also known as *task-centric business services* or *business process services*. Orchestrated task services are also known as *process services*, *business process services*, or *orchestration services*.

> ### NOTE
>
> There is a potential point of confusion when referring to these types of services as "business process services" or when renaming the task service layer to "business process layer." Just about every capability within every business service encapsulates an extent of business process logic. Establishing a task service layer does not abstract or centralize all business process logic. Its purpose is primarily to abstract non-agnostic process logic in support of agnostic service models. If there's a preference to incorporate the term "business process" within the title of this service layer, then it's recommended that it be further qualified with "parent" (as in the "parent business process layer").

Utility Services

Each of the previously described service models has a very clear focus on representing business logic. However, within the realm of automation, there is not always a need to associate logic with a business model or process. In fact, it can be highly beneficial to deliberately establish a functional context that is *non*-business-centric. This essentially results in a distinct, technology-oriented service layer.

The *utility service* model (Figure 3.20) accomplishes this. It is dedicated to providing reusable, cross-cutting utility functionality, such as event logging, notification, and exception handling. It is ideally application agnostic in that it can consist of a series of capabilities that draw from multiple enterprise systems and resources, while making this functionality available within a very specific processing context.

Utility services are also known as *application services*, *infrastructure services*, or *technology services*.

Figure 3.20

An example of a utility service providing a set of capabilities associated with proprietary data format transformation.

SOA and Web Services

It is very important to view and position SOA as an architectural model that is agnostic to any one technology platform (Figure 3.21). By doing so, an enterprise is given the freedom to continually pursue the strategic goals associated with service-oriented computing by leveraging future technology advancements. In the current marketplace, the technology platform most associated with the realization of SOA is Web services.

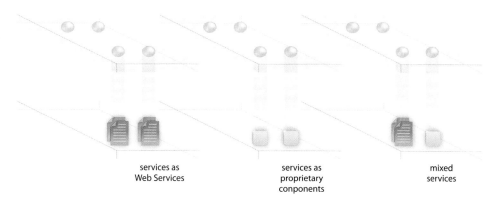

services as
Web Services

services as
proprietary
conponents

mixed
services

Figure 3.21

Service-oriented solutions can be comprised of services built as Web services, components, or combinations of both.

Web Services Standards

The Web services platform is defined through a number of industry standards that are supported throughout the vendor community. This platform can be partitioned into two clearly identifiable generations, each associated with a collection of standards and specifications:

- *First-Generation Web Services Platform*

  The original Web services technology platform is comprised of the following core open technologies and specifications: Web Services Description Language (WSDL), XML Schema Definition Language (XSD), SOAP (formerly the Simple Object Access Protocol), UDDI (Universal Description, Discovery, and Integration), and the WS-I Basic Profile.

  These specifications have been around for some time and have been adopted across the IT industry. However, the platform they collectively represent seriously lacks several of the quality of service features required to deliver mission critical, enterprise-level production functionality.

- *Second-Generation Web Services Platform (WS-* extensions)*

  Some of the greatest quality of service-related gaps in the first-generation platform lie in the areas of message-level security, cross-service transactions, and reliable messaging. These, along with many other extensions, represent the second-generation Web services platform. Consisting of numerous specifications that build upon the fundamental first-generation messaging framework, this set of Web services technologies (generally labeled as "WS-*") provides a rich feature-set far more sophisticated both in technology and in design. An example of a WS-* standard referenced throughout this book is WS-Policy.

Web Services Architecture

A typical Web service is comprised of the following:

- A physically decoupled technical *service contract* consisting of a WSDL definition, an XML schema definition, and possibly a WS-Policy definition. This service contract exposes public functions (called operations) and is therefore comparable to a traditional application programming interface (API).

- A body of programming logic. This logic may be custom-developed for the Web service, or it may exist as legacy logic that is being wrapped by a Web service in order for its functionality to be made available via Web services communication standards. In the case that logic is custom-developed, it generally is created as components and is referred to as the *core service logic* (or *business logic*).

- *Message processing logic* that exists as a combination of parsers, processors, and service agents. Much of this logic is provided by the runtime environment, but it can also be customized. The programs that carry out message-related processing are primarily event-driven and therefore can intercept a message subsequent to transmission or prior to receipt. It is common for multiple message processing programs to be invoked with every message exchange.

A Web service can be associated with temporary *roles*, depending on its utilization at runtime. For example, it acts as a service provider when it receives and responds to request messages, but can also assume the role of service consumer when it is required to issue request messages to other Web services.

When Web services are positioned within service compositions, it is common for them to transition through service provider and service consumer roles (additional composition-related roles are explained in Chapter 13). Note also that regular programs, components, and legacy systems can also act as Web service consumers as long as they are able to communicate using Web services standards.

Figure 3.22 introduces the symbols used to illustrate physical representations of Web services in this book. Service-orientation principles can affect the design of all displayed parts.

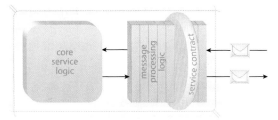

Web service acting as a service provider

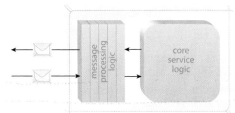

Portions of a Web service acting as a service consumer

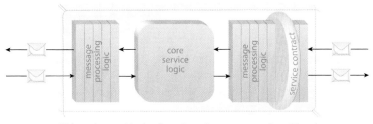

Web service transitioning through service consumer and provider roles

Figure 3.22

Three variations of a single Web service showing the different physical parts of its architecture that come into play, depending on the role it assumes at runtime.

Web Services and Service-Oriented Computing

The popularity of Web services preceded that of service-oriented computing. As a result, their initial use was primarily within traditional distributed solutions wherein they were most commonly used to facilitate point-to-point integration channels. As the maturity and adoption of Web services standards increased, so did the scope of their utilization.

With service-oriented computing comes a distinct architectural model that has been positioned by the vendor community as one that can fully leverage the open interoperability potential of Web services, especially when individual services are consistently shaped by service-orientation. For example, when exposing reusable logic as Web services, the reuse potential is significantly increased. Because service logic can now be accessed via a vendor-neutral communications framework, it becomes available to a wider range of service consumer programs.

Additionally, the fact that Web services provide a communications framework based on physically decoupled contracts allows each service contract to be fully standardized independently from its implementation. This facilitates a potentially high level of service abstraction while providing the opportunity to fully decouple the service from any proprietary implementation details. As explored in Part II, all of these characteristics are desirable when pursuing key principles, such as Standardized Service Contracts, Service Reusability, Service Loose Coupling, Service Abstraction, and Service Composability.

For example, transformation avoidance is a key goal of Standardized Service Contracts. As explained in Chapter 6, this principle advocates the standardization of the data model expressed by the service contract so as to increase intrinsic interoperability by reducing the need for transformation technologies. As illustrated in Figure 3.23, services delivered via disparate component platforms still require the transformation of technology regardless of whether data types are standardized. Services expressed through Web service contracts have the potential to avoid transformation altogether.

> **NOTE**
>
> To learn more about first and second-generation Web services technologies, read the tutorials posted at `www.ws-standards.com` or visit `www.soaspecs.com` and browse through the actual specifications. It is also important to acknowledge service communication mediums that provide an alternative to SOAP-based messaging, such as Representational State Transfer (REST) and Plain Old XML (POX). While these are not covered in this book, it would be worthwhile reading up on them to understand how they differ and where they are most commonly encountered.

Scenario #1: Communication between disparate components

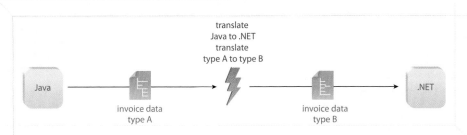

Scenario #2: Communication between non-standardized Web Services

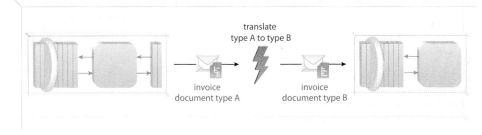

Scenario #3: Communication between standardized Web services with intrinsic interoperability

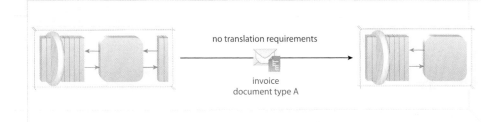

Figure 3.23
Three common data exchange scenarios demonstrating the effect of transformation avoidance.

Service Inventory Blueprints

An ultimate goal of an SOA transition effort is to produce a collection of standardized services that comprise a service inventory. The inventory can be structured into layers according to the service models used, but it is the application of the service-orientation paradigm to all services that positions them as valuable IT assets in full alignment with the strategic goals associated with the SOA project.

However, before any services are actually built, it is desirable to establish a conceptual blueprint of all the planned services for a given inventory. This perspective is documented in the *service inventory blueprint*. There are several common business and data models that, if they exist within an organization, can provide valuable input for this specification. Examples include business entity models, logical data models, canonical data and message models, ontologies, and other information architecture models.

A service inventory blueprint is also known as a *service enterprise model* or a *service inventory model*.

Service-Oriented Analysis and Service Modeling

To effectively deliver standardized services in support of building a service inventory, it is recommended that organizations adopt a methodology specific to SOA and consisting of structured analysis and design processes.

Within SOA projects, these processes are centered around the accurate expression of business logic through technology, which requires that business analysts play a more active role in defining the conceptual design of solution logic. This guarantees a higher degree of alignment between the documented business models and their implementation as services. Agnostic business services especially benefit from hands-on involvement of business subject matter experts, as the improved accuracy of their business representation increases their overall longevity once deployed.

Service-oriented analysis establishes a formal analysis process completed jointly by business analysts and technology architects. *Service modeling,* a sub-process of service-oriented analysis, produces conceptual service definitions called *service candidates*. Iterations through the service-oriented analysis and service modeling processes result in the gradual creation of a collection of service candidates documented as part of a service inventory blueprint.

While the collaborative relationship between business analysts and architects depicted at the lower half of Figure 3.24 may not be unique to an SOA project, the nature and scope of the analysis process is.

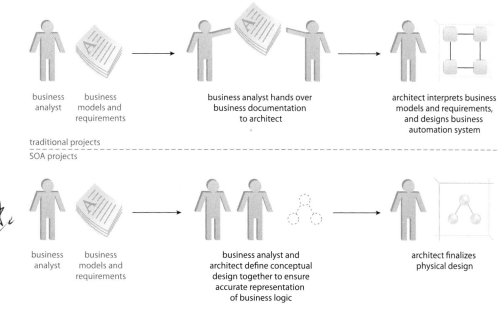

Figure 3.24

A look at how the collaboration between business analysts and technology architects changes with SOA projects.

Service-Oriented Design

The *service-oriented design* process uses a set of predefined service candidates from the service inventory blueprint as a starting point from which they are shaped into actual physical service contracts.

When carrying out service-oriented design, a clear distinction is made between service candidates and services. The former represents a conceptual service that has not been implemented, whereas the latter refers to a physical service.

As shown in Figure 3.25, the traditional (non-standardized) means by which Web service contracts are generated results in services that continue to express the proprietary nature of what they encapsulate. Creating the Web service contract *prior* to development allows for standards to be applied so that the federated endpoints established by Web services are consistent and aligned. This "contract first" approach lies at the heart of service-oriented design and has inspired separate design processes for services based on different service models.

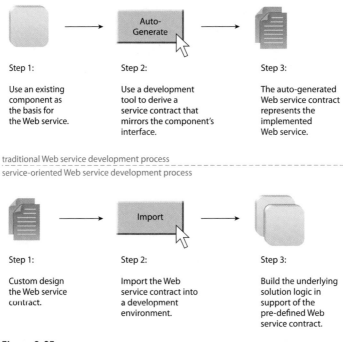

Step 1:

Use an existing component as the basis for the Web service.

Step 2:

Use a development tool to derive a service contract that mirrors the component's interface.

Step 3:

The auto-generated Web service contract represents the implemented Web service.

traditional Web service development process

service-oriented Web service development process

Step 1:

Custom design the Web service contract.

Step 2:

Import the Web service contract into a development environment.

Step 3:

Build the underlying solution logic in support of the pre-defined Web service contract.

Figure 3.25

Unlike the popular process of deriving Web service contracts from existing components, SOA advocates a specific approach that encourages us to postpone development until after a custom designed, standardized contract is in place.

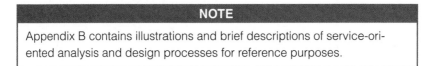

NOTE

Appendix B contains illustrations and brief descriptions of service-oriented analysis and design processes for reference purposes.

"Service-Oriented Architecture: Concepts, Technology, and Design"

Descriptions of first and second-generation Web services technologies, service models, service layers and variations of SOA, as well as a mainstream SOA methodology providing step-by-step process descriptions for service-oriented analysis, service modeling, and service-oriented design are explained in detail in the book *Service-Oriented Architecture: Concepts, Technology, and Design*. SOA is fundamental to all of the content in the remaining chapters and therefore a solid understanding of the concepts behind its architectural model and technologies commonly used for its implementation is recommended.

SUMMARY OF KEY POINTS

- The service-oriented computing platform is comprised of a distinct set of elements, each of which represents a specific aspect of service-oriented computing, and all of which are collectively applied to achieve its goals.

- Service models are used to establish service layers by categorizing services based on the type of logic they encapsulate.

- SOA represents an implementation-agnostic architectural model. However, Web services currently provide the foremost means of implementing services.

3.3 Goals and Benefits of Service-Oriented Computing

It is very important to establish why both vendor and end-user communities within the IT industry are going through the trouble of adopting the service-oriented computing platform and embracing all of the change that comes with it.

The vision behind service-oriented computing is extremely ambitious and therefore also very attractive to any organization interested in truly improving the effectiveness of its IT enterprise. A set of common goals and benefits has emerged to form this vision. These establish a target state for an enterprise that successfully adopts service-orientation.

The upcoming set of sections describe each of these strategic goals and benefits (also displayed in Figure 3.26):

- Increased Intrinsic Interoperability

- Increased Federation

- Increased Vendor Diversification Options

- Increased Business and Technology Domain Alignment

- Increased ROI

- Increased Organizational Agility

- Reduced IT Burden

It is beneficial to understand the significance of these goals and benefits prior to studying and applying service-orientation so that design principles are consistently viewed within a strategic context.

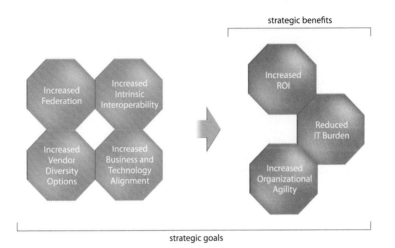

Figure 3.26

The seven identified goals are inter-related and can be further categorized into two groups: strategic goals and resulting benefits. Increased organization agility, increased ROI, and reduced IT burden are concrete benefits resulting from the attainment of the remaining four goals.

An important message of this book in general is that there is a concrete link between successfully applying service-orientation design principles and successfully attaining these specific goals and benefits (a point which is further detailed in Chapter 16).

> **NOTE**
>
> As previously explained, the term "SOA" has been used so much in the media and within marketing literature that it has become synonymous with what the entire service-oriented computing platform represents. Therefore, the goals and benefits listed here are frequently associated with SOA as well.

Increased Intrinsic Interoperability

Interoperability refers to the sharing of data. The more interoperable software programs are, the easier it is for them to exchange information. Software programs that are not interoperable need to be integrated. Therefore, integration can be seen as a process that enables interoperability. A goal of service-orientation is to establish native interoperability within services in order to reduce the need for integration (Figure 3.27). In fact, integration as a concept begins to fade within service-oriented environments (as further explained in the *Effects of Service-Orientation on the Enterprise* section in Chapter 4).

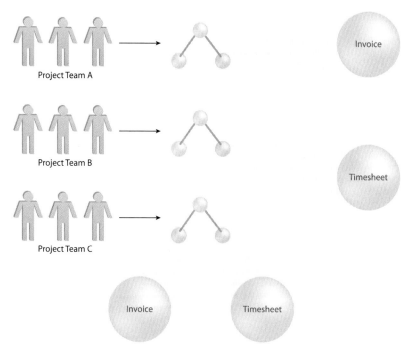

Figure 3.27

Services are designed to be intrinsically interoperable regardless of when and for which purpose they are delivered. In this example, the intrinsic interoperability of the Invoice and Timesheet services delivered by Project Teams A and B allow them to be combined into a new service composition by Project Team C.

Interoperability is specifically fostered through the consistent application of design principles and design standards. This establishes an environment wherein services produced by different projects at different times can be repeatedly assembled together into a variety of composition configurations to help automate a range of business tasks.

Intrinsic interoperability represents a fundamental goal of service-orientation that establishes a foundation for the realization of other strategic goals and benefits. Contract standardization, scalability, behavioral predictability, and reliability are just some of the design characteristics required to facilitate interoperability, all of which are addressed by the service-orientation principles documented in this book.

How specifically service-orientation design principles foster interoperability within services is explained in the *Service-Orientation and Interoperability* section of Chapter 4.

Increased Federation

A federated IT environment is one where resources and applications are united while maintaining their individual autonomy and self-governance. SOA aims to increase a federated perspective of an enterprise to whatever extent it is applied. It accomplishes this through the widespread deployment of standardized and composable services each of which encapsulates a segment of the enterprise and expresses it in a consistent manner.

In support of increasing federation, standardization becomes part of the extra up-front attention each service receives at design time. Ultimately this leads to an environment where enterprise-wide solution logic becomes naturally harmonized, regardless of the nature of its underlying implementation (Figure 3.28).

Figure 3.28

Three service contracts establishing a federated set of endpoints, each of which encapsulates a different implementation.

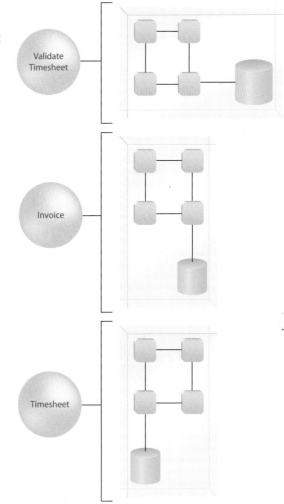

When service-oriented solutions are built via the Web services technology platform, the level of attainable federation is further elevated because services can leverage the non-proprietary nature of the technologies themselves. However, even when using Web services the key success factor to achieving true unity and federation remains the application of design principles and standards.

Increased Vendor Diversification Options

Vendor diversification refers to the ability an organization has to pick and choose "best-of-breed" vendor products and technology innovations and use them together within one enterprise. It is not necessarily beneficial for an organization to have a vendor-diverse environment; however, it is beneficial to have the *option* to diversify when required. To have and retain this option requires that its technology architecture not be tied or locked into any one specific vendor platform.

This represents an important state for an enterprise in that it provides the constant freedom for an organization to change, extend, and even replace solution implementations and technology resources without disrupting the overall, federated service architecture. This measure of governance autonomy is attractive because it prolongs the lifespan and increases the financial return of automation solutions.

By designing a service-oriented architecture in alignment with but neutral to major vendor SOA platforms and by positioning service contracts as standardized endpoints throughout a federated enterprise, proprietary service implementation details can be abstracted to establish a consistent inter-service communications framework. This provides organizations with constant options by allowing them to diversify their enterprises as needed (Figure 3.29).

Vendor diversification is further supported by taking advantage of the standards-based, vendor-neutral Web services framework. Because they impose no proprietary communication requirements, Web services further decrease dependency on vendor platforms. As with any other implementation medium, though, Web services need to be shaped and standardized through service-orientation in order to become a federated part of an SOA.

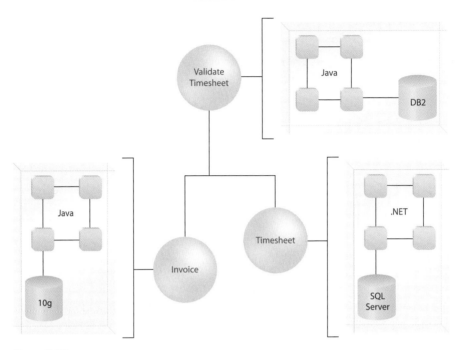

Figure 3.29

A service composition consisting of three services, each of which encapsulates a different vendor automation environment. If service-orientation is adequately applied to the services, underlying disparity will not inhibit their ability to be combined into effective compositions.

Increased Business and Technology Domain Alignment

The extent to which IT business requirements are fulfilled is often associated with the accuracy with which business logic is expressed and automated by solution logic. Although initial applications have traditionally been designed to address immediate and tactical requirements, it has historically been challenging to keep applications in alignment with business needs when the nature and direction of the business changes.

Service-oriented computing introduces a design paradigm that promotes abstraction on many levels. One of the most effective means by which functional abstraction is applied is the establishment of service layers that accurately encapsulate and represent business models. By doing so, common, pre-existing representations of business logic (business entities, business processes) can exist in implemented form as physical services.

This is accomplished by incorporating a structured analysis and modeling process that requires the hands-on involvement of business subject matter experts in the actual definition of the conceptual service candidates (as explained in the *Service-Oriented Analysis*

and Service Modeling section). The resulting service designs are capable of align-
ing automation technology with business
intelligence on an unprecedented level
(Figure 3.30).

Furthermore, the fact that services are
designed to be intrinsically interoperable
directly facilitates business change. As
business processes are augmented in
response to various factors (business
climate changes, new competitors, new
policies, new priorities, etc.) services can
be reconfigured into new compositions
that reflect the changed business logic.
This allows a service-oriented technology architecture to evolve in tandem
with the business itself.

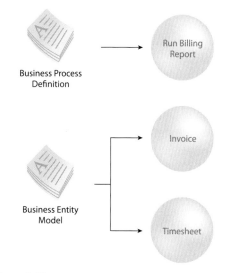

Figure 3.30

Services with business-centric functional contexts are carefully modeled to express and encapsulate corresponding
business models and logic.

Increased ROI

Measuring the return on investment (ROI) of automated solutions is a critical factor in
determining just how cost effective a given application or system actually is. The greater
the return, the more an organization benefits from the solution. However, the lower the
return, the more the cost of automated solutions eats away at an organization's budgets
and profits.

Traditional, silo-based applications tend to get extended over time, resulting in potentially complex environments with effort-intensive maintenance requirements. Combined
with the emergence of ever-growing, non-federated integration architectures that can be
even more difficult to maintain and evolve, the average IT department can demand a significant amount of an organization's overall operational budget. For many organizations,
the financial overhead required by IT is a primary concern because it often continues to
rise without demonstrating any corresponding increase in business value.

Service-oriented computing advocates the creation of agnostic solution logic—logic that
is agnostic to any one purpose and therefore useful for multiple purposes. This multi-
purpose or reusable logic fully leverages the intrinsically interoperable nature of services. Agnostic services have increased reuse potential that can be realized by allowing

them to be repeatedly assembled into different compositions. Any one agnostic service can therefore find itself being repurposed numerous times to automate different business processes as part of different service-oriented solutions.

With this benefit in mind, additional up-front expense and effort is invested into every piece of solution logic so as to position it as an IT asset for the purpose of repeatable, long-term financial returns. As shown in Figure 3.31, the emphasis on increasing ROI typically goes beyond the returns traditionally sought as part of past reuse initiatives. This has much to do with the fact that service-orientation aims to establish reuse as a common, secondary characteristic within most services.

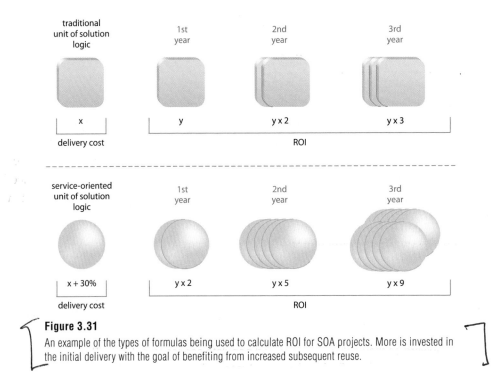

Figure 3.31
An example of the types of formulas being used to calculate ROI for SOA projects. More is invested in the initial delivery with the goal of benefiting from increased subsequent reuse.

It is important to acknowledge that this goal is not simply tied to the benefits traditionally associated with software reuse. Proven commercial product design techniques are incorporated and blended with existing enterprise application delivery approaches to form the basis of a distinct set of service-oriented analysis and design processes (as described earlier in the *Service-Oriented Analysis and Service Modeling* and *Service-Oriented Design* sections).

Increased Organizational Agility

Agility, on an organizational level, refers to the efficiency with which an organization can respond to change. Increasing organizational agility is very attractive to corporations, especially those in the private sector. Being able to more quickly adapt to industry changes and outmaneuver competitors has tremendous strategic significance.

An IT department can sometimes be perceived as a bottleneck, hampering desired responsiveness by requiring too much time or resources to fulfill new or changing business requirements. This is one of the reasons agile development methods have gained popularity as they provide a means of addressing immediate, tactical concerns more rapidly.

Service-oriented computing is very much geared toward establishing wide-spread organizational agility. When service-orientation is applied throughout an enterprise, it results in the creation of services that are highly standardized and reusable and therefore agnostic to parent business processes and specific application environments.

As a service inventory is comprised of more and more of these agnostic services, an increasing percentage of its overall solution logic belongs to no one application environment. Instead, because these services have been positioned as reusable IT assets, they can be repeatedly composed into different configurations. As a result, the time and effort required to automate new or changed business processes is correspondingly reduced because development projects can now be completed with significantly less custom development effort (Figure 3.32).

The net result of this fundamental shift in project delivery is heightened responsiveness and reduced time to market potential, all of which translates into increased organizational agility.

NOTE

Organizational agility represents a target state that organizations work toward as they deliver services and populate service inventories. The organization benefits from increased responsiveness *after* a significant amount of these services is in place. The processes required to model and design services require more up-front cost and effort than building the corresponding quantity of solution logic using traditional project delivery approaches.

It is therefore important to acknowledge that service-orientation has a strategic focus that intends to establish a highly agile enterprise. This is different from agile development approaches that have more of a tactical focus due to an emphasis on delivering solution logic more rapidly. From a delivery perspective, service-orientation does not tend to increase agility.

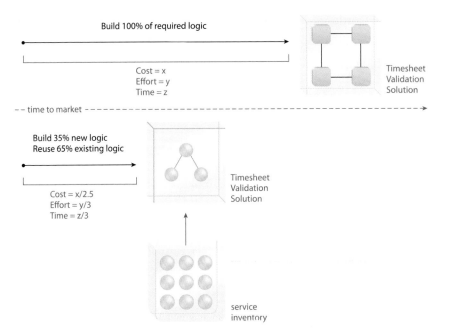

Figure 3.32

Another example of a formula used in SOA projects. This time, the delivery timeline is projected based on the percentage of "net new" solution logic that needs to be built. Though in this example only 35% of new logic is required, the timeline is reduced by around 50% because additional effort is still required to incorporate existing, reusable services from the inventory.

Reduced IT Burden

Consistently applying service-orientation results in an IT enterprise with reduced waste and redundancy, reduced size and operational cost (Figure 3.33), and reduced overhead associated with its governance and evolution. Such an enterprise can benefit an organization through dramatic increases in efficiency and cost-effectiveness.

In essence, the attainment of the previously described goals can create a leaner, more agile IT department; one that is less of a burden on the organization and more of an enabling contributor to its strategic goals.

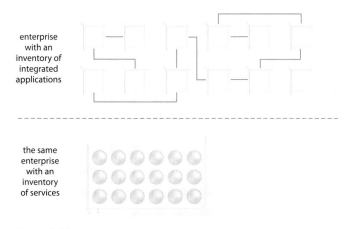

enterprise
with an
inventory of
integrated
applications

the same
enterprise
with an
inventory
of services

Figure 3.33

If you were to take a typical automated enterprise and redevelop it entirely with
custom, normalized services, its overall size would shrink considerably, resulting in a reduced operational scope.

SUMMARY OF KEY POINTS

- Key benefits of service-oriented computing are associated with the standardization, consistency, reliability, and scalability established within services
  through the application of service-orientation design principles.

- The service-oriented computing platform provides the potential to elevate the
  responsiveness and cost-effectiveness of IT through a design paradigm that
  emphasizes the realization of strategic goals and benefits.

3.4 CASE STUDY BACKGROUND

The Cutit ownership team has nowhere near the resources or in-house expertise to plan a transition toward an SOA-based automation environment. They therefore engage a local consulting firm to take charge of the planning and analysis effort. The goal is to complete this project within a month and then use the resulting reports to decide on a delivery strategy.

The consultants spend the next few weeks invading Cutit's environments to document technology and business requirements. They look at service encapsulation options for legacy systems and service-based middleware platforms as part of a marketplace survey but also perform some analysis around the creation of custom services to replace the outdated automation hub.

As part of the final analysis, a preliminary service-oriented architecture is conceptualized and supplemented with a list of Web service-centric technology components required to establish it. Cutit reviews the reports and takes the consultants' recommendations into consideration. The report emphasizes the pursuit of reuse, but Cutit is more interested in leveraging service-oriented computing to establish unity across its modest enterprise and to achieve a state where solution logic can be more easily extended in response to unpredictable business demands.

Regardless, Cutit decides to proceed to the next step. Before moving ahead and building actual services, they invest in the creation of a service inventory blueprint. Cutit cannot afford to wait more than three weeks before entering the development stage, so this model will need to be high-level and therefore somewhat incomplete.

Chapter 4

Service-Orientation

H aving covered some of the basic elements of service-oriented computing, we now narrow our focus on service-orientation. The next set of sections establish the paradigm of service-orientation and explain how it is changing the face of distributed computing.

4.1 Introduction to Service-Orientation

In the every day world around us, services are and have been commonplace for as long as civilized history has existed. Any person carrying out a distinct task in support of others is providing a service (Figure 4.1). Any group of individuals collectively performing a task is also demonstrating the delivery of a service.

Figure 4.1

Three individuals, each capable of providing a distinct service.

Similarly, an organization that carries out tasks associated with its purpose or business is also providing a service. As long as the task or function being provided is well-defined and can be relatively isolated from other associated tasks, it can be distinctly classified as a service (Figure 4.2).

Certain baseline requirements exist to enable a group of individual service providers to collaborate in order to collectively provide a larger service. Figure 4.2, for example, displays a group of employees that each provide a service for ABC Delivery. Even though each individual contributes a distinct service, for the company to function effectively, its staff also needs to have fundamental, common characteristics, such as availability, reliability, and the ability to communicate using the same language. With all of this in place, these individuals can be composed into a productive working team. Establishing these types of baseline requirements is a key goal of service-orientation.

Figure 4.2

A company that employs these three people can compose their capabilities to carry out its business.

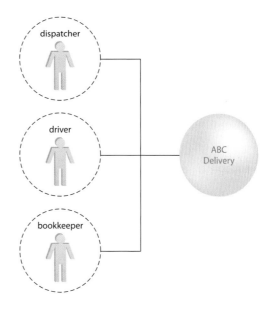

Services in Business Automation

In the world of SOA and service-orientation, the term "service" is not generic. It has specific connotations that relate to a unique combination of design characteristics. When solution logic is consistently built as services and when services are consistently designed with these common characteristics, service-orientation is successfully realized throughout an environment.

For example, one of the primary service design characteristics explored as part of this study of service-orientation is reusability. A strong emphasis on producing solution logic in the format of services that are positioned as highly generic and reusable enterprise resources gradually transitions an organization to a state where more and more of its solution logic becomes less dependent on and more agnostic to any one purpose or business process. Repeatedly fostering this characteristic within services eventually results in wide-spread reuse potential.

Consistently realizing specific design characteristics requires a set of guiding principles. This is what the service-orientation design paradigm is all about.

Services Are Collections of Capabilities

When discussing services, it is important to remember that a single service can provide a collection of capabilities. They are grouped together because they relate to a functional context established by the service. The functional context of the service illustrated in Figure 4.3, for example, is that of "shipment." Therefore, this particular service provides a set of capabilities associated with the processing of shipments.

Figure 4.3
Much like a human, an automated service can provide multiple capabilities.

"I can:
- drive
- fill out a waybill
- collect payment
etc."

Shipment

o Get
o Add
o Report
etc.

A service can essentially act as a container of related capabilities. It is comprised of a body of logic designed to carry out these capabilities and a service contract that expresses which of its capabilities are made available for public invocation.

References to service capabilities in this book are specifically focused on those that are defined in the service contract. For a discussion of how service capabilities are distinguished from Web service operations and component methods, see the *Principles and Service Implementation Mediums* section in Chapter 5.

Service-Orientation as a Design Paradigm

As established in Chapter 3, a design paradigm is an approach to designing solution logic. When building distributed solution logic, design approaches revolve around a software engineering theory known as the *separation of concerns*. In a nutshell, this theory states that a larger problem is more effectively solved when decomposed into a set of smaller problems or *concerns*. This gives us the option of partitioning solution logic into capabilities, each designed to solve an individual concern. Related capabilities can be grouped into units of solution logic.

The fundamental benefit to solving problems this way is that a number of the solution logic units can be designed to solve immediate concerns while still remaining agnostic to the greater problem. This provides the constant opportunity for us to reutilize the capabilities within those units to solve other problems as well.

Different design paradigms exist for distributed solution logic. What distinguishes service-orientation is the manner in which it carries out the separation of concerns and how it shapes the individual units of solution logic. Applying service-orientation to a meaningful extent results in solution logic that can be safely classified as "service-oriented" and units that qualify as "services." To understand exactly what that means requires an appreciation of the strategic goals covered in Chapter 3 combined with knowledge of the associated design principles documented in Part II.

For now, let's briefly introduce each of these principles:

Standardized Service Contract

Services express their purpose and capabilities via a service contract. The Standardized Service Contract design principle is perhaps the most fundamental part of service-orientation in that it essentially requires that specific considerations be taken into account when designing a service's public technical interface and assessing the nature and quantity of content that will be published as part of a service's official contract.

A great deal of emphasis is placed on specific aspects of contract design, including the manner in which services express functionality, how data types and data models are defined, and how policies are asserted and attached. There is a constant focus on ensuring that service contracts are both optimized, appropriately granular, and standardized to ensure that the endpoints established by services are consistent, reliable, and governable.

Chapter 6 is dedicated to exploring this design principle in detail.

Service Loose Coupling

Coupling refers to a connection or relationship between two things. A measure of coupling is comparable to a level of dependency. This principle advocates the creation of a specific type of relationship within and outside of service boundaries, with a constant emphasis on reducing ("loosening") dependencies between the service contract, its implementation, and its service consumers.

The principle of Service Loose Coupling promotes the independent design and evolution of a service's logic and implementation while still guaranteeing baseline interoperability with consumers that have come to rely on the service's capabilities. There are numerous types of coupling involved in the design of a service, each of which can impact the content and granularity of its contract. Achieving the appropriate level of coupling requires that practical considerations be balanced against various service design preferences.

Chapter 7 provides an in-depth exploration of this principle and introduces related patterns and concepts.

Service Abstraction

Abstraction ties into many aspects of service-orientation. On a fundamental level, this principle emphasizes the need to hide as much of the underlying details of a service as possible. Doing so directly enables and preserves the previously described loosely coupled relationship. Service Abstraction also plays a significant role in the positioning and design of service compositions.

Various forms of meta data come into the picture when assessing appropriate abstraction levels. The extent of abstraction applied can affect service contract granularity and can further influence the ultimate cost and effort of governing the service.

Chapter 8 covers several aspects of applying abstraction to different types of service meta data, along with processes and approaches associated with information hiding.

Service Reusability

Reuse is strongly advocated within service-orientation; so much so, that it becomes a core part of typical service analysis and design processes, and also forms the basis for key service models. The advent of mature, non-proprietary service technology has provided the opportunity to maximize the reuse potential of multi-purpose logic on an unprecedented level.

The principle of Service Reusability emphasizes the positioning of services as enterprise resources with agnostic functional contexts. Numerous design considerations are raised to ensure that individual service capabilities are appropriately defined in relation to an agnostic service context, and to guarantee that they can facilitate the necessary reuse requirements.

Variations and levels of reuse and associated agnostic service models are covered in Chapter 9, along with a study of how commercial product design approaches have influenced this principle.

Service Autonomy

For services to carry out their capabilities consistently and reliably, their underlying solution logic needs to have a significant degree of control over its environment and resources. The principle of Service Autonomy supports the extent to which other design principles can be effectively realized in real world production environments by fostering design characteristics that increase a service's reliability and behavioral predictability.

This principle raises various issues that pertain to the design of service logic as well as the service's actual implementation environment. Isolation levels and service normalization considerations are taken into account to achieve a suitable measure of autonomy, especially for reusable services that are frequently shared.

Chapter 10 documents the design issues and challenges related to attaining higher levels of service autonomy, and further classifies different forms of autonomy and highlights associated risks.

Service Statelessness

The management of excessive state information can compromise the availability of a service and undermine its scalability potential. Services are therefore ideally designed to remain stateful only when required. Applying the principle of Service Statelessness requires that measures of realistically attainable statelessness be assessed, based on the adequacy of the surrounding technology architecture to provide state management delegation and deferral options.

Chapter 11 explores the options and impacts of incorporating stateless design characteristics into service architectures.

Service Discoverability

For services to be positioned as IT assets with repeatable ROI they need to be easily identified and understood when opportunities for reuse present themselves. The service design therefore needs to take the "communications quality" of the service and its individual capabilities into account, regardless of whether a discovery mechanism (such as a service registry) is an immediate part of the environment.

The application of this principle, as well as an explanation of how discoverability relates to interpretability and the overall service discovery process, are covered in Chapter 12.

Service Composability

As the sophistication of service-oriented solutions continues to grow, so does the complexity of underlying service composition configurations. The ability to effectively compose services is a critical requirement for achieving some of the most fundamental goals of service-oriented computing.

Complex service compositions place demands on service design that need to be anticipated to avoid massive retro-fitting efforts. Services are expected to be capable of participating as effective composition members, regardless of whether they need to be immediately enlisted in a composition. The principle of Service Composability addresses this requirement by ensuring that a variety of considerations are taken into account.

How the application of this design principle helps prepare services for the world of complex compositions is described in Chapter 13.

Service-Orientation and Interoperability

One item that may appear to be absent from the preceding list is a principle along the lines of *"Services are Interoperable."* The reason this does not exist as a separate principle is because interoperability is fundamental to every one of the principles just described. Therefore, in relation to service-oriented computing, stating that services must be interoperable is just about as basic as stating that services must exist. Each of the eight principles supports or contributes to interoperability in some manner.

Here are just a few examples:

- Service contracts are standardized to guarantee a baseline measure of interoperability associated with the harmonization of data models.

- Reducing the degree of service coupling fosters interoperability by making individual services less dependent on others and therefore more open for invocation by different service consumers.

- Abstracting details about the service limits all interoperation to the service contract, increasing the long-term consistency of interoperability by allowing underlying service logic to evolve more independently.

- Designing services for reuse implies a high-level of required interoperability between the service and numerous potential service consumers.

- By raising a service's individual autonomy, its behavior becomes more consistently predictable, increasing its reuse potential and thereby its attainable level of interoperability.

- Through an emphasis on stateless design, the availability and scalability of services increase, allowing them to interoperate more frequently and reliably.

- Service Discoverability simply allows services to be more easily located by those who want to potentially interoperate with them.

- Finally, for services to be effectively composable they must be interoperable. The success of fulfilling composability requirements is often tied directly to the extent to which services are standardized and cross-service data exchange is optimized.

A fundamental goal of applying service-orientation is for interoperability to become a natural by-product, ideally to the extent that a level of intrinsic interoperability is established as a common and expected service design characteristic. Depending on the architectural strategy being employed, this extent may or may not be limited to a specific service inventory.

Of course, as with any other design characteristic, there are levels of interoperability a service can attain. The ultimate measure is generally determined by the extent to which service-orientation principles have been consistently and successfully realized (plus, of course, environmental factors such as the compatibility of wire protocols, the maturity level of the underlying technology platform, and adherence to technology standards).

NOTE

Increased intrinsic interoperability is one of the key strategic goals associated with service-oriented computing (as originally established in Chapter 3). For more detailed information about how service-orientation principles directly support this and other strategic goals, see Chapter 16.

SUMMARY OF KEY POINTS

- The service-orientation paradigm consists of eight distinct design principles, each of which fosters fundamental design characteristics, such as interoperability. These principles are explored individually in subsequent chapters.

- Interoperability is a natural by-product of applying service-orientation design principles.

4.2 Problems Solved by Service-Orientation

To best appreciate why service-orientation has emerged and how it is intended to improve the design of automation systems, we need to compare before and after perspectives. By studying some of the common issues that have historically plagued IT, we can begin to understand the solutions proposed by this design paradigm.

> **NOTE**
>
> This book fully acknowledges that past design paradigms have advocated similar principles and strategic goals as service-orientation. Several of these design approaches, in fact, directly inspired or influenced service-orientation (as explained further in the *Origins and Influences of Service-Orientation* section of this chapter). The following section is focused specifically on a comparison with the silo-based design approach because it has persisted as the most common means by which applications are delivered.

Life Before Service-Orientation

In the world of business it makes a great deal of sense to deliver solutions capable of automating the execution of business tasks. Over the course of IT's history, the majority of such solutions have been created with a common approach of identifying the business tasks to be automated, defining their business requirements, and then building the corresponding solution logic (Figure 4.4).

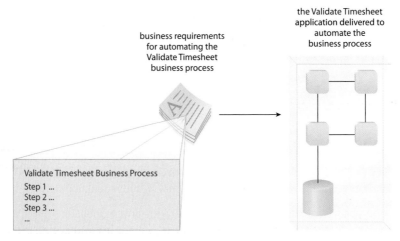

Figure 4.4

A ratio of one application for each new set of automation requirements has been common.

This has been an accepted and proven approach to achieving tangible business benefits through the use of technology and has been successful at providing a relatively predictable return on investment (Figure 4.5).

Figure 4.5

A sample formula for calculating ROI is based on a predetermined investment with a predictable return.

Development cost = x

Yearly operational cost = y

Estimated yearly savings
due to increased productivity = (x/2) - y

Validate Timesheet
Application

The ability to gain any further value from these applications is usually inhibited because their capabilities are tied to specific business requirements and processes (some of which will even have a limited lifespan). When new requirements and processes come our way, we are forced to either make significant changes to what we already have, or we may need to build a new application altogether.

In the latter case, although repeatedly building "disposable applications" is not the perfect approach, it has proven itself as a legitimate means of automating business. Let's explore some of the lessons learned by first focusing on the positive.

- Solutions can be built efficiently because they only need to be concerned with the fulfillment of a narrow set of requirements associated with a limited set of business processes.

- The business analysis effort involved with defining the process to be automated is straight forward. Analysts are focused only on one process at a time and therefore only concern themselves with the business entities and domains associated with that one process.

- Solution designs are tactically focused. Although complex and sophisticated automation solutions are sometimes required, the sole purpose of each is to automate just one or a specific set of business processes. This predefined functional scope simplifies the overall solution design as well as the underlying application architecture.

- The project delivery lifecycle for each solution is streamlined and relatively predictable. Although IT projects are notorious for being complex endeavors, riddled with unforeseen challenges, when the delivery scope is well-defined (and doesn't change), the process and execution of the delivery phases have a good chance of being carried out as expected.

- Building new systems from the ground up allows organizations to take advantage of the latest technology advancements. The IT marketplace progresses every year to the extent that we fully expect technology we use to build solution logic today to be different and better tomorrow. As a result, organizations that repeatedly build disposable applications can leverage the latest technology innovations with each new project.

These and other common characteristics of traditional solution delivery provide a good indication as to why this approach has been so popular. Despite its acceptance, though, it has become evident that there is still lots of room for improvement.

It Can Be Highly Wasteful

The creation of new solution logic in a given enterprise commonly results in a significant amount of redundant functionality (Figure 4.6). The effort and expense required to construct this logic is therefore also redundant.

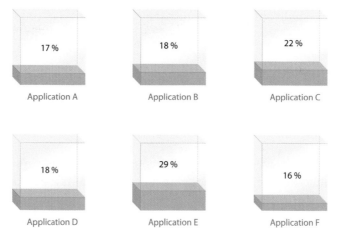

Figure 4.6
Different applications developed independently can result in significant amounts of redundant functionality. The applications displayed were delivered with various levels of solution logic that, in some form, already existed.

It's Not as Efficient as it Appears

Because of the tactical focus on delivering solutions for specific process requirements, the scope of development projects is highly targeted. Therefore, there is the constant perception that business requirements will be fulfilled at the earliest possible time. However, by continually building and rebuilding logic that already exists elsewhere, the process is not as efficient as it could be if the creation of redundant logic could be avoided (Figure 4.7).

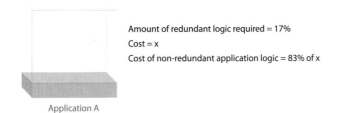

Amount of redundant logic required = 17%
Cost = x
Cost of non-redundant application logic = 83% of x

Application A

Figure 4.7
Application A was delivered for a specific set of business requirements.
Because a subset of these business requirements had already been ful-
filled elsewhere, Application A's delivery scope is larger than it has to be.

It Bloats an Enterprise

Each new or extended application adds to the bulk of an IT environment's system inventory (Figure 4.8). The ever-expanding hosting, maintenance, and administration demands can inflate an IT department in budget, resources, and size to the extent that IT becomes a significant drain on the overall organization.

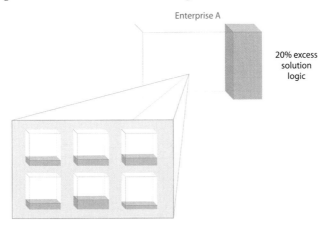

Enterprise A

20% excess
solution
logic

Figure 4.8
This simple diagram portrays an enterprise environment containing applications with redundant functionality. The net effect is a larger enterprise.

It Can Result in Complex Infrastructures and Convoluted Enterprise Architectures

Having to host numerous applications built from different generations of technologies and perhaps even different technology platforms often requires that each will impose unique architectural requirements. The disparity across these "siloed" applications can lead to a counter-federated environment (Figure 4.9), making it challenging to plan the evolution of an enterprise and scale its infrastructure in response to that evolution.

Figure 4.9
Different application environments within the same enterprise can introduce incompatible runtime platforms as indicated by the shaded zones.

Integration Becomes a Constant Challenge

Applications built only with the automation of specific business processes in mind are generally not designed to accommodate other interoperability requirements. Making these types of applications share data at some later point results in a jungle of convoluted integration architectures held together mostly through point-to-point patchwork (Figure 4.10) or requiring the introduction of large middleware layers.

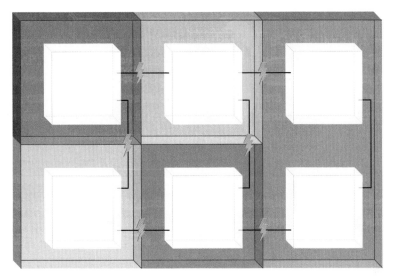

Figure 4.10

A vendor-diverse enterprise can introduce a variety of integration challenges, as expressed by the little lightning bolts that highlight points of concern when trying to bridge proprietary environments.

The Need for Service-Orientation

After repeated generations of traditional distributed solutions, the severity of the previously described problems has been amplified. This is why service-orientation was conceived. It very much represents an evolutionary state in the history of IT in that it combines successful design elements of past approaches with new design elements that leverage conceptual and technology innovation.

The consistent application of the eight design principles listed earlier results in the widespread proliferation of the corresponding design characteristics:

- increased consistency in how functionality and data is represented

- reduced dependencies between units of solution logic

- reduced awareness of underlying solution logic design and implementation details

- increased opportunities to use a piece of solution logic for multiple purposes

- increased opportunities to combine units of solution logic into different configurations

- increased behavioral predictability

- increased availability and scalability

- increased awareness of available solution logic

When these characteristics exist as real parts of implemented services, they establish a common synergy. As a result, the complexion of an enterprise changes as the following distinct qualities are consistently promoted:

Increased Amounts of Agnostic Solution Logic

Within a service-oriented solution, units of logic (services) encapsulate functionality not specific to any one application or business process (Figure 4.11). These services are therefore classified as agnostic and reusable IT assets.

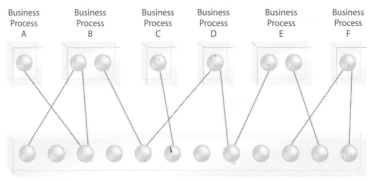

business process agnostic services

Figure 4.11
Business processes are automated by a series of business process-specific services
(top layer) that share a pool of business process-agnostic services (bottom layer). These
layers correspond to the task, entity, and utility service models described in Chapter 3.

Reduced Amounts of Application-Specific Logic

Increasing the amount of solution logic not specific to any one application or business process decreases the amount of required application-specific logic (Figure 4.12). This blurs the lines between standalone application environments by reducing the overall quantity of standalone applications. (See also the *Service-Orientation and the Concept of "Application"* section later in this chapter.)

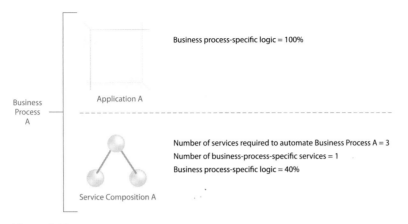

Figure 4.12

Business Process A can be automated by either Application A or Service Composition A. The delivery of Application A can result in a body of solution logic that is specific to and tailored for the business process. Service Composition A would be designed to automate the process with a combination of agnostic services and 40% of additional logic specific to the business process.

Reduced Volume of Logic Overall

The overall quantity of solution logic is reduced because the same solution logic is shared and reused to automate multiple business processes, as shown in Figure 4.13.

Figure 4.13

The quantity of solution logic shrinks as an enterprise transitions toward a standardized service inventory comprised of "normalized" services.

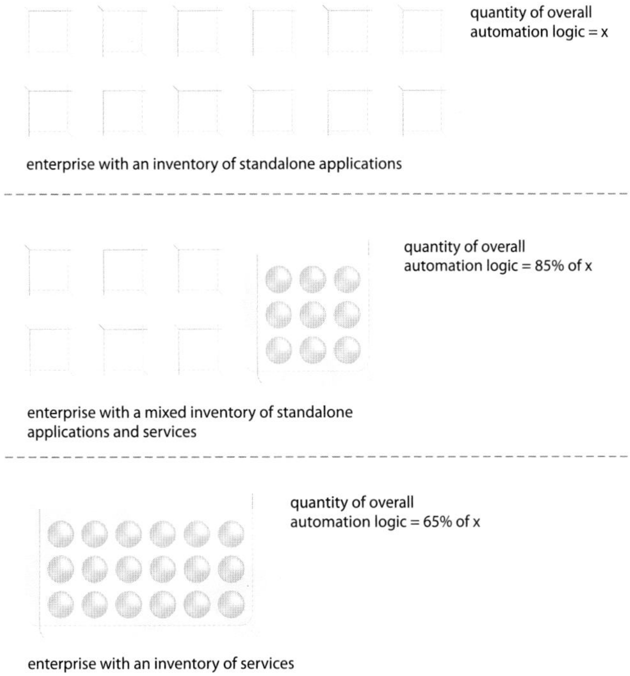

quantity of overall
automation logic = x

enterprise with an inventory of standalone applications

quantity of overall
automation logic = 85% of x

enterprise with a mixed inventory of standalone
applications and services

quantity of overall
automation logic = 65% of x

enterprise with an inventory of services

Inherent Interoperability

Common design characteristics consistently implemented result in solution logic that is naturally aligned. When this carries over to the standardization of service contracts and their underlying data models, a base level of automatic interoperability is achieved across services, as illustrated in Figure 4.14. (See also the *Service-Orientation and the Concept of "Integration"* section later in this chapter.)

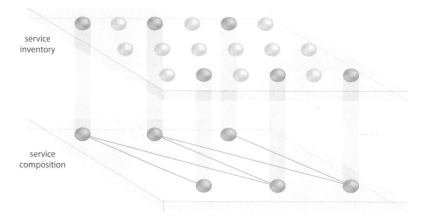

Figure 4.14

Services from different parts of a service inventory can be combined into new compositions. If these services are designed to be intrinsically interoperable, the effort to assemble them into new composition configurations is significantly reduced.

SUMMARY OF KEY POINTS

- The traditional silo-based approach to building applications has been successful at providing tangible benefits and measurable returns on investment.

- This approach has also caused its share of problems, most notably an increase in integration complexity and an increase in the size and administrative burden of IT enterprises.

- Service-orientation establishes a design paradigm that leverages and builds upon previous approaches and proposes a means of avoiding problems associated with silo-based application delivery.

4.3 Challenges Introduced by Service-Orientation

As much as service-orientation can solve some of the more significant historical problems in IT, its application in the real world can make some serious impositions. It is necessary to be aware of these challenges ahead of time because being prepared is key to
overcoming them.

Design Complexity

With a constant emphasis on reuse, a significant percentage of a service inventory can
ultimately be comprised of agnostic services capable of fulfilling requirements for multiple potential service consumer programs.

Although this can establish a highly normalized and streamlined architecture, it can also
introduce an increased level of complexity for both the architecture as well as individual service designs.

Examples include:

- increased performance requirements resulting from the increased reuse of agnostic
  services

- reliability issues of services at peak concurrent usage times and availability issues
  of services during off-hours

- single point of failure issues introduced by excessive reuse of agnostic services
  (and that may require the need for redundant deployments to mitigate risks)

- increased demands on service hosting environments to accommodate autonomy-
  related preferences

- service contract versioning issues and the impact of potentially redundant service
  contracts

Design issues such as these can be addressed by a combination of sound technology
architecture design, modern vendor runtime platform technology, and the consistent
application of service-orientation design principles. Solving service reliability and performance issues in particular are primary goals of those design principles more focused
on the underlying service logic, such as Service Autonomy, Service Statelessness, and
Service Composability.

The Need for Design Standards

Design standards can be healthy for an enterprise in that they "pre-solve" problems by making several decisions for architects and developers ahead of time, thereby increasing the consistency and compatibility of solution designs. Their use is required in order to realize the successful propagation of service-orientation.

Although it can be a straight-forward process to create these standards, incorporating them into a (non-standardized) IT culture already set in its ways can be demanding to say the least. The usage of design standards can introduce the need to enforce their compliance, a policing role that can meet with resistance. Additionally, architects and developers sometimes feel that design standards inhibit their creativity and ability to innovate.

A circumstance that tends to aid the large-scale realization of standardization is when the SOA initiative is championed by an executive manager, such as a CIO. When an individual or a governing body has the authority to essentially "lay down the law," many of these cultural issues resolve themselves more quickly. However, within organizations based on peer-level departmental structures (which are more common in the public sector), the acceptance of design standards may require negotiation and compromise.

The best weapon for overcoming cultural resistance to design standards is communication and education. Those resisting standardization efforts are more likely to become supporters after gaining an appreciation of the strategic significance and ultimate benefits of adopting and respecting the need for design standards.

Top-Down Requirements

A preferred strategy to delivering services is to first conceptualize a service inventory by defining a blueprint of all planned services, their relationships, boundaries, and individual service models. This approach is very much associated with a top-down delivery strategy in that it can impose a significant amount of up-front analysis effort involving many members of business analysis and technology architecture groups.

Though preferred, achieving a comprehensive blueprint prior to building services is often not feasible. It is common for organizations to face budget and time constraints and tactical priorities that simply won't permit it. As a result, there are phased and iterative delivery approaches that allow for services to be produced earlier on. These, however, often come with trade-offs in that they can require the service designs to be revisited and revised at a later point. While this can introduce risks associated with

Design Service blueprints prior to Service Contracts.

the implementation of premature service designs, it is often considered an acceptable compromise.

The principles of service-orientation can be applied to services on an individual basis, allowing a reasonable degree of service-orientation to be achieved regardless of the approach. However, the actual quality of the resulting service designs is typically tied to how much of the top-down analysis work was completed prior to their delivery.

> ### BEST PRACTICE
>
> It is recommended that, at minimum, a high-level service inventory blueprint always be defined prior to creating physical service contracts. This establishes an important "broader" perspective in support of service-oriented analysis and service modeling processes and, ultimately, results in stronger and more durable service designs.

Counter-Agile Service Delivery in Support of Agile Solution Delivery

Irrespective of the potential top-down efforts needed for some SOA projects, the additional design considerations required to implement a meaningful measure of each of the eight design principles increases both the overall time and cost to deliver service logic.

This may appear contrary to the attention SOA has received for its ability to increase agility. To achieve the state of organizational agility described in Chapter 3 requires that service-orientation already be successfully implemented. This is what establishes an environment in which the delivery of solutions is much more agile.

However, given that it takes more initial effort to design and build services than it does to build a corresponding amount of logic that is not service-oriented, the process of delivering services in support of SOA can actually be *counter*-agile. This can cause issues for an organization that has tactical requirements or needs to be responsive while building a service inventory.

> ### BEST PRACTICE
>
> An effective approach, when sufficient resources are available, is to allow SOA initiatives to be delivered alongside existing legacy development and maintenance projects. This way, tactical requirements can continue to be fulfilled by traditional applications while the enterprise works toward a phased transition toward service-oriented computing.
>
> Appendix B provides additional coverage of SOA delivery strategies that address tactical versus strategic service delivery requirements.

Governance Demands

The eventual existence of one or more service inventories represents the ultimate deliverable of the typical large-scale SOA initiative. A service inventory establishes a powerful reserve of standardized solution logic, a high percentage of which will ideally be classified as agnostic or reusable. Subsequent to their implementation, though, the management and evolution of these agnostic services can be responsible for some of the most profound changes imposed by service-orientation.

In the past, a standalone application was typically developed by a single project team. Members of this team often ended up remaining "attached" to the application for subsequent upgrades, maintenance, and extensions. This ownership model worked because the application's overall purpose and scope remained focused on the business tasks it was originally built to automate.

The body of solution logic represented by agnostic services, however, is intentionally positioned to *not* belong to any one business process. Although these services may have been delivered by a project team, that same team may not continue to own the service logic as it gets repeatedly utilized by other solutions, processes, and compositions.

Therefore, a special governance structure is required. This can introduce new resources, roles, processes, and even new groups or departments. Ultimately, when these issues are under control and the IT environment itself has successfully adapted to the required changes, the many benefits associated with this new computing platform are there for the taking. However, the process of moving to this new governance model can challenge traditional approaches and demand time, expense, and a great deal of patience.

SUMMARY OF KEY POINTS

- Applying service-orientation on a broad scale can introduce increased design complexity and the need for a consistent level of standardization.

- The construction of services can be expensive and time-consuming, introducing a more burdensome project delivery lifecycle, further compounded by some of the common top-down analysis requirements that may need to be in place before services can be built.

- Service inventory governance requirements can impose significant changes that can shake up the organizational structure of an IT department.

4.4 Additional Considerations

To supplement the benefits and challenges just covered, this section discusses some further aspects of service-orientation.

It Is Not a Revolutionary Paradigm

Service-orientation is not a brand new paradigm that aims to replace all that preceded it. It, in fact, incorporates and builds upon proven and successful elements from past paradigms and combines these with design approaches shaped to leverage recent technology innovations.

This is why we do not refer to SOA as a revolutionary model in the history of IT. It is simply the next stage in an evolutionary cycle that began with the application of modularity on a small scale (by organizing simple programming routines into shared modules for example) and has now spread to the potential modularization of the enterprise.

Enterprise-wide Standardization Is Not Required

There is a common misperception that unless design standardization is achieved globally throughout the entire enterprise, SOA will not succeed. Although design standardization is a critical success factor for SOA projects that is *ideally* achieved across an enterprise, it only needs to be realized to a meaningful extent for service-orientation to result in strategic benefit.

For example, service-orientation emphasizes the need for standardizing service data models to avoid unnecessary data transformation and other problematic issues that can compromise interoperability. The extent to which data model standardization is achieved determines the extent to which these problems will be avoided.

The goal is not always to eliminate problems entirely because that can be an unrealistic objective, especially in larger enterprises. Therefore, the goal is sometimes to just minimize problems by taking special considerations into account during service design.

In support of this approach, design patterns exist for organizing the division of an enterprise into more manageable domains. Data standardization is generally more easily attained within each domain, and transformation is then only required when exchanging data across these domains. Even though this does not achieve a global data model, it can still help establish a very meaningful level of interoperability.

Reuse Is Not an Absolute Requirement

Increasing reusability of solution logic is a fundamental goal of service-orientation, and reuse is clearly one of the most associated benefits of SOA. As a result, organizations that have had limited success with past reuse initiatives, or with concerns that significant amounts of reuse cannot be achieved within their enterprise, are often hesitant about SOA in general.

While reuse, especially over time, can be one of the most rewarding parts of investing in SOA, it is not the sole primary benefit. Perhaps even more fundamental to service-orientation than promoting reuse is fostering interoperability. Enabling an enterprise to connect previously disparate systems or to make interconnectivity an intrinsic quality of new solution logic is extremely powerful.

You could ignore the principle of Service Reusability in service designs and still achieve significant returns on investment based solely on raising the level of enterprise-wide interoperability.

> **NOTE**
>
> One could argue that reuse and interoperability are very closely related in that if two services are interoperable, there is always the opportunity for reuse. However, traditional perspectives of reusable solution logic focus on the nature of the logic itself. A service that is designed to be specifically agnostic to business processes and cross-cutting to address multiple concerns will have a particular functional context associated with it. Therefore, reuse can be seen as a separate design characteristic that relies and builds upon interoperability. See Chapter 9 for more details.

SUMMARY OF KEY POINTS

- Service-orientation has deep roots in several past computing platforms and design approaches, and is therefore not considered a revolutionary design paradigm.

- Global standardization within an enterprise is not a requirement for creating service-oriented enterprises because individual service inventories can be established (and separately standardized) within different enterprise domains.

- Although fundamental to much of service-orientation, if reusability were to be omitted as a design characteristic, significant interoperability-related benefit would still be attainable.

4.5 Effects of Service-Orientation on the Enterprise

There are good reasons to have high expectations from the service-orientation paradigm. But, at the same time, there is much to learn and understand before it can be successfully applied. The following sections explore some of the more common examples.

Service-Orientation and the Concept of "Application"

Having just stated that reuse is not an absolute requirement, it is important to acknowledge the fact that service-orientation does place an unprecedented emphasis on reuse. By establishing a service inventory with a high percentage of reusable and agnostic services, we are now positioning those services as the primary (or only) means by which the solution logic they represent can and should be accessed.

As a result, we make a very deliberate move away from the silos in which applications previously existed. Because we want to share reusable logic whenever possible, we automate existing, new, and augmented business processes through service composition. This results in a shift where more and more business requirements are fulfilled not by building or extending applications, but by simply composing existing services into new composition configurations.

When compositions become more common, the traditional concept of an application, a system, or a solution actually begins to fade, along with the silos that contain them. Applications no longer consist of self-contained bodies of programming logic responsible for automating a specific set of tasks (Figure 4.15). What was an application is now just another service composition. And it's a composition made up of services that very likely participate in other compositions (Figure 4.16).

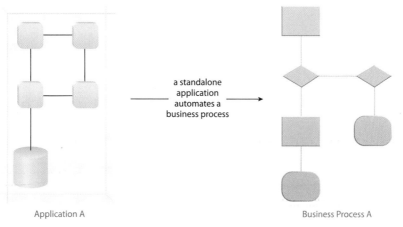

a standalone application automates a business process

Application A

Business Process A

Figure 4.15
The traditional application, delivered to automate specific business process logic.

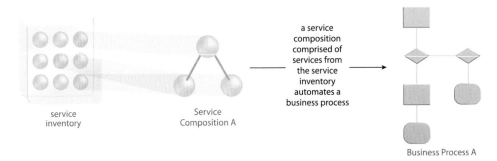

Figure 4.16

The service composition, intended to fulfill the role of the traditional application by leveraging agnostic and non-agnostic services from a service inventory. This essentially establishes a "composite application."

An application in this environment loses its individuality. One could argue that a service-oriented application actually does not exist because it is, in fact, just one of many service compositions. However, upon closer reflection, we can see that some of the services are actually not business process-agnostic. The task service, for example, intentionally represents logic that is dedicated to the automation of just one business task and therefore is not necessarily reusable.

What this indicates is that non-agnostic services can still be associated with the notion of an application. However, within service-oriented computing, the meaning of this term can change to reflect the fact that a potentially large portion of the application logic is no longer exclusive to the application.

Service-Orientation and the Concept of "Integration"

When we revisit the idea of a service inventory consisting of services that have, as per our service-orientation principles, been shaped into standardized and (for the most part) reusable units of solution logic, we can see that this can challenge the traditional perception of "integration."

In the past, integrating something implied connecting two or more applications or programs that may or may not have been compatible (Figure 4.17). Perhaps they were based on different technology platforms or maybe they were never designed to connect with anything outside of their own internal boundary. The increasing need to hook up disparate pieces of software to establish a reliable level of data exchange is what turned integration into an important, high profile part of the IT industry.

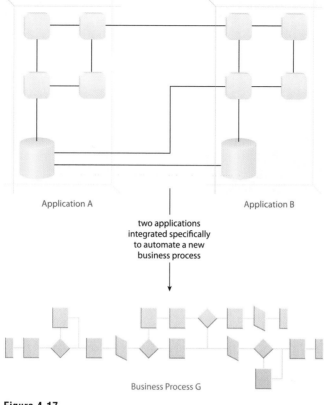

Application A   Application B

**two applications
integrated specifically
to automate a new
business process**

Business Process G

Figure 4.17
The traditional integration architecture, comprised of two or more applications
connected in different ways to fulfill a new set of automation requirements (as
dictated by the new Business Process G).

Services designed to be "intrinsically interoperable" are built with the full awareness
that they will need to interact with a potentially large range of service consumers, most
of which will be unknown at the time of their initial delivery. If a significant part of our
enterprise solution logic is represented by an inventory of intrinsically interoperable
services, it empowers us with the freedom to mix and match these services into infinite
composition configurations to fulfill whatever automation requirements come our way.

As a result, the concept of integration begins to fade. Exchanging data between different
units of solution logic becomes a natural and secondary design characteristic (Figure
4.18). Again, though, this is something that can only transpire when a substantial percentage of an organization's solution logic is represented by a quality service inventory.

While working toward achieving this environment, there will likely be many requirements for traditional integration between existing legacy systems and also between legacy systems and these services.

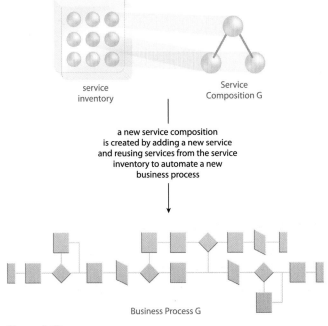

Figure 4.18
A new combination of services is composed together to fulfill the role of traditional integrated applications.

The Service Composition

Applications, integrated applications, solutions, systems, all of these terms and what they have traditionally represented can be directly associated with the service composition (Figure 4.19). However, given the fact that many SOA implementations consist of a mixture of legacy environments and services, these terms are sure to survive for quite some time.

In fact, as SOA transition initiatives continue to progress within an enterprise, it can be helpful to make a clear distinction between a traditional application (one which may reside alongside an SOA implementation or which may be actually encapsulated by a service) and the service compositions that eventually become more commonplace.

Figure 4.19

A service-oriented solution, application, or system is the equivalent of a service composition. If we were to build an enterprise-
wide SOA from the ground up, it would likely be comprised of
numerous service compositions capable of fulfilling the traditional
roles associated with these terms.

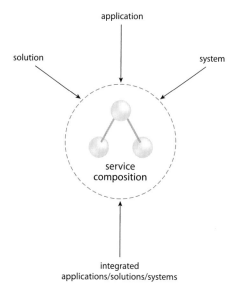

Application, Integration, and Enterprise Architectures

Because applications have existed for as long as IT, when technology architecture as a
profession and perspective within the enterprise came about, it made perfect sense to
have separate architectural views dedicated to individual applications, integrated applications, and the enterprise as a whole.

When standardizing on service-orientation, the manner in which we document technology architecture is also in for a change. The enterprise-level perspective becomes pre-
dominant as it represents a master view of the service inventory. It can still encompass
the traditional parts of a formal architecture, including conceptual views, physical
views, and supporting technologies and governance platforms—but all these views are
likely to now become associated with the service inventory.

A new type of technical specification that gains prominence in service-oriented enterprise initiatives is the *service composition architecture*. Even though we talk about the simplicity of combining services into new composition configurations on demand, it is by
no means an easy process. It is a design exercise that requires the detailed documentation of the planned composition architecture.

For example, each service needs to be assessed as to its competency to fulfill its role as a
composition member, and foreseeable service activity scenarios need to be mapped out.

Message designs, messaging routes, exception handling, cross-service transactions, policies, and many more considerations go into making a composition capable of automating its designated business process.

BEST PRACTICE

Although the structure and content of traditional application architecture specifications are augmented when documenting composition architectures, there can still be a natural tendency to refer to these documents as architecture specifications for applications.

While an organization is undergoing a transition toward SOA, it can be helpful to make a clear distinction between an application consisting of a service composition and traditional, standalone or legacy applications.

One approach is to consistently qualify the term "application." For example, it can be prefixed with "service-oriented," "composite," "standalone," or "legacy." Another option is to simply limit the use of the term "application" to refer to non-service-composed solutions only.

Furthermore, a composed service encapsulating a legacy application can be documented in separate specifications: a composition architecture specification that identifies the service and points to an application architecture specification that defines the corresponding application.

SUMMARY OF KEY POINTS

- The traditional concept of an application can change as more agnostic services become established parts of the enterprise.

- The traditional concept of integration can change as the proliferation of standardized, intrinsic interoperable services increases.

- Architectural views of the enterprise shift in response to the adoption of service-orientation. Principally, the enterprise perspective becomes increasingly prominent.

4.6 Origins and Influences of Service-Orientation

It is often said that the best way to understand something is to gain knowledge of its history. Service-orientation, by no means, is a design paradigm that just came out of nowhere. It is very much a representation of the evolution of IT and therefore has many roots in past paradigms and technologies (Figure 4.20). At the same time, it is still in a state of evolution itself and therefore remains subject to influences from on-going trends and movements.

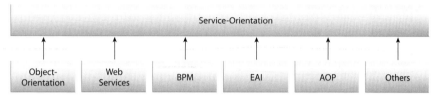

Figure 4.20
The primary influences of service-orientation also highlight its many origins.

The sections that follow describe some of the more prominent origins and thereby help clarify how service-orientation can relate to and even help further some of the goals from past paradigms.

Object-Orientation

In the 1990s the IT community embraced a design philosophy that would lead the way in defining how distributed solutions were to be built. This paradigm was object-orientation, and it came with its own set of principles, the application of which helped ensure consistency across numerous environments. These principles defined a specific type of relationship between units of solution logic classified as objects, which resulted in a predictable set of dynamics that ran through entire solutions.

Service-orientation is frequently compared to object-orientation, and rightly so. The principles and patterns behind object-oriented analysis and design represent one of the most significant sources of inspiration for this paradigm.

In fact, a subset of service-orientation principles (Service Reusability, Service Abstraction, and Service Composability, for example) can be traced back to object-oriented counterparts. What distinguishes service-orientation, though, are the parts of the object-oriented school of thought that were left out and the other principles that were added. See Chapter 14 for a comparative analysis of principles and concepts associated with these two design approaches.

Web Services

Even though service-orientation as a paradigm and SOA as a technology architecture are each implementation-neutral, their association with Web services has become common-place—so much so that the primary SOA vendors have shaped their respective platforms around the utilization of Web services technology.

Although service-orientation remains a fully abstract paradigm, it is one that has historically been influenced by the SOA platforms and roadmaps produced by these vendors. As a result, the Web services framework has influenced and promoted several service-orientation principles, including Service Abstraction, Service Loose Coupling, and Service Composability.

Business Process Management (BPM)

BPM places a significant emphasis on business processes within the enterprise both in terms of streamlining process logic to improve efficiency and also to establish processes that are adaptable and extensible so that they can be augmented in response to business change.

The business process layer represents a core part of any service-oriented architecture. From a composition perspective, it usually assumes the role of the parent service composition controller. The advent of orchestration technology reaffirmed this role from an implementation perspective.

A primary goal of service-orientation is to establish a highly agile automation environment fully capable of adapting to change. This goal can be realized by abstracting business process logic into its own layer, thereby alleviating other services from having to repeatedly embed process logic.

While service-orientation itself is not as concerned with business process reengineering, it fully supports process optimization as a primary source of change for which services can be recomposed.

Enterprise Application Integration (EAI)

Integration became a primary focal point in the late 90's, and many organizations were ill prepared for it. Numerous systems were built with little thought given to how data could be shared outside of the system boundary. As a result, point-to-point integration channels were often created when data sharing requirements emerged. This led to well known problems associated with a lack of stability, extensibility, and inadequate interoperability frameworks.

EAI platforms introduced middleware that allowed for the abstraction of proprietary applications through the use of adapters, brokers, and orchestration engines. The resulting integration architectures were, in fact, more robust and extensible. However, they also became notorious for being overwhelmingly complex and expensive, as well as requiring long-term commitments to the middleware vendor's platform and roadmap.

The advent of the open Web services framework and its ability to fully abstract proprietary technology changed the face of integration middleware. Vendor ties could be broken by investing in mobile services as opposed to proprietary platforms, and organizations gained more control over the evolution of their integration architectures.

Several innovations that became popularized during the EAI era were recognized as being useful to the overall goals associated with building SOA using Web services. One example is the broker component, which allows for services using different schemas representing the same type of data to still communicate through runtime transformation. The other is the orchestration engine, which can actually be positioned to represent an entire service layer within larger SOA implementations. These parts of the EAI platform support several service-orientation principles, including Service Abstraction, Service Statelessness, Service Loose Coupling, and Service Composability.

Aspect-Oriented Programming (AOP)

A primary goal of AOP is to approach the separation of concerns with the intent of identifying specific concerns that are common to multiple applications or automation scenarios. These concerns are then classified as "cross-cutting," and the corresponding solution logic developed for cross-cutting concerns becomes naturally reusable.

Aspect-orientation emerged from object-orientation by building on the original goals of establishing reusable objects. Although not a primary influential factor of service-orientation, AOP does demonstrate a common goal in emphasizing the importance of investing in units of solution logic that are agnostic to business processes and applications and therefore highly reusable. It further promotes role-based development, allowing developers with different areas of expertise to collaborate.

> **NOTE**
>
> The actual events and timeline associated with the emergence of SOA are documented in Chapter 4 of the book *Service-Oriented Architecture: Concepts, Technology, and Design*.

SUMMARY OF KEY POINTS

- Service-orientation represents a design paradigm that has its roots in several origins. It emphasizes successful and proven approaches and supplements them with new principles that leverage recent conceptual and technology innovation.

- Service-orientation, as a design paradigm, is comparable with object-orientation. In fact, several key object-oriented principles have persisted in service-orientation.

- The Web services technology platform is primarily responsible for the popularity of SOA and is therefore also a significant influence in service-orientation. Conversely, the rise of service-oriented computing has repositioned and formalized the Web services technology set from its original incarnation.

4.7 CASE STUDY BACKGROUND

Cutit's immediate priority is to streamline their internal supply chain process. The order process in particular needs to be supported by the planned services so that orders and back-orders can be fulfilled as soon as possible.

Below are brief descriptions of the service candidates shown in Figure 4.21 in relation to how they inter-relate based on their entity-centric functional contexts:

- Everything originates with the manufacturing of chain blades in the Cutit lab, which requires the use of specific *materials* that are applied as per predefined *formulas*.

- The assembly of *chains* results in products being added to their overall *inventory*.

- *Saws* and *kits* are items Cutit purchases from different manufacturers to complement their chain models.

- *Notifications* need to be issued when stock levels fall below certain levels or if other urgent conditions occur.

- Finally, a periodic *patent sweep* is conducted to search for recently issued patents with similarities to Cutit's planned chain designs.

Note that all services shown are entity services, with the exception of Patent Sweep and Notifications, which are based on the utility service model. A task service is added in Part II.

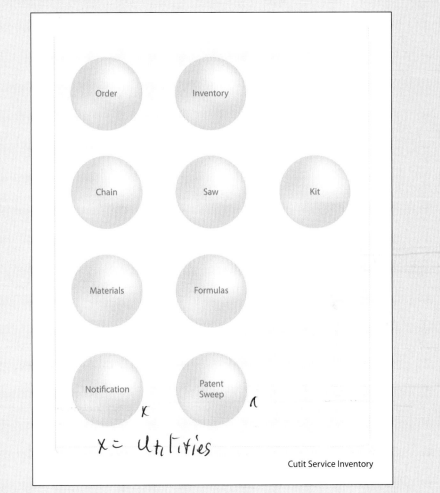

Cutit Service Inventory

Figure 4.21
The initial set of services planned to support the following types of processes: keeping track of orders and backorders, chain manufacturing, tracking required manufacturing materials, and inventory management of manufactured and purchased products. All of the displayed services are based on the entity service model, except for the bottom two, which are utility services.

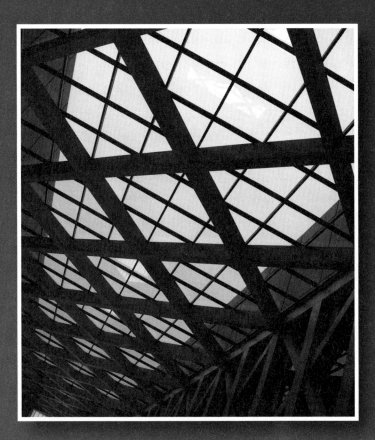

Chapter 5

Understanding Design Principles

Principles help shape every aspect of our world. We navigate ourselves through various situations and environments, guided by principles we learned from our family, society, and from our own experiences. Historically, many parts of the IT world encouraged the use of design principles so that when you did something, you would "do it right" on a consistent basis. Often, though, their use was optional or just recommended. They were viewed more as guidelines than standards, providing advice that we could choose to follow.

When moving toward a service-oriented architecture, principles take on renewed importance primarily because the stakes are higher. Instead of concentrating on the delivery of individual application environments, we usually have a grand scheme in mind that involves a good part of the enterprise. A "do it right the first time" attitude has therefore never been more appropriate. SOA projects have the potential to shape and position solution logic in ways that can significantly transform an enterprise. We want to make sure we steer this transformation effort in the right direction.

As documented in Chapter 4, the design principles explored in this book establish a paradigm with many roots in previous computing generations. None of them are really that new. What is distinct about service-orientation is which of these existing principles have been included and excluded—that and the high-minded goals promised by its successful application.

5.1 Using Design Principles

The *Design Fundamentals* section of Chapter 3 formally defined the term "design principle" and determined that it essentially is "a recommended guideline for shaping solution logic with certain goals in mind." We subsequently covered the following list of service-oriented computing benefits:

- Increased Intrinsic Interoperability
- Increased Federation
- Increased Vendor Diversification Options
- Increased Business and Technology Domain Alignment

- Increased ROI

- Increased Organizational Agility

- Reduced IT Burden

These benefits represent the most common strategic goals associated with service-orientation. The application of the eight principles explored in this book results in the realization of very specific design characteristics, all of which support these goals.

We therefore need to ensure that the principles are effectively applied. Following is a set of best practices for getting the most out of the design principles in this book.

Incorporate Principles within Service-Oriented Analysis

Because we have labeled the principles in this book as *design* principles, there is a natural tendency to focus on their application during the design stage only. However, because of the unique form of analysis carried out as part of the common SOA delivery lifecycle, it can be highly beneficial to begin working with a subset of the principles during the analysis phase.

While iterating through the service modeling process of a typical service-oriented analysis, we are tasked with defining a conceptual blueprint for the inventory of services we will eventually be designing and building. This provides us with an opportunity to begin conceptually forming some of the key service design characteristics ahead of time.

Of the eight service-orientation design principles, the following three are most commonly incorporated within the service modeling process:

- *Service Reusability*—Reusability considerations are highly relevant to defining the inventory blueprint because they help us group logic within the contexts of proposed agnostic service candidates and further encourage us to refine the definition and functionality behind agnostic capability candidates.

- *Service Autonomy*—One of the goals of the information gathering steps that comprise the parent service-oriented analysis process is to determine where, within an enterprise, autonomy will ultimately be impacted. Knowing this in advance allows us to adjust service candidate granularity and capability candidate grouping in response to practical concerns. This prevents the inventory blueprint from becoming too abstract and out of touch with the realities of its eventual implementation.

- *Service Discoverability*—Although service meta data can be added to a contract at any time prior to deployment, the analysis stage enables us to leverage the expertise of subject matter experts that will not be participating in subsequent project phases. This is particularly relevant to the definition of business services. Analysts with a deep insight into the history, purpose, and potential utilization of business logic can provide quality descriptions that go far beyond the definition of the candidate service contract.

As illustrated in Appendix B, a separate step dedicated to applying select service-orientation principles is part of a standard service modeling process.

FOR EXAMPLE

A US-based shipping company created their own expanded variation of the service modeling process documented in Appendix B. Instead of bundling service-orientation considerations into one step, it included the following separate steps:

- *Business Reusability Survey*—A step during which representatives from different business domains were questioned as to the applicability of a given service that was being modeled. Those surveyed were asked to provide feedback about how any agnostic service could be potentially extended in support of business processes that resided in their domains.

- *COTS Evaluation*—This was carried out for each service capability candidate required to encapsulate functionality that resided in an existing COTS environment. It provided insight into potential autonomy constraints for some of the planned services.

- *Service Profile Copyedit*—This was a step toward the end of the modeling process during which the service profile document was refined by one of the on-staff technical writers (which is also a best practice discussed in Chapter 12).

Each of these steps was carried out by different individuals, all part of the service modeling project team.

Incorporate Principles within Formal Design Processes

The key success factor to leveraging service-orientation design principles is in ensuring that they are applied consistently. When services are delivered as part of different projects that are perhaps even carried out in different geographical locations, there is a constant danger that the resulting service inventories will be comprised of incompatible and misaligned services, varying in both quality and completeness.

Design synchronicity is important to achieving the harmonization and predictability required to ultimately compose services into different configurations. Establishing formal service design processes that exist as part of the organization's over-arching project delivery methodology requires that project teams give serious thought as to how each principle can or should be applied to their planned services.

The design processes listed in Appendix B have steps dedicated to applying service-orientation principles. These processes can be further customized and expanded to incorporate a dedicated step for each principle.

FOR EXAMPLE

The aforementioned shipping company formalized service design processes that included separate steps for applying Service Reusability, Service Autonomy, and Service Composability principles. The remaining principles were also incorporated in the design processes but grouped together with other design considerations.

The Service Composability step actually introduced a sub-process during which service contracts were combined into a variety of composition configurations in order to assess data exchange compatibility.

Establish Supporting Design Standards

Design principles are design guidelines, essentially recommended approaches to designing software programs. Due to the importance of creating consistent programs (services) in support of service-oriented computing, it is highly recommended that design principles take on a larger, more prominent role.

Once an organization has determined to what extent it wants to realize service-orientation, design standards need to be put in place in full support of the consistent application of these design principles. This often leads to the principles themselves forming the basis for multiple design standards.

Either way, if you are expecting to attain meaningful strategic benefit from a transition toward SOA, design standards need to be in place to ensure the consistent realization and proliferation of service-orientation across all affected services.

> ### FOR EXAMPLE
>
> An enterprise design specification for a government agency contained upwards of 300 separate design standards, many of which were directly or indirectly defined in support of service-orientation.
>
> One of these standards, for example, required that all XML schema definitions support null values by allowing an element to exist zero or more times (via the `minOccurs="0"` attribute setting). If the element was not present, its value was considered to be null.
>
> This simple design standard ensured that null values were consistently expressed across all XML document instances, thereby supporting the Service Contract Standardization and Service Reusability principles and also avoiding some of the negative coupling types described in Chapter 7.

Apply Principles to a Feasible Extent

Each of the eight service-orientation design principles can be applied to a certain extent. It is rare that any one principle will be fully and purely realized to its maximum potential. A fundamental goal when applying any principle is to implement desired, corresponding design characteristics consistently within each service to whatever measure is realistically attainable.

The fact that principles are always implemented to some extent is something we need to constantly keep in the back of our minds as we are working with them. For example, it's not a matter of whether a service is or is not reusable; it's the degree of reusability that we can realize through its design that we are primarily concerned with.

Most of the chapters in this book explore specific measures to which a principle can be applied and further provide recommendations for how these levels can be classified and documented. Additional supporting practices are provided in Chapter 15.

SUMMARY OF KEY POINTS

- Design principles can be effectively realized by applying them as part of formal analysis and design processes.
- Design principles can be further applied consistently by incorporating them into official design standards.
- Every principle can be applied to a certain extent.

5.2 Principle Profiles

Each of the chapters in Part II contains a section that summarizes a design principle within a standard profile table. Provided here are brief descriptions of the fields within the standard profile table:

- *Short Definition*—A concise, single-statement definition that establishes the fundamental purpose of the principle.

- *Long Definition*—A longer description of the principle that provides more detail as to what it is intended to accomplish.

- *Goals*—A list of specific design goals that are expected from the application of the principle. Essentially, this list provides the ultimate results of the principle's realization.

- *Design Characteristics*—A list of specific design characteristics that can be realized via the application of the principle. This provides some insight as to how the principle ends up shaping the service.

- *Implementation Requirements*—A list of common prerequisites for effectively applying the design principle. These can range from technology to organizational requirements.

- *Web Service Region of Influence*—A simple diagram that highlights the regions within a physical Web service architecture affected by the application of the principle. The standard Web service representation (consisting of core service logic, messaging logic, and the service contract) is used repeatedly. Red shaded spheres indicate the areas of the Web service the principle is most likely to affect. The darker the shading, the stronger the potential influence.

Chapters are further supplemented with the following sections:

- *Abstract*—An introductory section that explains each design principle outside of the context of SOA. This is a helpful perspective in understanding how service-orientation positions design principles. The title of this section incorporates the name of the principle as follows: *[Principle Name] in Abstract*.

- *Origins*—A section that establishes the roots of a given principle by drawing from past architectures and design approaches. By understanding the history of each design principle, it becomes clear how service-orientation is truly an evolutionary paradigm. The format of this section's title is as follows: *Origins of [Principle Name]*.

- *Levels*—As explained earlier in the *Apply Principles to a Feasible Extent* section, each principle can be realized to a certain degree. Most chapters provide suggested labels for categorizing the level to which a principle has been applied, primarily for measuring and communication purposes. The section title is structured as follows: *Levels of [Principle Name].*

- *Service Design*—Several chapters explore supplementary topics that highlight additional design considerations associated with a principle. These are found in a section called *[Principle Name] and Service Design*. (Note that the following *Service Models* and *Relationships* sections exist as sub-sections to the *Service Design* section.)

- *Granularity*—Whenever the application of a design principle raises issues or concerns regarding any of the four design granularity types (as explained in the upcoming *Principles and Design Granularity* section) a separate section entitled *[Principle Name] and Granularity* is added.

- *Service Models*—Where appropriate, a principle's influence on the design of each of the four primary service models (entity, utility, task, and orchestrated task) is described in a section titled *[Principle Name] and Service Models.*

- *Relationships*—To fully appreciate the dynamics behind service-orientation, an understanding of how the application of one principle can potentially affect others is required. Each chapter provides a section titled *How [Principle Name] Affects Other Principles* wherein inter-principle relationships are explored.

- *Risks*—Finally, every chapter dedicated to a design principle concludes with a list of risks associated with using or abstaining from the use of the principle. This list is provided in a section titled *Risks Associated with [Principle Name].*

Every effort was made to keep the format of the next eight chapters consistent so that aspects of individual principles can be effectively compared and contrasted.

NOTE

Principle profiles should not be confused with service profiles. The former represents a regular section format within the upcoming chapters, whereas the latter is a type of document for recording service meta details. Service profiles are described in Chapter 15.

SUMMARY OF KEY POINTS

- Each chapter summarizes a design principle using a standard profile section.

- Design principles are further documented with additional sections that explore various aspects of their origin and application.

5.3 Design Pattern References

The eight design principles in this book were documented in alignment with an SOA design pattern catalog published separately in the book *SOA: Design Patterns,* another title that is part of the *Prentice Hall Service-Oriented Computing Series from Thomas Erl.* This book expresses service-orientation through a fundamental pattern language and provides a collection of advanced design patterns for solving common problems.

Because these two books were written together, there is a strong correlation between the utilization of design principles and select design patterns that provide related solutions in support of realizing service-orientation. Fundamental design patterns are often tied directly to the design characteristics established by a particular design principle, whereas advanced design patterns more commonly solve problems that can be encountered when attempting to apply a principle under certain circumstances.

Throughout the chapters in Part II, references to related design patterns are provided. These references are further summarized in Appendix C.

5.4 Principles that Implement vs. Principles that Regulate

Before exploring the design principles individually, it is worth positioning them as they relate to the realization of physical service design characteristics. On a fundamental level we can group principles into two broad categories:

- Principles that primarily result in the implementation of specific service design characteristics.

- Principles that primarily shape and regulate the application of other principles.

The following principles fall into the first category:

- Standardized Service Contract

- Service Reusability

- Service Autonomy

- Service Statelessness

- Service Discoverability

As explained throughout Chapters 6, 9, 10, 11, and 12, the application of any one of these principles results in very specific design qualities. Some affect the service contract, while others are more focused on the underlying service logic. However, all result in the implementation of characteristics that shape the physical service design.

This leaves us with the remaining three that fall into the "regulatory" category:

- Service Loose Coupling

- Service Abstraction

- Service Composability

After studying Chapters 7, 8, and 13, it becomes evident that while these principles also introduce some new characteristics, they primarily influence how and to what extent the service design characteristics associated with other principles are implemented (Figure 5.1).

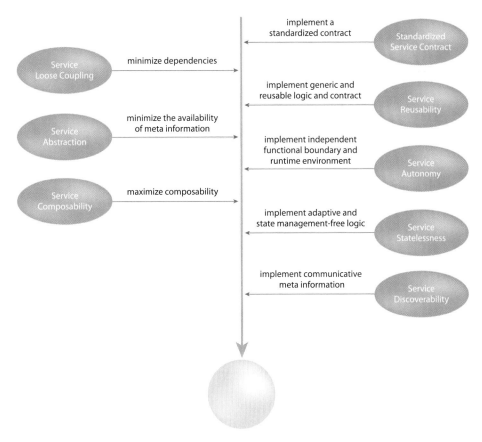

Figure 5.1

While the principles on the right-hand side want to add specific physical characteristics to the service design, the principles on the left act as regulators to ensure that these characteristics are implemented in a coordinated and appropriate manner.

Furthermore, each chapter explores how principles inter-relate. Specifically, the manner in which a design principle affects the application of others is documented. Figure 5.2, for example, provides an indication as to how two of the "regulatory" principles relate to each other.

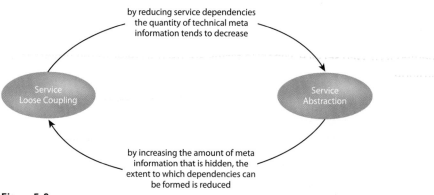

Figure 5.2

The Service Loose Coupling and Service Abstraction principles share a common dynamic in that the application of each supports the other.

SUMMARY OF KEY POINTS

- Five of the eight design principles establish concrete service design characteristics.

- The remaining three design principles also introduce design characteristics but act more as regulatory influences.

5.5 Principles and Service Implementation Mediums

Service logic can exist in different forms. It can be implemented as the core logic component within a Web service, as a standalone component with a public interface, or even within an event-driven service agent. The choice of implementation medium or format can be influenced by environmental constraints, architectural considerations, as well as the application of various design patterns.

Service-orientation design principles shape both service logic and service contracts. There is an emphasis on the Web service medium because it provides the most potential to apply key principles to the greatest extent. For example, contract-related principles may not apply as much to logic encapsulated within an event-driven service agent. This does not make the logic any less service-oriented; it only limits the principles that need to be taken into account during its development.

"Capability" vs. "Operation" vs. "Method"

To support the on-going distinction between a service in abstract and a service implemented as a Web service, separate terms are used to refer to the functions a service can provide.

A *service capability* represents a specific function of a service through which the service can be invoked. As a result, service capabilities are expressed within the service contract. A service can have capabilities regardless of how it is implemented.

A *service operation* specifically refers to a capability within a service that is implemented as a Web service. Similarly, a *service method* represents a capability that is part of a service that exists as a component.

Note that as mentioned early on in Chapter 3, when the term "capability" is used in this book, it implicitly refers to capabilities expressed by the service contract. If there is a need to reference internal service capabilities that are not part of the contract, they will be explicitly qualified as such.

5.6 Principles and Design Granularity

The term "granularity" is most commonly used to communicate the level of (or absence of) detail associated with some aspect of software program design. Within the context of service design, we are primarily concerned with the granularity of the service contract and what it represents.

Within a service, different forms of granularity exist, all of which can be impacted by how service-orientation design principles are applied. The following sections document four specific types of design granularity, three of which are further referenced in Figure 5.3.

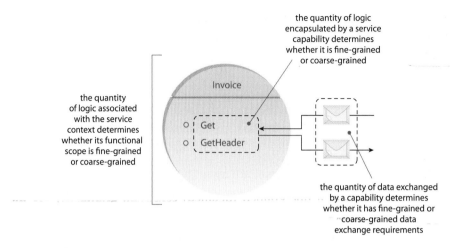

the quantity of logic encapsulated by a service capability determines whether it is fine-grained or coarse-grained

the quantity of logic associated with the service context determines whether its functional scope is fine-grained or coarse-grained

the quantity of data exchanged by a capability determines whether it has fine-grained or coarse-grained data exchange requirements

Figure 5.3

In this example, an Invoice entity service will tend to have a coarse-grained functional scope. However, it is exposing both coarse-grained (Get) and fine-grained (GetHeader) capabilities. Furthermore, because the GetHeader capability will return less data than the Get capability (which returns an entire invoice document), the GetHeader capability's data granularity is also considered fine.

Service Granularity

The granularity of the service's functional scope, as determined by its functional context, is simply referred to as *service granularity*. A service's overall granularity does not reflect the amount of logic it currently encapsulates but instead the quantity of potential logic it could encapsulate, based on its context. A coarse-grained service, for example, would have a broad functional context, regardless of whether it initially expresses one or ten capabilities.

Capability Granularity

Capability granularity represents the functional scope of a specific capability as it currently exists. As a rule of thumb, a fine-grained capability will have less work to do than a coarse-grained one.

Data Granularity

The quantity of data a capability needs to exchange in order to carry out its function represents its level of *data granularity*. There has been a tendency for services implemented as Web services to exchange document-centric messages—messages containing entire information sets or business documents. Because the quantity of data is larger, this would be classified as coarse-grained data granularity.

Document-centric messages are in sharp contrast to traditional RPC-style communication, which typically relies on the exchange of smaller (fine-grained) amounts of parameter data.

Constraint Granularity

The amount of detail with which a particular constraint is expressed is referred to as a measure of *constraint granularity*. The schema or data model representing the structure of the information being exchanged by a capability can define a series of specific validation constraints (data type, data length, data format, allowed values, etc.) for a given value. This would represent a fine-grained (detailed) constraint granularity for that value, as opposed to a coarse-grained level of constraint granularity that would permit a range of values with no predefined length or format restrictions, as represented by the first element definition in Example 5.1.

```
<xsd:element name="ProductCode" type="xsd:string"/>      Coarse Grain

<xsd:element name="ProductCode">                         Fine Grain 1
  <xsd:simpleType>
    <xsd:restriction base="xsd:string">
      <xsd:minLength value="1"/>
      <xsd:maxLength value="4"/>
    </xsd:restriction>
  </xsd:simpleType>
</xsd:element>
                                                         Fine Grain
<xsd:element name="ProductCode">
<xsd:simpleType>
  <xsd:restriction base="xsd:string">
    <xsd:pattern value="[0-9]{4}"/>
  </xsd:restriction>
</xsd:simpleType>
</xsd:element>
```

Example 5.1

Three variations of the same XML schema element definition. The first is clearly a coarse-grained constraint because it allows the product code to exist as an open-ended string value. The second is less coarse-grained because it restricts the product code length to one to four characters. The last element is a fine-grained constraint because it dictates that the product code must be four characters and that each character be a number between 0 and 9.

Constraint granularity can be associated with individual parameters processed by a capability or with the capability as a whole. For example, the same capability may accept a body of input data comprised of two separate values, one of which is subject to fine-grained constraints and the other of which is validated against a coarse-grained constraint. The three code samples in Example 5.1 could alternatively exist as different types with different names but with the same constraints and as part of the same service capability (or Web service operation).

It is also important to note that constraint granularity is generally measured in relation to the validation logic present in the service contract only. This measure therefore excludes validation constraints that may be applied by the underlying service logic. Whereas a capability defined within a contract may have coarse constraint granularity, the actual capability logic may apply more fine-grained constraints after input values have been validated against the service contract.

NOTE
There are no rules about how forms of granularity can be combined. For example, it would not be uncommon for a coarse-grained service to provide fine-grained capabilities that exchange coarse-grained data validated against fine-grained constraints.

Sections on Granularity Levels

There is no one principle that dictates granularity levels for a service design. Instead, several service-orientation principles impact the various types of granularity in different ways. Those chapters that cover principles affecting design granularity typically address this issue within the standard *[Principle Name] and Service Design* section.

SUMMARY OF KEY POINTS

- Service granularity refers to the functional scope of the service as a whole, as defined by its functional context.

- Capability granularity refers to the functional scope of a specific capability.

- Data granularity refers to the volume of data exchanged by a service capability.

- Constraint granularity refers to the level of detail to which validation logic is defined for a particular parameter or capability within the service contract.

5.7 CASE STUDY BACKGROUND

Each of the upcoming eight chapters concludes with a case study example that demonstrates the application of a principle. Specifically, a service delivery project underway at Cutit Saws forms the basis for these examples, as a modest set of services are developed to automate the Lab Project business process.

Up next is a description of this process that will help establish some overall context. Note, however, that the focus of subsequent case study examples is not on the nature of the business process logic but more so on the design issues pertaining to the incorporation of service-orientation principles.

The Lab Project Business Process

The following is a highly simplified version of a lab project in which the assembly of materials and the application of predefined (and sometimes newly created) formulas undergoes a series of verification checks and then a final simulation. Note that in order to preserve clarity surrounding the flow of the process logic, regular industry terms and chemistry-related terminology is intentionally avoided.

A lab project, within the context of this solution, is the equivalent of a simulated experiment. Using a customized user-interface, a lab technician assembles a combination of ingredients (purchased and/or developed materials) and retrieves either one or more existing base formulas or creates one or more newly developed base formulas. A base formula is essentially a documentation of existing compounds (previous mixtures of ingredients or elements).

Once all of the information is in place, the lab project is executed ("run"), and the solution retrieves the required information, as per the process description that follows. If all of the needed ingredients are available, the solution interacts with a simulator program to graphically display the results of the experiment. If any ingredients are missing or certain formula combinations are not possible, the solution will reject the experiment configuration and terminate the project.

Here are descriptions for the primary process steps, which are further displayed in the workflow diagram in Figure 5.4.

1. Issue a stock level check on all required materials. If any stock levels are lower than the requested quantities, terminate the process.

2. Retrieve information about required purchased materials. This can include lab equipment, tools, and disposable materials (gloves, swabs, etc.) in addition to materials used as ingredients for experiments.

3. Retrieve a list of the requested base formulas, filtered using criteria pertinent to the current project.

4. If a new base formula is being added, generate the base formula record and add the formula to the base formulas list for this project.

5. If developed materials are required, retrieve their corresponding data. This step is performed after the base formulas are defined to ensure that all required ingredients are accounted for.

6. Perform a validation check to ensure that all purchased and developed ingredients are available in order for the defined formulas to be applied.

7. Submit the collected data to the simulator.

8. Output the results in a predefined report format.

Note that the process contains one additional step that has been excluded from the preceding description and workflow diagram. If the simulation attempt fails, the returned report contains error information, and a separate sub-process is invoked that contains compensation steps including notification. This sub-process is only somewhat relevant to the case study example in Chapter 10 where processing subsequent to the completion of the report generation is referenced.

Figure 5.4

The workflow logic for the Lab Project business process.

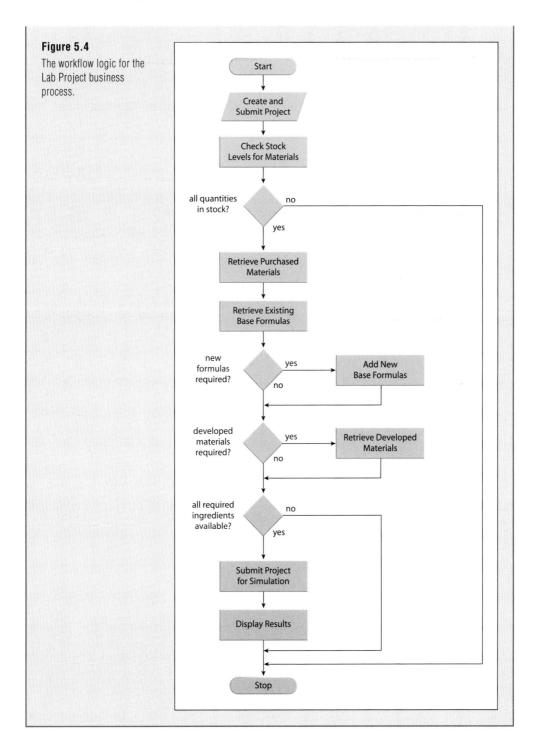

> **NOTE**
>
> Just a reminder that, as explained in the *What this Book Does Not Cover* section of Chapter 1, the focus of this book and the upcoming chapters in Part II is on the design of *services* for SOA, not the design of SOA itself. Architectural design issues are addressed separately as part of the book *SOA: Design Patterns*.

Part II

Design Principles

Chapter 6

Service Contracts (Standardization and Design)

S ervice contracts are a focal point of service design because they are central to just about everything services do. Although at a fundamental level this principle simply requires the use of formal or *standardized* contracts (Figure 6.1), it actually implies much more. Each individual part of the contract needs to be carefully measured and refined and because contracts are also core architectural components of service-oriented solutions, several of the other principles directly influence how they are positioned, designed, and ultimately utilized.

Figure 6.1

The fundamental role of this principle is to ensure the consistent expression of service capabilities and the overall purpose of the service as defined by the parent service context.

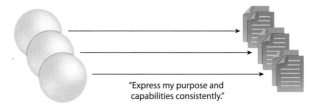

"Express my purpose and capabilities consistently."

6.1 Contracts Explained

Before we explore the meaning, dynamics, and application of this principle, let's first establish some general background information as to how contracts have been used in different types of computing platforms and vendor products.

Technical Contracts in Abstract

As with many terms in the IT industry, "contract" is one that can have different meanings when associated with automation solutions. For example, it is relatively common to view a contract as the equivalent of a technical interface. When it comes to services within SOA, we have a slightly broader definition. A contract for a service (or a *service contract*) establishes the terms of engagement, providing technical constraints and requirements as well as any semantic information the service owner wishes to make public.

A service contract can consist of a group of *service description* documents, each of which describes a part of the service. A Web service contract, for example, can be comprised of the following service description documents:

- WSDL definition

- XML schema definition

- WS-Policy description

A service contract is always comprised of one or more technical service descriptions designed for runtime consumption, but there are also cases when non-technical documents are required to supplement the technical details. Both are considered valid parts of the overall contract (Figure 6.2).

Figure 6.2

Possible service description documents that can comprise a contract for a service implemented as a Web service. The subset of these documents that establishes the technical interface for the service can be considered the technical service contract.

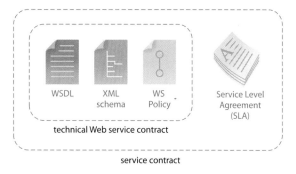

NOTE

This chapter is primarily concerned with technical service description documents. Therefore, when we refer to the service contract, a *technical service contract* is implied unless otherwise indicated. Having stated that, it should be further noted that service level agreements and other human consumable service description documents can contain highly technical content. The term "technical service contract" is used simply to refer to service description documents that are programmatically consumed at runtime.

Origins of Service Contracts

Contracts have been used by different types of automation systems almost for as long as information technology has existed. Interactions between two standalone software programs are based on a fundamental design where the data required to invoke and exchange information between the programs is pre-defined and based on a formal, technical specification. This is what is expressed in a technical contract. Figures 6.3 and 6.4 show examples of traditional forms of technical contracts.

Figure 6.3

In a classic client-server model, the client
program connects to a server-side program, such as a database. In this case, a
technical contract may be comprised of the
database protocol and a predefined query
syntax or language.

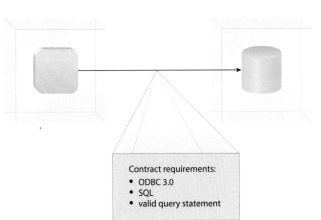

Contract requirements:
- ODBC 3.0
- SQL
- valid query statement

Figure 6.4

In a traditional distributed model, a component existing as a
standalone program interacts with other components. Each
provides a technical interface that can be accessed by any
compatible program.

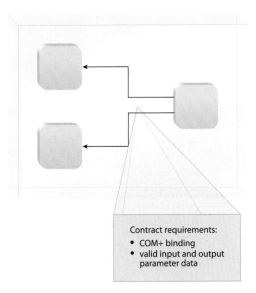

Contract requirements:
- COM+ binding
- valid input and output
  parameter data

In the past, technical contracts have commonly been represented by a form of technical
interface known as the application programming interface (API). An API library can be
accessed by a client program installed locally on the same computer as the API, or
remotely. The latter variation is most common in distributed architectures, where components require local representations of the contracts (called proxies) to interact with
components located on different servers. The Interface Definition Language (IDL) and
the Abstract Syntax Notation 1 (ASN.1) were frequently used to express technical contracts for remote invocation frameworks, such as those based on remote procedure calls
(RPCs). A sample fragment of IDL syntax is provided in Example 6.1.

```
long Multiply([in] long number1, [in] long number2);
```

Example 6.1

A Multiply capability expressed in traditional IDL. It receives two input values and returns the result of the multiplication.

Web services established a non-proprietary distributed communications framework that introduced the Web Services Description Language (WSDL) as the core part of a technical service contract (Example 6.2). Closely associated with WSDL is the XML Schema language used to define the data model for messages exchanged via Web services and the WS-Policy language through which policy assertions can be defined and attached to various parts of the WSDL.

```
<operation name="Multiply">
  <input message="tns:NumbersMessage"/>
  <output message="tns:ResultMessage"/>
</operation>
```

Example 6.2

A Multiply capability partially expressed as part of a WSDL definition. Input values are received via a message that is separately defined from the message that returns the results of the multiplication. (Not shown are the corresponding message and data type constructs.)

Historically, technical contracts created as part of custom designed automation solutions have been tailored to represent software programs for one or more specific and pre-identified clients. Exceptions to this include packaged software systems that supply a generic API (or API set) based on a specific development platform. The API would provide common functions, openly accessible to any compatible client programs (for example class libraries or GUI frameworks).

A common principle associated with object-oriented design encouraged the creation of reusable components. This often implied that the resulting component interface would be sufficiently generic to facilitate reuse. The advent of service-oriented computing has placed an unprecedented emphasis on reuse and the design of agnostic solution logic, elevating the importance of this style of contract design. The more a service can be reused, the more entrenched its contract will become and, as a result, the more pressure there is to deliver service contracts capable of standing the test of time.

As we will discover in this and subsequent chapters, much of service-orientation is dedicated to ensuring that service contracts establish a balanced expression of a service's purpose and capabilities in support of reuse and other key strategic goals of service-oriented computing.

SUMMARY OF KEY POINTS

- Technical contracts are an established part of IT. Whenever two programs or two units of programming logic need to connect, some form of technical contract is required.

- A service contract can consist of technical and non-technical service description documents.

6.2 Profiling this Principle

Table 6.1 provides a concise profile of the principle with a focus on its definition and the primary design characteristics it is expected to foster.

Principle Profile	
Short Definition	*"Services share standardized contracts."*
Long Definition	*"Services within the same service inventory are in compliance with the same contract design standards."*
Goals	• To enable services with a meaningful level of natural interoperability within the boundary of a service inventory. This reduces the need for data transformation because consistent data models are used for information exchange. • To allow the purpose and capabilities of services to be more easily and intuitively understood. The consistency with which service functionality is expressed through service contracts increases interpretability and the overall predictability of service endpoints throughout a service inventory. Note that these goals are further supported by other service-orientation principles as well.
Design Characteristics	• A service contract (comprised of a technical interface or one or more service description documents) is provided with the service. • The service contract is standardized through the application of design standards.

Implementation Requirements	The fact that contracts need to be standardized can introduce significant implementation requirements to organizations that do not have a history of using standards.
	For example:
	• Design standards and conventions need to ideally be in place prior to the delivery of *any* service in order to ensure adequately scoped standardization. (For those organizations that have already produced ad-hoc Web services, retro-fitting strategies may need to be · employed.)
	• Formal processes need to be introduced to ensure that services are modeled and designed consistently, incorporating accepted design principles, conventions, and standards.
	• Because achieving standardized Web service contracts generally requires a "contract first" approach to service-oriented design, the full application of this principle will often demand the use of development tools capable of importing a customized service contract without imposing changes.
	• Appropriate skill-sets are required to carry out the modeling and design processes with the chosen tools. When working with Web services, the need for a high level of proficiency with XML schema and WSDL languages is practically unavoidable. WS-Policy expertise may also be required.
	These and other requirements can add up to a noticeable transition effort that goes well beyond technology adoption.
Web Service Region of Influence	Because this principle is focused solely on the content of the service contract, its influence is limited to the contract and related processing logic within a typical Web service.

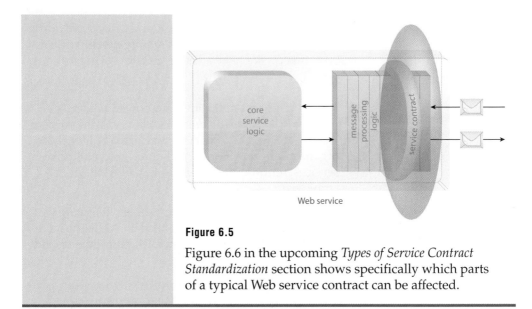

Figure 6.5

Figure 6.6 in the upcoming *Types of Service Contract Standardization* section shows specifically which parts of a typical Web service contract can be affected.

Table 6.1

A profile for the Standardized Service Contract principle.

NOTE
Design standards and standardization in general are first explained in the *Design Fundamentals* section of Chapter 3. Furthermore, this principle is also commonly defined as "Services share a formal contract." The term "standardized" is used here to more clearly communicate the relationship of this design principle with the use of design standards.

SUMMARY OF KEY POINTS

- This principle advocates the use of formal, standardized service contracts.

- The standardization of service contracts can be challenging, especially within larger service inventories.

6.3 Types of Service Contract Standardization

As part of a transition toward a service-oriented architecture, we need to assemble an inventory of services, many of which will have been deliberately designed as reusable resources. Ultimately, our goal is to reach a state where we can fulfill new business automation requirements by minimizing the amount of custom development effort and instead reuse more and more of the available services. This sounds like a logical plan in theory, but to carry this out in real life requires some serious attention to the design of each service contract, as standardization is applied on several primary levels.

Standardization of Functional Service Expression

When services become commonplace within an enterprise, there is significant benefit to having each service express the details of its respective functional domains using the same conventions. Specifically, the application of functional expression conventions to services increases the ease with which they are eventually interpreted by humans (and tools) at design-time and ultimately results in a service-oriented enterprise that is intuitive and easily navigated.

Because effort is made to consistently clarify the meaning of each service, reuse opportunities for those with an agnostic context are more easily identified. Also because the chances of misinterpretation are reduced, the risk of project teams inadvertently creating new services with conflicting or redundant logic is mitigated.

As illustrated in Figure 6.6, the application of design standards that affect functional service expression can shape many parts of a typical Web service contract. Example 6.3 demonstrates the application of a functional expression standard.

Listing #1

```
<message name="GetInvoiceRequest">
  <part name="InvoiceCriteria"
    element="bus:GetInvoiceRequestType"/>
</message>
<message name="GetInvoiceResponse">
  <part name="InvoiceDocument"
    element="bus:GetInvoiceResponseType"/>
</message>
```

Listing #2

```
<message name="GetInvoiceRequest">
  <part name="RequestValue"
    element="bus:InvoiceNumber"/>
</message>
<message name="GetInvoiceResponse">
  <part name="ResponseValue"
    element="bus:Invoice"/>
</message>
```

Example 6.3

The message definitions in Listing #1 are awkward and reference XML schema element names that seem very specific to this operation. Listing #2 represents a version of the same message definitions to which functional expression standards were applied, resulting in the use of more generic naming conventions and generic data type references.

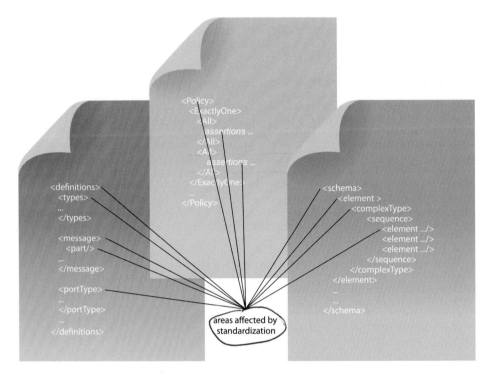

Figure 6.6

Specific constructs within common Web service description documents that are affected by functional expression design standards.

Standardization of Service Data Representation

The technical interface description that forms the base of any service contract will almost always include a formal definition of the input and/or output data required by each service capability. The detail of this definition generally includes a data type. When working with Web services and associated XML schemas, data models are typically comprised of complex data types that organize related pieces of information into a formal structure. This form of standardization advocates keeping schemas and associated data types for specific sets of data in alignment across services to whatever extent feasible.

For example, when building services as Web services in larger enterprise environments, the context established by each service boundary will usually not be exclusive to one body of data. An Invoice Web service will represent a collection of invoice-related functions and will therefore be primarily responsible for processing invoice data. However, even though it will be positioned as a primary endpoint for that body of functionality, it will likely not be the only service to work with invoice data. There could easily be several services that represent functionality requiring access to invoice-related information.

It is easy to create schemas for specific services that are tailored to how these services need to represent data (Figure 6.7). It can lead to very efficient schema designs that are streamlined to only represent data that is relevant to the functionality encapsulated by the service. However, this approach can cause many problems.

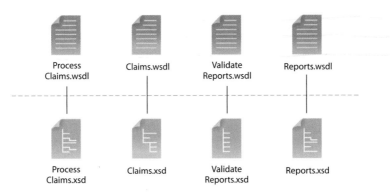

Figure 6.7

A set of WSDL definitions for which a corresponding set of XML schemas has been custom tailored. This has the appearance of a very clean contract architecture, but it can seriously undermine the interoperability potential of an SOA.

One of the key goals of service-oriented computing is to allow for the agile and even ad-hoc assembly of service compositions. It is through service compositions that we will be exercising most of the reuse opportunities that come our way. If two service capabilities within a composition represent the same type of data using different representations (data models, schemas), then their relationship is based on non-standardized data representation. This scenario usually leads to the need for data transformation.

Even though adequate transformation technology is available to overcome data model disparity, it is undesirable to use it. In fact, much of the standardization effort around service contract design is focused on "transformation avoidance," as explained in the *Contracts and Service Design* section of this chapter.

In the Web services world, schemas can be designed and implemented separately from the service capabilities (operations) that utilize them to represent the structure and typing of message content. As a result, a data representation architecture can be established and standardized somewhat independently from the parent service layer. This allows for the application of a design pattern known as Schema Centralization, which advocates the definition of one "official" schema for each information set. Web service contracts can then share these centralized schemas.

For example, if one schema representing invoice data is defined, any Web service with an operation that needs to access or process invoice data would use the same invoice schema. The result is standardized service data representation. The application of this pattern also encourages the creation of *entity schemas*—schemas that represent data associated with a particular business entity, as illustrated by the use of the ClaimHeader and ClaimsDetail schemas in Figure 6.8.

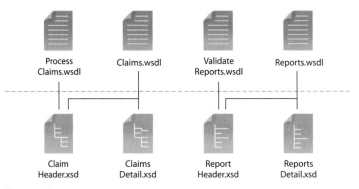

Figure 6.8

WSDL definitions that share common XML schemas end up sharing the same data models for messages. Should the Web services represented by these WSDL definitions ever need to interact as part of a composition, they will already have established a meaningful extent of intrinsic interoperability.

It is worth noting that in the *real* Web services world, this level of data representation standardization can pose daunting challenges, many of which revolve around the governance of the standards and the schemas themselves. As we established in Chapter 4, SOA does not require *global* data model standardization. An established design pattern called the Domain Inventory pattern supports the partitioning of an enterprise into separate domains that can be independently standardized and governed.

Achieving a meaningful level of standardization can prove to be highly beneficial in that it supports the creation of effective service compositions and improves both the efficiency with which these services can be delivered and the efficiency with which they carry out their functions at runtime.

Note also that when applying the Schema Centralization pattern, service contracts are not limited to the use of centralized schemas (such as entity schemas). Additional schemas providing service-specific types are frequently also required. However, the notable benefit to incorporating a centralized set of schemas is that this one set of schemas can be maintained in support of multiple services (as opposed to multiple sets of disparate schemas requiring separate, on-going maintenance).

> ### FOR EXAMPLE
>
> An international financial services company divided its enterprise up into business domains, each representing a boundary in which XML schemas were standardized (an implementation of the aforementioned design patterns). This established an autonomous data representation architecture in each domain. Services are currently being designed for two of these domains with the goal of establishing separately governed service inventories.
>
> Within each inventory, services are expected to repeatedly share centralized XML schemas representing common business documents (also referred to as "entity-centric schemas"). A primary objective of this effort is a dramatic reduction in data transformation requirements.

Standardization of Service Policies

WS-Policy definitions add a separate layer of potential abstraction to service contracts, allowing for policy logic to be expressed through individual policy assertions that can be contained within physically separate policy definition documents. Standardization comes into play on a number of levels, depending on the nature of the policies and the extent to which polices are used in general.

Proprietary Assertion Vocabularies

When standardizing services with separate policy definitions, the focal point is generally on the syntax used to express policy assertions. Whereas some policy assertions are predefined via existing specifications (such as WS-SecurityPolicy and WS-ReliableMessaging), others can be customized using proprietary vocabularies that express business rules or internal corporate business policies.

Much in the same way XML schema supports the creation of an abstract data representation layer (by allowing for the expression of data models that are not bound to any one proprietary database platform), policy definitions introduce an opportunity to establish abstract vocabularies used specifically to extend the Web service contract with policy-related validation logic.

This, however, can only be achieved when such vocabularies are standardized across a service inventory. Otherwise, service consumers are in constant danger of forming unhealthy dependencies on a service's underlying implementation (as explained in the *Contract-to-Implementation Coupling* section of Chapter 7).

Parameters and Nested Polices

Policy assertions can be nested or expressed through the use of parameters. Nested policy assertions are always checked and validated by the system policy processor. Assertions expressed with parameters are ignored by most processors and therefore need to be checked by the underlying service logic. An exception to this is when the service is hosted by a proprietary vendor runtime environment that provides a policy processor capable of validating parameters expressing assertions that were pre-defined and provided by the vendor platform itself.

It is generally considered a best practice to always use nested policy assertions. However, it may sometimes be suitable to use parameters when having to absolutely express proprietary assertions or when requiring the flexibility to express assertions that only apply to a subset of consumers. In this case, the consumer program requires a foreknowledge of how the service will process the assertions within its underlying logic. This, of course, ties back to the need for standardized assertion vocabularies, as explained in the previous section. However, it also raises the need for a related design convention associated with the use of parameters and nested policies. How and when these parts of the WS-Policy language should be applied needs to be explicitly stated within design standards to avoid the creation of inconsistent policy definitions.

Modularizing and Centralizing Policies

While it is relatively common for custom policy definitions to be created for individual Web services, because policy assertions can be separated into separate policy definition documents, policies can be modularized allowing some to even be centralized.

Applying the concept of centralization to polices essentially allows for the creation of a base policy definition containing broad, generalized assertions. More specialized assertions can be placed into separate policy definitions that can then be attached to the same WSDL definition when the Web service is invoked during a specific runtime scenario or if variations of the service contract need to be created for different types of consumers (Figure 6.9).

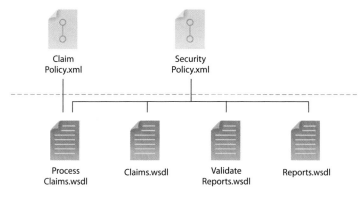

Figure 6.9

A security policy is defined containing assertions that apply to all WSDL definitions. However, only one of these Web service contracts needs to be further extended with a specialized assertion associated with claims processing.

Structural Standards

Policies can impact service contract structure in a variety of ways. Individual policy assertions can apply to different parts of a WSDL definition and can be attached to those parts in different ways. Furthermore, the manner in which some assertions are structurally expressed can also vary. For example, optional assertions can be defined using a compact form that relies upon the use of the `wsp:optional` attribute, or a normalized form that explicitly defines each option.

These types of structural design considerations need to be taken into account when standardizing service contracts. Structural disparity, especially within highly reused and centralized policy definitions, can lead to eventual governance challenges.

<hr>

SUMMARY OF KEY POINTS

- The main areas in which standardization is applied to services are functional expression, data representation, and policies.

- Naming conventions play a large role in ensuring that the functionality of services is consistently expressed.

- Data representation standardization comes down to how the underlying data model of a service is defined. By increasing the consistency between service data models, interoperability is improved.

- Policy standardization primarily revolves around the creation of standardized assertion vocabularies and the consistent use of WS-Policy language features.

6.4 Contracts and Service Design

Contracts form the foundation for communication between services and therefore represent the most fundamental architectural element of an SOA. Service-oriented design is a process dedicated to ensuring that necessary factors and issues are taken into account when shaping a service contract through service-orientation. Up next is a collection of design considerations specific to the application of this principle.

Data Representation Standardization and Transformation Avoidance

A key to understanding what it takes to make the standardization of data models happen within an organization is knowing more about why it has historically been such a challenging goal to accomplish.

With a focus on Web services, here are some common reasons contracts are *not* standardized:

- they were auto-generated by development tools
- they were part of purchased service adapters
- no design standards were in place when they were created
- design standards were ignored

Once implemented and part of the production environment, non-standardized Web service contracts result in the creation and implementation of different data models representing the same bodies of data. To overcome these differences requires the use of a data transformation technology and the definition of mapping logic between one schema and another. This map is implemented into an actual software component, such as an XSLT style sheet, which subsequently executes transformation logic at runtime *every time* the services need to exchange information.

Data transformation technologies provide important features essential to enabling connectivity within integrated enterprise architectures. However, when standardizing the design of services as part of a well-defined service inventory, one of our primary objectives is to avoid having to resort to data transformation wherever possible.

Data transformation introduces a number of problems, including:

- increased integration development effort required to create the mapping logic
- increased performance overhead resulting from the need to execute the mapping logic at runtime with every data exchange

- increased architectural complexity due to the incorporation of transformation layers

- increased governance burden due to the need to maintain and evolve transformation layers along with the rest of the architecture

The consistent application of data representation standards avoids these issues by keeping service contract data models in alignment, as illustrated in Figure 6.10.

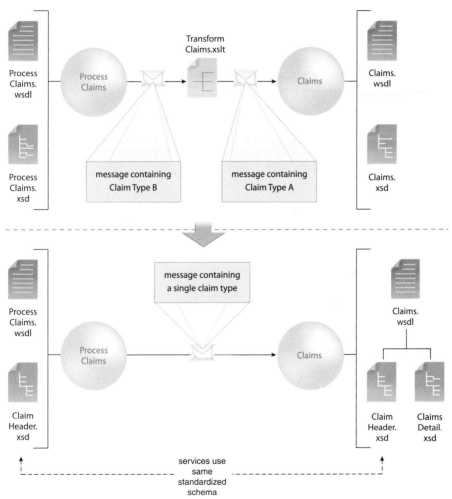

Figure 6.10

By increasing the standardization of service contracts and the resulting message data representation, the quantity of required transformation layers is reduced. This results in more efficient and simplified interoperability, as shown in this diagram where runtime message transformation is avoided when two services share data based on a common XML schema.

While transformation avoidance via data representation standardization is feasible within a controlled environment, it is often more challenging when sharing data between organizations. The use of industry schemas or an unwillingness for organizations to agree on the same schema predictably leads to the need for data transformation. A foreknowledge of these issues places even more emphasis on successfully realizing this principle *within* organization boundaries so that the overall impact and burden of transformation layers can be mitigated.

> **NOTE**
>
> Although this chapter emphasizes data transformation avoidance, it is worth noting that the standardization of service contracts can also overcome other forms of undesirable transformation layers, such as the use of proprietary adapters and bridging products used to translate disparate communication protocols.

Standardization and Granularity

The use of design standards can impact all four types of service-related design granularity.

Service-level granularity is impacted and often determined by the choice of service model. Basing functional context on service models is, in fact, a form of standardization in itself. A service based on the entity service model, for example, will inherit a predefined functional scope that will determine the overall measure of service granularity (as shown in Example 6.4).

```
<definitions name="Invoice" ...>
  ...
  <operation name="Get">
    ...
  </operation>
  <operation name="Update">
    ...
  </operation>
  <operation name="Add">
    ...
  </operation>
  <operation name="Delete">
    ...
  </operation>
  ...
</definitions>
```

Example 6.4

A standardized WSDL definition representing an Invoice service will likely have a predetermined functional scope associated with a range of invoice-related processing. The result is a coarse level of service granularity.

While capability granularity is often initially defined when carrying out the service modeling process (see Appendix B), design standards derived from or based on design patterns concentrated on the service contract will often further shape the granularity of a capability or add capabilities with different granularity levels.

Data granularity can also be directly defined by data representation standards and further affected by architectural design standards concerned with regulating message sizes and service-roundtrips for scalability and performance reasons. Example 6.5 shows how standardization affects both the capability and data granularity of two operations.

```
<operation name="Update">
  ...
</operation>
<operation name="UpdateStatus">
  ...
</operation>
```

Example 6.5

Design standards may require a combination of coarse and fine-grained service capabilities. In this example, the Update operation receives an entire invoice document as input and updates any changed values. As a result, both capability and data granularity are coarse. The finer-grained UpdateStatus operation receives a status value as input and is only responsible for updating that value. This would represent fine-grained capability and data granularity.

Finally, constraint granularity is often directly dictated by a series of detailed design standards. These are usually validation-centric conventions that specify how flexible constraints may be (in terms of allowing ranges of input or output data values) and how, specifically, the constraints themselves are to be expressed.

Incorporating pre-determined code values into data types, for example, can dramatically increase constraint granularity (as shown in Example 6.6). On the other hand, when working with policy definitions, the use of policy alternatives and the application of the `wsp:optional` and `wsp:ignorable` attributes can introduce some "validation leeway" and can therefore lead to more coarse-grained constraints.

```
<xsd:simpleType name="status">
  <xsd:restriction base="xsd:string">
    <xsd:enumeration value="P"/>
    <xsd:enumeration value="A"/>
  </xsd:restriction>
</xsd:simpleType>
```

Example 6.6

An example of a very fine-grained constraint using standardized single character codes to represent pending ("P") and approved ("A") status values.

Design standards may furthermore determine the quantity and type of validation logic that should be located in the service contract. For example, there may be a design standard that requires validation logic associated with business rules to be carried out within the underlying service logic—not within the service contract. While the overall amount of validation logic remains the same, the application of this particular design standard would result in coarser-grained constraint granularity because this form of granularity is concerned with the contract only.

Standardized Service Contracts and Service Models

As we learned in Chapter 3, service models provide us with templates for common types of services. The two models that boast high reuse potential are entity and utility services. Contracts for these service types receive a great deal of attention in that they are highly streamlined and tuned so as to facilitate numerous usage scenarios.

Task services are often delivered to represent just a single task. This reduces the chances of them being shared, thereby also reducing the need to optimize the contract beyond the immediate requirements the service is being delivered for. Similarly, orchestrated task services (responsible for encapsulating business process logic hosted by orchestration platforms) also require contracts that are more specific to the process logic they represent.

Another characteristic that distinguishes process-agnostic from process-specific services is the average size of the contracts they tend to establish. Because agnostic services need to provide a range of generic functionality, they are usually equipped with several finely tuned capabilities. Process-specific services, on the other hand, sometimes require only a single capability that allows an external service consumer to "kick-off" the process logic they encapsulate.

Regardless of the nature of the logic represented by these service models, all benefit from being subjected to the same set of design standards and naming conventions to whatever extent feasible.

How Standardized Service Contract Design Affects Other Principles

With an insight into how principles inter-relate, we can gain a better understanding of how to optimize service designs. Let's begin with a look at the principles that directly relate to the standardization and overall design of service contracts (Figure 6.11).

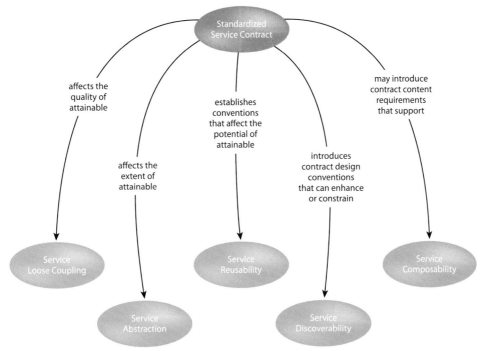

Figure 6.11

The manner in which service contracts are designed directly affects the extent to which some of the most important service-orientation principles can be realized.

Standardized Service Contract and Service Loose Coupling

A service consumer program is designed specifically to comply with the technical inter-face requirements dictated by the contract of the service it will be binding to, creating a very real dependency between consumer and service.

As explained in Chapter 7, the principle of Service Loose Coupling emphasizes that services should be designed to have minimal dependencies on other services. By limit-ing cross-service dependencies to the service contract, a reduced amount of overall cou-pling is attained between the solution logic encapsulated by each respective service. This is one of the primary goals of the Service Loose Coupling principle. To fully achieve this goal requires that we pay special attention to the content and design of each service contract.

Even though a loosely coupled relationship may have been formed between a service and its consumers, there are degrees of "looseness" that can be attained. Specifically, the more detailed and content-rich a technical service contract is, the greater the depend-ency consumers will form on the service.

From an architectural perspective, it is often desirable to defer lots of detail to the service contract layer. In a Web service, for example, numerous validation constraints, complex type constructs, and detailed policy assertions can be placed in WSDL, XML schema, and WS-Policy definitions. This guarantees two important results: First, that the service contract will be very communicative to those who need to develop potential service consumer programs, and secondly, that the service itself can be designed to process a very predictable set of data.

Although from a service developer's perspective this all makes sense, the principle of Service Loose Coupling pushes back and asks us to reconsider. Chapter 7 explores the details of this dynamic, but for the purpose of this chapter, it is important to understand that the extent of loose coupling that is achieved between two services is directly tied to the quantity of dependencies placed into the service contract. It is therefore during the design of the contract that cross-service coupling is determined.

A side note to this discussion is the fact that contracts that are standardized will tend to improve the consistency and *quality of coupling* between services. An exception to this is when the standards themselves impose an increased quantity of contract content. This can happen inadvertently when multiple design standards are created independently and their collective effect is not considered.

Standardized Service Contract and Service Abstraction

As with Service Loose Coupling, this principle encourages us to limit what is expressed in the service contract. In fact, abstraction asks us to streamline the contract to the extent that all non-essential information about a service is hidden.

The details of Service Abstraction and the different levels at which it can be applied are covered in Chapter 8. From the perspective of a service designer, it is important to note that what is documented in the service contract may very well be the only piece of information available to describe its purpose, capabilities, and interaction requirements.

Therefore, there is a tendency to put more information into the contract to ensure that its meaning is correctly understood and it is properly utilized. While this may seem to run contrary to the Service Loose Coupling principle that encourages us to minimize contract content, it simply emphasizes the need for balanced contract design. In other words, it is again the design of the service contract that determines the extent of abstraction. The more detail in the contract, the less information about the service is abstracted.

Standardized Service Contract and Service Reusability

The principle of Service Reusability is often focused on the logic encapsulated by the service. If this logic is sufficiently generic and common, the service can be classified as reusable. However, it comes down to how the service contract is designed that determines how reusable solution logic relates to data exchange. As established in Chapter 9, there are different levels of reuse attainable by a service.

Because we want reusable services to be as agnostic as possible to parent business processes and tasks, the underlying service logic often needs to include a series of highly generic routines capable of processing a range of message content.

Keeping the overall service design more reusable therefore implies that constraints on the contract layer be lifted so as to allow a wider range of input and output data to be processed. It also places an emphasis on designing extensible contracts so that as a reusable service matures, new capabilities can be added without compromising existing consumer dependencies (in other words, without requiring a new version of the contract to be released).

What all of this amounts to is the fact that service contract design can indeed affect the extent to which a service can be reused. Essentially, the more generic, flexible, and extensible a contract is, the greater the long-term reuse potential of the service.

Standardized Service Contract and Service Discoverability

If a service can't be found or if its capabilities aren't clearly understood, opportunities for the service to be utilized will likely be missed. Discoverability mechanisms, such as service registries, provide a means of locating service contracts. Often, though, contracts are simply published somewhere or need to be "dug out" from a remote folder or directory on a LAN. Either way, when searching for and assessing reusable services within the enterprise, it is imperative that what the contract represents is clearly documented and communicated.

Although the clarity of contracts can be improved by adding human-readable annotations, formal standardization plays a key role in making a contract more easily interpretable. The more consistently contracts are labeled and structured, the more predictable they become to those who need to use them.

A strong naming convention, for example, can immediately convey the purpose and requirements of individual capabilities belonging to a service you may have never seen before. Furthermore, the aforementioned use of standardized policy assertion vocabularies can also improve the communication quality of service contracts when optional or ignorable assertions are used to hint at behavioral service characteristics or preferences.

Chapter 12 is dedicated to discussing the importance of making services discoverable. Here, we just want to establish that the design characteristic of discoverability is directly tied to the content of the service contract. The more standardized a contract is and the more the technical interface details are supplemented with meta information, the more discoverable the service will become.

Standardized Service Contract and Service Composability

As discussed in Chapter 13, individual services need to be capable of acting as effective composition members in order for a service inventory to facilitate repeated compositions in support of fulfilling a wide range of automation requirements.

From a contract design perspective, this means viewing the service from two perspectives:

- as though it will be accessed by just one consumer to perform a specific task

- as though it will be accessed by a consumer that is coordinating the service's involvement as part of a larger composition

These two scenarios may seem identical to the service (it is still just one consumer invoking the service), but the circumstances often introduce different interaction requirements.

Note that Service Composability requirements frequently relate to the granularity with which the service contract expresses its capabilities. Coarse-grained capabilities, for example, are usually structured to receive larger, more complete documents and to respond with the same. While this saves on roundtrips, it can also introduce extra bandwidth and processing demands because not all of the data being exchanged is actually necessary for the capability to carry out its task.

Therefore, overly coarse-grained capabilities are often less suitable for when the service needs to participate in a larger composition. This means alternative design characteristics may have to be provided, even if they result in a degree of interface redundancy or specificity. Several design patterns can be used to address this issue, in particular the Contract Denormalization pattern.

There are many issues that affect the ultimate composability of a service. Service contracts can certainly play a significant part in supporting or hindering the realization of this principle.

SUMMARY OF KEY POINTS

- Both the quantity of service contract content and the extent to which it is standardized have a direct bearing on how other design principles can be realized.

- This design principle has especially close relationships with the Service Loose Coupling and Service Abstraction principles.

6.5 Risks Associated with Service Contract Design

The stage at which the design of a service contract is determined is considered a critical decision point in service delivery projects. In fact, entire service-oriented analysis and service-oriented design processes have been developed solely to provide a series of formal steps, each of which raises considerations that go into finalizing the service contract.

As a result, there are several pitfalls that lie between the idea for a service and its eventual concrete expression. Here we take a look at some of the primary risks associated with designing the contract and then implementing the service based on that design. All of these risks essentially come down to the level of judgment exercised by the contract designer.

Versioning

One of the most challenging aspects of managing service-oriented enterprise environments is dealing with the evolution of service contracts. Once an implemented service has been in use for some time, it is likely that several dependencies will have been formed on it by service consumers. This is generally tied to the reuse potential of the service—essentially the more reusable its underlying logic, the greater the volume and frequency with which programs that need to consume it will be built.

Service reuse is a positive and planned dynamic of SOA, but it does result in an increasing amount of enterprise-wide coupling being placed onto a single service contract. This amplifies the need for the design of a service to be appropriately balanced and extensible because once it is implemented, significant changes that can effectively "break" the established contract may introduce the need for new service versions to be released.

> **NOTE**
>
> Much of service-orientation is geared toward producing services with long life-spans. In fact, longevity, is a highly desirable design characteristic of service contracts and is also a measurable success indicator as to how well service-orientation was originally applied. If new versions of service contracts need to be released on a regular basis, it is often an indication that principles related to composability, reuse, and coupling were not given sufficient attention. Note that the book *SOA: Design Patterns* provides several patterns that address versioning concerns, and the *Web Service Contract Design for SOA* title (described in the *More About Service Contracts* section) has a chapter dedicated to versioning techniques specifically for Web service contracts.

Technology Dependencies

There are options when it comes to choosing an implementation technology for services. For example, services can be built using different programming languages and development platforms. An implementation option provides a valid approach to building SOA as long as the underlying technology is capable of realizing a significant extent of service-orientation.

Both open and proprietary technologies are available in the SOA marketplace. Non-industry standard approaches usually involve the utilization of component-based systems with RPC technology augmented to support service-orientation. Industry standard technologies generally refer to the Web services platform and its non-proprietary communications framework (which may also necessitate the use of WS-I compliant service contracts).

Because service contracts need to be physically implemented using some form of technology, there is a risk associated with the maturity and lifespan of the technology itself. Once the contract is in place, it establishes itself as the sole entry point into the service's encapsulated functionality. If new, enhanced technology platforms emerge the existing service contract can become outdated, not because of the solution logic it is representing, but because the medium by which the service can communicate is subject to a non-backwards-compatible upgrade.

> **BEST PRACTICE**
>
> Steps can be taken to mitigate this risk when designing solution logic (proprietary or otherwise) capable of encapsulation via Web services. As per fundamental service design patterns, service contracts can be designed according to existing conventions so that if a Web service contract needs to later be derived, it will mirror a technical interface that is already standardized.

Development Tool Deficiencies

Service contracts themselves can't be ignored because we need them to create services. However, the design of service contracts can certainly be neglected. Depending on the implementation platform used to realize services, it is often easy to allow a development tool to derive and auto-generate the contract from an arbitrary source, such as a database or a programmatic interface. This feature has led to the creation of many non-standardized Web service contracts.

We can avoid the problems associated with auto-generated contracts by introducing standards that require that service contracts be custom-designed. A potential challenge to accomplishing this, though, lies with the ability of development tools to accept and preserve the custom contract content after the developer proceeds to build the supporting service logic.

Some Web services development tools, for example, offer limited support for importing custom-coded WSDL and XML schema definitions. Even if they can be imported, the program may attempt to alter some of the code or may raise errors because it does not support the full range of WSDL and XML schema features. Further limitations may be encountered when attempting to customize and then import WS-Policy definitions.

BEST PRACTICE

When building services as Web services, it is worth taking the time to assess the marketplace. Commercial tools have different features and limitations as to the amount of support and control they offer for customizing the actual Web service markup code.

Some of the key considerations to look out for include the following:

- It can be very helpful to have the option to view service contracts graphically so as to display a tree view of the various element constructs. Although this feature is common, it varies in sophistication. For example, it is preferable to be able to view a WSDL definition in relation to numerous external schema definitions on one screen.

- All tools provide some sort of validation checking. However, the quality of feedback can vary. It can be invaluable to the contract designer for the tool to provide highly descriptive error and warning messages that naturally incorporate WS-I basic profile checking.

- To properly apply detailed contract design standards requires the ability to fully customize the contract markup code. Some tools have limitations as to the range of support they provide for Web services specifications. This can cause problems in that the tool may not be able to properly validate the code or may actually modify it.

- Some tools may provide little to no support for service contracts that include WS-Policy definitions. There may be development environments that assume you want to create policies only through graphical user interfaces. It is therefore a good idea to investigate whether custom coded policies can be imported along with other service description documents.

NOTE

This book repeatedly emphasizes the need to avoid the use of Web service contract auto-generation features. The intent is not to state that these features represent poor product design. In fact, auto-generation utilities helped popularize Web services by making their development easier. However, when pursuing service-oriented design, their use is generally limited due to contract standardization requirements.

SUMMARY OF KEY POINTS

- The quality of the initial release of a service contract often determines its ultimate longevity within a given enterprise. The sooner it needs to be changed in a non-backwards-compatible manner, the sooner version control enters the picture.

- Service-orientation can be applied to proprietary components and Web services. Either is a valid option, but having both types of services co-exist within the same inventory can lead to interoperability issues due to different communications standards and technologies.

- A desired level of standardization can be inhibited by development tools incapable of properly importing and preserving custom designed service contracts.

6.6 More About Service Contracts

Provided in this section are some supplementary notes and resources regarding the design of standardized service contracts.

Non-Technical Service Contract Documents

At the beginning of this chapter it was established that a service contract typically consists of a collection of technical service descriptions, but that it can also include non-technical documents. A classic example is the service level agreement (SLA), a document that establishes a contract associated with quality of service characteristics, such as availability, accessibility, and performance. Though not technically binding, this agreement is often legally binding and therefore considered an important extension of the technical interface.

An SLA can provide additional semantic details about a service, thereby reducing its level of abstraction while preserving (or perhaps even enhancing) the existing level of required technical coupling.

Some examples include:

- guaranteed availability schedule

- guaranteed response times for service capabilities

- response time averages for service capabilities

- usage statistics (concurrency and variance of service consumers)

- a rating based on feedback from service consumer owners

- charge-back costs (which may be required if the service is a third-party product or part of an infrastructure department that charges project teams for its usage)

- coupling, reusability, autonomy, statelessness meta details (as explained in Chapters 7, 9, 10, and 11)

Note that the service profile document described in Chapter 15 can be used to collect various types of information during the definition and development of a service that can later be carried over into the SLA.

"Web Service Contract Design for SOA"

The purpose of this chapter is to establish standardized service contract design as a core and governing principle that shapes a fundamental part of the service-orientation paradigm. The focus has therefore been on the influence of this principle and conceptual topics associated with the positioning and utilization of service contracts.

This book has deliberately not delved into the specific technical details of designing WSDL, XML schema, and WS-Policy definitions for Web services to avoid overlap with *Web Service Contract Design for SOA*, a separate book in the *Prentice Hall Service-Oriented Computing Series from Thomas Erl*. This title is dedicated to exploring the details of designing Web service contracts and supplies examples based on the use of WSDL, XML schema, SOAP, WS-Policy, and WS-Addressing.

6.7 CASE STUDY EXAMPLE

Cutit Saws has made the automation of the business process associated with experimental simulation projects a priority and has therefore decided to proceed with the implementation of services required to carry out this process (as described in the *Case Study Background* section of Chapter 5).

Planned Services

In the service inventory established in the Cutit example at the end of Chapter 4, the following two Web services were identified to represent business entities involved in the manufacturing of saw blades:

- Materials

- Formulas

These agnostic services are used to support various lab projects in which different materials are combined as per new and existing formulas. Both materials and formulas are stored in repositories and modeled as separate information sets.

Cutit sets out to build these services in addition to a service called Run Lab Project. This new task-centric service will encapsulate the automation requirements of the entire business process and will fulfill these requirements by composing the Materials and Formulas services (Figure 6.12).

Figure 6.12

A high-level look at the simple composition represented by the Cutit services responsible for automating the lab project processes.

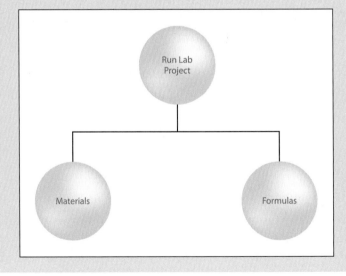

Design Standards

Although Cutit did not have the time to develop a comprehensive service inventory blueprint, it takes the time to put design standards in place to address both the functional expression and data representation aspects for the initial set of service contracts, as follows:

Functional Expression Standards

- Entity services will be named in accordance with the corresponding business entities from which they are derived.

- The names of task services will be based on the process the service is responsible for automating, further prefixed with an appropriate verb.

- Operations for all services will be based on the following naming format: verb + noun.

- The operation name cannot repeat the name of the service.

Data Representation Standards

- Whenever complex types representing data constructs already established by entity schemas are required, the existing complex types must be used. Therefore, all-encompassing, service-specific schema definitions are prohibited.

- Only when services need new complex types that fulfill processing requirements unique to the service are service-specific schema definitions allowed.

- All XML schema definitions must exist in separate files that are linked to the WSDL definitions.

Standardized WSDL Definition Profiles

Cutit uses the functional expression standards to define preliminary service contract profiles. The following tables establish the operations related to the automation of the Lab Project Process for each of the three services. (See the *Service Profiles* section in Chapter 15 for more information about service profile documents.)

Materials Service	
GetDeveloped Operation	Input: unique material identifier and employee identifier Output: developed material document
GetPurchased Operation	Input: unique material identifier Output: purchased material document
ReportStockLevels Operation	Input: unique material identifier Output: stock level value

Table 6.2

The three operations of the Materials Web service and their respective input and output requirements. Separate operations are provided for the two types of materials records.

Formulas Service	
AddBase Operation	Input: formula document and employee identifier Output: acknowledgement code
Simulate Operation	Input: materials and formula identifiers required for this project plus an employee identifier Output: simulation report document
Get Operation	Input: unique formula identifier and employee identifier Output: formula document

Table 6.3

In addition to the retrieval of formula documents, the operations of the Formulas Web service allow for the creation of base formula records as well as the combining of base formulas into compound formulas.

Run Lab Project Service	
Start Operation	Input: employee identifier and date value Output: acknowledgement code

Table 6.4
The Run Lab Project task service has a simple operation that kicks off the Lab Project Process.

Standardized XML Schema Definitions

As part of this service delivery project, XML schema definitions are also defined. These schemas are required to provide the necessary complex types for the input and output message definitions listed in the preceding service description tables. Extra effort is made to ensure that they are modeled in accordance with existing logical data models so that they preserve the overall structure of the data records that already exist.

- DevelopedMaterial.xsd (entity)

- PurchasedMaterial.xsd (entity)

- Materials.xsd

- Formula.xsd (entity)

- Formulas.xsd

- Employee.xsd (entity)

- RunLabProject.xsd

As indicated in the preceding list, four of the schema definitions are derived from data models based on existing information sets or business entities. The other schemas provide complex types that support service-specific data exchange requirements.

Standardized Service and Data Representation Layers

Figure 6.13 shows the functional expression layer established by the service WSDL definitions and the data representation layer consisting of XML schema definitions used in the service contracts.

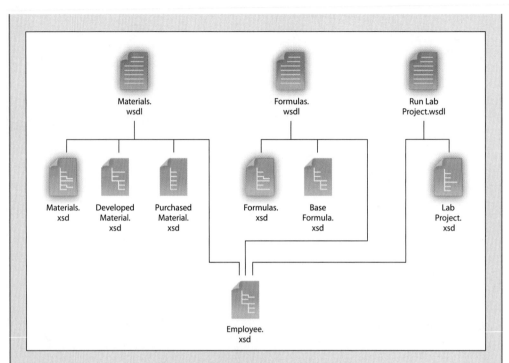

Figure 6.13

The seven operations provided by the three services require the involvement of seven schema definitions. Highlighted symbols represent service-specific schemas, whereas the other schemas represent document structures derived from existing business entity models.

Note how the Employee.xsd definition is used by all three services; this requirement ties into the fundamental need for standardization (as discussed at the end of this section) and is also an implementation of the Schema Centralization design pattern.

Service Descriptions

At this stage we are not that interested in the process being automated or even how these services are composed. Our focus is on the design of the individual service contracts and the manner in which service description documents have been standardized in consideration of this principle. However, before we look at the underlying contract details, let's briefly establish how the WSDL definitions relate to the schema definitions.

Materials Service

- Materials in the Cutit inventory are grouped into two categories: developed and purchased. Each represents a type of material document with different attributes and characteristics.

- The Materials.wsdl definition needs to expose the ability for consumer programs to process data associated with these two types of materials. Separate GetDeveloped and GetPurchased operations are therefore provided, each of which represents logic that accesses different databases that return different document structures.

- Almost all of the complex types required to define the input and output messages for the GetDeveloped and GetPurchased operations are defined in the respective DevelopedMaterial.xsd and PurchasedMaterial.xsd schema definitions.

- Because the GetDeveloped operation retrieves documents representing internally created materials considered intellectual property, it also requires the employee ID of the person issuing the request. The complex type for this identifier is defined in the Employee.xsd schema.

- Also provided is the GetStockLevels operation, which returns the current in-stock value of a given material. The input and output messages for this operation are defined separately in the Materials.xsd definition.

Formulas Service

- Formulas exist as separate records within the Cutit labs. There are base formulas that are created and defined individually but which can also be combined.

- The Formulas.wsdl definition provides operations for the creation of base formulas and the simulated application of formulas via the AddBase and Simulate operations. Also defined is a simple Get operation that retrieves one or more formula documents.

- The input message for the AddBase operation and the output message for the Get operation are defined in the Formula.xsd schema which represents the official document structure for formula records.

- The acknowledgement code values required by the output messages for the AddBase operation are defined in the service-specific Formulas.xsd definition as is the simulation report structure that is output by the Simulation operation.

- Formula records are also considered private and secured information. The identifiers of employees working with formulas therefore always need to be supplied. The employee identifier required as an input value by all three operations is defined in the Employee.xsd schema.

Run Lab Project Service

- The RunLabProject.wsdl definition exposes a Start operation that requests a date value as well as an employee identifier for the process to begin.

- The input date value and the acknowledgement code that is output when the process has been successfully initiated are defined in the RunLabProject.xsd definition.

- The employee identifier needed as input for the Start operation is defined in the Employee.xsd schema.

Conclusion

The use of the functional expression and data representation design standards established prior to the delivery of the planned services allowed Cutit service designers to pursue key design benefits:

- By using naming conventions, a consistent expression of service capabilities was ensured, regardless of how the individual services were implemented. This ends up establishing each service as a standardized endpoint easily understood by humans and consistently consumed by client programs.

- Requiring that the complex types defined by entity schemas be used where appropriate by all standardized service contracts *within the boundary of a specific service inventory* guarantees that these services will be able to exchange data defined by these schemas while minimizing transformation requirements. For example, the employee identifier defined by the Employee.xsd schema was incorporated into all three contracts. The Run Lab Project service may collect the identifier upon invocation and can then pass the same value (or set of values) to the other two services without the need to convert it to and from other formats.

- The fact that entity schemas were established independently of the WSDL definitions allowed for the creation of a data representation layer that fully supports these and future services but can also exist on its own in support of other (non-Web services-based) parts of the enterprise that also need to exchange XML data.

The delivery of the initial three services fulfilled tactical requirements while also allowing Cutit to take an important step toward establishing a standardized service inventory.

Chapter 7

Service Coupling (Intra-Service and Consumer Dependencies)

When assembling the pieces of a machine with nuts and bolts, you want to tighten each part just the right amount. If you over-tighten one, you risk stripping the bolt. If you don't tighten it enough, the machine won't be robust. Each tightened bolt represents a coupling between two parts.

Along those same lines, we need to pay attention not just to where service coupling occurs, but the extent to which the parts of a service composition as well as the parts that comprise its individual services should be coupled.

7.1 Coupling Explained

The term "coupling" is a pretty straight-forward part of the IT vocabulary: Anything that connects has coupling and coupled things can form dependencies on each other. However, when we qualify coupling with "loose" or "tight," we get into a more ambiguous realm. Who's to say what is considered more or less dependent? We will need a firm understanding of how to measure and allocate appropriate levels of coupling (Figure 7.1) in order to effectively apply this principle. Let's therfore begin with a brief exploration of how coupling relates to automation environments in general.

Figure 7.1

This principle emphasizes the reduction ("loosening") of coupling between the parts of a service-oriented solution, especially when compared to how applications have traditionally been designed. Specifically, loose coupling is advocated between a service contract and its consumers and between a service contract and its underlying implementation.

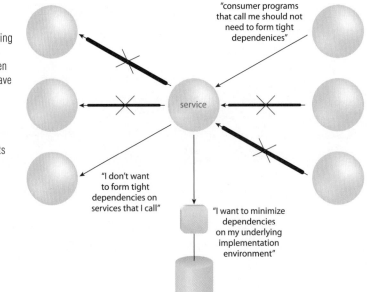

> **NOTE**
>
> In this chapter thicker arrow lines represent tighter coupling requirements.

Coupling in Abstract

Any part of an automation environment that's separable has the potential (and usually the need) to be coupled to something else for the sake of imparting its value. The root of the term (couple) itself implies that two of something exist and have a relationship.

The most common way of explaining coupling is to compare it to dependency. A measure of coupling between two things is equivalent to the level of dependency that exists between them. For example, the relationship between one software program and another represents a measure of coupling associated with interoperability. Or the relationship a technical contract has to the solution logic it is representing indicates a measure of coupling associated with the behind-the-scenes structure of the software program.

This also highlights the fact that the directionality of coupling can vary as well. Two applications tightly coupled by a point-to-point integration channel may have formed a bidirectional dependency in that each application requires the existence (and perhaps even the availability) of the other to function properly. Alternatively, unidirectional coupling is also common where one program may depend on another, but the reverse is not true. The relationship between applications and databases, for example, is a common form of unidirectional coupling (an application may depend on a database, but the database may not depend at all on the application).

Coupling is unavoidable. What we are most interested in when exploring coupling within IT automation is how close this relationship actually is or should be.

Origins of Software Coupling

In the past, many custom applications were developed with certain types and levels of coupling that were simply pre-set by the programming environments or surrounding technology architectures. More often than not, coupling between software programs or components was tight.

For example:

- In a traditional two-tier client-server architecture, the clients were developed specifically to interact with a designated database (or specific process servers).

Proprietary commands were embedded within the client programs, and changes to this binding affected all client installations.

- In a typical multi-tier component-based architecture, components were often developed to work with other specific components. Even shared components that became more popular after OO principles were applied still required tight levels of coupling when made part of inheritance structures.

- When Web services emerged, they were often mistakenly perceived to automatically establish a looser form of coupling within distributed architectures. While Web services can naturally decouple clients from proprietary technology, they can just as easily couple client programs to many other service implementation details.

Interestingly, it is one of the earliest architectures that implemented a more loosely coupled paradigm. Mainframe environments imposed little dependencies on client terminals, allowing the same terminal to be used for multiple types of mainframe applications (a loosely coupled client-server relationship that was later revived with the browser and Web server).

However, while there is some conceptual commonality in this comparison, it's important to point out that loose coupling is a very specific design characteristic that service-orientation aims to establish across all services, especially throughout solution back-ends. Even though mainframe environments had loosely coupled workstation clients, their server-side applications were monolithic and self-contained. Because they weren't typically distributed, there was little emphasis on regulating back-end coupling.

Loose coupling, as a design concept, has historically been a greater part of commercial software design. The use of drivers, for example, allowed client programs to tightly bind to the driver software, which, in turn, decoupled the client programs from underlying hardware and system programs. Similarly, database connection protocols and associated software (such as ODBC and JDBC) also introduce a loosely coupled relationship between the client programs and underlying database environments.

This past emphasis on reducing coupling between programs in general highlights commercial design as a primary influence of service-orientation, as further discussed in Chapters 8 and 9.

7.2 Profiling this Principle

Service coupling is a multi-faceted, dynamic design characteristic that ties into and influences several other principles. On a fundamental level, this principle is concerned with the relationship between a service, its underlying environment, and its consumers (as previously illustrated in Figure 7.1).

As further detailed in Table 7.1, when trying to determine suitable levels of service coupling, our goal is to position the service as a continually useful and accessible resource while also protecting it and its consumers from forming any relationships that may constrain or inhibit them in the future (Figure 7.2).

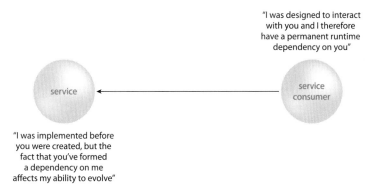

Figure 7.2

The fundamental impacts of coupling on the service and consumer. The constraints expressed in this figure are amplified when the measure of coupling and the quantity of consumers is increased.

NOTE
Because the scope of this chapter (and this book) is focused on service design, we are only concerned with coupling issues internal to the service architecture and between a service and its immediate consumers. There are various architectural design options for reducing coupling levels via the use of middleware and intermediaries. Some of these architectural coupling issues are also addressed by design patterns.

Principle Profile	
Short Definition	*"Services are loosely coupled."*
Long Definition	*"Service contracts impose low consumer coupling requirements and are themselves decoupled from their surrounding environment."*
Goals	By consistently fostering reduced coupling within and between services we are working toward a state where service contracts increase independence from their implementations and services are increasingly independent from each other. This promotes an environment in which services and their consumers can be adaptively evolved over time with minimal impact on each other.
Design Characteristics	• The existence of a service contract that is ideally decoupled from technology and implementation details. • A functional service context that is not dependent on outside logic. • Minimal consumer coupling requirements.
Implementation Requirements	• Loosely coupled services are typically required to perform more runtime processing than if they were more tightly coupled. As a result, data exchange in general can consume more runtime resources, especially during concurrent access and high usage scenarios. • To achieve the right balance of coupling, while also supporting the other service-orientation principles that affect contract design, requires increased service contract design proficiency.

Web Service Region of Influence	As we explore different coupling types in the next section, it will become evident that applying this principle touches numerous parts of the typical Web service architecture. However, the primary focal point, both for internal and consumer-related design considerations, remains the service contract.

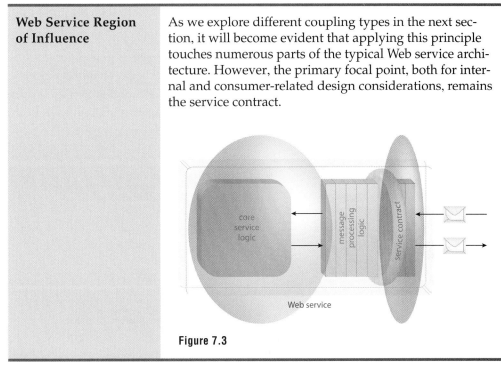

Figure 7.3

Table 7.1
A profile for the Service Loose Coupling principle.

SUMMARY OF KEY POINTS

- The scope of this principle affects both the design of a service, as well as its relationship with consumer programs.

- While we are concerned with how coupling affects service logic, the primary emphasis is on the design of the service contract.

7.3 Service Contract Coupling Types

To gain a better appreciation of the extent to which coupling can become part of service design, we need to take a look at the common types of relationships that need to be created within and outside of the service boundary.

This, the first of two sections that explores coupling types, is focused on dependencies that originate from within the service. How these relate to and influence the service contract directly ties into the subsequent *Service Consumer Coupling Types* section that explores how less desirable forms of intra-service coupling can make their way into consumer program designs.

The service contract is the core element around which most coupling-related design considerations revolve. The basis of these issues is the relationship between the service contract and whatever logic and resources it encapsulates. As shown in Figure 7.4, we can design the contract with dependencies on the underlying service logic—or—we can choose to design the service logic with dependencies on the service contract.

Figure 7.4

The illustrated forms of coupling are described in the upcoming *Contract-to-Logic Coupling* and *Logic-to-Contract Coupling* sections.

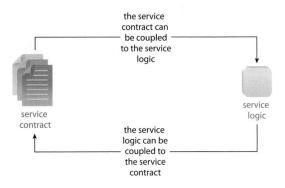

Understanding these two fundamental coupling types and the impact of proceeding with either is key to identifying the link between the design of individual services and the direction in which an entire service inventory will ultimately evolve. The design-time dependencies established between a service contract and its underlying logic have a direct bearing on the ultimate strategic potential of each service within a service inventory and, therefore, on the inventory as a whole.

Figure 7.5 positions the contract and its logic within the scope of common service-related dependencies that can exist as part of a typical SOA. This perspective also highlights the potential design complexity introduced by coupling-related issues.

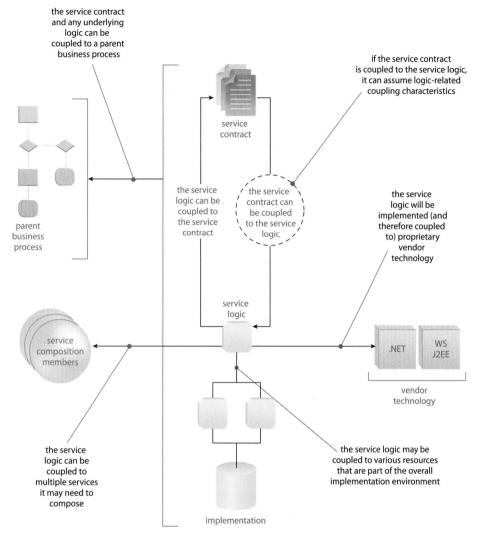

the service contract
and any underlying
logic can be
coupled to a parent
business process

if the service contract
is coupled to the service logic,
it can assume logic-related
coupling characteristics

service
contract

the service
logic can be
coupled to
the service
contract

the service
contract can
be coupled
to the service
logic

the service
logic will be
implemented (and
therefore coupled
to) proprietary
vendor
technology

parent
business
process

service
logic

service
composition
members

.NET

WS
J2EE

vendor
technology

the service
logic can be
coupled to
multiple services
it may need to
compose

the service logic may be
coupled to various resources
that are part of the overall
implementation environment

implementation

Figure 7.5

Coupling is a natural and unavoidable part of service architecture. It's knowing how and when to adjust the extent of coupling that gives us the ability to tune this architecture in support of service-orientation.

Various types of service-related coupling are represented in Figure 7.5, all of which can relate to both the service logic and contract. The same coupling types are re-displayed as part of a conceptual view in Figure 7.6.

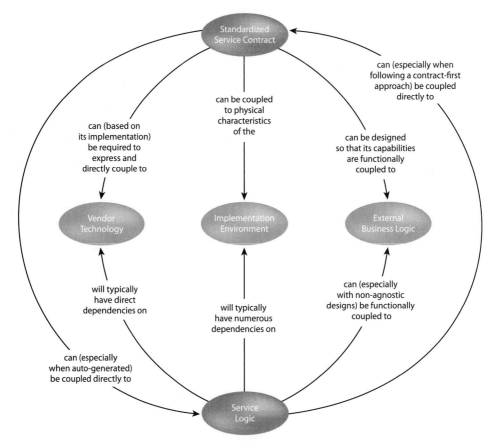

Figure 7.6
Both service contract and service logic can form dependencies on parts of the service environment and on each other.

From the relationships and dependencies depicted in Figures 7.5 and 7.6 we can extract a specific set of coupling types that are directly relevant to the design of services:

- Logic-to-Contract Coupling
- Contract-to-Logic Coupling
- Contract-to-Technology Coupling

- Contract-to-Implementation Coupling

- Contract-to-Functional Coupling

Except for logic-to-contract coupling, the goal behind this principle is to reduce the extent of all these coupling types. The following sections explore each type in more detail:

Logic-to-Contract Coupling (the coupling of service logic to the service contract)

A recommended approach to building a service is to design its physical contract prior to its underlying solution logic. This "contract first" process is very effective at ensuring that contract design standards are consistently incorporated. It also allows us to tune the underlying logic in support of the service contract, which can optimize runtime performance and reliability.

Following the contract-first process can result in the service logic being tightly coupled to the service contract (known as *logic-to-contract coupling*) because it is created specifically in support of the independently designed contract, as shown in Figure 7.7.

Figure 7.7

A Web service created through the contract-first process will naturally result in the service logic forming a tightly coupled relationship on the service contract. The contract, though, is not really coupled to the logic at all, allowing the service logic to be replaced in the future without affecting service consumers that have formed dependencies on the contract.

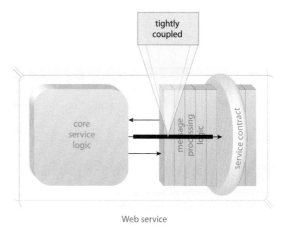

Despite the tight, unidirectional dependency formed by the logic on the contract, this is considered a positive type of coupling and a proven means of customizing services in support of service-orientation. It is further supported through the application of the Standardized Service Contract principle, which fundamentally preaches the contract-first design approach.

Of course, controlling the amount of required coupling between contract and logic is something we can only really accomplish when custom-developing services. In environments where service contracts need to be auto-generated or are provided by service adapter extensions, the level of coupling is often predetermined. In these cases there may be a need to resort to wrapper services, as further explored in the case study example at the end of this chapter.

FOR EXAMPLE

A multi-national pharmaceutical firm carried out a two-year SOA pilot program during which 47 Web services were created to automate 12 business processes within the human resources segment of the organization. A service design process was custom tailored for this project requiring that each Web service contract be fully developed prior to any further programming effort. Before the project could start, several of the programmers on the team had to undergo training in order to gain the required proficiency with WSDL and XML schema.

The end result was a moderately sized service inventory wherein 85% of services achieved high logic-to-contract coupling. Various capabilities within the remaining services were required to encapsulate legacy systems to one extent or another. This resulted in some service contracts having no logic-to-contract coupling at all (or having mixed levels of this coupling as implemented by a subset of the contract capabilities).

Note that in this project some legacy system encapsulation restrictions were overcome through the use of dedicated utility services that provided native translation of proprietary legacy APIs. (Specific design patterns exist to address legacy abstraction for service inventories.)

Contract-to-Logic Coupling (the coupling of the service contract to its logic)

The previous section described a coupling type based on the customization of the service contract prior to the development of the underlying service logic. This positions the contract as a relatively independent part of the service architecture, which maximizes the freedom with which the service can be evolved over time.

However, many contracts for Web services in particular have been derived from existing solution logic. This reverses the coupling dynamic, in that once these types of contracts come into existence, they find themselves immediately dependent on the underlying logic and implementation. As explained in Figure 7.8, this dependency of the contract upon its underlying logic is referred to as *contract-to-logic coupling*.

Figure 7.8

In environments where contracts can be auto-generated, the service logic is not dependent on the contract because if the logic changes, a new contract can be created at any time. The contract, however, is tightly coupled to the underlying service logic because the logic determines its design. Every time the logic changes and a new contract is generated, a new version of the service is effectively published, which raises numerous coupling and governance issues with consumers.

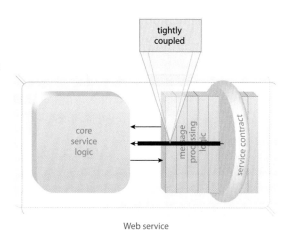

Web service

The most common examples have been the auto-generation of WSDL definitions using component interfaces as the basis for the contract design, as well as the auto-generation of XML schemas from database tables and other parts of physical data models. In both cases, the design of the resulting service contract is hardwired to the characteristics of its implementation environment. This is an established anti-pattern that shortens the lifespan of the service contract and inhibits the long-term evolution of the service.

NOTE

Services with contract-to-logic coupling will tend to have increased levels of technology, functional, and implementation coupling (as described in the upcoming sections).

FOR EXAMPLE

The aforementioned pharmaceutical company initiated the SOA pilot program to replace an integration architecture that had only existed for two years but had caused many problems. A legacy system acted as a hub for several custom-developed, distributed applications that exchanged data via five Web service endpoints.

A development tool had been used to auto-generate the source markup code that comprised each of the Web service contracts. As a result, the five WSDL definitions closely mirrored the five corresponding component interfaces. Each Web service contract therefore had a high level of contract-to-logic coupling. All of these Web services were eventually replaced.

Contract-to-Technology Coupling (the coupling of the service contract to its underlying technology)

A service that exists as a traditional proprietary component generally requires that the service contract be tightly coupled to the service's associated communications technology. As shown in Figure 7.9, the resulting *contract-to-technology* coupling may impose technology-specific characteristics on the contract as proprietary as the development technology used to build the service itself.

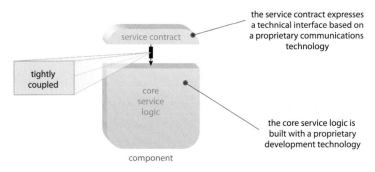

Figure 7.9

A service developed as a proprietary component can require that the service contract exist as a proprietary extension of the service. This couples the contract to the implementation technology which, in turn, imposes the requirement that all service consumers support the same proprietary (or non-industry standard) communications protocol.

As further explained in the *Consumer-to-Contract Coupling* section of this chapter, making the technical service contract dependent on proprietary technology limits the potential consumers to those who are capable of supporting the technology.

The ability to abstract proprietary technology in support of a non-proprietary framework is what has made Web services so successful. A Web service contract is not required to express proprietary details of the underlying solution logic and can be positioned to exist as an independent part of the service architecture. This not only frees consumer programs from having to comply with proprietary communication protocols, it also gives the service owner the ability to swap service implementation technologies without affecting the service's existing consumer base.

> ## FOR EXAMPLE
>
> In its initial incarnation, the pharmaceutical company's human resource integration environment consisted of .NET components only. Data sharing was effectively accomplished as long as both ends of every integration channel supported the .NET Remoting protocol they had standardized on at the time. Each of the components involved therefore exposed technical interfaces with contract-to-technology coupling.
>
> As interoperability demands increased, the existing architecture was deemed too restrictive because it limited interaction to programs capable of supporting .NET Remoting. The previously mentioned Web services were introduced and strategically positioned to allow for messaging-based data exchange over HTTP. These Web service endpoints overcame the contract-to-technology coupling limitations by exposing vendor technology-neutral contracts.
>
> The subsequent SOA program that replaced these Web services introduced new, standardized Web services to continue to avoid contract-to-technology coupling.

Contract-to-Implementation Coupling (the coupling of the service contract to its implementation environment)

Any physically deployed service will be comprised of or will require access to a collection of implementation technologies and products beyond the core service logic.

Examples include:

- physical databases and associated physical data models
- legacy system APIs
- user and group accounts and associated physical directory structures
- physical server environments and associated domains
- file names and network paths

It is relatively normal for some forms of service logic to be bound and connected to these details. This enables the logic to effectively access and interact with these resources as required at runtime.

When deriving service contracts from logic bound to an implementation environment, implementation-specific characteristics and details can become embedded within the contract content. In the case of XML, the auto-generation of the schema from database tables or views will similarly end up placing physical data model details into the service contract. The result is a direct dependency formed by the service contract on the underlying implementation, referred to as *contract-to-implementation coupling* (Figure 7.10).

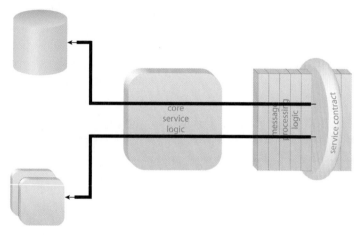

Figure 7.10

A Web service consisting of service logic, external components, and a database, the latter two of which impose implementation-specific details onto the service contract content.

Note that the manner in which the service logic itself relates to its underlying implementation can also establish a related form of coupling called *logic-to-implementation coupling*. As we will learn in Chapter 10, it is highly preferable for the implementation resources required by a service to be dedicated. However, almost every service architecture is unique, and desired levels of autonomy are not always possible. Therefore, we need to account for situations where the parts of the service logic that are dedicated are required to access (and therefore form dependencies on) parts of the enterprise that exist external to the service boundary.

The extent to which the service relies on external resources determines the level of coupling the service forms on its surrounding implementation environment. There are concrete benefits to minimizing this form of coupling, all of which are addressed by the Service Autonomy principle.

FOR EXAMPLE

A corporation owning several lumber mills had a centralized IT department that custom developed a handful of applications to manage some of the more unique aspects of their business. Subsequent integration requirements prompted IT managers to explore XML as a standard data representation format. For each data exchange requirement a utility was used to derive one or more XML schemas from existing database tables and views.

This approach fulfilled immediate requirements but caused some challenges when several Web services were later introduced to accommodate a new business process that imposed changes on the integration architecture. The schemas became part of the Web service contracts. They introduced an extent of contract-to-implementation coupling because their complex types were directly derived from composites of table columns and fields.

Here is a sampling of one of the complex types containing embedded table column names and the questionable use of an attribute:

```
<xsd:element name="BZN_TAB22">
  <xsd:complexType>
    <xsd:sequence>
      <xsd:element name="BZN_DET_SHP"
          type="xsd:string"/>
      <xsd:element name="BZN_TS_DAT67"
          type="xsd:base64Binary"/>
    </xsd:sequence>
    <xsd:attribute name="BZN_A_EMP_NAME"
        type="xsd:string" use="required"/>
  </xsd:complexType>
</xsd:element>
```

NOTE

Service contracts can include WS-Policy definitions capable of expressing a variety of policy assertions. Some of these assertions may be comprised of syntax or characteristics proprietary to the vendor platform used to generate the definition or perhaps proprietary to business rules and polices predefined within vendor products or legacy systems. These cases could also be classified as forms of contract-to-implementation coupling.

Contract-to-Functional Coupling (the coupling of the service contract to external logic)

When the logic encapsulated by a service (or, more specifically, by one of its capabilities) is specifically designed in support of a body of functionality that exists outside of the service boundary, then the corresponding service contract can become functionally coupled, resulting in *contract-to-functional coupling*.

There can be many variations of functional coupling. Provided here are some common examples:

Parent Process Coupling

Functional coupling can exist between the logic encapsulated by service capabilities and business process logic represented and implemented elsewhere in the enterprise. If a service has been designed specifically to support a particular business process, its logic as well as its contract might well be tightly coupled to the logic of that process.

Service-to-Consumer Coupling

A service can be designed to support a particular (usually pre-existing) service consumer program. This is common in B2B architectures, where an established organization already has a service consumer in place. Partners wishing to participate online are required to deliver services according to design standards dictated by the organization and their environment. Another typical occurrence of consumer coupled services is within internal point-to-point integration architectures, where both service and consumer are built only to work with each other to establish a specific integration channel.

Either way, intentionally designing a service for a single consumer (or for a limited amount of consumers) typically results in consumer-specific functional coupling. Note that this may or may not also result in parent process coupling, depending on the nature of the functionality being delivered by the service.

Functional Coupling and Task Services

In the case of a task service, we are deliberately limiting the functional scope to that of a business process. We generally do so with the assumption that the service encompasses the scope of the process and therefore acts as the parent controller. Other services avoid this type of coupling by basing their functional scope on an agnostic context (such as a business entity). A task service can be considered an example of intentional or *targeted* functional coupling.

> **NOTE**
>
> Focusing on logic-to-contract coupling and avoiding the other negative forms of coupling described in this section leads to increased design-time control of a service, as explained in the *Design-Time Autonomy* section of Chapter 10.

SUMMARY OF KEY POINTS

- There are many forms of coupling that relate to internal and external service design and runtime processing. All represent relationships and dependencies that exist between different architectural components.

- Numerous coupling-related concerns revolve around the service contract. If the contract for a service can be standardized, many undesirable types of coupling between the contract and its underlying implementation can be avoided.

7.4 Service Consumer Coupling Types

Ultimately, it is the service and one of its consumers that will need to interact to carry out some form of business task. How their relationship is defined at design-time determines the level of cross-service coupling they will need to live with, as explained in Figure 7.11. This relationship is therefore a core design consideration.

Two very specific types of consumer coupling are explored in this section:

- Consumer-to-Implementation Coupling
- Consumer-to-Contract Coupling

The primary distinction between these types is whether or not the service contract is accessed as the sole or primary endpoint into service logic and resources.

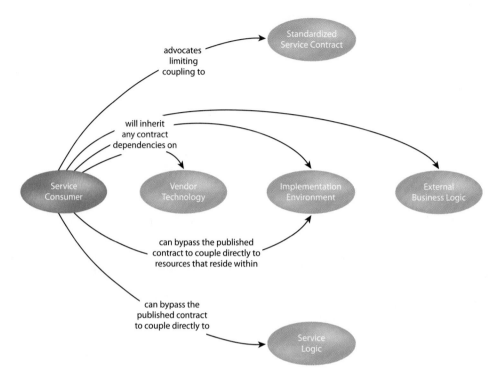

Figure 7.11

Consumer programs can form various types of dependencies on service resources, either via the service contract or by circumventing it.

Consumer-to-Implementation Coupling

A service consumer is technically not forced to access a service via its contract, as evidenced by Figure 7.12. There are often other entry points that may seem more attractive for reasons such as improved performance and design simplicity. However, these result in undesirable forms of *consumer-to-implementation coupling* that can inhibit both service and consumer in the future.

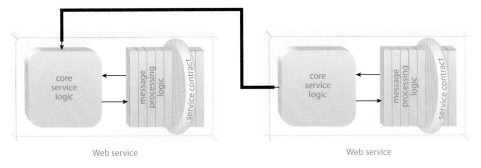

Figure 7.12

The service consumer bypasses the published service contract and accesses (and tightly couples to) the underlying service logic directly.

The first question a consumer program designer needs to answer is whether a service's published contract will be used at all. When designing a program to access or use a resource or capability that belongs within the boundary of a service, there are usually several options that exist as to how the consumer's data sharing requirements can be fulfilled.

Many of these options are reminiscent of past integration architectures, where often performance and ease of connectivity helped determine the most suitable integration channel between two applications. As illustrated in Figure 7.13, consumer programs can be designed with this approach in mind, leading them to disregard the service contract and connect directly to underlying resources.

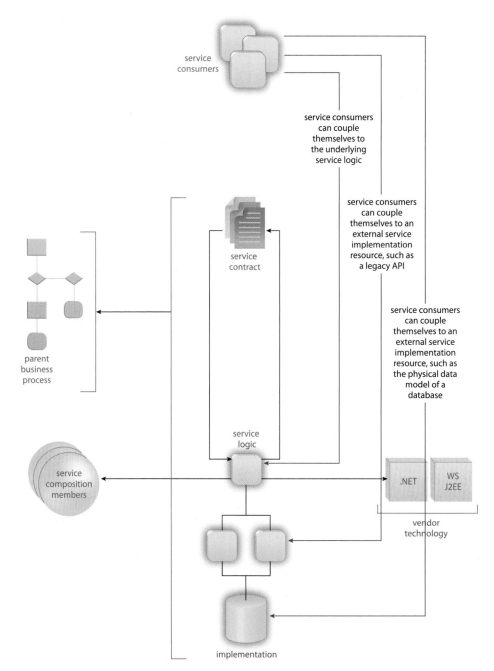

Figure 7.13

Consumer programs are designed to disregard the service contract and access underlying resources directly. While this may lead to more efficient data sharing channels, it is in fact an anti-pattern that severely undermines the goals of service-orientation.

Standardized Service Coupling and Contract Centralization

To address the pitfalls associated with bypassing the service contract, a standards-related design pattern known as Contract Centralization provides a simple solution for effectively and consistently implementing the appropriate form of consumer coupling.

Centralization simply means limiting the options of something to one. From a consumer's perspective, this pattern simply asks us to restrict access to a service to its contract only (thereby reducing or eliminating consumer-to-implementation coupling). Consumer programs either adhere to centralization, or they don't. If they do, then they only establish connections as described in the upcoming *Consumer-to-Contract Coupling* section.

> **NOTE**
>
> The centralization of service contracts is a standards-based concept also relevant to furthering the application of the Service Reusability principle. As explained in the *Standardized Service Reuse and Logic Centralization* section in Chapter 9, the associated Logic Centralization design pattern requires that certain bodies of logic be accessed only through certain (centralized) services. Contract Centralization and Logic Centralization therefore can be positioned as cornerstone enterprise standards that directly support SOA.

Consumer-to-Contract Coupling

Regardless of whether a service contract is fully centralized, any time a consumer binds to its contract, the resulting relationship can simply be referred to as *consumer-to-contract coupling* (Figure 7.14).

This is a recommended and desirable form of coupling because it achieves the greatest amount of independence between the consumer and the service. Consumer-to-contract coupling essentially forms the basis of a loosely coupled cross-service relationship, as promoted by this principle. However, the extent of "coupling looseness" actually attained is determined by the content of the service contract.

All variations of coupling we covered in the *Service Contract Coupling Types* section are relevant to consumer-to-contract coupling because the consumer program is required to physically bind to a capability expressed as part of the technical service contract. As a result, it will end up forming a dependency on anything to which that part of the service contract is coupled.

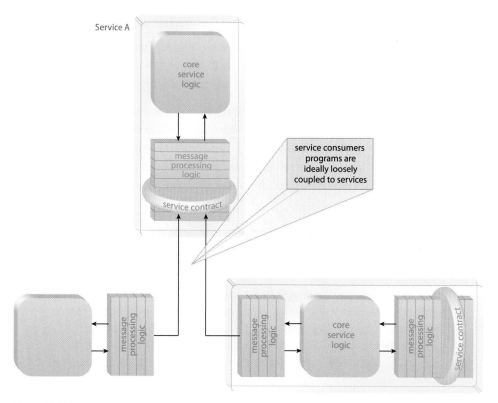

Figure 7.14

In this scenario, a Web service (bottom right) and a regular component (bottom left) are both designed to work with Service A (a Web service). The contract published by Service A was designed specifically to minimize consumer dependencies, resulting in loosely coupled consumer relationships.

This form of "coupling inheritance" is a constant concern, especially with agnostic services, because we want to avoid the proliferation of undesirable coupling characteristics throughout multiple service consumers, as highlighted in Figure 7.15.

Direct and Indirect Coupling Scenarios

A service contract tightly coupled to other parts of the service architecture will find itself expressing (usually physical) details about its underlying implementation. As we've established, this has a domino effect in that all subsequent service consumer programs that end up forming dependencies on the service contract also become coupled to the very same implementation characteristics.

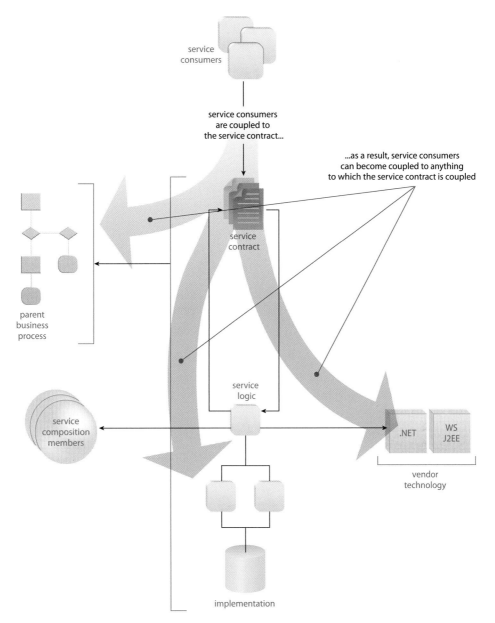

Figure 7.15

Service consumers inherit undesirable coupling characteristics embedded within the service contract, which can lead to the consumer programs forming dependencies on the underlying service environment.

The next set of figures revisits three of the previously explained service contract coupling types to demonstrate how each can result in *direct* or *indirect* consumer coupling.

Figure 7.16 shows that when the service contract is technology-coupled, its consumers will likewise become technology-coupled. This is a direct form of negative coupling because the consumer designer is fully aware of the coupling-related technology requirements during design-time.

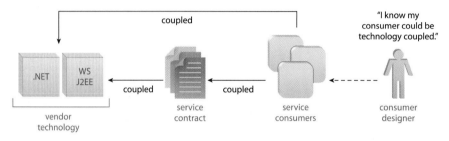

Figure 7.16
When the service contract is technology coupled, its service consumers will be forced to become coupled to the service's underlying technology.

Figure 7.17 illustrates that if the service logic is functionally coupled to external business logic AND if the service contract is coupled to the same service logic, then the resulting contract-to-functional coupling can be imposed on consumers. This can be an indirect form of negative coupling because the consumer designer may not know of the service's dependency on a parent business process.

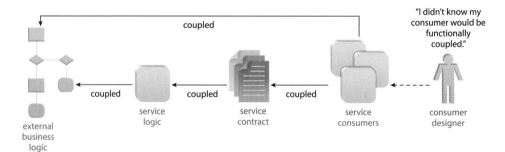

Figure 7.17
When the service contract is functionally coupled, its service consumers are required to couple to the service's underlying functional dependencies.

Figure 7.18 further proves that if the service logic is coupled to implementation resources AND if the service contract is (partially or entirely) derived from these resources, then the resulting contract-to-implementation coupling can lead to further proliferation of implementation coupling by service consumers. This is perhaps the most common form of indirect negative coupling.

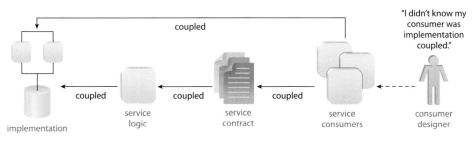

Figure 7.18

When the service contract is derived from parts of the service's implementation resources, its consumers will also become coupled to those parts of the implementation environment. This is especially undesirable when the resources do not belong exclusively to the service but are instead shared parts of the overall architecture.

One of the greatest challenges to avoiding indirect coupling is that, due to deliberate information hiding policies that result from the application of the Service Abstraction principle, many service consumer designers may be completely unaware of the fact that their programs are in fact being (indirectly) coupled to underlying service details. It is therefore the responsibility of the service designers to minimize negative forms of contract coupling in the first place.

The level of dependency we establish between individual, physically separate services can have profound implications as to how effective a service inventory can become in support of future service composition requirements. We therefore need to pay close attention to the extent of coupling a service demands of its consumers.

Contract Centralization and Technology Coupling

When standardizing on the service contract as the sole service endpoint, we are forcing all consumers to comply with the interaction requirements expressed by that contract. If the contract technology is proprietary or requires the use of proprietary communication protocols, then we limit the consumer base to those programs compatible with the proprietary requirements (Figure 7.19).

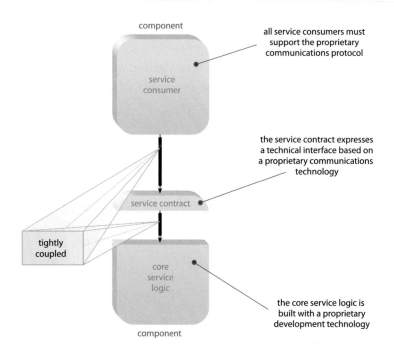

Figure 7.19

The figure originally displayed in the *Contract-to-Technology Coupling* section is revisited to show how the tight technology coupling of the service contract is passed on to a service consumer.

If the centralization of contracts is enforced to a meaningful extent, we make the service contract a focal point for a great deal of interaction. From a long-term evolutionary perspective, therefore, Web services provide an effective means of establishing a service contract that can be customized and standardized, while remaining decoupled from the service's underlying technology.

Without the use of an open technology platform, such as Web services, Contract Centralization can result in the proliferation of technology coupling throughout an enterprise.

Validation Coupling Considerations

Regardless of the extent of indirect coupling a service contract imposes, there will always be the requirement for the consumer program to comply to the data model defined in the technical service contract definitions.

In the case of a Web service, this form of *validation coupling* refers to the XML schema complex types that represent individual incoming and outgoing messages. Schemas establish data types, constraints, and validation rules based on the size and complexity of the information being exchanged as well as the validation requirements of the service itself.

The extent of validation coupling required by each individual service capability can vary dramatically and is often tied directly to the measure of constraint granularity of service capabilities. As per the validation-related design patterns, each contract can be individually assessed as to the quantity of actual constraints required to increase its longevity.

Consumer Coupling and Service Compositions

What happens when a service composes another that has a particular level of coupling established with a third service? Are negative coupling characteristics (such as those related to the implementation) passed on from the third service through to the first? These types of issues will arise when designing service compositions. Chapter 13 explores service composition, and the corresponding Service Composability principle addresses some of the concerns associated with cross-service relationships. However, inter-service coupling measures still deserve individual attention.

> **NOTE**
>
> The case study at the end of this chapter documents the scenario just described and further addresses commonly raised questions.

Measuring Consumer Coupling

Because of the uniqueness of service capabilities and consumer requirements, each inter-action between a consumer and a service capability will be distinct. It is therefore help-ful to establish a set of categories that we can use to represent measures of consumer coupling.

Based on the possible variations of consumer coupling that are technically possible, there are many classifications one could come up with to label different coupling levels. Because the Contract Centralization pattern is so fundamental to establishing the most beneficial forms of consumer coupling, we can define two basic levels that address the following questions:

- Is the coupling centralized?

- If it is, what is the degree of required contract coupling?

The following generic categories define corresponding coupling levels and provide a means of communicating the coupling requirements of individual service capabilities.

Non-Centralized Consumer Coupling

The body of logic represented by the service is not accessed solely by consumer programs via the service contract. The actual coupling requirements are therefore dependent on the individual access points chosen by the consumer.

Centralized Consumer Coupling

To measure the level of a centralized coupling relationship requires the identification and assessment of each of the coupling types that can affect the content and coupling requirements of the service contract.

Therefore, one approach for documenting coupling levels is to create a profile for every service capability in which the dependency level of each of the previously described coupling types is assessed. A numeric rating system can be used (ranging from 1 to 5, for example), or standard classification terms (such as "low," "moderate," and "high") can be applied.

BEST PRACTICE

The environment in which you are required to create Web services will often dictate constraints that make some negative forms of coupling unavoidable. Wherever possible, apply this principle to reduce the *extent* of these coupling types prior to implementing the service for production use. At a minimum, this principle can be used to establish an awareness of negative coupling types associated with a service so that service consumer designers are fully cognizant of how these intra-service dependencies may impact their use of the service over the long-term.

Specifically, coupling levels can be documented as part of a service profile for communication purposes during service design processes. These levels can be furthermore made available as part of the overall service contract to openly reveal negative forms of coupling to whatever extent allowed when taking Service Abstraction considerations into account.

SUMMARY OF KEY POINTS

- The key motivation for decoupling a service contract from its implementation is to avoid having service consumers indirectly couple to service implementation details.

- The Contract Centralization pattern requires that consumers interface only with the official service contract and not with other potentially available service entry points.

- Consumer-to-contract coupling is an approach used to avoid consumer-to-implementation coupling. However, when based on a poorly designed service contract, consumer-to-contract coupling can still result in the consumer becoming coupled to the service implementation.

7.5 Service Loose Coupling and Service Design

The following sections position previously discussed coupling types and Contract Centralization within the service-orientation paradigm as a whole and also take a look at how service coupling affects the design of individual service models.

Coupling and Service-Orientation

We've defined an array of coupling types and discussed how they relate to the notion of Contract Centralization. When we tie all this together we can see how, through this principle and others, service-orientation promotes loose coupling within and between services.

As mentioned in point number 2 in Figure 7.20, other service-orientation principles get involved in shaping the structure and content of service contracts. Table 7.2 explores this further by listing coupling types along with associated principles.

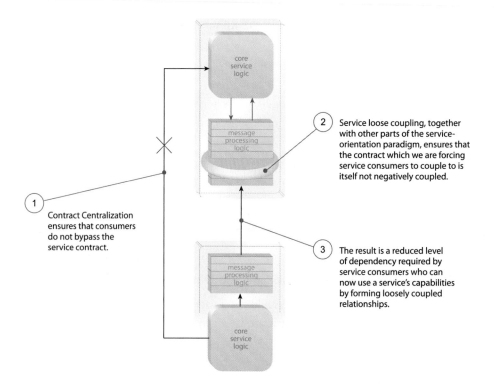

Figure 7.20

Through Contract Centralization we place the service contract front and center within a service-oriented architecture. This is why much of service-orientation is focused on contract design.

Coupling Type	Negative?	Note
Logic-to-Contract	No	Tight coupling of the service logic to the contract is acceptable and supported by the Standardized Service Contract principle.
Contract-to-Logic	Yes	This form of coupling is not recommended and can be avoided through the use of "contract first" design approaches.
Contract-to-Technology	Yes	The service contract is ideally decoupled from vendor technology, as supported by the use of open XML and Web services standards.

Coupling Type	Negative?	Note
Contract-to-Functional	Yes	This negative coupling type is avoidable through the application of the Service Reusability principle but may still be required for certain types of services.
Contract-to-Implementation	Yes	This form of coupling is not recommended, especially in relation to external and shared implementation resources.
Consumer-to-Implementation	Yes	The Contract Centralization design pattern is used specifically to avoid this coupling type.
Consumer-to-Contract	No	This is a positive form of coupling, but its benefit is related to the extent to which negative service contract coupling levels have been avoided.

Table 7.2
A summary of coupling types and associated influences.

Service Loose Coupling and Granularity

Granularity concerns associated with this principle primarily relate to consumer-to-contract coupling, which can affect capability, data, and constraint granularity levels.

The functional scope of a capability exposed by a service contract is what the service consumer is required to commit to when forming a design-time dependency on the contract. If the capability performs too much work, the consumer may be negatively affected by the extra processing overhead. Alternatively, if the functional scope of the capability is too fine-grained, the consumer may be negatively affected by increased service roundtrips (either by having to call the same capability repeatedly or by having to call additional capabilities).

Consumers are further required to submit to whatever level a capability's data granularity is set at. If the required data exchanges are too fine-grained, the consumer may not receive sufficient information and may be required to invoke additional services. And on the flipside, if the data is too coarse, the consumer may receive more information than it actually needs, which can waste bandwidth and consumer processing cycles.

Constraint granularity can also play a role in determining coupling requirements. Larger amounts of fine-grained constraints can increase the amount of validation logic consumers are required to comply with (as also discussed in the aforementioned *Validation Coupling* section).

Clearly, determining the appropriate granularity levels is important for a service to be effectively utilized, especially when providing reusable functionality. There is no one level that is perfect for all possible consumers. In fact, the Contract Denormalization pattern advocates providing similar capabilities with different granularity levels to accommodate different types of consumers.

Fundamentally, though, it is the service contract designer's understanding of how granularity directly influences consumer coupling requirements that helps determine the right balance of capability, data, and constraint granularity.

Coupling and Service Models

Because there are so many types of dependencies that can exist to varying extents, the actual coupling that results really comes down to the nature of the service logic as well as the manner in which it is delivered and then implemented, regardless of service model. However, there are some coupling-related tendencies associated with service models worth mentioning:

Entity Services

Entity services are generally delivered as part of a service inventory modeling project supplemented with design standards required to establish the entity service layer. They are ideally custom designed to make the most of top-down analysis efforts required to properly model service boundaries. They therefore present an ideal opportunity to create services that avoid many of the negative coupling types by establishing highly independent (and decoupled) service contracts.

The only external part of the enterprise to which entity services are tightly coupled is the business entities themselves. Therefore, if an organization's fundamental lines of business change, so too can the complexion of its information architecture and associated enterprise entity model. However, in most cases, business entities provide a safe functional context that is business-centric while remaining agnostic to multiple business processes. In fact, it is the increased longevity of business entities within the lifespan of an organization that makes the entity service model so attractive.

Utility Services

Because utility services are often required to encapsulate existing enterprise resources (including legacy systems), they can easily become implementation-coupled. In this case, it is important to design a standardized service contract whenever possible to avoid indirect consumer coupling to the implementation as well.

Utility services are also frequently developed as components using native vendor technology. Often this approach is taken out of necessity for performance and reliability reasons when the surrounding vendor platform's support for Web services technology is deemed insufficient. This will result in technology coupling requirements until these services can be wrapped with and exposed via open Web service contracts.

Task Services

Due to their specific functional context, task services are sometimes functionally coupled. If the business process logic encapsulated by the service represents a sub-process of a larger parent process, then the service logic will be directly dependent on that external business logic.

Furthermore, task services required to perform unique (and especially smaller scoped) activities are sometimes created for single clients, making them service-to-consumer coupled.

Orchestrated Task Services

Because orchestrated task services rely on the deployment environment provided by a vendor orchestration platform, there is a natural dependency between the solution logic and its implementation.

The use of open Web services standards, such as WS-BPEL, can (to a large extent) avoid technology coupling. However, because some of these standards require that the Web service contract be appended with orchestration-specific constructs, a level of contract implementation coupling may be unavoidable.

How Service Loose Coupling Affects Other Principles

With such an emphasis on how dependencies relate to and originate from within service contracts, the application of this principle naturally affects other principles also concerned with service contract design or influenced by reduced coupling levels (Figure 7.21).

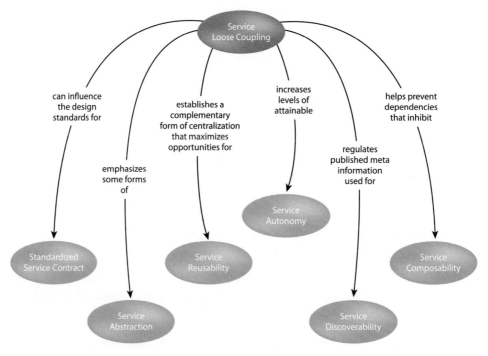

Figure 7.21

Service coupling emphasizes a reduction of internal and external service dependencies, which ends up supporting and affecting various aspects of other principles.

Service Loose Coupling and Standardized Service Contract

Establishing consistently standardized service contracts requires the existence and use of contract design standards. Often these standards will be rigid with many requirements related to schema structure, data types, validation constraints, and business rules. Loose coupling encourages us to moderate the quantity and complexity of technical contract content so as to minimize consumer dependency requirements and maximize the freedom service owners can have to evolve and change the service over time without affecting existing consumers.

Service Loose Coupling and Service Abstraction

As established in Chapter 5, Service Loose Coupling and Service Abstraction go hand-in-hand. The emphasis on creating less coupled consumer relationships specifically requires well-defined levels of functional and technology abstraction to be applied (as explained in Chapter 8).

Service Loose Coupling and Service Reusability

Decreasing dependencies allows us to do more with services in the long-term. They can be more easily composed, evolved, and even augmented in support of changing business requirements and directions. The ability to effectively reutilize and repurpose existing services is what reuse is all about. The enablement of loosely coupled relationships within a service and across a service inventory maximizes the potential for leveraging enterprise-wide reuse opportunities.

Service Loose Coupling and Service Autonomy

Reduced levels of negative coupling types support the realization of higher runtime and design-time autonomy levels. There is also a direct correlation between consumer coupling levels and service autonomy in that the more cross-service dependencies a service consumer has, the less autonomous it can become.

Service Loose Coupling and Service Discoverability

Because Service Discoverability is concerned with making services easily located and understood, it tends to encourage us to outfit service contracts with meta rich content. The Service Loose Coupling principle can sometimes push back at this requirement and help regulate the amount of contract content to what is actually necessary. Note that unlike Service Abstraction, Service Loose Coupling is primarily concerned with technical contract content or any part of the published meta information that would allow a consumer program to form a direct dependency.

Service Loose Coupling and Service Composability

Negative forms of coupling within a composed service can have a direct impact on the larger composition, as follows:

- *Contract-to-Logic Coupling*—If the service contract is auto-generated, it will likely not conform to standards in use by other services, therefore resulting in the need for transformation between it and other composition members.

- *Contract-to-Technology Coupling*—If a combination of open and proprietary service technologies are in use as part of the same composition, native technology conversion layers might be required. For example, Web services can compose services that exist as components; however, if those components then compose services that exist as Web services, data exchanges need to undergo two levels of technology transformation.

- *Contract-to-Implementation Coupling*—When a service contract is coupled to underlying implementation characteristics, it ends up imposing those characteristics upon the composition as a whole.

Using the previously described coupling levels to communicate the nature and extent of service dependencies can therefore be highly beneficial when modeling service compositions.

SUMMARY OF KEY POINTS

- Service Loose Coupling helps shape the application of other principles because much of general service design ties into or affects some form of coupling.

- This principle introduces concepts and considerations that go beyond the scope of other principles.

7.6 Risks Associated with Service Loose Coupling

There are obvious risks that come with allowing negative coupling types within a service contract. For example, it is evident that long-term issues will arise when a technology or implementation-coupled service contract passes on these coupling requirements to all of its consumer programs. However, even when pursing the loosely coupled ideal, there are additional risk factors that deserve to be taken into account.

Limitations of Logic-to-Contract Coupling

The contract first approach is a recommended process for delivering services that leads to tight logic-to-contract coupling because service logic is built after and tailored for the customized service contract.

However, a design concern raised by this approach is the limitation of having just one service contract associated with the core service logic. There are times when it is preferable to have two or more contracts for the same underlying logic so as to establish multiple points of entry, each exposing different service capabilities for different types of consumers.

As shown in Figure 7.22, this type of service design requires us to establish a lower degree of coupling between logic and its contract. By taking multiple potential service contracts into account early in the design and development of the core logic, the risk of limiting the service to one contract can be mitigated. The use of the Service Façade design pattern accommodates this issue by introducing a separate layer of abstraction within the underlying service logic.

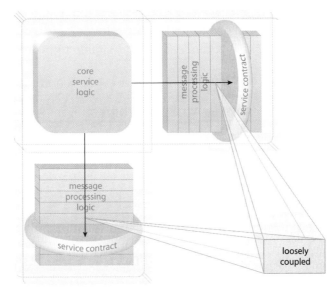

Figure 7.22
The same core service logic now accessible via two separate service contracts. This effectively establishes two Web services based on the same underlying logic.

Note also that this form of logic normalization (using the same underlying service logic in support of multiple services) can result from the discovery of similar but physically separate services and the application of refactoring-related design patterns to consolidate service logic into one location.

Problems when Schema Coupling Is "too loose"

Sometimes in pursuit of reducing consumer dependencies, contract schemas are "over-streamlined," resulting in a weakly typed, bare bones data model that does little more than establish some very generic data types.

The rationale behind this approach is to enable the service to accept and transmit a range of data via request and response messages, allowing both service and consumer owners to make more changes without affecting the published service contract.

By building in too much flexibility, the service logic is required to perform extra runtime processing just to interpret the data it receives for any given invocation instance. The net result of over-emphasizing a lower consumer coupling level can therefore increase service performance requirements.

Furthermore, the less that is published in a service contract, the more consumer programs may need to know about how the underlying solution logic is designed. Depending on the nature of the logic, this can lead to undesirable forms of implementation coupling.

SUMMARY OF KEY POINTS

- A common design concern with the logic-to-contract approach is limiting the logic to just one service contract.

- Another possible risk associated with loosely coupled consumer relationships is the introduction of runtime performance overhead and inadvertent implementation coupling.

7.7 CASE STUDY EXAMPLE

The following three services defined by Cutit Saws in the case study example from Chapter 6 are revisited to ensure that appropriate coupling levels are implemented:

- Materials Service

- Formulas Service

- Run Lab Project Service

Coupling Levels of Existing Services

Because all three are custom services for which standardized service contracts were delivered, each exhibits a high level of logic-to-contract coupling and negligible contract-to-logic coupling.

The Materials and Formulas services were based on the entity service model, which deliberately decreases potential functional coupling to external or parent business process logic.

Run Lab Project, being a task-centric service, is bound to the Lab Project business process, which is a very specific procedure within the Cutit labs. As a result, the targeted functional coupling of this service is an intentional part of its design.

On the surface, everything appears to be acceptable in terms of coupling-related design requirements. However, upon closer examination of some of the individual service operations, Cutit architects notice some problem areas.

Introducing the InvLegacyAPI Service

Both the GetPurchased and ReportStockLevels operations (Table 6.2 from Chapter 6) of the Materials service are required to interact with the legacy inventory management system that has been an entrenched part of the Cutit enterprise for some time. This system is technologically archaic and offers limited integration capabilities. An API is available, but it is crude and primitive.

It is determined that (fortunately), the two operations from the Materials service do not need to interface directly with the proprietary API. A separate Web service named InvLegacyAPI is already in place (Figure 7.23 and Table 7.3).

InvLegacyAPI Service	
AddItem Operation	Input: non-standard inventory item document Output: acknowledgement code
GetItem Operation	Input: unique inventory identifier Output: non-standard inventory item document
GetItemCount Operation	Input: unique inventory identifier Output: stock level value
RemoveItems Operation	Input: unique inventory identifier for each item to be removed from inventory Output: acknowledgment code

Table 7.3
The InvLegacyAPI service is defined to encapsulate Cutit's legacy inventory control system.

Because the InvLegacyAPI service abstracts the legacy environment, it lowers the Materials service's overall implementation coupling level. Though it encapsulates inventory-related processing, it is considered a utility service because it essentially acts as a wrapper endpoint for a proprietary legacy API.

Of the four operations listed in the InvLegacyAPI profile, AddItem, RemoveItems, and GetItem interact with the published legacy API. This requires these operations to preserve the cryptic XML schema accepted by the API functions. This schema is primarily a reflection of the inventory system's underlying inventory items database table.

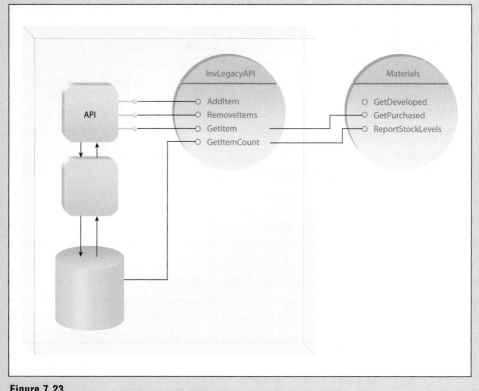

Figure 7.23

The back-end implementation details of the InvLegacyAPI service operations. Notice how the GetItemCount operation bypasses the API to access the database directly.

Due to the functional limitations of the native API, retrieving a total stock level for a particular item is not supported. In order to expose this capability via a Web service, the logic for the GetItemCount operation was built to access the inventory system's database directly.

GetItem and GetItemCount provide the functionality required to carry out the Materials service's GetPurchased and ReportStockLevels operations respectively. Even though the InvLegacyAPI Web service offers these operations via standard SOAP message exchanges, it incorporates the proprietary inventory system schema into the service contract.

The InvLegacyAPI service is therefore classified as having a significant level of contract-to-logic coupling. As a result, the Materials service will need to inherit an extent of indirect implementation coupling due to the physical characteristics of the GetItem and GetItemCount schema designs.

Service Design Options

The Cutit architects are leery about this extension of the overall Run Lab Project service composition. Before agreeing to build on the existing InvLegacyAPI Web service, they take the time to identify at least one alternative design.

The two options they end up with are as follows:

Option 1   Accept the contract requirements of the InvLegacyAPI service and allow the Materials service to bind to the Inventory service's GetItem and GetItemsCount operations "as is."

Option 2   Introduce a service that provides a contract based on the existing, standardized Inventory Item schema definition. This would establish a true Inventory entity service that would still wrap the existing legacy system but would be built to perform internal conversion between the legacy API schemas and the standard Inventory Item schema at runtime.

Option 1 (Figure 7.24) is attractive because the project team would simply be able to use what is already there. Given the time pressure they are under to automate the Lab Project process, there is little room for scope creep. However, the downside is that by building on an inferior service contract, they will be further entrenching this service as a part of the overall service inventory.

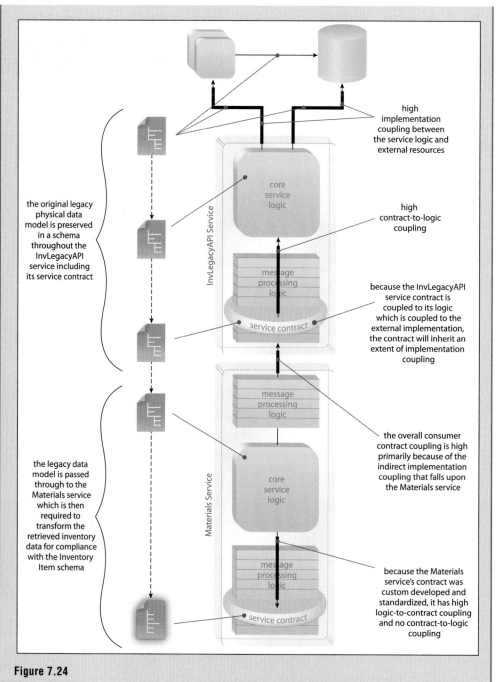

the original legacy physical data model is preserved in a schema throughout the InvLegacyAPI service including its service contract

the legacy data model is passed through to the Materials service which is then required to transform the retrieved inventory data for compliance with the Inventory Item schema

high implementation coupling between the service logic and external resources

high contract-to-logic coupling

because the InvLegacyAPI service contract is coupled to its logic which is coupled to the external implementation, the contract will inherit an extent of implementation coupling

the overall consumer contract coupling is high primarily because of the indirect implementation coupling that falls upon the Materials service

because the Materials service's contract was custom developed and standardized, it has high logic-to-contract coupling and no contract-to-logic coupling

Figure 7.24

The increased consumer contract coupling imposed by the InvLegacyAPI service can be traced to the persistence of the physical legacy data model.

The Materials service can perform internal transformation of the non-standardized schema prior to relaying the data to its service consumers. However, any other services that need access to the central inventory system will need to do the same. This is expected to result in a large amount of redundant processing, adding to the expense of subsequent service delivery and also increasing the looming impact due to occur on the day the legacy system is replaced with a new solution that introduces new data representation models for inventory item records.

This last point makes Option 2 (illustrated in Figure 7.25) look pretty good. However, that approach comes with an immediate impact that is difficult to absorb. It requires the delivery of a new service with sophisticated transformation logic, which also introduces a new runtime processing layer. It is uncertain as to what the performance impact of this layer will be, especially considering how different the legacy and standardized inventory item schema structures are.

From a coupling perspective, Option 1 introduces indirect implementation coupling upon the Materials service and any other service consumers that are required to interact with the GetItem and GetItemCount operations. In fact, because the GetItemCount operation bypasses the legacy API to perform direct data access, it actually deepens the potential proliferation of indirect implementation coupling.

Option 2 (Figure 7.25) limits implementation coupling to within the boundaries of a new Inventory service wherein it resolves schema disparity. Therefore, a healthy level of loose coupling is preserved between the Inventory service, the Materials service, and future service consumers.

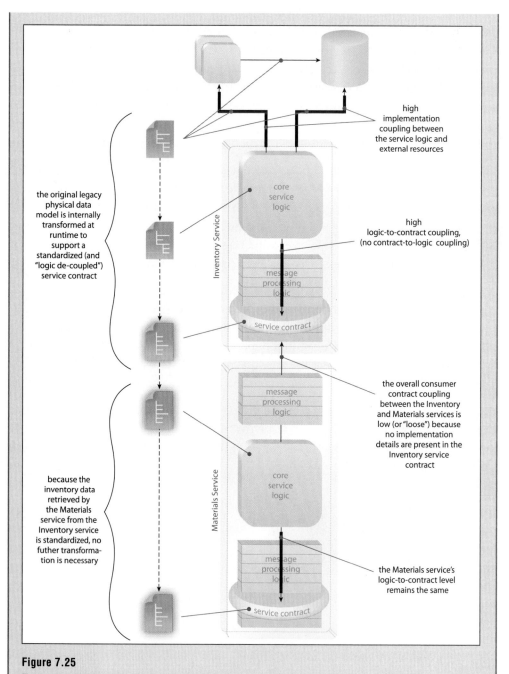

the original legacy physical data model is internally transformed at runtime to support a standardized (and "logic de-coupled") service contract

high implementation coupling between the service logic and external resources

high logic-to-contract coupling, (no contract-to-logic coupling)

the overall consumer contract coupling between the Inventory and Materials services is low (or "loose") because no implementation details are present in the Inventory service contract

because the inventory data retrieved by the Materials service from the Inventory service is standardized, no futher transformation is necessary

the Materials service's logic-to-contract level remains the same

Figure 7.25

The new Inventory service shields the Materials service (and other future service consumers) from its underlying implementation details, resulting in a lower overall level of coupling.

For the benefit of their target SOA, Cutit ultimately decides to go ahead with the delivery of the new Inventory service. Cutit's collection of deliverable services for the automation of the Lab Project process therefore increases to four (Figure 7.26).

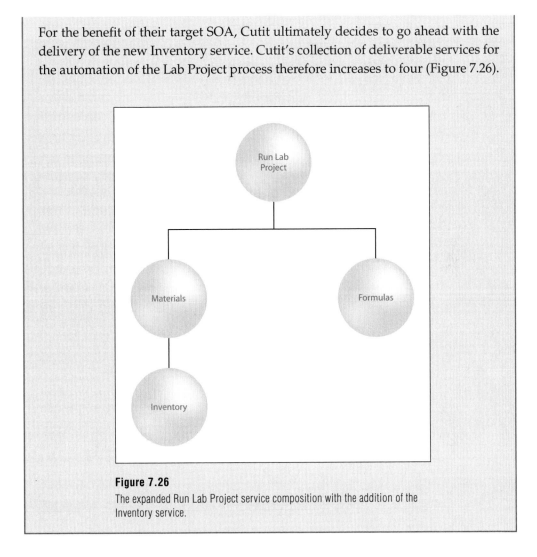

Figure 7.26

The expanded Run Lab Project service composition with the addition of the Inventory service.

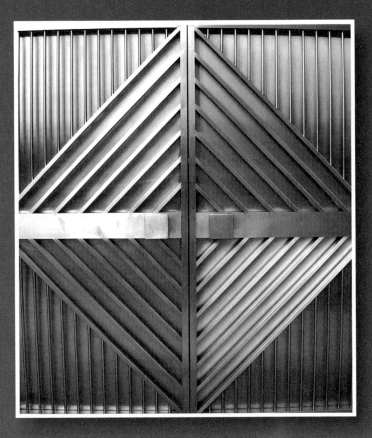

Chapter 8

Service Abstraction (Information Hiding and Meta Abstraction Types)

We can only assess and judge the value of something for which information is made available to us. What we publish about a service communicates its purpose and capabilities and provides details to potential consumers about how it can be programmatically invoked and engaged.

The information we *don't* publish about a service protects the integrity of the coupling formed between it and its future consumers. By keeping specific details hidden, we allow the service logic and its implementation to evolve over time while continuing to fulfill its obligations in relation to what was originally published in its contract (Figure 8.1).

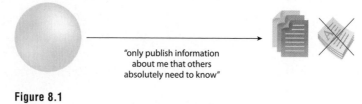

"only publish information
about me that others
absolutely need to know"

Figure 8.1
The fundamental purpose of this principle is to avoid the proliferation of unnecessary service information, meta or otherwise.

Achieving the right balance of information hiding is what Service Abstraction is all about. As explained in this chapter, abstraction goes beyond what is expressed in the service contract. There are additional aspects of abstraction that, when properly applied, can each further service-orientation in its own way.

8.1 Abstraction Explained

The notion of abstraction is very simple on the surface: hide information about a program not absolutely required for others to effectively use that program. However, applying this principle can raise a series of design-time considerations. Too little or too much of something abstracted away from the outside world can constrain the potential for a program to be repeatedly utilized (reused) by others throughout its lifespan.

The first step to attaining the understanding required to determine the right amount of abstraction is to study how this broad design characteristic has been applied in the past.

Origins of Information Hiding

As with several of the other concepts that have inspired service-orientation, abstraction is one that has deep roots in the history of automation systems.

Compilers provided one of the most effective and widespread means of containing the internals of a software program within a protected package while exposing a specific public contract. This black box concept enabled software designers to firmly control levels of abstraction within self-contained program files. For example, the contract could be as simple as a command line function provided by an executable file or more targeted for programmatic consumption, such as a technical interface exposed by a dynamic link library. Information hiding was furthermore promoted by the object-oriented design paradigm that formally positioned abstraction as a key principle. (See the *Abstraction* section in Chapter 14 for a more detailed comparison.)

The demand for inter-application connectivity caused a surge of interest in integration that led many vendors to expose functional and even programmatic details of their products via commercially released APIs and adapters. The subsequent era of integration architectures opened up previously abstracted environments. New entry points into application environments were identified and used to fulfill tactical data exchange requirements.

After it was recognized that the point-to-point integration channels created to exploit these entry points resulted in convoluted and unmanageable environments, middleware came into the picture. The middle tier introduced by EAI vendor platforms was positioned as a prominent layer of abstraction in an attempt to decouple previously tightly coupled legacy systems. Instead of connecting to each other, applications now all connected to the middleware product.

Building an architecture around the concept of intentional information hiding proved effective. The abstraction of legacy functionality, technology, and implementation details allowed for the evolution and eventual replacement of legacy systems to occur with less impact to the overall enterprise. Legacy applications did not even need to have knowledge of each other because the middleware established a centralized access point and performed all the necessary translation and mediation.

Of course these are just some past examples of information hiding. Abstraction has taken on a greater significance in distributed solution architectures where automation logic is regularly decomposed into standalone units, each of which abstracts a portion of the greater whole.

> **NOTE**
>
> We revisit this chronology in the *Types of Meta Abstraction* section later in this chapter in order to explore how different forms of abstraction are implemented to varying extents in different types of programs.

SUMMARY OF KEY POINTS

- The commercial "black box" concept, APIs, and middleware are all historic applications of abstraction that have influenced this principle.

- By wrapping commercial software programs into compiled black boxes, a high level of intentional abstraction is attained.

- The advent of the commercial API enabled programs to expose specific subsets of their functionality, while continuing to abstract the rest.

8.2 Profiling this Principle

Abstraction and the black box concept have traditionally been important to the development of commercial products. Because service-orientation treats individual services similar to standalone commercial products, abstraction within the enterprise now becomes a key design consideration (as profiled in Table 8.1).

Why Service Abstraction Is Needed

The more information we publish in a service contract, the deeper subsequent consumer-to-contract coupling can become. Additionally, the more information made available to humans responsible for the delivery of service consumers, the greater their awareness of the underlying logic, platform, and proprietary details of the service. As a result, they may naturally make assumptions and judgments about a service based on this "extra knowledge."

This introduces a risk in that it can subsequently influence the design of service consumer programs (Figure 8.2), which can effectively lead to a form of consumer-to-implementation coupling, even though the consumer is adhering to a standardized service contract. This risk is further amplified by the fact that other service-orientation principles advocate more generic and lenient service contract design characteristics for the sake of supporting agnostic functional contexts and improving overall reusability.

By increasing the flexibility of capabilities to process a wider range of values, there is a greater opportunity for implementation-specific data to creep into consumer-service data exchanges.

Figure 8.2

This principle discourages making superfluous information about a service available to humans responsible for the design of service consumer programs.

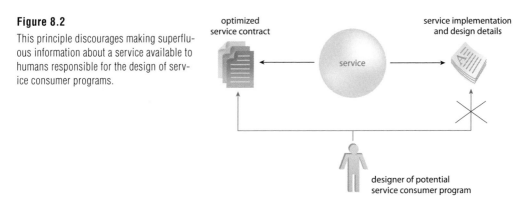

One of the primary reasons to hide details about a service is to empower the service owner with the freedom to evolve the service implementation as required. Service Abstraction therefore raises post-implementation, organizational issues (such as access control) that can also be part of a governance methodology. However, because it directly affects the service design process and specifically influences design-time decision points as to what should be published in the official service contract, it is very much part of the service design stage as well.

Principle Profile	
Short Definition	*"Non-essential service information is abstracted."*
Long Definition	*"Service contracts only contain essential information and information about services is limited to what is published in service contracts."*
Goals	Many of the other principles emphasize the need to publish *more* information in the service contract. The primary role of this principle is to keep the quantity and detail of contract content concise and balanced and prevent unnecessary access to additional service details.

Design Characteristics	• Services consistently abstract specific information about technology, logic, and function away from the outside world (the world outside of the service boundary).
	• Services have contracts that concisely define interaction requirements and constraints and other required service meta details.
	• Outside of what is documented in the service contract, information about a service is controlled or altogether hidden within a particular environment.
Implementation Requirements	The primary prerequisite to achieving the appropriate level of abstraction for each service is the level of service contract design skill applied.
Web Service Region of Influence	The *Region of Influence* part of this profile has been moved to the *Types of Meta Abstraction* section where a separate Web service figure is provided for each form of abstraction.

Table 8.1

A profile for the Service Abstraction principle.

FOR EXAMPLE

A public agency has, for many years, outsourced various custom development projects. Different divisions within the organization have their own IT support departments and therefore also have complete autonomy over their respective technical environments. As a result, some of the solutions have been delivered as .NET applications, whereas others were built using Java technologies.

Four years ago an enterprise-wide initiative resulted in the required use of Web services within all divisional IT domains for the purpose of establishing strategic integration endpoints. Two years later, this initiative was further extended by a formal adoption of SOA. Existing Web services were standardized and further refined by taking various reusability considerations into account. The subsequent enterprise architecture was evolved beyond an integration architecture to one that somewhat resembled a cross-domain service inventory.

The outsourcing of applications continued throughout this time. The solution providers delivering the applications respected the new contract design standards and also took reusability considerations into account with any new service they created.

One of the divisions within the agency recently decided to transition a specific, componentized .NET environment over to a Java platform in order for it to better interface with a recently purchased COTS product. Several of the .NET components were exposed as standardized Web services, which raised the expectation that their redevelopment as Enterprise Java Beans would not disrupt existing service consumers.

However, after the redevelopment project completed, some problems arose:

- Although the original Web service contracts remained unchanged, the behavior of the new service logic was noticeably different and, at times, erratic.

- New runtime exceptions occurred, sometimes causing the services to fail altogether.

- Performance latency was increased at peak times, reducing the usage threshold of two of the services.

Subsequent to a post-project analysis, the source of these problems was revealed. Even though the contractors hired to build the original service consumer programs that accessed the Web service-enabled .NET components complied with the use of the published standardized contracts, they were still able to incorporate a number of .NET-specific characteristics into the service data exchanges.

Because of the emphasis on Service Reusability, constraint granularity had been reduced, allowing for a wider range of data values to be passed to each Web service operation. Additional proprietary details made their way into the messages, including security tokens, Active Directory references, and processing instructions intended for other .NET components encapsulated by the service.

Developers were able to add these details because they had access to the underlying service design and implementation specifications. This allowed them to fully optimize their programs and make the most out of every message exchange. Streamlining performance was considered a priority because the success of their projects was partially measured by the applications' runtime response times.

However, when the .NET components were replaced, many of the data exchanges turned out to be invalid. Even though Contract Centralization was adhered to, a form of consumer-to-implementation coupling was still able to creep into the solution designs. It was later recognized that the formal abstraction of underlying service information would be required to prevent this from recurring.

SUMMARY OF KEY POINTS

- The Service Abstraction principle requires that we take the time to assess the value and risk associated with publishing service meta information.

- Service Abstraction balances and regulates the tendency of other service-orientation principles to add content to the service contract.

8.3 Types of Meta Abstraction

The term "service abstraction" on its own is quite vague. When we discuss abstraction and information hiding, we need to understand what kinds of information can actually be abstracted.

Figure 8.3

Common types of service meta information, each describing something distinct about the service.

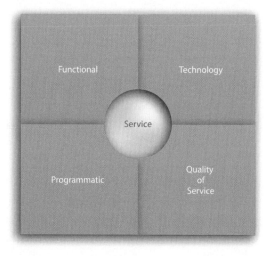

As introduced in Figure 8.3, there are different types of meta information we are interested in when it comes to applying this principle, as follows:

- *Technology Information*—Meta data that describes the technical implementation of the underlying service logic.

- *Functional Information*—Meta data that describes what the service is capable of.

- *Programmatic Logic Information*—Meta data that describes how the service carries out its capabilities.

- *Quality of Service Information*—Meta data that describes service behavior, limitations, and interaction requirements.

Individual meta types can be expressed and documented with different mediums, requiring abstraction to be applied in different ways. It helps to keep in mind that software programs can attain different measures of each abstraction type. As with other principles, it doesn't come down to whether to abstract or not, but to what extent abstraction should be applied and in what manner.

Technology Information Abstraction

It can be beneficial to hide details of the technology used to build a software program so that we retain the freedom to make technical changes without affecting existing users.

A fundamental example is a simple commercial software product, such as a calculator. This program is implemented as a compiled and linked executable file. It has a straightforward invocation interface (or contract) accessible to a human who only needs to double-click the Calculator.exe file to start the program (Figure 8.4).

Figure 8.4

Some details of the Calculator.exe program are hidden from potential consumers, whereas others are openly published and available.

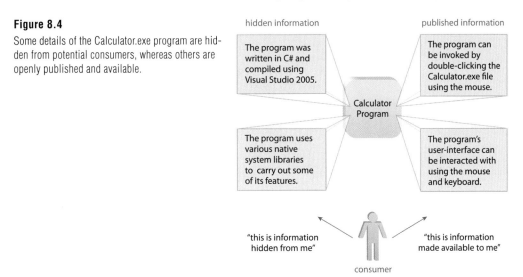

In this case, the human is made aware of the following information:

- the technology required to invoke the program
- the technology required to interact with the program

Examples of technology information intentionally hidden from the user include:

- the programming language used to write the program
- the system resources used by the program

By abstracting technology details, we (the calculator program development team) have a measure of freedom as to how we can choose to evolve our program in the future. For example, if the program had originally been written in Java, we can choose to rewrite it in C# as long as we provide the same original contract (which, in this case, consists of the executable file name and the human user-interface). Those who have come to rely on the use of the calculator will continue to do so in the same manner, even after we upgrade the program with a new version.

In distributed computing, technology information abstraction becomes an information hiding issue that applies to back-end consumers as much as front-end users. As illustrated in Figure 8.5, the abstraction-related considerations we take into account for a Web service are similar to our calculator product. In both cases we hide information from humans who have an interest in using our program.

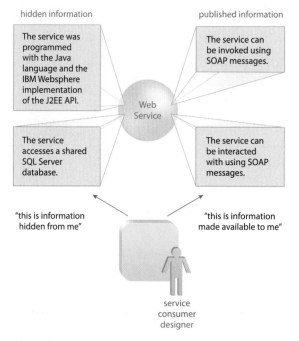

Figure 8.5

Components and Web services within a distributed environment only reveal information to each other relevant to their runtime invocation and interaction requirements.

> **NOTE**
>
> It is important to qualify this form of abstraction with the word "information." When we discuss technology abstraction in general, we might be referring to the fact that proprietary technology was successfully abstracted through the use of a standards-based service contract. In this context, the mere use of Web services can achieve high levels of technology abstraction. However, from an information hiding point of view, we are concerned with the amount of information made available about the type of technology used to implement the service.
>
> So while a Web service achieves a high degree of technology abstraction, it would have a low level of technology information abstraction if the nature of its implementation was openly accessible to others. (Note that technology abstraction is also addressed by the Service Loose Coupling principle.)

Functional Abstraction

Functional abstraction determines which of a program's capabilities are made public through its technical contract. The level of functional abstraction applied may or may not be equal to the actual range of functionality contained by the program.

A classic example is a software product that supplies an API. Often the API will be comprised of a set of generic functions considered those most likely to be useful to clients that may need to build programs capable of connecting and interoperating with the product (Figure 8.6).

In this example, the designer of the program may supply an API consisting of what are considered the most popular arithmetic functions: addition, subtraction, division, multiplication. This API establishes an alternative contract to the user-interface described earlier, targeted at a consumer base consisting of programs instead of humans (although the ultimate consumer in a value chain is always a human).

The level of functional abstraction is relatively high because the API only exposes a subset of the program's overall capabilities.

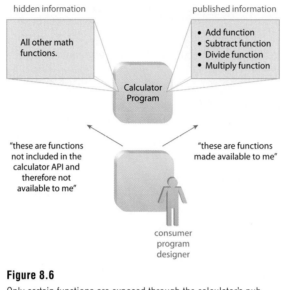

Figure 8.6

Only certain functions are exposed through the calculator's published API. This limits the extent to which a consumer program can be built to programmatically interface and interact with the calculator program.

Programmatic Logic Abstraction

Programmatic logic abstraction (or just *logic abstraction*) refers to internal details about a program that are deliberately hidden from the outside world. This will typically represent low-level design details, such as algorithms, exception handling and logging routines, and other logic associated with how the program is constructed.

The calculator example demonstrated how an automation client interacting with a program via an API has to contend with an interface providing a much higher level of functional abstraction as that provided by the human user-interface. Neither type of consumer, however, is granted access to the specific routines, algorithms, and exception handling logic that are programmed into the calculator (Figure 8.7). Consumers are not given this access because the owner of the program saw no reason to grant it.

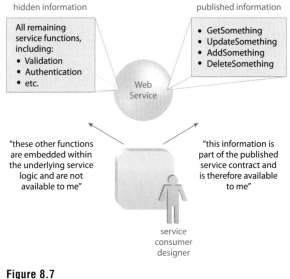

Figure 8.7

If the service consumer designer does not have access to the service design specifications or source code, the consumer program can only be designed based on information provided by the published service contract.

Having stated that, though, it would be possible for the human designer of a consumer program to gain this knowledge if access to technical specifications and source code was made available (Figure 8.8). Open source projects are a good example of environments in which access control and programmatic logic tend to be reduced.

Figure 8.8

In some organizations, design specifications and source code are readily accessible to others in the IT division. This can make programmatic logic difficult to abstract.

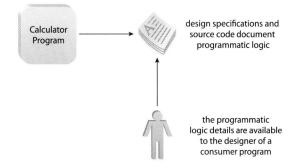

Quality of Service Abstraction

Quality of service data is an umbrella term for a range of behavioral, rules-based, and reliability-related meta information about a service (Figure 8.9).

Examples include:

- concurrent access thresholds at which point a service becomes less or non-responsive

- availability limitations, such as regular scheduled outages

- business rules that determine how a service processes or responds to different types of input data

Figure 8.9

Several quality of service details need to be made available to service consumer designers so that they can fully understand what to expect from a service.

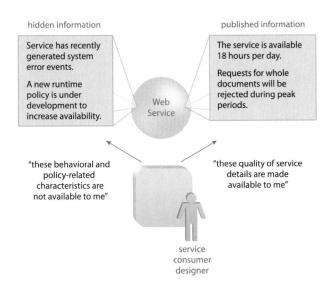

Policies are a common form of service description document used to define quality of service characteristics. Depending on whether a runtime environment is capable of supporting a technical policy expression syntax as part of the core service contract, it may very well be necessary to place some or all of this meta information in a supplemental, non-technical document, such as an SLA.

For our calculator service, we may choose to publish an SLA along with the technical service contract that describes various runtime policies, including an availability limit of 18 out of 24 hours each day.

Meta Abstraction Types and the Web Service Regions of Influence

If we take a closer look at the specific types of meta information that can be abstracted, we can gain a better understanding of how each affects the design of a Web service (as illustrated in Figures 8.10, 8.11, 8.12, and 8.13).

Functional Abstraction Region

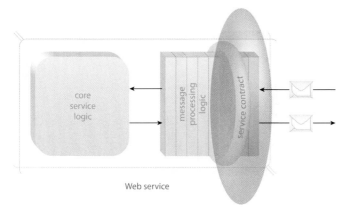

Figure 8.10
Functional abstraction is generally limited to the service contract because that is where we formally express the service's capabilities.

Technology Information Abstraction Region

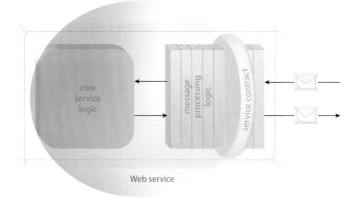

Figure 8.11
Technology information abstraction affects the underlying implementation of a service, both in terms of its core solution logic and its message processing logic. It only reaches the service contract when (non-industry-standard) technology-specific requirements need to be expressed.

Programmatic Logic Abstraction Region

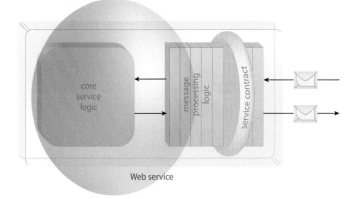

Figure 8.12

Whether it's the underlying routines used by a message processing service agent or the code representing the implementation logic of the service, all have programmatic logic.

Quality of Service Abstraction Region

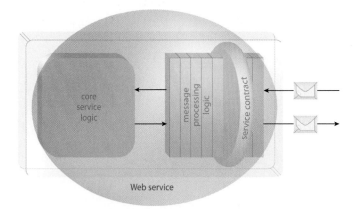

Figure 8.13

Because this is a broad form of meta information, it can represent all types of behavioral and reliability related meta details. Furthermore, technical policy documents and business rules implemented in the schema can bring quality of service data right up into the technical service contract.

Meta Abstraction Types in the Real World

Let's take a brief look at the extent to which common forms of solution logic already implement the previously described meta abstraction types. These examples provide a further indication as to how design approaches associated with commercial product development have influenced this principle.

> **NOTE**
>
> This section is provided for reference purposes only and is not essential to understanding this principle. Feel free to skip ahead to the *Measuring Service Abstraction* section if you're not interested in studying how meta abstraction types typically relate to common software programs.

Commercial and Open Source Products

A product built for commercial sale (Figure 8.14) will have naturally high levels of all three forms of meta abstraction. The average human consumer does not need to know what programming language a packaged product was written in or how it was designed. Furthermore, some quality of service details may be published as part of the product documentation (but most are not). The only information typically made available is functional in nature so that consumers can interact with the program. Otherwise, a commercial product exists as a classic black box.

Figure 8.14
A program designed for sale to the public will almost always hide as many of its underlying details as possible.

Open source programs (Figure 8.15) are the complete opposite in that pretty much everything there is to know about the program is made available to whoever is interested. Abstraction levels can be managed when a program designer creates a variation of the open source and hides details of the implementation at the programming logic level.

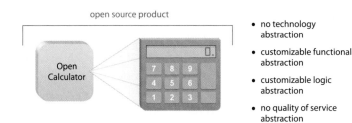

open source product

- no technology abstraction
- customizable functional abstraction
- customizable logic abstraction
- no quality of service abstraction

Figure 8.15

All details of an open source product are openly available.

Custom-Developed Applications

When we compare different custom-developed application designs, we can see comparable levels of meta abstraction between standalone and distributed, component-based environments—the key difference being that a componentized application will often decrease some abstraction levels when there is the possibility of some of the components being shared.

A standalone application (Figure 8.16) is frequently designed, developed, and implemented by a project team that continues to own and maintain it over time. Therefore, functional and logic abstraction levels can vary, depending on how accessible source code and design details are in the organization.

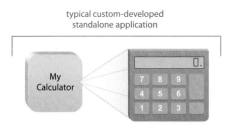

typical custom-developed standalone application

- low technology abstraction (technical environment is well known)
- targeted and flexible functional abstraction (APIs are customized as required)
- low-to-medium logic abstraction (source code and design specifications are often published on the local network)
- low quality of service abstraction (runtime behavior, policies are well known)

Figure 8.16

A standalone application's abstraction levels tend to be low in organizations that don't have access control processes in place. Often abstraction is not a primary concern due to the self-sufficient nature of the application.

Although individual components in distributed applications (Figure 8.17) are designed to provide specific subsets of functionality, little effort is made to hide information about them. A low emphasis on reuse results in less need to protect component consumer designers from changes to underlying component implementations.

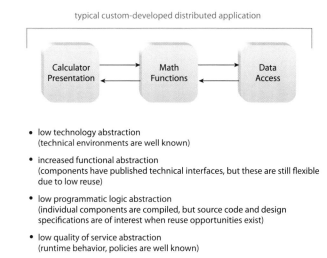

typical custom-developed distributed application

- low technology abstraction
  (technical environments are well known)

- increased functional abstraction
  (components have published technical interfaces, but these are still flexible
  due to low reuse)

- low programmatic logic abstraction
  (individual components are compiled, but source code and design
  specifications are of interest when reuse opportunities exist)

- low quality of service abstraction
  (runtime behavior, policies are well known)

Figure 8.17

Similarly, low abstraction levels have been common for distributed application environments.

Web Services-Based and Service-Oriented Solutions

The more recent distributed application architectures have placed a greater emphasis on abstraction and have therefore shifted some of the meta abstraction types. The use of Web services (Figure 8.18), for example, can introduce an opportunity to increase technology information abstraction.

The fundamental advantage of the Web services platform is that it can free applications from proprietary communication constraints, which is why many organizations are more motivated to keep underlying programmatic logic details hidden. However, within most IT environments, this information is still accessible to those who really want to find it.

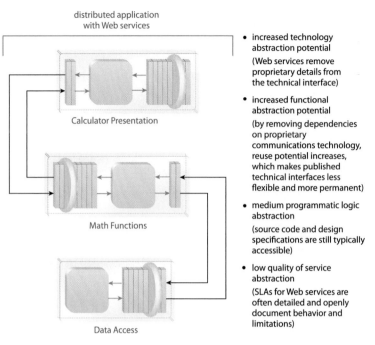

distributed application
with Web services

- increased technology
  abstraction potential
  (Web services remove
  proprietary details from
  the technical interface)

- increased functional
  abstraction potential
  (by removing dependencies
  on proprietary
  communications technology,
  reuse potential increases,
  which makes published
  technical interfaces less
  flexible and more permanent)

- medium programmatic logic
  abstraction
  (source code and design
  specifications are still typically
  accessible)

- low quality of service
  abstraction
  (SLAs for Web services are
  often detailed and openly
  document behavior and
  limitations)

Calculator Presentation

Math Functions

Data Access

Figure 8.18

Web services within distributed applications require individual parts of the application to
express functionality through a non-proprietary service contract.

When building components or Web services as service-oriented solution logic (Figure
8.19), we pay the most attention to abstraction for each type of service meta information.
Our goal is to achieve the appropriate levels of meta abstraction while still supporting
the objectives of the other service-orientation principles.

Figure 8.19

A composition consisting of services that are
each designed to maximize technology, functional, and programmatic logic abstraction.

service-oriented solution

Calculator   Math   Data
Access

- high technology abstraction
  (proprietary technology details are intentionally hidden)

- streamlined functional abstraction
  (service contracts are carefully designed to express just the
  right amount of functionality)

- high programmatic logic abstraction
  (underlying service logic details are intentionally hidden)

- targeted quality of service abstraction
  (aqnostic services especially need to publish select details)

SUMMARY OF KEY POINTS

- There are four primary types of meta information we are interested in abstracting when applying this principle: technology, functionality, programmatic logic, and quality of service.

- Achieving high levels of abstraction has both technical design and organizational implications associated with the deliberate hiding of information.

- Past architectural models have generally not emphasized meta abstraction to the extent of SOA.

8.4 Measuring Service Abstraction

It can be beneficial to have labels that we apply to services and service capabilities in order to communicate the extent of content abstraction and associated access control measures that are in place.

Contract Content Abstraction Levels

Based on the quantity and detail of information in a contract, its measure of content abstraction can be classified using categories such as those provided in this section (Figure 8.20). Note that these levels are used specifically to measure functional abstraction.

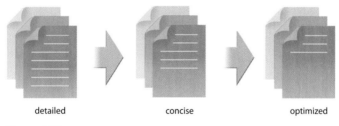

detailed   concise   optimized

Figure 8.20

Applying this principle changes a contract's level of content abstraction, which tends to reduce the overall quantity of contract content.

Detailed Contract

The content within the contract is elaborate, with many explicit constraints. This abstraction level is common when the bulk of validation logic and associated business rules have been deferred to a service contract along with additional types of supplemental information. This category generally represents a service contract to which the principle of Service Abstraction has not been seriously applied.

Concise Contract

A concise contract will attempt to balance content with known usage scenarios. Even though a significant amount of validation logic and constraints can still be present, meta data that is clearly not required will have been removed. This category essentially represents the minimal level of abstraction required to indicate that this principle has been applied to a meaningful extent.

Optimized Contract

A contract is considered optimized when it has undergone a formal audit and has subsequently been trimmed of unnecessary content and constraints. These steps are commonly taken to maximize the consumer potential of a service that encapsulates reusable logic. Generally, detailed validation constraints are sparse within optimized contracts to enable the service to process a range of input and output values.

Mixed Detailed Contract

When service contracts are evolved or extended at different stages or by different designers, the level of abstraction of individual service capabilities can vary. Some capabilities may be detailed, whereas others may be concise or even optimized. Due to its inconsistency, this form of contract content abstraction is undesirable. It is generally most common when contract design standards are not consistently used.

Access Control Levels

Whereas content abstraction is, for the most part, associated with the functionality expressed in the technical contract interface, access control is related to the ability of humans to learn about a service's underlying logic and implementation (which is different from *consumer* access control we may apply to a deployed service). Access control levels are therefore an indication of the extent to which technology information and programmatic logic abstraction (or information hiding) are enforced on an organizational level.

It is important to establish that these levels are used as labels for non-service owners. Obviously those who are responsible for maintaining and governing a service will have direct access to a service and knowledge about its implementation. Access control applies to service meta information not "officially" published to the outside world.

In other words, it is primarily geared toward potential service consumer program designers (the humans on the bottom of the dashed line in Figure 8.21).

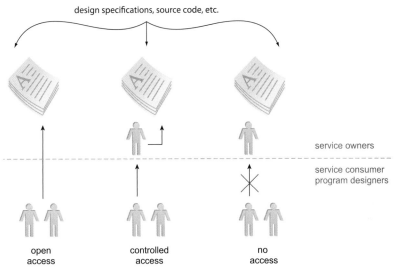

Figure 8.21
Higher levels of access control allow for abstraction levels to be consistently preserved during the lifetime of a service.

The following categories can be used to indicate measures of privacy applied to the actual service design specifications.

Open Access

The design specifications of a service are openly available and as accessible as the service contract itself. This is relatively common in IT environments where design documents are published on a shared LAN.

Controlled Access

Security measures are in place to limit access to service design documents. In this case, projects delivering service consumer programs will often require that consumer designers request formal approval to view design specifications. Clearly, there are different levels of control that can be applied based on the criteria used to grant approval.

One example of controlled access is when a collection of services are owned by a particular group or custodian, but another IT department with an enterprise focus (such as an Enterprise Architecture group) would be given open read-only access to all service design specifications.

BEST PRACTICE

When using controlled access measures, many of the labels used to identify implementation levels of other principles can be applied within the controlled groups. For example, the labels used to define measures of autonomy (as described in the *Levels of Service Autonomy* section in Chapter 10) may be useful for communication purposes within the team that owns a particular service. However, it may be deemed necessary to hide autonomy levels from those outside of this group.

No Access

Service design specifications are essentially considered off limits and are accessed and maintained solely by the service owners or custodians. Access to anyone else is only granted under specific circumstances, and even then, access to potential consumer program designers would be denied.

Abstraction Levels and Quality of Service Meta Information

The previously described forms of measuring and controlling access to meta data can apply to quality of service information. Through the use of policy technologies (as provided by the WS-Policy framework), quality of service details can also be implemented as an extension of the technical service contract of a Web service.

However, quality of service characteristics are most commonly documented and maintained as part of SLAs. Note that there can be situations where the published SLA is not made openly available, in which case access control measures may apply.

SUMMARY OF KEY POINTS

- There are commonly defined levels of content abstraction that are primarily associated with the quantity of content in the service contract.

- There are commonly defined levels of access control that can be used to ensure that content abstraction levels are preserved.

8.5 Service Abstraction and Service Design

Achieving the right measure of abstraction for a given service can be one of the most challenging parts of the service design process. Because abstraction affects so many other principles, it is often a constant concern. This section raises a variety of common design considerations associated with incorporating all forms of service abstraction.

Service Abstraction vs. Service Encapsulation

It is important to make a clear distinction between what a service encapsulates and what it abstracts. Encapsulation refers to the logic, resources, and information contained within the service boundary. A service, in its entirety, is comprised of a contract and what it encapsulates.

Abstraction refers to the parts of what the service encapsulates that are exposed to and hidden from consumer programs outside of the service boundary. In other words, the application of this principle determines how much of the encapsulated logic we make public. The primary reason for us to share less information about what a service encapsulates is so that we can make changes to what is encapsulated without affecting consumer programs that are already using the service.

How Encapsulation Can Affect Abstraction

From a service design perspective, we are very interested in what each service capability encapsulates because that will often influence the extent of attainable abstraction, as illustrated in Figure 8.22 and discussed in the following examples.

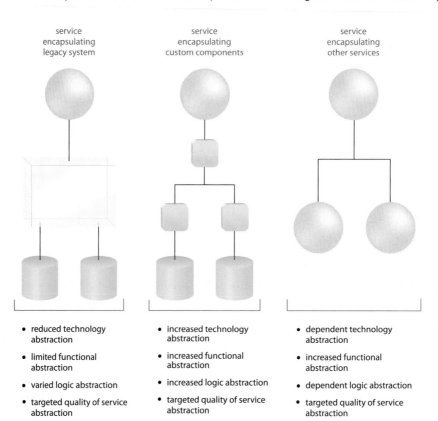

Figure 8.22

The nature of the logic and implementation of what a service encapsulates can have a direct bearing on the attainable levels of meta abstraction types.

Services Encapsulating Legacy Environments

As with other principles, legacy environments can pose significant challenges to attaining balanced Service Abstraction. The extent to which content can be abstracted may need to be dependent on the underlying service adapter and the corresponding legacy APIs. Specifications for the legacy system may have been widely accessible for years, prior to service encapsulation. Therefore, access control may be difficult to implement.

Services Encapsulating Custom Logic

The freedom that comes with building custom solution logic in support of services allows for the greatest opportunities to achieve balanced levels of content and access abstraction.

For example, validation logic associated with each input and output message of a Web service operation can be assessed and tuned accordingly. Constraints that may inhibit the service's overall ability to interoperate can be moved away from the contract to the underlying logic. Furthermore, subsequent to service deployment, immediate measures can be put in place to ensure the required level of privacy for the service design specifications.

Services Encapsulating Services

As we will study in Chapter 13, service compositions introduce some unique design considerations, especially when it comes to abstraction. For example, a controller service with optimized content abstraction will need to ensure that its role as controller is not revealed to its consumers. On the other hand, a service that is known to be a controller will then have a cumulative level of content abstraction that is determined collectively by its own measure of abstraction as well as that of all its composition members.

This, of course, can lead to all kinds of scenarios. A controller service may encapsulate a composition that consists of several services that compose others. Each of these additional controller services may support different levels of content and access abstraction.

NOTE
The only meta data typically not directly affected is quality of service information. Regardless of what is encapsulated, it is usually considered preferable for these details to be consistently documented, published, and shared.

Service Abstraction and Non-Technical Contract Documents

When applying this principle the focus is often on two specific service design aspects: the content of the technical service contract and access to design specifications and source code. One type of document in which we therefore also need to carefully weigh the abstraction level is the *non-technical* service description. The classic example is an SLA that accompanies the technical contract with additional rules, constraints, policies, guarantees, and assurances documented by the service owner for interpretation by human service consumer program designers.

Even though we don't programmatically bind to an SLA, we will naturally make a series of assumptions based on what it expresses. These assumptions will find their way into the design of our consumer programs. For example, if we know the service will not be available for two specific hours out of each day, we may design the consumer program to automatically deactivate itself during that time period.

We need to ensure that the SLA is not over-documented so that it can accommodate future change without impacting all of the consumer programs that have formed dependencies on the service. For example, if new infrastructure constraints require us to extend the downtime of our service from two to five hours daily, consumer programs designed specifically to accommodate the two-hour outage will need to be revised, retested, and redeployed.

In an SLA it's not always a matter of reducing the amount of content. Sometimes, the wording in the agreement simply needs to be altered. In the case of the aforementioned example, the service could have been originally delivered with an SLA that stated its current unavailability at two hours but then also stated that this amount of downtime (as well as the specific time during which it occurs) is subject to change. This simple wording change provides a heads up to consumer program designers to not tightly couple their designs to specific service implementation characteristics that are not explicitly fixed. Instead, the consumer program can be outfitted with extra exception handling logic that detects when the service is not available and gracefully deactivates itself or perhaps enters a polling cycle.

Service Abstraction and Granularity

The validation rules and data types established by capabilities can vary in rigidity and detail, especially with Web service contracts where operations can be defined with complex types originating from different schemas. Service Abstraction encourages us to publish less detail so as to give the service owners the maximum amount of freedom in evolving the service over time. This can directly influence service constraint granularity with a tendency toward coarser-grained constraint levels.

The use of policy definitions in particular can raise abstraction concerns. WS-Policy provides a number of ways to express policy assertions for which consumer compliance is *not* required. For example, assertions can be grouped into alternatives, appended with `wsp:optional` or `wsp:ignorable` attributes, or expressed via parameters. A common reason for using these extensions is to accommodate multiple groups of consumers, each with its own policy requirements. While all of these features allow for rich, diverse, and flexible service contracts, their use can result in contracts that reveal too many details about a service's underlying logic, behavior, and preferences. This is why the Service Abstraction principle asks us to moderate their use.

Other service-orientation principles, such as Service Loose Coupling and Service Autonomy, also advocate placing fewer constraints into the service contract. While this imposes fewer dependency requirements on service consumers, it leaves more room for interpretation (and speculation) because less detailed information is available. Therefore, determining how much validation logic and data constraints should be published as part of a service contract is a key decision point. Several patterns provided in the book *SOA: Design Patterns* address this issue.

Service Abstraction and Service Models

The unique design considerations that go into each service model also carry forward into how abstraction can be incorporated and applied, as follows.

Entity Services and Utility Services

Agnostic service models are often required to encapsulate a variety of environments. Utility services especially can have diverse capabilities that represent custom logic, legacy APIs, or a combination of both. Therefore, the type of service model used may have little impact on the extent of attainable content abstraction.

When it comes to access control, however, agnostic services often demand stricter governance procedures that are put in place to protect the longevity of the service contract and the reuse potential of the underlying logic. With a dedicated ownership group, controlled or even restricted access to design specifications is much more feasible.

Task Services and Orchestrated Task Services

If we label a service as a task service, then it's almost a dead giveaway that it will act as a controller of a composition. Therefore, when optimized content abstraction is being pursued, removing this service model classification may be necessary. However, normally that would be considered an extreme measure.

Orchestrated task services that exist as Web services encapsulating WS-BPEL process logic will have their WSDL definitions appended with WS-BPEL constructs that also advertise their role and responsibilities, as well as the fact that they are implemented as part of an orchestration platform.

How Service Abstraction Affects Other Principles

Because this principle emphasizes the reduction of service contract content, it ties directly into how other principles that also shape service contracts are applied (Figure 8.23).

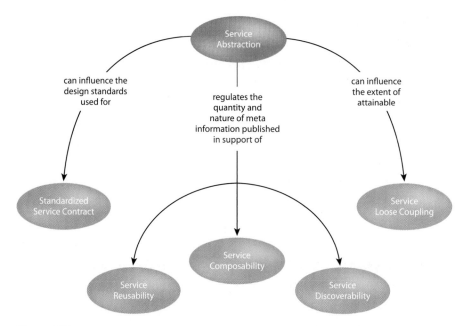

Figure 8.23

Besides directly influencing Standardized Service Contract and Service Loose Coupling principles, Service Abstraction shapes the application of other principles and pushes back against some of the tendencies for them to publish more content in support of their specific goals.

Service Abstraction and Standardized Service Contract

As we've established, the base amount of information that is abstracted from the service and made available to the outside world is the service contract. Therefore, this principle's emphasis on abstracting *more* away from the outside world can have a significant impact on what we originally were planning to publish in the contract documents.

The nature of the content within a standardized service contract will generally be influenced (if not determined by) the design standards in use. However, these conventions will often be focused on naming, data types, policy expression, and overall contract structure. The volume of detail and the types of constraints we choose to include are impacted by the levels of functional, technology, and logic abstraction we decide to apply. Therefore, Service Abstraction will often end up shaping service contract content indirectly by influencing the governing contract design standards.

Service Abstraction and Service Loose Coupling

On the surface it may appear as though Service Abstraction has a lot in common with Service Loose Coupling. They are indeed related, but each still represents a design characteristic that is exclusive of the other (see Figure 5.2 in the *Principles that Implement vs. Principles that Regulate* section from Chapter 5).

The level of abstraction applied to a service determines how much information about the service is available. The availability of this information makes the formation of dependencies from service consumers possible. Therefore, the extent of abstraction can have a direct bearing on the extent of possible coupling.

If this is the case, then how are these principles separated? It is possible to make a great deal of information available about a service and still not enable an excessive amount of coupling. *It comes down to what the information actually is.* A small amount of highly detailed technical interface constraints can result in much tighter coupling requirements than a larger amount of technical interface information with vague or open (range-based) data constraints.

So while these two very fundamental principles usually find themselves intertwined within service designs, the extent of coupling is generally determined by a combination of the quantity of information abstracted *and* the nature of the information itself. Because of this relationship, the application of both Service Loose Coupling and Service Abstraction design principles can have a great deal of influence over a service contract's ultimate granularity.

Service Abstraction and Other Principles

As explained in upcoming chapters, principles such as Service Reusability, Service Composability, and Service Discoverability all encourage us to make more meta information about a service available to further their respective goals. For example, a service can be considered more discoverable if a larger amount of information about the service is published.

In relation to these principles, Service Abstraction is very much like a regulatory presence that asks us to assess the necessity of each piece of meta data before choosing to make it available to the outside world. To continue our example, the information we choose *not* to abstract sets the limit as to what data becomes available for external discovery and interpretation purposes.

SUMMARY OF KEY POINTS

- Service Abstraction raises design-time considerations associated with the technical service contract, service design specifications, and source code, as well as non-technical contract documents, such as SLAs.

- The location of data constraints and validation logic is a primary (long-term) contract design consideration when it comes to applying this principle.

- Service Abstraction directly affects the Standardized Service Contract and Service Loose Coupling principles but also helps shape the application of others.

8.6 Risks Associated with Service Abstraction

Because this principle results in the deliberate hiding of information, we need to carefully determine what information should be exposed. Each piece of available meta data can be used in some way that may have unforeseen consequences in the future.

Multi-Consumer Coupling Requirements

Some level of required coupling for consumer programs needs to be established to connect to and interact with a service at runtime. For this reason the technical service contract is exposed as an interface that details the terms of runtime engagement.

However, for agnostic service contracts it is often difficult to design capabilities that are just right for all possible consumers. Some may require more technical interface detail, while others would have actually benefited from less.

The challenge of striking the right balance for numerous potential interaction scenarios can sometimes be near impossible. However, this issue cannot be ignored, as abstracting the wrong amount of functionality can limit the consumer's ability to use the service.

The application of the Contract Denormalization pattern can alleviate this design risk, as it provides the option of exposing redundant functionality through different levels of abstraction granularity to facilitate different consumer requirements.

Misjudgment by Humans

With an emphasis on hiding more comes the danger of hiding too much. The service contract is what we rely on to communicate the purpose and capabilities of a service or service capability. If we make our contract too lean, we run the risk of it not containing enough information to properly express these qualities. This, in turn, can lead to humans misinterpreting or not sufficiently understanding a service. When this happens, we lose opportunities for potential reuse and increase the chances of redundant service logic being developed and deployed within the same inventory.

The flipside is the risk of human misjudgment resulting from an excess of available information. An example of this relates back to our discussion of access control. If humans have access to the underlying design details of a service, they risk making assumptions about the service's behavior that will carry over to the design of their consumer programs. Design characteristics implemented as a result of these assumptions will jeopardize their consumer programs the day the service implementation changes.

Human misjudgment is a constant and unavoidable risk. We can strive to find the right balance of abstraction with any given service, but even then, no two humans are the same, and no one service contract will ever be perfect for everyone. To maximize the chances of broad interpretability, this risk can be significantly alleviated through the application of the Service Discoverability principle.

Security and Privacy Concerns

Anything we publish about a service holds us accountable. We have to pay special attention to not just the quantity of information being abstracted, but the nature of the data itself. For example, if a service is initially delivered for internal use within a controlled environment and then made available to service consumers external to the organization, the original service contract may inadvertently expose private or sensitive information. (Design patterns are available to address this risk through the use of concurrent and redundant service contract content.)

SUMMARY OF KEY POINTS

- Once a service is implemented, its abstraction levels are established and difficult to change thereafter. This introduces the potential for risks that can typically be avoided at design-time.

- Common risks associated with service contract abstraction are service granularity and security considerations, as well as the on-going possibility of human misjudgment.

8.7 CASE STUDY EXAMPLE

Each of the services documented in the previous two case study examples for Cutit Saw's Lab Project process has its own set of abstraction levels. Even though the services are being built with similar development technologies and deployed in similar environments, they are distinguished by the logic they represent.

Service Abstraction Levels

Before we get into individual service encapsulation, let's revisit the four services and take a brief look at what each has under the hood:

- Materials (Table 8.2)
- Formulas (Table 8.3)
- Inventory (Table 8.4)
- Run Lab Project (Table 8.5)

Following are a set of tables that summarize the technology, functional, programmatic, and quality of service abstraction for these four services. Toward the end of this example, we'll discover how, upon review of the current abstraction levels, Cutit makes some changes to refine and better support this principle.

NOTE

As indicated within the tables, the categories established in the *Contract Content Abstraction Levels* section are used to label functional abstraction levels. Technology, programmatic, and quality of service abstraction levels are classified as per the categories described in the *Access Control Levels* section.

Materials Service	
Functional Abstraction (Content Abstraction)	Concise (the service contract provides targeted functionality with limited constraints)
Technology Information Abstraction (Access Control)	Open Access (the technologies used to build and implement this service are openly documented and published as part of architecture specifications)
Programmatic Abstraction (Access Control)	Open Access (source code and design specifications are openly available on the local LAN)
Quality of Service (Access Control)	Open Access (SLA is published alongside service contract)

Table 8.2
Abstraction levels for the Materials service.

Formulas Service	
Functional Abstraction (Content Abstraction)	Detailed (due to complex rules associated with the exchange of formula data this service's contract has a low level of functional abstraction)
Technology Information Abstraction (Access Control)	Open Access (the technologies used to build and implement this service are openly documented and published as part of architecture specifications)
Programmatic Abstraction (Access Control)	Open-to-Controlled Access (source code and design specifications for the Web service are openly available on the local LAN, but information about the Formulas database is tightly guarded by a group of DBAs)
Quality of Service (Access Control)	Open Access (SLA is published alongside service contract)

Table 8.3
Abstraction levels for the Formulas service.

Inventory Service	
Functional Abstraction (Content Abstraction)	Concise (a limited amount of available functionality is exposed via the service contract)
Technology Information Abstraction (Access Control)	Controlled Access (access to documentation of the older, more proprietary technology behind the legacy system encapsulated by this service is not openly available and requires permission)
Programmatic Abstraction (Access Control)	Controlled Access (source code and the original system design specifications are kept on a separate server with limited access)
Quality of Service (Access Control)	Open Access (SLA is published alongside service contract)

Table 8.4
Abstraction levels for the Inventory service.

Run Lab Project Service	
Functional Abstraction (Content Abstraction)	Optimized (the sole operation provided by this Web service has few constraints and could likely not be more efficiently designed)
Technology Information Abstraction (Access Control)	Open Access (the technologies used to build and implement this service are openly documented and published as part of architecture specifications)
Programmatic Abstraction (Access Control)	Open Access (source code and design specifications are openly available on the local LAN)
Quality of Service (Access Control)	Open Access (SLA is published alongside service contract)

Table 8.5
Abstraction levels for the Run Lab Project service.

Cutit architects compile a report that highlights the alarmingly high amount of openly accessible meta information available for most of these services. The report points out that external consultants (that will need to be hired to staff upcoming service delivery projects) will be able to read up on any existing service details unless an access control process is put in place.

Outside contractors will often choose the path of least resistance when building new solutions so as to fulfill immediate performance and budgetary requirements (because that is how their work has traditionally been measured). As a result, they will tend to tune or optimize consumer programs in any way possible. Technology and programmatic meta information about services they will be required to work with will provide them with valuable background details that can be used to achieve this end.

The report points out that one of the more glaring risks associated with not hiding excessive meta information is related to the encapsulation of the legacy inventory control system. Although the Inventory service has a measure of access control in place, it is still relatively easy for anyone with a manager's approval to receive permission to view solution code and specifications.

Furthermore, just the knowledge of the fact that the legacy system is a central part of the overall automation of the Run Lab Project process introduces the potential for other service designs to be skewed.

Upon review of this report, Cutit IT management decides to assign a service custodian responsible for the ownership of all entity services, including the Inventory service. This will effectively make technology and programmatic meta information off-limits to future project teams responsible for delivering service consumer programs.

Operation-Level Abstraction Examples

In this section we'll choose three operations from the four Cutit Web services (Figure 8.24) and drill down to discuss how the increased access control levels established by IT managers affect their abstraction levels.

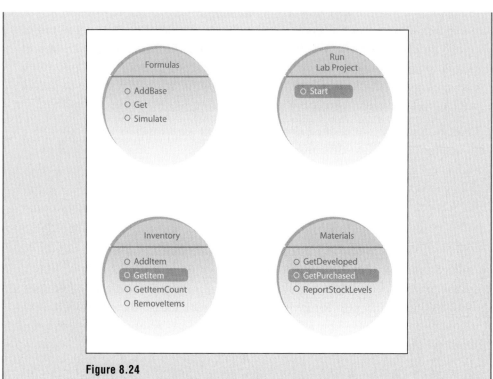

Figure 8.24

Encapsulated environments for the highlighted operations within these services are explored.

GetItem Operation of the Inventory Service

The GetItem operation encapsulates logic within a custom component that interacts with the legacy system's published API. The corresponding API function that is invoked triggers internal legacy logic that ends up accessing the legacy repository to retrieve the requested inventory item record (Figure 8.25).

As established in the case study example at the end of Chapter 7, the custom logic added to the Inventory service transforms the retrieved record data to conform to the standard Inventory Item schema. The fact that the GetItem operation can incorporate complex types from this standard schema allows it to establish a concise level of functional abstraction (because the schema types were intentionally streamlined for message exchanges).

Both technology and programmatic abstraction levels for this operation are elevated because it is part of an entity service for which increased access control measures have been put in place. The fact that it encapsulates older technology is considered classified. However, known operational limitations (resulting from the legacy system) are documented in an SLA published alongside the Inventory service contract.

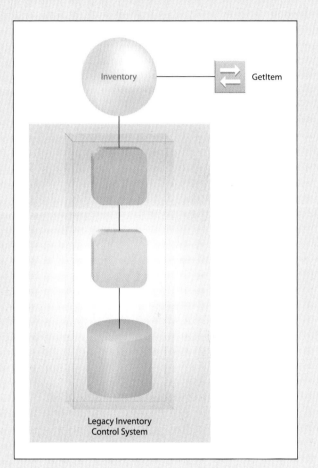

Figure 8.25

The Inventory service's GetItem operation encapsulates legacy inventory control system functionality but expresses it as part of a standardized service contract. The shaded area indicates what about the service is intentionally hidden.

GetPurchased Operation of the Materials Service

When the GetPurchased operation of the Materials service is invoked, it is required to compose the Inventory service's GetItem operation (Figure 8.26). As a result, it indirectly encapsulates (and triggers) all of the functionality we just described in association with what the GetItem operation encapsulates.

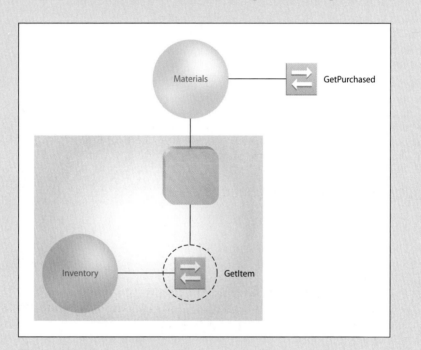

Figure 8.26

The GetPurchased operation encapsulates logic that invokes the Inventory service's GetItem operation. However, as indicated by the shaded zone, that interaction is intentionally hidden from service consumers.

The functional abstraction level is not directly influenced by the composition of the Inventory service because this form of abstraction is associated solely with the content of the contract published by the Materials service. Because the contract is based on standardized schemas that have been streamlined for message exchange, the operation is classified as concise.

Note that even if Cutit had decided to continue with the InvLegacyAPI service described in the case study example from Chapter 7, the GetPurchased operation would still be considered optimized. This is because its underlying logic would still have performed the transformation necessary to keep its part of the service contract compliant with the standard schemas.

With regards to technology and programmatic information abstraction, the interaction with the Inventory service is deliberately hidden. The Materials service is also an entity service that now falls under the ownership of the newly hired service custodian. However, because this service does compose a service that encapsulates legacy logic (and is subject to legacy constraints), portions of the Inventory service SLA are carried forward to the Materials service SLA, specifically for this and other operations that need to interact with the Inventory service.

Start Operation of the Run Lab Project Service

As illustrated in Figure 8.27, underlying details of the Run Lab Project service are not hidden. Because this is a task service, its meta information is not protected by the entity service custodian. This is considered acceptable because architects are comfortable with others knowing what service operations task services need to compose.

However, because its composition logic is limited to invoking other entity services, service consumer designers do not gain access to any meta information beyond which entity service operations are invoked.

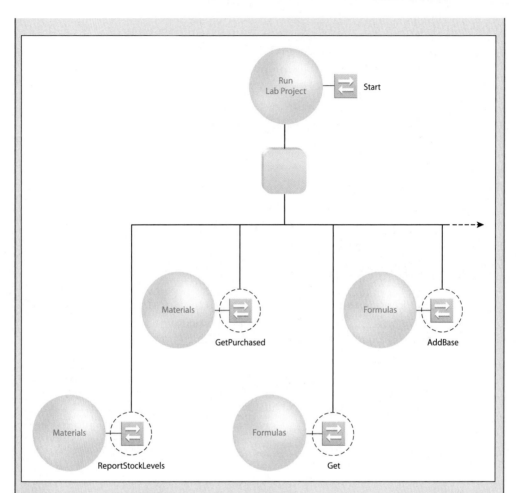

Figure 8.27

The Start operation kicks off service composition logic that includes the composition of several operations from at least two services. In addition to its implementation via a custom component, the composed service operations are not hidden.

Chapter 9

Service Reusability
(Commercial and Agnostic Design)

The three principles we've discussed so far primarily concentrate on the design and positioning of the service contract. While service contract design continues to remain an important consideration, our focus now goes well beyond the contract layer as we need to take a close look at the manner in which the actual underlying service logic needs to be shaped.

From this perspective, there is perhaps no principle more fundamental to achieving the goals of service-oriented computing than that of reusability (Figure 9.1). It can even be argued that several of the other principles would not exist if the service-orientation paradigm did not place such a core emphasis on fostering reuse.

Figure 9.1
By advocating repeated reuse, this principle strives to get the most possible value out of each piece of software.

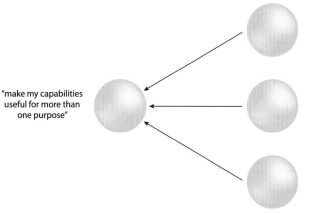

"make my capabilities useful for more than one purpose"

9.1 Reuse Explained

Before we cover the details of this principle, let's first take some time to explain the general concept of reuse within automation environments and its colorful history in IT.

Reuse in Abstract

In theory, reuse is a pretty straight-forward idea: simply make a software program useful for more than just one single purpose. The reasons for doing so are also quite evident. Whereas something that is useful for a single purpose will provide value, something that is *repeatedly* useful will provide repeated value and is therefore a more attractive investment.

The rationale is logical, but it also brings to light the difference between something that is simple and something that is easy. Reuse is a simple concept, but history has taught us that effectively achieving reuse is not easy.

Single-Purpose Programs

Building a software program for one purpose allows us to focus only on one set of very specific requirements (Figure 9.2). Everything within the program can be optimized and customized in support of its sole purpose and the predictable usage scenarios it will need to facilitate.

Its narrow scope affects all parts of the program's delivery lifecycle. Design, development, and testing are easier because the scope of usage is limited and predictable. Furthermore, the deployment and subsequent administration of the program are straight forward because again, we only need to make sure it continues to fulfill its one purpose.

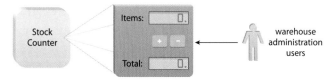

Figure 9.2
A simplistic example of a primitive program that can only perform the addition and subtraction of values, tailored to help warehouse employees take or adjust the stock of inventory. This program was designed with a specific purpose and user-base in mind.

Multi-Purpose Programs

As software designers, we have the option to design a program so that it is useful for more than just one purpose (Figure 9.3). To accomplish this, we need to take numerous new considerations into account.

For example, when designing a multi-purpose program, we have to determine how it will be utilized within multiple known usage scenarios. This tends to change and expand its programming logic in that it is required to become more generic and perhaps offer a wider range of functions. The design grows more complex, which carries over to an increased development effort to accommodate all of the scenarios associated with the range of planned capabilities.

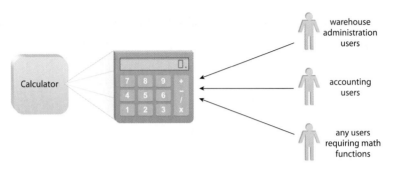

Figure 9.3

A generic calculator program can be designed providing the same functionality originally
supplied by the Stock Counter program, but packaging it in a generic user-interface
equipped with several additional calculation features. This program continues to fulfill the
requirements of the warehouse administration users while also being useful to several other
types of users.

Testing is another impacted phase—larger programs especially can require many new
test cases and additional exception handling logic. A reusable program may furthermore
require a hosting environment capable of fulfilling increased availability and scalability
requirements (unless it is redundantly implemented, which also places extra demands
on the infrastructure).

Finally, once the program has been implemented and is in use, we need to pay special
attention to how we decide to evolve it. Regardless of whether the program is being used
by humans or other programs, once it has been released, we lose the freedom to make
arbitrary changes. Its existing clients will have formed dependencies on it and, especially if it is being programmatically interfaced with, those dependencies will be very
specific to the design of the program in its initial release.

These are examples of some of the factors that have traditionally inhibited the success of
achieving reuse in IT. Service-orientation deals with these issues head-on by providing
principles that prepare a service for reuse from the very beginning.

NOTE
At this point it is worth highlighting the difference between the terms *reusability* and *reuse*. The former is a design characteristic we look to foster with this principle, while the latter is the end result we aim to achieve by applying the principle. As we will discuss in the *Measuring Service Reusability and Applying Commercial Design* section later in this chapter, the extent of reusability we are able to realize within a service determines its ultimate reuse potential.

Origins of Reuse

Any software program ever built for sale to the general public was designed with reuse in mind. Whether it's an operating system, a shrink-wrapped accounting product, or an entire middleware platform, in the initial design stages of these programs, the considerations we listed in the previous section were very likely taken into account.

This makes the notion of reuse just about as old as the commercial software industry itself. It also gives us a clear understanding of what it takes to deal with the additional requirements reusability adds to the delivery lifecycle. Reuse increases the complexity, cost, effort, and time to build software. Furthermore, it can be awkward and challenging to build solutions that incorporate software programs developed by other teams. Reusability has therefore not always been a design characteristic organizations have chosen to pursue for their internal solutions.

Why should we care about future potential usage scenarios that may or may not exist, when we have a specific set of business requirements we need to fulfill right now? As explained in Chapter 4, building programs for just a single purpose does have a certain pay off. There is a measurable investment and a measurable return. This type of reasoning is what has led to the popularity of siloed application environments.

The advent of object-orientation is credited with boosting awareness of the potential gain to be had when building distributed solutions out of components (objects) capable of serving more than just an immediate purpose. Reuse through the application of object-oriented design was attempted and achieved mixed levels of success.

Many of those who were part of less successful reuse initiatives became disillusioned with the vision of establishing an inventory of shareable objects that would reap large returns over years to come. A number of common problems emerged from these projects. Some examples include:

- The reuse potential of a component was limited to proprietary runtime environments and/or proprietary consumer programs.

- Reusable components suffered from too much overhead resulting from tight dependencies on other components (via inheritance structures and other tight coupling design approaches).

- Components that were legitimately reusable were simply not used enough.

- Reusable components were outfitted with too much functionality that ended up not actually being required (see the *Commercial Design and Gold-Plating* section later in this chapter).

Although previous reuse initiatives were not always successful, vendors and standards organizations continued to work toward a vision of enabling organizations to establish effective, shared enterprise resources.

The subsequent emergence of the Web services technology platform was seen as a significant step ahead in that its vendor-neutral communications framework directly addressed the limitations associated with proprietary runtime boundaries (the first item on the preceding list).

Web services did succeed in increasing reuse potential. A body of logic exposed as a Web service can be made accessible to any part of the enterprise that also supports the corresponding Web service messaging technology. Therefore, as long as technology constraints imposed by the Web services framework are not a factor, the range of potential consumer programs naturally increases.

However, it has become evident that technology innovation alone is insufficient to overcome many of the other obstacles that held back past reuse efforts. The fact remains that no one innovation (including SOA) can overcome endemic organizational problems. These need to be resolved within the organization itself.

Several of the service-orientation design principles were inspired by these past challenges. They establish a paradigm in which reusability is a core and central consideration. For organizations interested in attaining reuse on a broad scale, a commitment to service-orientation creates a clear path. It is up to the organization to see this commitment through.

SUMMARY OF KEY POINTS

- Designing software to be reusable opens the door to increased ROI but also introduces changes to the traditional application delivery lifecycle.

- "Reusability" is a term used to indicate the potential for a software program to be reused, whereas "reuse" is the actual act of reusing the program.

- The concept of reusability and the goal of attaining reuse has been floating around the IT world for some time. However, past attempts to achieve significant enterprise-wide reuse have had mixed results.

9.2 Profiling this Principle

Service Reusability is a core service-orientation principle to the extent that its realization is considered an expected, secondary characteristic in most services. The profile in Table 9.1 provides further details.

Principle Profile	
Short Definition	*"Services are reusable."*
Long Definition	*"Services contain and express agnostic logic and can be positioned as reusable enterprise resources."*
Goals	The goals behind Service Reusability are tied directly to some of the most strategic objectives of service-oriented computing: • To allow for service logic to be repeatedly leveraged over time so as to achieve an increasingly high return on the initial investment of delivering the service. • To increase business agility on an organizational level by enabling the rapid fulfillment of future business automation requirements through wide-scale service composition. • To enable the realization of agnostic service models. • To enable the creation of service inventories with a high percentage of agnostic services.
Design Characteristics	• *The service is defined by an agnostic functional context*—The logic encapsulated by the service is associated with a context that is sufficiently agnostic to any one usage scenario so as to be considered reusable. • *The service logic is highly generic*—The logic encapsulated by the service is sufficiently generic, allowing it to facilitate numerous usage scenarios by different types of service consumers. • *The service has a generic and extensible contract*—The service contract is flexible enough to process a range of input and output messages. • *The service logic can be accessed concurrently*—Services are designed to facilitate simultaneous access by multiple consumer programs.

Implementation Requirements	From an implementation perspective, Service Reusability can be the most demanding of the principles we've covered so far. Below are common requirements for creating reusable services and supporting their long-term existence:
	• A scalable runtime hosting environment capable of high-to-extreme concurrent service usage. Once a service inventory is relatively mature, reusable services will find themselves in an increasingly large number of compositions.
	• A solid version control system to properly evolve contracts representing reusable services.
	• Service analysts and designers with a high degree of subject matter expertise who can ensure that the service boundary and contract accurately represent the service's reusable functional context.
	• A high level of service development and commercial software development expertise so as to structure the underlying logic into generic and potentially decomposable components and routines.
	These and other requirements place an emphasis on the appropriate staffing of the service delivery team, as well as the importance of a powerful and scalable hosting environment and supporting infrastructure.
Web Service Region of Influence	This principle can affect all parts of a Web service. Contract design, the use of system messaging agents, and the underlying core logic can all be shaped by a service's reusability requirements.
	When we view the service as an IT asset that requires an investment but provides the potential for repeated returns, we can appreciate why more care needs to be taken when designing each part of the service architecture.

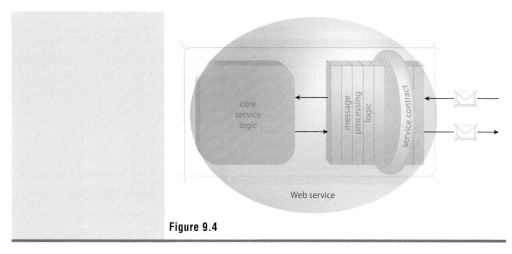

Web service

Figure 9.4

Table 9.1

A profile for the Service Reusability principle.

NOTE
A service capability can be reused in two different ways. It can be repeatedly invoked by the same service consumer program automating the same business task—or—it can be invoked by different service consumers automating different business tasks. While both scenarios can be viewed as a form of service reuse, it is the latter situation that this principle is focused on promoting. We want services and their capabilities to be multi-purpose so that they help automate multiple business tasks. The extent to which a service is repeatedly invoked for a specific business task is an issue of scalability that is addressed by other design principles, such as Service Autonomy and Service Statelessness.

SUMMARY OF KEY POINTS

- Service Reusability is a core principle that represents fundamental design characteristics key to achieving many strategic goals associated with SOA.

- Reusable service logic needs to be grouped within and expressed via an agnostic context.

- An emphasis on reusability introduces design considerations that can shape all parts of a Web service.

9.3 Measuring Service Reusability and Applying Commercial Design

The ability to realize the reuse potential of a service is often equated with the ability to predict the future. This is, for the most part, an inaccurate statement. In commercial product development, the key to building a successful product is understanding its target user market. Similarly, the key to building custom program logic that is successfully reused is understanding its potential users.

In an enterprise, this understanding comes from a knowledge of the organization's business models, technology environments, and user communities. This is one of the major reasons as to why service-oriented analysis requires the up-front involvement of both business and technology subject matter experts (as explained in Chapter 3).

Commercial design considerations tie into the established service-oriented analysis and design processes in that they are drawn from established commercial product development lifecycles and are fundamental to planning, conceptualizing, and ultimately designing reusable resources as services.

As illustrated in Figure 9.5, the service-orientation design paradigm can be seen as the merging of commercial product design with traditional enterprise design and delivery methods.

Commercial Design Considerations

The purpose of the commercial design approach is not to guarantee absolute reuse, but to instead apply expert judgment when determining:

- the most suitable *type* of logic, and…
- the most suitable *quantity* of logic

…to be provided by a particular version of a reusable service.

By doing so, reuse potential is maximized, while the risk of over-equipping a service with excessive features that may not actually be required is alleviated. The extra design considerations introduced by commercial design almost always require the involvement of both business and technology subject matter experts.

Common factors that form the criteria applied to the service design include:

- Strategic goals and vision statements associated with the organization as a whole. (*How can we design the service to best support these goals?*)

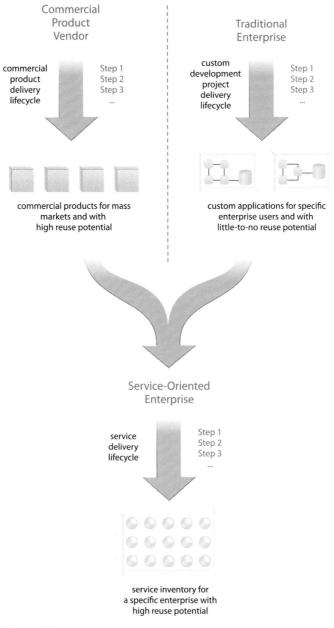

Figure 9.5

Service-orientation has deep roots in past software delivery approaches. It essentially brings commercial software design methods into the targeted environment of the enterprise.

- Existing models, such as the service inventory blueprint. (*How does a service fit into the overall service inventory, and how does it relate to other services?*)

- Current business requirements and the definition of common usage scenarios. (*Which requirements is a service expected to fulfill upon implementation and in the foreseeable future?*)

- Known historical business patterns which help predict future changes. (*Are there past trends and predictable changes in how an organization carries out its lines of business?*)

- Any known corporate acquisitions that may impact IT. (*Do we know of any foreign technology, systems, or platforms that we will need to incorporate into our enterprise?*)

- The urgency of service delivery requirements and associated timelines. (*What sacrifices will we need to make in order to fulfill high-priority tactical requirements?*)

- Existing legacy environments and any known upgrade or replacement plans. (*What types of service adapters or wrapper services will we be forced to work with or create?*)

Answering these types of questions with research, analysis, and input from various subject matter experts allows us to determine the nature and extent of reusable logic to place within agnostic services. With the considerations just highlighted, it is evident that guesswork is generally not required. When we build a program we intend to resell to a mass market, we are essentially interested in making this program as reusable as possible. The greater its reusability, the more useful it will be to more consumers and the greater its sales potential.

To accomplish this goal, we don't blindly design the program and just hope it "does well" in the end. We survey the marketplace, perform various types of demographic analysis, bring in subject matter experts to test alpha and beta releases, and so on. We do the up-front work required and make educated decisions as to the feature set the product will offer. This is very much the mentality required to build reusable services for an enterprise. There is a wealth of information available to us within an organization, much of which will tell us exactly what belongs in each agnostic service.

While a commercial product mindset is beneficial, it is worth noting that when designing services for an enterprise, we actually avoid many of the pressures of the commercial world. For example, unlike commercial vendors who need to perform anonymous surveys or cold calling, marketing research is easier to carry out within an organization because the target end-user communities are clearly identified and much more accessible. This increased accessibility gives us the ability to focus feature-sets on the specific needs of the enterprise, resulting in improved efficiency and accuracy and an overall increased quality of the reusable software.

Furthermore, commercial software is built for the open marketplace where competitive considerations, such as pricing, distribution channels, and uncompromising time-to-market pressures, can skew product designs. Within an enterprise, we generally don't encounter these types of circumstances (perhaps some, but rarely all) and can focus designs on the needs of the known end-users.

Leveraging proven and well established methods for building commercial products within a more predictable, accessible, and targeted enterprise environment maximizes the potential for achieving wide-spread reuse. To manage this eventuality, common levels of planned and actual reuse are described in the upcoming sections.

Measures of Planned Reuse

Categories such as the following can be used to refer to or label services during analysis and design phases.

Tactical Reusability

If project delivery requirements demand that services be developed and deployed as soon as possible, then reuse efforts need to be concentrated on the immediate functional requirements (Figure 9.6). In this case, the scope of the service-oriented analysis will be limited to the range of features required only by the current service delivery project.

Figure 9.6

A tactical measure of reuse only results in the implementation of service capabilities that address immediate needs. But the service is designed in such a manner that the immediate capability is still reusable so that the service can be safely extended in the future.

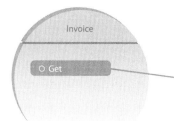

We only need for the service to retrieve invoice documents, so we will only equip it with that capability.

However, we will design the service so that it offers this capability within an agnostic context. That way the service is still reusable and can be further extended in the future with additional capabilities also associated with the agnostic functional context.

Targeted Reusability

If a project team has the ability to deliver a service with functionality that provides features beyond what is immediately required, then this approach adds only extensions that have the highest degree of guaranteed reuse potential (Figure 9.7). In other words, a service-oriented analysis will have been performed, and only those features at the top of the list are implemented. Others are added later, as required.

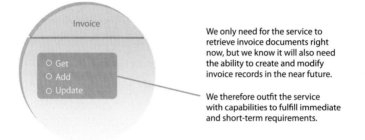

We only need for the service to retrieve invoice documents right now, but we know it will also need the ability to create and modify invoice records in the near future.

We therefore outfit the service with capabilities to fulfill immediate and short-term requirements.

Figure 9.7

A targeted enhancement measure represents a limited scope of reusability that, in this case, addresses well known functional requirements anticipated in the near future.

Complete Reusability

Based on the scope of the service boundary, an effort is made to equip the service with a complete range of functionality (Figure 9.8). This approach is only recommended if a well-defined service inventory blueprint exists, as it will have formed the basis for a comprehensive service-oriented analysis and service modeling effort.

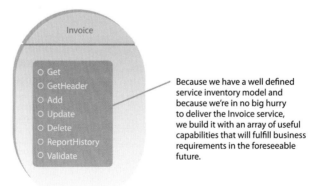

Because we have a well defined service inventory model and because we're in no big hurry to deliver the Invoice service, we build it with an array of useful capabilities that will fulfill business requirements in the foreseeable future.

Figure 9.8

The Invoice service is outfitted with a range of established capabilities, all of which address known requirements.

Measuring Actual Reuse

Of course, the ultimate measure of *accomplished* reuse is how much a service actually is and has been used subsequent to its implementation. This can be determined by analyzing the following statistics:

- The amount of service consumers that were built to use the service.

- The frequency with which these service consumers have used the service.

This information allows us to judge the success of the service as an investment, thereby giving us the ability to calculate a relatively accurate return on the cost originally required for its delivery and on-going maintenance.

Additionally, we are provided with enough detail to assess the accomplished reuse of each actual service *capability*. This allows us to measure the return right down to individual service capabilities and also supplies us with performance indicators as to which parts of a service are being taxed more than others.

Commercial Design Versus Gold-Plating

The term "gold-plating" arose from the object-oriented design era and generally referred to the approach of adding features to a program that go beyond its defined requirements.

The common risks associated with gold-plating are:

- The extra features added increase delivery expense and time.

- The extra features may end up conflicting with the program's existing design goals.

- Some of the extra features may end up not being required in the end and may have unnecessarily burdened delivery projects.

The proper application of the Service Reusability principle does not result in gold-plating, even when attempting the complete reusability measure. Any features added to a service that provide functionality beyond what is immediately required are done so only after careful consideration of how these tie into known usage scenarios and requirements. This is where proven commercial design approaches become so important to achieving "true" reuse.

SUMMARY OF KEY POINTS

- Reusability can be more effectively built into a service by applying common commercial design considerations.

- The three common levels of reusability are tactical, targeted, and complete.

- When higher measures of reusability are pursued through established methods, we avoid issues (such as gold-plating) that have inhibited reuse success in the past.

9.4 Service Reuse in SOA

Repeatedly delivering services with high levels of reusability can have a tremendous impact on the complexion of an enterprise. In the following sections we examine the relationship between Service Reusability, the service inventory blueprint, and common service models.

Reuse and the Agnostic Service

Because we have traditionally been focusing on the delivery of solution logic for a single purpose, programs have typically been associated with the automation of a particular business task via a specific application environment. Pursuing Service Reusability requires us to position logic so that it is as neutral or agnostic as possible to its surrounding environment. This establishes the concept of the *agnostic service*.

So what's the difference between an agnostic service and a reusable service? Both have specific design characteristics, and though related, each is distinct. A service is agnostic when its logic is independent from its business processes and proprietary technology or application platforms. The more agnostic the service is, the more generic its capabilities. Generic logic is multi-purpose logic. Therefore, the more agnostic the service, the greater its reuse potential.

For example, a service has reuse potential if it:

- provides capabilities that are not specific to any one business process

- is useful to the automation of more than one business process

The former characteristic classifies the service as agnostic, and the latter deems it reusable.

Utility services are frequently process-agnostic because they are intentionally designed to not encapsulate business logic. Business services, though, need to be carefully crafted to avoid being tied to parent business logic (which is why business service models are so helpful).

Other examples of agnostic design include limiting proprietary platform dependencies by making the service capable of encapsulating logic from different application environments. A service providing a logging capability could, for instance, be writing logs to three different proprietary databases. However, its processing context is considered agnostic because it is about logging only and not about any proprietary details related to the databases it interacts with to carry out its logging capabilities (all of those details can be abstracted and hidden from the context expressed in a standardized service contract).

Freeing services from ties to specific processes and proprietary implementation details furthers the vision of building an inventory of services that can be reused through recomposition as new requirements arise. Because of their reuse potential, well-designed agnostic services provide the most repeated value in a given inventory.

The Service Inventory Blueprint

The goal of the service inventory blueprint is to establish a complete perspective of solution logic across the enterprise or within a predefined enterprise domain as represented by an inventory of service *candidates* (Figure 9.9). Defining this perspective requires significant effort and a great deal of involvement from business analysts and information architects.

Each service boundary is carefully modeled so that it accurately represents the service's functional context while not overlapping with other service boundaries. Furthermore, how services relate to each other is frequently mapped out so as to better gauge and refine the type and quantity of logic each should encapsulate.

The availability of a service inventory blueprint dramatically reduces the effort and risk associated with the design of reusable services. The service candidates established in this model form the basis for service contracts with well-defined functional scopes. Furthermore, they establish service layers based on the chosen service models. It is these service models that provide both agnostic and non-agnostic (or less-agnostic) functional contexts for services, allowing for the initial identification and classification of service logic with reuse potential.

Figure 9.9

A segment of a service inventory modeled after a service inventory blueprint. The top highlighted row represents a layer of non-agnostic task services.

Note that service inventory blueprints were first introduced in the *Introduction to Service-Oriented Computing* section of Chapter 3.

SUMMARY OF KEY POINTS

- Services with agnostic functional contexts provide the highest reusability potential.

- The definition of a service inventory blueprint helps maximize the opportunities to identify and define agnostic services.

9.5 Standardized Service Reuse and Logic Centralization

Reusability represents a key characteristic that typically needs to be realized on a broad scale for some of the more strategic goals of service-orientation to be attained. To pursue these goals, reuse itself must form the basis of supporting internal design standards. The foremost of these standards needs to dictate that services classified as reusable must become a primary (or even sole) means by which the logic they encapsulate is accessed. This leads us to a standards-related design pattern known as Logic Centralization.

Understanding Logic Centralization

As we originally established in Chapter 7, centralization simply means limiting the options of something to one. This intentional limitation can support our efforts to establish a highly "normalized" service inventory blueprint.

Within a normalized service inventory each service represents a distinct functional domain, which essentially means that service boundaries do not overlap. In order to see this perspective through in the real world, services need to be positioned as the official access points for the logic they encapsulate, as demonstrated in Figure 9.10. The level to which Logic Centralization is achieved determines the extent to which it becomes an enterprise-wide standard.

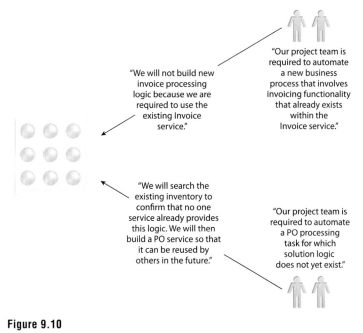

Figure 9.10

Logic Centralization introduces rules as to how solution logic is built in relation to a service inventory that acts as a central repository for agnostic services. These rules affect project teams regardless of whether logic already exists for the systems they are building.

Although this fundamental design pattern applies to all services, it is the reusable services that require extra attention. Services that provide business process-specific functionality are less likely to be duplicated as they are responsible for automating specific business tasks.

> **NOTE**
>
> Service Normalization is the basis of its own design pattern which is further discussed in the *Service Contract Autonomy* section in Chapter 10.

Logic Centralization as an Enterprise Standard

When solution logic for new processes is being created, there is always the risk that the project team will build logic that already resides within an existing reusable service.

Common reasons for this are:

- The project team is not aware of the service's existence or capabilities because the service is not sufficiently discoverable or interpretable.

- The project team refuses to use the service because it is considered burdensome to do so.

While the former scenario can be avoided through the application of the Service Discoverability principle and the existence of a central service registry (see Chapter 12), the latter issue is generally addressed by the use of an enterprise design standard that dictates that reusable services must always be used as intended, even if they do not yet possess all required functions. For example, if a new capability needed by a project team clearly falls within the boundary of an existing service, the corresponding functionality needs to be added to that service instead of ending up elsewhere (as illustrated by the project team dialog at the bottom of Figure 9.10).

Logic Centralization and Contract Centralization

In Chapter 6 we introduced Contract Centralization, another fundamental design pattern that focuses on the standardized positioning of the service contract as the primary (or sole) entry point into service logic.

As important as it is to clearly differentiate Logic and Contract Centralization, it is equally important to understand how these two patterns can and should be used together:

- While Logic Centralization asks designers to build consumer programs that only invoke designated services when specific types of information processing are required, it does not address how this logic is to be accessed.

- While Contract Centralization asks designers to build consumer programs that access a service only via its published contract, it does not specify which services should be accessed for what purpose.

As illustrated in Figure 9.11, combining these patterns forms an architecture that is not just highly standardized, but also naturally normalized and in which loosely coupled service-consumer relationships are intrinsically fostered.

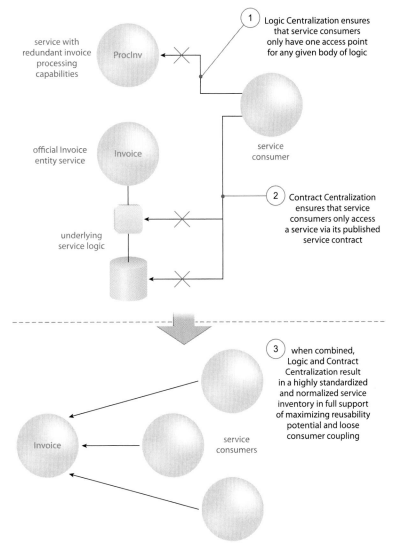

Figure 9.11

Combining Logic and Contract Centralization results in the positioning of central entry points into central bodies of logic.

Centralization and Web Services

When implementing centralized services as Web services, there is increased emphasis on the design of the Web service contract. The fact that a service's WSDL, XML schema, and WS-Policy definitions must now accurately represent an official endpoint (as per Contract Centralization) to an official body of logic (as per Logic Centralization) requires that contract details be carefully designed to accommodate the service's role and position as a centralized resource (Figure 9.12).

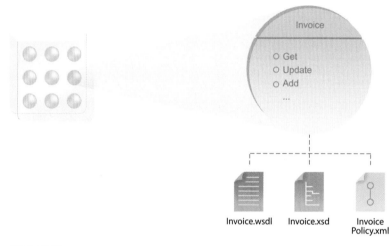

Figure 9.12

An Invoice service implemented as a Web service can support Logic and Contract Centralization by establishing a central Web service contract.

These considerations need to be balanced against the possibilities of centralizing (and thereby sharing) the Web service's underlying schemas and policies. As previously illustrated in Figures 6.8 and 6.9 in Chapter 6, XML schemas and policies can establish separate architectural layers that may limit their ability to accommodate service-specific requirements. Often, however, this can be addressed with the right blend of generalized and specialized schema and policy definitions.

Challenges to Achieving Logic Centralization

As straight-forward as Logic Centralization may sound, it can be enormously difficult to achieve on an enterprise-wide basis. In larger organizations, attaining a state where all development project teams agree not to build redundant logic and instead use existing services is sometimes an unattainable ideal.

Several additional architectural design patterns exist to accommodate this very issue, the foremost of which is the Domain Inventory pattern, which allows for standardization requirements to be contained within domain-specific service inventories that each represent a subset of the overall enterprise. Not only does this make Logic Centralization more attainable, it allows for an SOA initiative to proceed in phases, on a per-domain basis.

Further details are discussed in the *Risks Associated with Service Reusability* section at the end of this chapter.

BEST PRACTICE

There is a common misperception that in order to attain the strategic benefits associated with SOA it must be implemented on an enterprise-wide basis. In larger environments, this can lead an organization to take on more than it can handle in terms of the scope and magnitude of change that can come with an enterprise-wide transition, or it can lead the organization to simply reject SOA altogether.

There is no disputing that building a global, enterprise-wide service-oriented architecture is ideal. However, as previously explained, it is not the sole option. For some organizations, a domain-based approach is the only feasible means of transitioning toward SOA. It is therefore highly recommended that as part of any SOA planning effort, the Domain Inventory pattern be seriously considered.

SUMMARY OF KEY POINTS

- Logic Centralization requires project teams and IT staff to use designated services as the primary or sole means of accessing information sets and associated capabilities.

- When positioned as an enterprise standard, it may be impractical to apply Logic Centralization across an entire enterprise, especially within larger organizations. Therefore, the option to apply it to subsets of the enterprise, as per the Domain Inventory pattern can be explored.

- Most of the obstacles to achieving Logic Centralization to a meaningful extent are organizational and cultural in nature.

9.6 Service Reusability and Service Design

The pursuit of reusability can shift design priorities and change the overall process by which we design self-contained software. In the following sections we explore some of the specific ways this principle impacts service design.

Service Reusability and Service Modeling

Service Reusability is one of the three service-orientation principles taken into account during the service-oriented analysis stage (the other two being Service Autonomy and Service Discoverability). When conceptualizing services as part of a service modeling exercise, we are specifically asked to further refine service candidates by taking reusability considerations into account.

Just about everything discussed so far in this chapter can be applied to the definition of a service candidate, including the positioning of "official" service candidates via Logic Centralization and classification via reusability levels. The commercial product design influences also come into play; modeling a service candidate is very much like the early drafting stages of a product design, except for the fact that we are continually interested in how a service candidate relates to others within an inventory.

In relation to Service Reusability, we are specifically focused on exploring the following aspects:

- The refinement of existing service capability candidates so as to make them more generic and reusable.

- The definition of additional service capability candidates that go beyond the functionality required for the automation of the business process that formed the basis of the service modeling process.

The latter point is more encouraged when modeling services as opposed to building them. Because we are not yet committing to a physical design and implementation, there is little risk in exploring how a service could be extended to provide a range of reusable capabilities.

Because services are being defined during a preliminary analysis phase, there is a real opportunity to leverage the insight and expertise of business subject matter experts that may not be as involved in subsequent project stages.

Any additional capabilities defined at this point are simply candidates for potential capabilities that we may or may not choose to build right away. Having documented them, though, provides us with a better understanding of the direction in which a service may evolve. Furthermore, defining a wider range of potential capabilities up-front helps us to better position and align the capabilities that will actually need to be delivered in the short-term.

Note that service candidates were first introduced in the *Service-Oriented Analysis and Design* section of Chapter 3. Additional information about service candidates and the service-oriented analysis and service modeling processes is provided in Appendix B.

Service Reusability and Granularity

Positioning a service as a reusable enterprise resource directly influences all forms of granularity considerations, as follows:

Service Granularity

Service granularity is often streamlined in support of reusability—the rationale being that a service with a narrower focus is more easily reused because it brings with it less baggage than one with a more coarse-grained level of service granularity. Reducing service granularity can also distribute the processing demands of agnostic logic across more service implementations.

Even though the Service Reusability principle will tend to raise service granularity levels, the performance repercussions of having to later compose together numerous fine-grained services need to be carefully assessed, as further discussed in Chapter 13.

Capability Granularity

Reusable service capabilities can be created to support a variety of usage scenarios and a range of input and output values. This approach leads to coarser-grained capabilities that appear to be more reusable because they truly are multi-purpose service extensions.

However, this can result in challenges associated with imposing excess data exchange and processing requirements upon service consumers and service-oriented solutions as a whole. For example, a coarse-grained capability may be so generic that it returns a large amount of data to consumers, many of which only require a subset.

Therefore, the application of the Service Reusability principle often leads to the necessity of defining coarse *and* fine-grained versions of similar capabilities. This is accomplished via the use of the Contract Denormalization design pattern, as explained in the *Service Contract Autonomy* section of Chapter 10.

Data Granularity

The document-centric messaging style of services has led to a noticeable reduction of data granularity, especially when compared to the fine-grained parameter data exchanges that were so common with RPC-based solutions. Although somewhat moderated through the use of the aforementioned Contract Denormalization pattern, the asynchronous exchange patterns and additional processing overhead that come with the use of a messaging framework have definitely increased the need for coarse data exchanges when building reusable services as Web services.

Constraint Granularity

To make service capabilities as reusable as possible requires that they be as easily consumed as possible. This places a direct emphasis on the reduction of detailed validation logic, leading to coarser-grained constraints.

Service Reusability and Service Models

Service models provide a proven means of planning and building services with reuse potential—and—providing criteria for clearly distinguishing reusable from non-reusable service contexts. In fact, the driving motivation behind creating service models was to support the definition of agnostic service logic. Therefore, all service models play a part in fostering reusability within a service inventory.

The agnostic focus of entity and utility services is clearly intended to provide a functional context suitable for the encapsulation of reusable logic. Because they provide a central location for non-agnostic logic, task services also support reusability by alleviating agnostic services from having to deal with business process logic.

How Service Reusability Affects Other Principles

Being such a prominent part of service-orientation, the principle of Service Reusability influences all other principles (Figure 9.13).

Service Reusability and Standardized Service Contract

Though contract standardization applies to any service, details of the technical interface (such as how data types are constructed and constraints are defined) are almost always influenced by the need for the contract to be kept as generic as possible. A reusable service needs to be flexible enough to support multiple consumers with reasonably different interaction requirements. This requirement can inspire design standards that reduce contract validation constraints (especially ones prone to change).

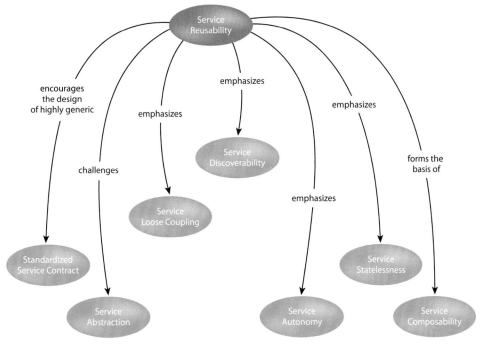

Figure 9.13
This principle is fundamental to service-orientation and therefore affects every other principle to various extents.

Service Reusability and Service Abstraction

For services to maximize their reuse potential, there is an inclination to make contracts as self-descriptive as possible. However, this must be balanced with the consideration that reusable services are positioned to facilitate multiple service consumers, some of which will be unknown at the time the service is deployed. As a result, it is also important for the service contract to be concise so that it does not describe or constrain itself in a way that would inhibit its future reuse. All of this comes down to how much service meta information should be abstracted.

Service Reusability and Service Loose Coupling

Service Reusability emphasizes loose service coupling because the lower the dependency requirements of a service, the more easily it can be reused. Therefore, when pursuing reusability in service logic, there is often a tendency to reduce constraints in service contracts.

For example, a service is more easily kept agnostic to business processes when validation rules can be deferred away from the contract and into the underlying service logic. Although this increases the processing burden of the logic, it prevents the initial service design from inadvertently becoming incompatible with future service consumers. Increasing the longevity or lifespan of a service contract enables the service to extend its availability and value as a reusable resource. Reducing and even minimizing coupling requirements is an effective means of achieving this.

Service Reusability and Other Principles

Because much of service-orientation is centered around the overall notion of fostering reuse, when we apply this principle the importance of others is further amplified.

- *Service Autonomy*—Because of the potentially high performance and concurrent usage demands on reusable services, the extent of control they can exercise over their underlying environment is an important design consideration in guaranteeing an acceptable level of predictable behavior. For example, Logic Centralization and composition requirements will demand increased autonomy for services to maintain this guarantee as the quantity of service consumers grows and the complexity of compositions increases.

- *Service Statelessness*—By minimizing the amount of its state management responsibilities, the availability of a service is increased. This is directly associated with the service's ability to be effectively scaled in response to high reuse requirements.

- *Service Discoverability*—For enterprise-wide reuse and Logic Centralization to be accomplished, reusable services must be discoverable and interpretable. A reusable service being delivered as part of a serious effort to build a service inventory must be equipped with all of the meta data required for it to be located and for its purpose and capabilities to be clearly understood.

- *Service Composability*—As explained in Chapter 13, composing services can be seen as a form of reuse. Our goal is usually not to design services for one specific composition, but instead to position each service as an effective composition member capable of participating in multiple composition configurations. The extent to which we can accomplish this goal is rooted in the degree of reusability the service offers. The greater the reuse potential, the greater the opportunities for the service to be repeatedly composed.

Reuse does not alter the way these principles are applied; it simply emphasizes their importance to the extent that the design characteristics they promote become required qualities of an effectively reusable service.

SUMMARY OF KEY POINTS

- Service Reusability is a fundamental principle that affects all others.

- Reusability amplifies the importance of service-orientation in that it asks us to ensure that supporting principles are successfully applied to achieve its goals.

9.7 Risks Associated with Service Reusability and Commercial Design

As much as reusability is considered a desirable quality, positioning reusable services as centralized enterprise resources introduces some potentially significant challenges.

Cultural Concerns

Introducing Service Reusability via Logic Centralization into an organization that does not have a history of fostering reuse or using design standards in general will almost always raise cultural issues with some of the groups affected by service delivery projects (Figures 9.14 and 9.15).

Examples of concerns common to IT departments and project teams are:

- Existing project plans and processes are impacted by requiring the involvement of reusable services as part of their existing development projects.

- There may be resistance to giving up control of solution designs if teams are forced to include existing reusable services or produce new services that need to be reusable.

- Some developers may resist having to work with reusable services as it can inhibit their creativity and may prevent them from fully customizing programming routines or streamlining solution logic.

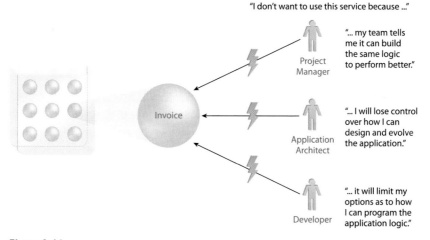

Figure 9.14

Common cultural concerns that arise when project teams are required to comply with the Logic Centralization of specific reusable services.

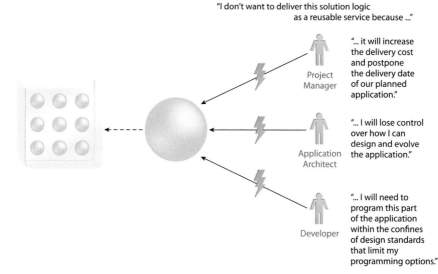

Figure 9.15

Even if project teams are required to build solution logic that does not yet exist, there are often issues with doing so when they are mandated to deliver this logic in the form of a reusable service that will be made available to other teams as well.

These concerns need to be addressed prior to the delivery of reusable services. Otherwise, the strategic goals associated with the overarching SOA initiative can be compromised. If only partial support for the delivery and usage of reusable services is received within an IT division, the risk of ending up with a denormalized service inventory and a potentially convoluted enterprise architecture is ever-present.

Governance Concerns

When a high percentage of a service inventory is comprised of reusable services, traditional governance approaches are no longer applicable. The agnostic nature of these services turns them into units of solution logic without any direct association to a business process, application, or user base.

Because traditional project teams are built around the delivery of standalone applications (as opposed to services), they typically own the maintenance responsibilities of the applications they deliver. Therefore, as illustrated in Figure 9.16, there is a lower demand for resources dedicated to the enterprise as a whole.

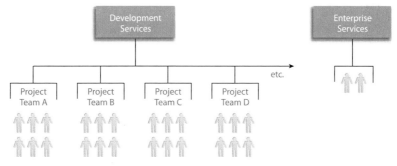

Figure 9.16

A look at resource allocation in traditional enterprises. Project teams own the development and maintenance of individual applications, carrying forward the well-known siloed approach. Enterprise architects and others concerned with the overall infrastructure comprise a fraction of the total IT staff.

The unique governance requirements of service-oriented architectures often introduce the need for the organizational structure of IT environments to be augmented. An infrastructure services group or an enterprise architecture group (often combined with business domain groups) is usually required to assume custodianship of agnostic services so as to ensure their usage and proper evolution.

Over time, this results in a shift where resources for individual project teams are decreased and the size of enterprise-centric groups increases, as shown in Figure 9.17.

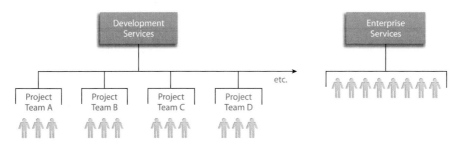

Figure 9.17

Because the delivery of solution logic requires less time and effort after a service inventory is established, the size of project teams is reduced. However, the increased governance requirements of the service inventory results in a need for larger enterprise groups.

Without a governance structure in place, reusable service designs run the risk of becoming skewed to suit the needs of the projects that are responsible for their immediate delivery or extension. Furthermore, an absence of governance processes decreases the likelihood of achieving and maintaining Logic Centralization.

NOTE

Governance is a large topic encompassing processes, technology platforms, and patterns of its own. A separate title as part of the *Prentice Hall Service-Oriented Computing Series from Thomas Erl* is being planned specifically about SOA governance.

FOR EXAMPLE

An organization in the regional public sector carried out an SOA initiative several years ago, resulting in the creation of over 100 services. The majority of these services was delivered specifically with reuse in mind. The standard project delivery stages were even further appended with an extra quality assurance phase dedicated to rigorous testing beyond the immediate requirements for which the services were being built.

As more and more services were delivered, an increasing amount of reuse opportunities did present themselves. Details about each completed service were posted on the local intranet as part of an online catalog, complete with links to the locations of the implemented service and its source code. Project teams interested in using existing services were encouraged to browse the catalog and choose those most suitable for their requirements.

Those who wanted to use existing services were only asked to notify the administrators of the servers hosting the services. Those who needed to extend a service could simply check out the source code and hand it over to their developers.

Over the next six months, the following occurred:

- Seven separate project teams had created different variations of several reusable services, each skewed toward their immediate requirements.

- Three solutions that accessed 12 of the existing reusable services ended up imposing unanticipated and erratic performance demands, causing periodic latency for all service consumer programs.

- During two of the seven projects, the logic that resided in an existing reusable service was simply rebuilt in a completely different manner (and in one case, not as a service at all).

A subsequent survey of the enterprise revealed a convoluted architecture comprised of several services providing redundant logic in different implementations. IT managers agreed that if this continued, none of their anticipated strategic goals would be attained. Several measures were then taken to introduce a formal governance methodology.

By defining the processes and roles required for the proper administration of reusable services, managers pinpointed the source of the original problem: they had allowed services intended as enterprise resources to be maintained within a project-and silo-centric culture.

The following are some highlights among the many changes they introduced:

- Designated service custodians were established to take ownership over reusable services.

- The Enterprise Architecture team, which previously consisted of three individuals, grew into a new IT department comprised of over 20 architects.

- Each new project team was required to work with service custodians and enterprise architects to ensure that reusable services were appropriately incorporated and extended.

For more information about organizational roles that relate to the application of service-orientation, see Chapter 15.

Reliability Concerns

Services that are successfully reused can introduce significant risk associated with enterprise-wide reliability. Reusable services essentially establish a single point of failure for multiple automated business processes.

For example, should the server hosting a centrally established service go down, all of the service consumers depending on its availability would need to go into exception handling mode, which could have a ripple effect throughout the enterprise.

There are design patterns that address this concern by proposing multiple implementations of key services. These patterns rely on traditional fail-over measures, such as the use of clustering technologies. Again, though, these measures need to be applied prior to the service becoming a physically centralized part of the enterprise.

Security Concerns

One of the most challenging parts of reusable service design is building the service so that it can accommodate the security requirements of the information it is responsible for processing, as well as the security requirements of its potential service consumers.

A service that is delivered without taking security constraints into account will likely introduce the need for new versions to be released, which predictably results in functional redundancy. For example, there may be three known types of consumers the service is expected to interact with. Each can represent a different level of security clearance, which may tie directly to the manner in which information is exchanged and perhaps even relate to the type of functions exposed by the service contract.

Commercial Design Requirement Concerns

Commercial design relies upon the judgment of the subject matter experts that conceptualize and design the commercial products. Similarly, subject matter experts play a critical role in SOA projects as key contributors to the service-oriented analysis and service modeling phases.

A measure of risk is therefore present when services are delivered in response to tactical delivery requirements. Decreasing the up-front analysis as part of reduced top-down efforts correspondingly decreases the amount of opportunity subject matter experts have to shape service candidates and the inventory blueprint as a whole.

Furthermore, analysts and architects involved with these processes need to be sufficiently proficient in dealing with the extra requirements that come with applying commercial design considerations. Even with the most generous timeline, having under-qualified resources involved in finalizing the service design can prove equally hazardous.

Agile Delivery Concerns

Building a highly reusable service is an investment in time and money. The required design effort often involves preparatory research and analysis phases that may need to be completed by multiple subject matter experts. All of this extra effort adds to the delivery overhead and, especially when required to produce the initial releases of reusable services, this overhead can significantly tax project resources.

In environments where agile development approaches are required to address short-term and tactical business goals, fostering Service Reusability can be difficult. Demanding that project teams build high levels of reusability into services can have potentially negative repercussions when critical business goals can only be fulfilled through rapid solution delivery.

Reuse is most commonly associated with the increase of ROI over the long-term and the eventual increase in organizational agility—a point at which the delivery of solutions becomes significantly more agile due to the availability of more standardized, reusable services. Once achieved, these strategic benefits can transform an IT enterprise into a highly effective, streamlined part of an organization. However, the pursuit of this future state needs to be balanced with tactical priorities so as to not put the organization itself in jeopardy.

SUMMARY OF KEY POINTS

- The greatest challenges and risks to achieving reusability within services on a consistent basis are primarily organizational.

- Infrastructures and architectures need to be designed to accommodate increased security, performance, and reliability concerns.

- Building services with high reusability results in prolonged delivery processes that can run contrary to tactical fulfillment requirements and agile development methodologies.

- The initial delivery of reusable services can be counter-agile but the availability of these services eventually leads to an environment in which the agility of solution delivery is dramatically increased.

9.8 CASE STUDY EXAMPLE

As explained in Chapter 7, the Inventory service was designed in response to the coupling-related limitations identified in the original InvLegacyAPI Web service. The primary enhancement introduced by the Inventory service was a customized service contract that supported the standardized complex types in the Inventory Item schema. Aside from that, though, the original InvLegacyAPI operations continued to be supported.

Both Materials and Formulas services were designed to support their agnostic entity contexts in order to maximize their reusability potential. Cutit architects now turn their attention to applying the same rigor to the Inventory service design.

The Inventory Service Profile

The operations listed in Table 9.2 were defined prior to the SOA initiative because the wrapper InvLegacyAPI Web service needed to be positioned as an endpoint into the inventory legacy system for (primarily point-to-point) integration requirements. Those operations that directly encapsulate legacy API functions had their names derived from the corresponding function names. The others were added using the same naming convention to keep the contract consistent.

Inventory Service	
AddItem Operation	Input: standard inventory item document Output: acknowledgement code
GetItem Operation	Input: unique inventory identifier Output: standard inventory item document
GetItemCount Operation	Input: unique inventory identifier Output: stock level value
RemoveItems Operation	Input: unique inventory identifier for each item to be removed from inventory Output: acknowledgment code

Table 9.2
The contract profile for the Inventory service.

Assessing Current Capabilities

The newly defined Inventory service has a greater responsibility than its predecessor. It is not only here to serve as an integration endpoint, but also as the official entry point for processing associated with the inventory item business entity. As a result, the service contract is closely reviewed with an emphasis on facilitating service consumers beyond the Run Lab Project service.

Cutit Saws cannot afford to outfit any of its initial services with a full range of reusable capabilities. However, it does want to make the most out of this delivery project and therefore decides to work toward a targeted enhancement measure for the Inventory service.

The Run Lab Project service needs to compose the following Inventory service operations:

- *GetItem*—Used to retrieve an inventory item record that can then be examined by a lab team member prior to deciding on whether to use it.

- *GetItemCount*—Used to retrieve the in-stock quantity of a particular item. Sometimes a certain quantity is required, and if the required amount is not available, an order needs to be immediately placed (or alternative items can be considered).

- *RemoveItems*—When one or more items are chosen, this operation decreases the stock level.

The existing AddItem operation has been in place to support other integration requirements.

Modeling for a Targeted Measure of Reusability

Business analysts responsible for various types of processes involving accounting and inventory control procedures are consulted to help assess the most immediate and critical inventory item-related functions that upcoming business processes will require.

The discussions identify the following additional capabilities:

- Revising the cost of an existing inventory item record (usually in response to changing vendor prices).

- Generating a particular type of stock levels report that, based on specific criteria, summarizes all items nearing dangerously low stock quantities. This report would be used as the basis for a regular re-ordering (or advance ordering) process.

The architects and analysts collaborated on a service modeling process where the existing Inventory service definition is subjected to the new requirements. Originally it was expected that this would simply end up extending the existing service contract. However, because this iteration through the service modeling steps was focused primarily on enhancing reuse, other ideas surfaced.

After various options were explored, the following changes were agreed upon:

The New EditItemRecord Operation

An EditItemRecord operation was added, specifically qualified with the term "Record" because it was determined that AddItemRecord and DeleteItemRecord operations would also soon be needed. These are different from the existing AddItem and RemoveItem operations in that the former actually inserts and deletes inventory item records in the legacy system database, whereas the latter two only increase and decrease inventory item quantity values.

Additionally, even though the immediate requirement was for the ability to change inventory item costs, this new operation allows any editable part of an inventory item record to be updated, including its cost.

The New ReportStockLevels Operation

Both analysts and architects agree that the Inventory service could do with a generic operation capable of accepting a range of criteria limited to generating stock quantity-related reports, including the specific "low stock quantity" report identified as an upcoming requirement. The new operation is tentatively called ReportStockLevels.

However, due to a convoluted physical data model and some technical limitations associated with the legacy systems database, it is discovered that the ability to generate the required stock levels report is actually not possible. Essentially, because of the specific search criteria, the query ended up running several hours before returning results.

Cutit has a modest but central data warehouse repository that receives periodic imports from all primary databases (including the inventory system database). Various queries probing stock levels are tried out, all with acceptable results. It is decided to implement the new operation so that it accesses the data warehouse instead of the legacy inventory system under the condition that data warehouse repository refresh cycles for inventory item data are increased.

The New AdjustItemsQuantity Operation

The original AddItem operation accepted a quantity value for a particular item record and then increased the recorded stock level of the item accordingly. The accompanying RemoveItems operation allowed multiple item ID and quantity values as input, subsequently reducing stock levels. The main reason an AddItems operation was not created to support a similar range of input values had to do with a limitation of the API.

It was originally thought that the new EditItemRecord operation could now replace these older operations by allowing service consumers to submit new item record documents with updated quantity values. However, during the service modeling process, it was discussed how this particular function is required repeatedly, not just within the Lab Project business process, but in several others as well. It therefore would make sense to define a more targeted operation, even if its functionality is somewhat redundant. Essentially, this operation would not accept an entire inventory item document as input, but only the inventory item ID and the revised quantity value.

Analysts suggest combining the original AddItem and RemoveItems operations into a single AdjustItemQuantity operation that would be able to increase or decrease the quantity of any given inventory item. Architects investigate the feasibility of accomplishing this, given the known API limitations. They come up with a solution that requires them to bypass the API and access the legacy database directly.

They furthermore suggest that the operation could also allow for a range of items to be received and processed at the same time. The result is the new AdjustItemsQuantity operation capable of accepting a range of item IDs and quantity values.

Revised Inventory Service Profile

Table 9.3 shows how the Inventory service's contract changed after a reusability-centric remodeling and redesign effort.

By working toward a targeted measure of enhancement for the Inventory service, several new processing requirements were accommodated. These establish capabilities that are known to be useful for multiple business processes and are also capable of carrying out their functions in an efficient manner.

Inventory Service	
AdjustItemsQuantity Operation	Input: unique inventory identifier for each item to be removed from inventory Output: acknowledgement code
EditItemRecord Operation	Input: standard inventory item document Output: acknowledgment code
GetItem Operation	Input: unique inventory identifier Output: standard inventory item document
GetItemCount Operation	Input: unique inventory identifier Output: stock level value
ReportStockLevels Operation	Input: query criteria Output: summary in report format

Table 9.3
The revised contract profile for the Inventory service.

Chapter 10

Service Autonomy
(Processing Boundaries and Control)

S ervice-orientation brings with it a serious attitude when it comes to decomposition. When assembling a service inventory, there is an extreme emphasis on positioning each service of that inventory as a standalone building block. Autonomy therefore almost always ties into the design of what lies beneath the service contract (Figure 10.1).

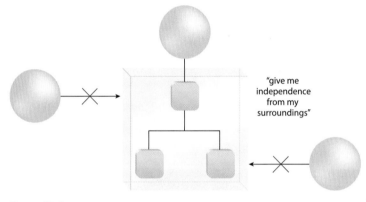

Figure 10.1
Autonomy represents the independence of a service implementation.

10.1 Autonomy Explained

Following is a brief overview of autonomy both as a general design concept and design characteristic. This abstract perspective helps us later associate autonomy with the overall goals of the service-orientation paradigm.

Autonomy in Abstract

Autonomy represents the ability to self-govern. Something that is autonomous has the freedom and control to make its own decisions without the need for external approval or involvement. Therefore, the level to which something is autonomous represents the extent to which it is able to act independently.

If a software program exists in an autonomous runtime state, it is capable of carrying out its logic independently from outside influences. It therefore must have the control to govern itself at runtime. The more control the program has over its runtime execution environment, the more autonomy it can claim.

To achieve increased levels of autonomy requires that program implementations be more isolated so as to increase corresponding levels of independence. The result of achieving enhanced autonomy in software programs is increased reliability and predictability due to the increased independence and isolation in which the programs operate.

NOTE
It is important to acknowledge that for a service, autonomy is a quality that represents its ability to carry out its core service logic independently. The level of a service's autonomy can be enhanced by increasing the amount of control it has over its runtime execution environment. For simplicity's sake, we refer to this level of control as a level of autonomy.

Origins of Autonomy

The more independent a system is from unpredictable outside influences, the more reliable it will be. Predictability and reliability are two of the main factors that make autonomy a key design consideration.

However, historically autonomy as a design characteristic of custom-developed solution logic has not always received as much attention as it does now. For example, it has traditionally been a quality more associated with a runtime platform or environment as a whole, rather than with individual components of solution logic. Often autonomy was sometimes pursued by deploying applications onto dedicated servers.

Autonomy within distributed architectures was frequently associated with the deployment environment for groups of related components. It started to become an issue for individual components when they were actually shared to a significant extent or if they provided some form of mission critical functionality. Autonomy is a quality we now look to establish on a service-by-service basis primarily because loss of autonomy is commonplace within service compositions (as explained further in this chapter).

SUMMARY OF KEY POINTS

- Autonomy, in relation to software, represents the independence with which a program can carry out its logic.

- Two primary benefits of raising the level of autonomy within a program are to increase its reliability and behavioral predictability.

10.2 Profiling this Principle

For services to provide a consistently reliable and predictable level of performance as members of a service inventory and as members of complex compositions, they must exist as self-sufficient parts of the enterprise. This requires services to possess a significant degree of control over their underlying resources. Autonomy represents this measure, and this principle emphasizes the need for individual services to have high levels of individual autonomy, as further described in Table 10.1.

Principle Profile	
Short Definition	*"Services are autonomous."*
Long Definition	*"Services exercise a high level of control over their underlying runtime execution environment."*
Goals	• To increase a service's runtime reliability, performance, and predictability, especially when being reused and composed.
	• To increase the amount of control a service has over its runtime environment.
	By pursuing autonomous design and runtime environments, we are essentially aiming to increase post-implementation control over the service and the service's control over its own execution environment.
Design Characteristics	• Services have a contract that expresses a well-defined functional boundary that should not overlap with other services.
	• Services are deployed in an environment over which they exercise a great deal (and preferably an exclusive level) of control.
	• Service instances are hosted by an environment that accommodates high concurrency for scalability purposes.
Implementation Requirements	• A high level of control over how service logic is designed and developed. Depending on the level of autonomy being sought, this may also involve control over the supporting data models.

	• A distributable deployment environment, so as to allow the service to be moved, isolated, or composed as required.
	• An infrastructure capable of supporting desired autonomy levels.
Web Service Region of Influence	Service Autonomy is almost exclusively focused on the service implementation, with an emphasis on the core service logic and any resources it may need at runtime. However, the service contract is also affected due to normalization considerations (as explained later). core service logic message processing logic service contract Web service **Figure 10.2**

Table 10.1
A profile for the Service Autonomy principle.

SUMMARY OF KEY POINTS

- Autonomy supports the reusability and composability of services.

- Achieving increased Service Autonomy can introduce significant infrastructure requirements.

10.3 Types of Service Autonomy

The following sections compare the two primary forms of autonomy associated with services. They are significantly different in the design considerations they raise but do share a link in our overall goal of positioning services as independent, self-governing members of a service inventory.

Runtime Autonomy (execution)

The level of control a service has over its processing logic at the time the service is invoked and executing is called *runtime autonomy*. The primary objective of increasing runtime autonomy is to guarantee the following to service consumers:

- consistently acceptable runtime execution performance

- a greater degree of performance reliability

- the option for it to be isolated in response to specific security, reliability, or performance requirements

- a greater level of behavioral predictability (especially when concurrently accessed)

The more a service is comprised of logic or resources that are shared by other parts of the enterprise, the less it is able to make the types of quality of service claims just listed. The primary reason these claims are so important to service-orientation is service composition. Because a composition exists as an aggregate of programs (services) that may also be participating in other compositions, it tends to be naturally *non*-autonomous.

Each service that encapsulates and composes logic from another forms a dependency on logic that resides outside of its boundary and therefore outside of its control. As a result, the autonomy of a service encapsulating a service composition is determined by the collective autonomy of all services that participate in the composition.

Further taking into consideration that complex compositions that draw from larger service inventories will have increased amounts of composition members, it becomes evident that the individual autonomy of each service in an inventory becomes increasingly important. When creating complex compositions, we fully accept the fact that an extent of autonomy is lost when composition members consist of agnostic services. This principle essentially attempts to minimize this loss by encouraging high levels of autonomy in all potentially composable services.

> **NOTE**
>
> See the *Task Services* part of the *Service Autonomy and Service Models* section in this chapter for a diagram that illustrates how autonomy levels decrease further up a typical composition hierarchy.

Design-Time Autonomy (governance)

Regardless of whether a service has control over its runtime execution environment, multiple service consumers will form design-time dependencies on it. This can restrict our ability to evolve a service in response to future change requirements. The level of freedom we, as service owners, have to make changes to a service over its lifetime can be referred to as *design-time autonomy*.

Once consumer programs programmatically bind themselves to a service's contract, the service can no longer escape its obligation to that contract. We therefore automatically lose a degree of control over how the service could be evolved. However, given that baseline constraint, we can still strive to maximize the level of attainable design-time autonomy.

There are several aspects of SOA that drive the need for this quality:

- the ability to scale a service in response to higher usage demands
- the option to further modify or enhance a service's hosting environment
- the freedom to augment, upgrade, or replace the technology of a service in response to new requirements or a desire to leverage new innovations

All of these forms of design-time autonomy can be attained by applying the Service Loose Coupling principle in pursuit of the positive contract coupling types documented in Chapter 7. This is because by fully abstracting the service contract from the underlying implementation environment, we gain the design-time control needed to evolve that environment independently from consumers that bind to the contract. Service Autonomy and Service Loose Coupling therefore have a close relationship, as further explained in the *Service Autonomy and Other Principles* section.

What is of particular importance is how design-time autonomy can relate to runtime autonomy. The more control we have over how a service is designed and developed, the greater our ability to establish a service implementation with increased runtime autonomy. Conversely, the higher the level of runtime autonomy we achieve, the more dedicated the underlying parts of the service implementation are to the service. This increases design-time autonomy because it increases the amount of control we have over how the service can be governed and evolved.

> **NOTE**
>
> The application of the Service Autonomy principle is primarily focused on increasing service runtime autonomy. However, its relationship to design-time autonomy is an important related design factor worth keeping in mind because it also ties into the close association between Service Autonomy and Service Loose Coupling principles.

SUMMARY OF KEY POINTS

- Runtime autonomy represents the amount of control a service has over its execution environment at runtime.

- Design-time autonomy represents the amount of governance control a service owner has over the service design.

- As a rule of thumb, the greater the amount of design-time autonomy, the greater the amount of attainable runtime autonomy.

10.4 Measuring Service Autonomy

Each service will naturally have requirements and constraints that will dictate the extent of achievable independence with which it can be evolved and operated. Even though Service Abstraction encourages us to hide information about the underlying environment of a service, it can be helpful to label services according to the level of autonomy they have to offer. Such labels can be used in documentation published alongside a technical service contract, such as an SLA.

Being able to clearly communicate a service's measure of autonomy can help set appropriate expectations in relation to performance and reliability. This, in turn, can aid service consumer designers in making better design decisions.

Provided in this section is a set of generic categories, each representing a common autonomy level. You will notice that these levels are sometimes directly associated with how a service is designed and the nature of the logic it is required to encapsulate. Feel free to use these categories as a starting point to derive your own.

- Service Contract Autonomy

- Shared Autonomy

- Service Logic Autonomy

- Pure Autonomy

Note that the latter three levels are usually measured on a per-capability basis but can also be applied to the service as a whole. Table 10.2 provides a brief summary of these levels and is followed by more detailed descriptions.

Level	Description	Focus	Scope	Implementation Isolation
Service Contract	Service contracts are designed in alignment with each other to avoid overlap of expressed functionality.	Contract	Contract	n/a
Shared	The logic and resources that comprise the underlying service implementation are shared with other parts of the enterprise.	Implementation	Capability	None
Service Logic	The underlying logic is isolated, but data resources are shared with other parts of the enterprise.	Implementation	Capability	Partial
Pure	The underlying logic and data resources are isolated and dedicated to the service.	Implementation	Capability	Full

Table 10.2

An overview of Service Autonomy levels, each of which is further explained in the upcoming sections.

Service Contract Autonomy (services with normalized contracts)

One of the primary considerations when populating a service inventory is ensuring that each service establishes a functional boundary that is its own. In other words, the range of capabilities expressed by one service contract should not overlap with the capabilities expressed by others.

Because service contract autonomy is tied to what a service expresses as opposed to how a service is implemented, it is a level that can be attained regardless of the *actual* runtime autonomy the physical service may have.

In other words, even if the expressed functionality does not overlap, underlying service implementations may still overlap. The remaining levels discussed in this section address the autonomy of the actual implementation by categorizing the measure of control the service has over its real-world environment.

Therefore, service contract autonomy can represent a design characteristic that is attainable independently or in addition to the shared, service logic, and pure autonomy levels.

> ### NOTE
>
> Service contract autonomy is more easily attained when the service contract is standardized and decoupled from its underlying implementation. This measure of autonomy is therefore directly supported by the application of the Standardized Service Contract principle, as well as the Service Loose Coupling principle to minimize undesirable contract-to-logic coupling.

Service Contract Autonomy and Service Normalization

"Normalization" is a term borrowed from the world of data modeling where it essentially refers to an approach to reduce or even eliminate redundancy across data entities and structures. For example, a normalized data model would allow only one table in one database to define and contain customer address information, whereas a denormalized data model might define multiple customer address tables.

In the world of service-orientation there is a specific Service Normalization pattern that, when applied, minimizes the amount of *functional* redundancy across a service inventory. Functional normalization is, in fact, one of the primary reasons to invest in the creation of a service inventory blueprint prior to actually building the service inventory. It is through service-oriented analysis and design, with an emphasis on reuse and logic centralization, that we are able to best apply this pattern.

As illustrated in Figure 10.3, if we do not pay attention to avoiding functional overlap, redundancy can creep into a service inventory, resulting in functional denormalization and potentially convoluted composition architectures. An adherence to service normalization results in a well aligned (and streamlined) service inventory, and because redundancy is avoided, the overall quantity of required services (and therefore the overall size of the inventory) is also reduced.

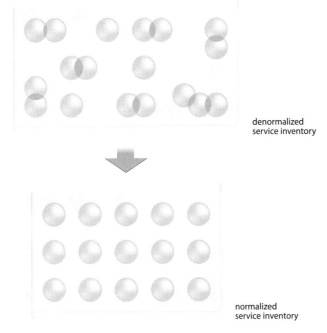

Figure 10.3

Because more redundant logic exists, the denormalized service inventory is required to contain more services (or more service logic) than its normalized counterpart.

Services that are functionally normalized make for better composition members, as their individual roles and capabilities are well-defined. Combine this with the reliability, performance, and predictability benefits that come with increased runtime autonomy, and we end up with services that can be assembled into highly effective compositions.

FOR EXAMPLE

A telecommunications company proceeded with their second SOA project one year ago. The first project was a pilot program that delivered 22 services over the course of eight months by three different project teams. It provided valuable lessons in both service design and governance.

One of the most challenging aspects of the delivery process was the avoidance of building similar services (or services with overlapping functionality). Of the 22 services, eight actually ended up with redundant logic. Though these services were still effective in fulfilling immediate requirements, their eventual governance (and the governance of the service inventory as a whole) became increasingly burdensome.

Project managers vowed not to let this happen again with this second initiative. Even though, as before, project teams would be working in parallel, designated coordinators were assigned to monitor individual service modeling and design efforts. These coordinators would meet regularly to go over the progress of each project and identify any potential service candidates (or service contracts) that had similar functional contexts and capabilities. (In this capacity, a coordinator is similar to the service analyst role described in Chapter 15.)

This project was more successful in achieving a normalized service inventory. However, several project team members expressed dissatisfaction with the quality of the inventory. Even though it was normalized, it was still somewhat project-centric in that the services were geared toward tactical requirements. It was therefore decided to invest in the formal creation of a service inventory blueprint the next time around.

Contract Denormalization

Within the parent context defined by a service, each capability establishes its own functional scope. This scope will usually be associated with a specific task or sub-task. Although capabilities have the luxury of sharing routines and resources *within* the service boundary, from a functional design perspective, we generally strive for each capability to be operationally distinct.

However, it is often unrealistic for one capability to fully accommodate the requirements of all possible consumers for whatever functionality the capability encapsulates. For this reason, the Contract Denormalization design pattern advocates the targeted, intentional denormalization of a service contract.

Figure 10.4, for example, illustrates how a normalized service contract can be further extended with redundant Get capabilities. Whereas the original Get capability retrieves an entire invoice document, GetDetail and GetHeader retrieve only specific subsets.

To keep the service contract fully normalized would require that all service consumers retrieve the entire document. While there is a purity to the contract from a design perspective, this would result in unnecessary data exchange and excess performance overhead for consumers that don't need the whole document each time the capability is invoked.

Figure 10.4

A service with normalized capabilities versus one with partially redundant capabilities.

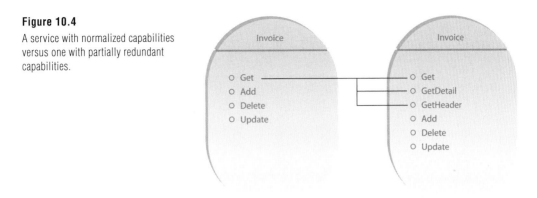

Normalization Patterns and Runtime Autonomy

How does an emphasis on Service Normalization relate to our goal of increasing runtime autonomy? Essentially, these design patterns provide us with an important insight as to how services can be fully optimized to support this principle.

Specifically…

- From a functional service boundary perspective, we want to ensure that services as a whole do not overlap with each other (as per the Service Normalization pattern) because if they do, runtime autonomy is compromised.

- From a functional capability boundary perspective, it is acceptable to denormalize a service contract (as per the Contract Denormalization pattern) because it allows us to maximize the fulfillment of consumer requirements without compromising service autonomy.

Shared Autonomy

For many organizations it is unrealistic to build all services from the ground up. The typical scenario is that some services can be custom programmed, whereas others must encapsulate older legacy technology or applications entrenched within integration architectures (Figure 10.5).

For the latter type of service, the chances of achieving a high level of autonomy can range from improbable to impossible. The service is limited to the characteristics and usage demands of a legacy environment that was most likely never designed with any form of foreign encapsulation in mind. In this case, it is beneficial to clearly categorize the service's autonomy as being low to non-existent. The "shared" label is used to simply indicate that other parts of the enterprise are expected to access (and perhaps even compete for) whatever processing logic may fall within the service boundary.

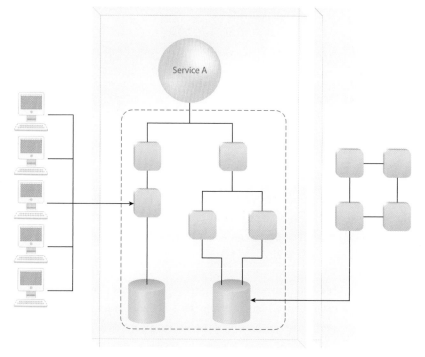

Figure 10.5

An example of shared autonomy: Service A encapsulates a legacy application with an existing user-base and a point-to-point integration channel.

NOTE
Service models are also commonly used to label services based on specific sets of design characteristics. The wrapper service model, for example, specifically represents a service responsible for encapsulating legacy logic and therefore generally implies that a service's autonomy is shared. Issues related to the use of wrapper services are discussed in the *Risks Associated with Service Autonomy* section.

Service Logic Autonomy (partially isolated services)

Service logic autonomy represents perhaps the most common level attained when custom-developing new services. It essentially indicates that underlying service components are dedicated and can be isolated. It is considered a form of partial autonomy because databases, directories, and other resources are still shared between services and other parts of the enterprise (Figure 10.6).

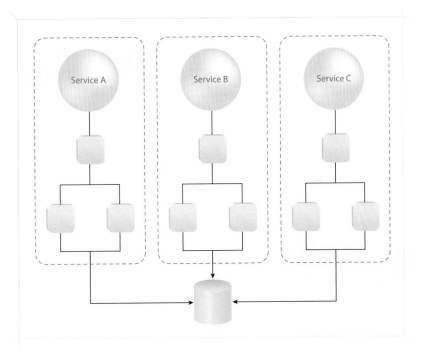

Figure 10.6
Services A, B, and C are each implemented with dedicated components, but all three services share the same database.

The common runtime issues that arise with the absence of a dedicated data access layer are:

- unpredictable levels of concurrent data access

- record or page locking

- prolonged query execution times

These events can affect service runtime performance as follows:

- inconsistent or even unacceptable response times

- occasional unpredictable behavior

- less than optimum scalability

Clearly it is a significant (and often monumental) effort for an organization to adjust or even redo physical data models in support of a service-oriented architecture, which is why this level of autonomy is so common.

Partially Isolated Services at Design-Time

Because distributed environments naturally abstract the data access layer into its own physical tier (usually represented by one or more database servers), we can claim full design-time control over the service's custom-developed components. The processing functionality of the components can be augmented and extended as we see fit, as long as the published service contract continues to be preserved. Further, the component technology itself can be altered or even replaced. For example, if the services are implemented as Web services, we should be able to replace the underlying component technology as long as the new platform is capable of preserving the existing Web service contract and supporting the protocols required to interact with the databases.

Pure Autonomy (isolated services)

The ideal implementation environment for a service is one where it has absolute ownership of its runtime existence and we have top-to-bottom governance over its design and architecture. Pure autonomy therefore represents a category where the service environment is isolated and firmly in our control.

Both functional and data access routines can be customized to provide optimum performance for each service capability. We can further take full advantage of the runtime and any vendor-specific features or extensions it may have to offer. Most importantly, the service can be presented with increased quality of service guarantees.

There are different levels of isolation that can be defined, each of which falls under this category:

Functional Isolation

Service components and physical data models are dedicated, but the service is hosted on a server with others (Figure 10.7).

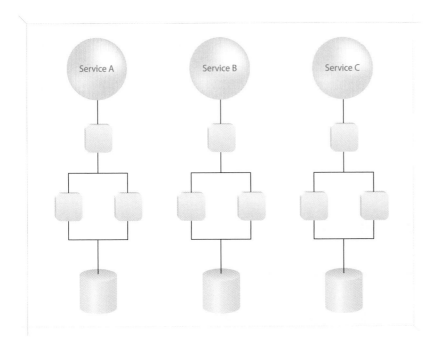

Figure 10.7
Services A, B, and C have separate dedicated databases but still share the system resources of a
single server and runtime.

Absolute Isolation

Service components and associated data models are on a dedicated server (Figure 10.8).

Other variations of this category can exist, some of which will depend on the process isolation features of the vendor platform being used to develop and host the services.

Isolated Services at Design-Time

As with the runtime benefits, pure autonomy also provides the most desirable environment for a service to be evolved over the long term. We have complete governance over its design and hosting environments, and even its data model can be augmented in relative isolation.

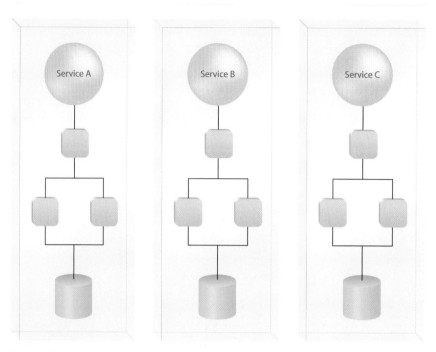

Figure 10.8

Services A, B, and C each have their own, physically isolated hosting environments, providing the ultimate in autonomous computing.

As explored in the *Case Study Example* section at the end of this chapter, the use of replication can be an effective means of supporting increased isolation levels.

Services with Mixed Autonomy

When we label a service with a measure of autonomy, we need to ensure that this measure is representative of the service as a whole. The overall autonomy of some services is relatively easy to assess because they are part of a custom-developed solution environment where all service capabilities draw from the same set of underlying resources.

However, it is not uncommon for services to consist of capabilities that need to access different parts of the enterprise, especially when legacy system encapsulation is required. In this case, the service may very well have capabilities with different autonomy levels, each of which can be assigned its own autonomy level. The service as a whole can then simply be classified as having *mixed autonomy*.

10.5 Autonomy and Service Design

Autonomy tends to be an "enabler" for a service, empowering it with increased self-reliance. Here we briefly explore how realizing this quality can tie into both the analysis and design of services.

Service Autonomy and Service Modeling

Service Autonomy is the second of the three principles that is applied to the analysis of services in addition to their physical design (Service Reusability and Service Discoverability being the other two).

The parent service-oriented analysis process contains an information gathering step dedicated to identifying systems associated with the automation of a particular business process. The collected information provides some insight into potential constraints and limitations in attaining higher levels of autonomy. It further helps technology architects judge the appropriate service granularity levels, as discussed in the upcoming *Service Autonomy and Granularity* section.

Service Autonomy considerations essentially provide some real-world context to the service modeling process. This can keep modeling efforts "down to earth" and prevent the definition of ideal yet unrealistic service inventory blueprints. For more information about service-oriented analysis and service modeling processes, see Appendix B.

Service Autonomy and Granularity

A service can consist of a collection of capabilities, each of which may encapsulate logic from a different system, platform, resource, or technical environment. While from the consumer's perspective, the service contract may provide a clear functional context, behind the scenes, autonomy levels can vary dramatically.

Furthermore, some capabilities may be more mission-critical than others. Perhaps there is a Tax service with a Calculate capability that is utilized far more often than any other in this service, or maybe the Tax service has a ModifyRate capability with strict security controls that don't apply to the remaining service capabilities.

Reliability, performance, and security requirements can motivate project teams to isolate specific capabilities into separate services, thereby resulting in a reduction of the original service granularity. There are several design patterns centered around the use of a façade layer that can accommodate these situations while preserving the service's original functional context.

Also worth noting is that the use of the Contract Denormalization pattern described earlier in the *Service Contract Autonomy* section will lead to the creation of multiple (albeit redundant) finer-grained service capabilities.

Service Autonomy and Service Models

The real-world limitations of most SOA projects will generally not allow each service to attain its optimal autonomy level. The expense required to give a service its own execution environment may be too high, or perhaps legacy encapsulation constraints prohibit attaining a meaningful level of independence.

Therefore, when required to prioritize, it is best to understand which services will benefit the most from increased autonomy. These benefits are especially important when looking ahead to the long-term utilization and evolution of services within a given inventory. Often, an exercise in prioritization will reveal what parts of the inventory blueprint warrant an investment in custom development as opposed to others for which legacy encapsulation may still be adequate.

Entity Services

Services based on business entities benefit the most from increased autonomy levels. These types of business services tend to establish the core service layer within an enterprise and are very likely to be composed by others. (As explored in Chapter 13, individual service autonomy is an important factor of composition performance.)

Because of their intentionally agnostic functional context (and resulting high reuse potential), their runtime usage and design-time evolution become important (and eventually critical) success factors of a service-oriented enterprise effort. Therefore, entity services are prime candidates for pursuing pure autonomy levels, even to the extent of absolute isolation. Additionally, because entity services are often formally modeled as a centralized part of a service inventory blueprint, they are almost always expected to attain high levels of normalization.

Utility Services

Being another key source of agnostic solution logic, the ability for utility services to automate specific, cross-cutting functions is greatly supported when they are built with increased levels of autonomy. As with entity services, utility services are likely candidates for re-composition and similar considerations therefore apply.

Functional normalization and achieving service contract autonomy can sometimes be more challenging with utility services because, unlike entity services, they are not derived or required to be in synch with logical business and data models. They therefore tend to undergo less of a formal modeling effort when it comes to the definition of the service contract and especially its alignment with others.

It can be difficult to predict how a utility service will need to evolve over time and whether its processing context may be required to change. Scalability and concurrency are generally the paramount on-going issues so that all of the other services further up in the composition hierarchy that rely on their availability and predictable behavior are not compromised.

Also due to the fact that utility services are often assigned the responsibility of interacting with and encapsulating legacy APIs, mixed autonomy levels are common. Depending on the nature of the functions provided by a utility service, autonomy measures can easily range from absolute isolation to partial isolation to shared autonomy.

Task Services and Orchestrated Task Services

Because task services generally act as composition controllers, their ability to effectively compose and complete the processing of a given task in a predictable manner can be directly improved through higher levels of autonomy. Because of their dependency on service compositions, task services are often intentionally located within close geographic proximity of the services they need to compose.

Middleware products supplying orchestration engines often require dedicated and even isolated servers, which can naturally increase runtime autonomy. However, the actual gain in autonomy is ultimately related to the quantity of orchestrated task services and business process instances that the environment will need to host.

As controllers, the overall measure of a task service's autonomy is always dependent on the collective autonomy levels of the services (or, more specifically, the service capabilities) that comprise its composition (Figure 10.9). Chapter 13 discusses the relationship between Service Autonomy and service compositions in more in detail and also introduces the concept of "composition autonomy."

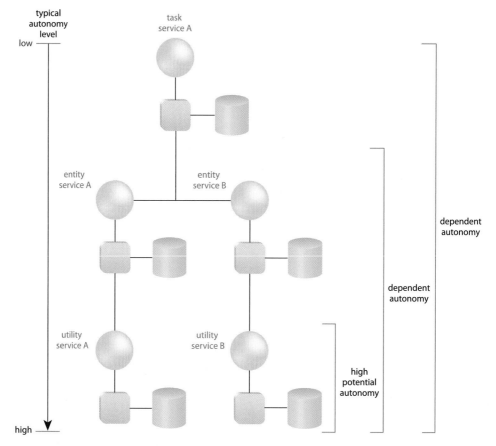

Figure 10.9

As a rule of thumb, the higher up we go in a service composition hierarchy, the more the autonomy of a service will depend on the collective autonomy of the underlying composition.

How Service Autonomy Affects Other Principles

As mentioned earlier, Service Autonomy helps support and even enable the realization of other design principles (Figure 10.10). The following sections explain how.

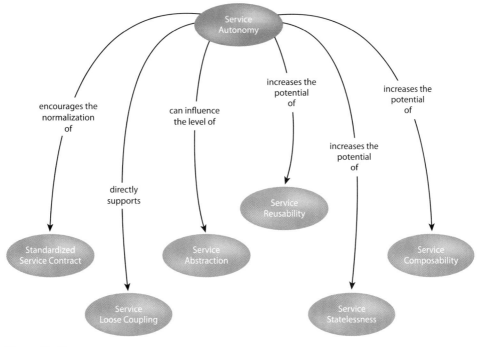

Figure 10.10

By establishing meaningful levels of Service Autonomy, several other principles are supported.

Service Autonomy and Standardized Service Contract

Service contract autonomy is directly tied to the service contract because normalization concerns affect how contracts are shaped and aligned in relation to each other. This principle therefore fully supports and leverages the standardization efforts of the Standardized Service Contract principle. The more control we have over the service contract, the more we can ensure the underlying implementation can be designed independently in support of autonomy, and, the more customized and standardized the service contract, the more we can guarantee this level of control.

Service Autonomy and Service Loose Coupling

When we pursue high levels of autonomy, we work toward establishing freedom and independence for a service. For a service to interact with and compose others, though, requires it to reduce its respective freedom by intentionally forming dependencies on (coupling with) other services.

Therefore, the principle of Service Autonomy very much supports Service Loose Coupling in that both want to minimize the extent of dependency between services. Essentially, autonomy considerations help shape the nature of inter-service coupling, especially in relation to how service coupling ties into the overall structure of service compositions.

These principles are furthermore related through how they affect the design of service contracts. As previously explained in the *Design-Time Autonomy* section, positive forms of contract coupling directly lead to increased design-time autonomy. Increased design-time autonomy, in turn, leads to the ability to further enhance and optimize service implementations in full support of runtime autonomy.

Service Autonomy and Service Abstraction

As we explained previously, it may be beneficial to communicate a service's autonomy level as part of the overall service contract. Therefore, it is one additional piece of information we are deliberately *not* hiding. This does not need to be seen as running contrary to the principle of Service Abstraction, but more so as an occasion to apply this principle with care. Publishing discreet information about a service's autonomy is an example of quality of service information abstraction.

Service Autonomy and Service Reusability

Increased autonomy improves the reuse potential of a service. By making the service more reliable and its behavior more predictable, its logic can be more easily made available to multiple service consumers. Further, by having an increased level of control over its governance, we can modify its hosting environment and scale it to whatever concurrency demands result from its logic being reused more frequently.

Service Autonomy and Service Statelessness

Increasing control over the design of a service enables us to better dictate the extent to which that service is able to manage state information. For example, shared wrapper services forced to encapsulate legacy environments will have little choice but to go along with whatever state management approaches those systems are using. But if a service has functional or pure autonomy, it has the option of being designed to maximize statelessness.

The internally deferred level of statelessness explained in Chapter 11, for example, represents the ultimate in state management deferral options in that it establishes the potential for services to attain a high measure of individual statelessness without having to rely on external architectural state management extensions. This level is only attainable when the service implementation achieves an absolute isolation level of pure autonomy.

Either way, the realization of higher Service Autonomy levels can directly support increased measures of service statelessness.

Service Autonomy and Service Composability

As mentioned previously in the *Task Services* section and as further explored in Chapter 13, the overall autonomy of a service composition can rely on the collective autonomy of its individual members. Therefore, the more reliable and predictable services are, the more effectively they can act as members of a larger service composition.

SUMMARY OF KEY POINTS

- Service Autonomy is one of the three principles applied during both analysis and design stages.

- The higher up a service is in a typical composition hierarchy, the less autonomy it tends to have due to dependencies on other composed services.

- Achieving a higher level of autonomy is an especially important consideration for agnostic services, such as those based on the entity and utility service models.

10.6 Risks Associated with Service Autonomy

Provided here are some common challenges and risks related to this principle.

Misjudging the Service Scope

Once we commit to isolating functionality and even data models in support of one specific service, we establish the service as a standalone, physically separate part of the enterprise architecture. Even though with a higher level of autonomy, we possess a greater deal of control, our control is limited to the scope of the service, as established by the functional context of its service contract.

If during the modeling of the service we miscalculate or misjudge the definition of its scope, it will become very difficult to change, especially after it has been deployed in an isolated environment. This is a risk not just associated with the service, but with each of its capabilities. The functional scope of every service capability needs to be properly measured, especially when capabilities represent different levels of autonomy.

Wrapper Services and Legacy Logic Encapsulation

Services required to encapsulate legacy logic to a significant extent are commonly referred to as *wrapper services*. There are inherent autonomy-related risks associated with these types of services including:

- The service adapter used to implement the service is inflexible and does not allow sufficient customization. This can compromise standardization and discoverability design characteristics.

- The underlying legacy environment is not customizable, thereby jeopardizing the application of other service-orientation principles.

The extent to which autonomy can be attained when implementing services that encapsulate legacy environments will almost always be significantly reduced. Understanding the benefits of autonomy therefore leads to an understanding as to how its loss in legacy-based service-oriented architectures can inhibit some of the strategic benefits of service-orientation.

BEST PRACTICE
It is a good idea to give encapsulated legacy environments a formal autonomy assessment and perhaps even a rating that is published along with the service contract. As long as this is considered acceptable after taking Service Abstraction considerations into account, it will provide potential service consumer designers with valuable insight as to the runtime constraints a service may need to impose.

Overestimating Service Demand

While it may be a safe practice to over-allocate resources for a service, this approach can result in a significant drain on the organization when applied to many highly autonomous services within an inventory. Physically isolating a service is an investment in hardware and software infrastructure and also impacts on-going administration and governance expense and effort. Therefore, even in resource-rich organizations, it is worth assessing the cost of attaining some of the higher levels of autonomy on a service-by-service basis.

Consistently overestimating service usage requirements can somewhat undermine the overarching service-oriented computing objective of creating a more lean and streamlined IT enterprise (as per the reduced IT burden goal).

SUMMARY OF KEY POINTS

- Legacy system encapsulation poses the greatest challenge to applying this principle.

- Providing isolated environments for services that don't require them can unnecessarily inflate implementation costs.

10.7 CASE STUDY EXAMPLE

To date, the architects at Cutit Saws have worked to refine the design of the services (in particular the design of service contracts) in support of automating the Lab Project business process. Now they turn their attention to ensuring that this collection of services will be capable of performing as expected, even considering that services within this planned composition will be reused by others.

The implementation environment for each of the four Web services described so far is studied with an emphasis on expected runtime autonomy levels. This study is performed on an individual operation basis. Following is a highlight of the study, focusing specifically on the architecture of the Inventory service's GetItem operation.

Existing Implementation Autonomy of the GetItem Operation

When required to retrieve an inventory item record, the Inventory service interacts with the legacy system's published API. The corresponding function invokes internal logic that eventually accesses the inventory database to fetch the requested data.

The legacy inventory system supports over 20 existing users that access it via rich client front-ends installed on workstations as part of a classic client-server application architecture. Additionally, several other systems integrate with its API and directly access its underlying database. The database is therefore in constant use. Although it rarely reaches its maximum performance threshold, increased concurrent usage affects its response times, especially for data retrieval commands.

The GetItem operation therefore has a shared level of autonomy, as illustrated in Figure 10.11. In its current state, the service cannot guarantee the response time associated with the execution of this operation.

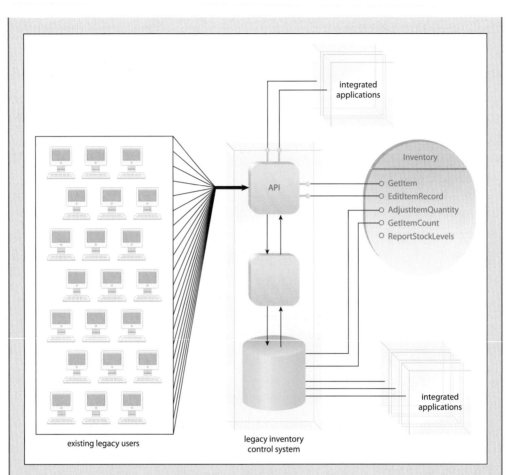

Figure 10.11

The current service operation-level architecture for the GetItem operation illustrates how busy the inventory control environment can get. Desktop users, integrated applications, and even other operations from the same service are all clients that will potentially compete for the same underlying resources at runtime.

New Operation-Level Architecture with Increased Autonomy

Cutit architects consult with analysts to explore the range of potential usage scenarios this operation may need to be involved with. They use the preliminary service inventory blueprint as a reference to map out anticipated service compositions based on known business processes.

It turns out that the retrieval of inventory item records will become one of the most popular pieces of logic within their planned service inventory. They estimate that at least a dozen more business processes will require this capability. This translates into the GetItem operation being reused a comparable amount of times in upcoming service compositions.

While the variation in response times is of some concern in relation to the Run Lab Project service composition, it is considered a major problem area when looking ahead at its repeated reuse. Not only will the existing user base of the legacy system affect the operation's predictability, increased reuse by additional compositions will only compound its potential unreliability, thereby jeopardizing these compositions as well as the current legacy users (not to mention its integrated applications).

It is decided to invest in an infrastructure upgrade. A new inventory database is established on a separate server. A replication channel is implemented keeping its data synchronized with the legacy repository at an hourly refresh cycle (Figure 10.12).

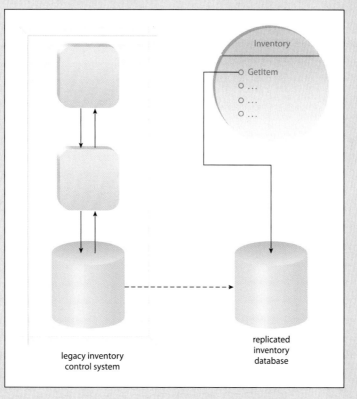

Figure 10.12

The revised service operation-level architecture for the GetItem operation. The new replicated database establishes a partially isolated access environment for the operation, significantly increasing autonomy and overall performance predictability.

The only data value of an inventory record that requires more current availability is its quantity. Because that value is retrieved by the separate GetItemCount operation, which will continue to access the legacy database directly, the hourly refresh rate is considered sufficient.

The replicated inventory database is not solely for use by the GetItem operation. Additional operations from this and other services will be able to utilize it as well. Therefore, this new partially isolated extension of the service architecture results in the GetItem operation achieving an increased measure of service logic-level autonomy. The operation's resources are still shared with other operations but not with the existing legacy user base.

Effect on the Run Lab Project Composition

Increasing the autonomy of the Inventory service's GetItem operation has a ripple effect in that this architectural improvement automatically ends up raising the autonomy of consumer service operations that invoke GetItem as well as operations that compose those operations (and so on).

In relation to the Lab Project business process for which services are currently being delivered, this improvement directly benefits the logic encapsulated by the GetPurchased operation of the Materials service, as well as the logic underlying the Run Lab Project service's Start operation (Figure 10.13).

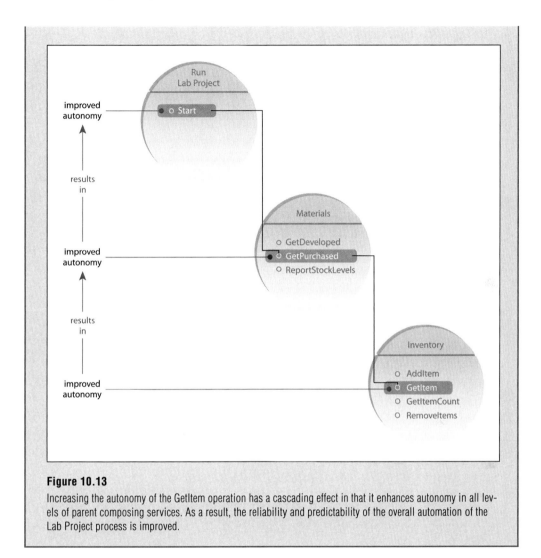

Figure 10.13

Increasing the autonomy of the GetItem operation has a cascading effect in that it enhances autonomy in all levels of parent composing services. As a result, the reliability and predictability of the overall automation of the Lab Project process is improved.

Chapter 11

Service Statelessness
(State Management Deferral
and Stateless Design)

A good indication that the design of an agnostic service was successful is when it is reused and recomposed on a regular basis. This outcome emphasizes the need to optimize the service processing logic so as to support the requirements of multiple consumer programs while the service itself consumes as little resources as possible.

As the complexity of service compositions increases, so does the quantity of activity-specific data that needs to be managed and retained throughout the lifespan of the composition. Services required to process and "hold" this data while waiting for other services in the composition to carry out their logic can tax the overall infrastructure. This is especially the case when numerous instances of those services need to exist concurrently, further compounding the drain on system resources.

To maximize service scalability and to make the most of whatever performance thresholds service inventories are required to work within, services and their surrounding architecture can be designed to support the delegation and deferral of state management responsibilities. This results in a service design streamlined by leveraging a condition called *statelessness* (Figure 11.1).

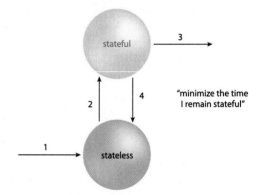

Figure 11.1

This principle encourages us to incorporate state management deferral extensions within our service designs so as to keep services in a stateless condition wherever appropriate.

<table>
<tr><td align="center">NOTE</td></tr>
<tr><td>There are various naming conventions used in the industry in relation to state information. For the purposes of this book, the terms defined in this chapter establish a modest taxonomy derived from how state and activity data has been referenced and described in past distributed models and Web services standards. Feel free to substitute any of these terms with your own.</td></tr>
</table>

11.1 State Management Explained

Unlike some of our other design principles that have roots in more widely established concepts, state management represents a dimension of solution design that can vary from platform to platform. Therefore, we'll take the time to explicitly define its meaning in relation to service-orientation.

State Management in Abstract

State refers to the general condition of something. A car that is moving is in a state of motion, whereas a car that is not moving is in a stationary state (Figure 11.2). In business automation, it is understood that a software program can also have and transition through different states usually because of its involvement in a runtime activity.

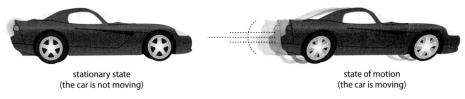

stationary state
(the car is not moving)

state of motion
(the car is moving)

Figure 11.2
The states of a car can be represented by two very fundamental categories.

Each state can be represented and described by data that typically has a lifespan equivalent to the duration at which the program remains active for a given task or purpose. As a result, all variations of state information tend to be temporary in nature. Therefore, *state management* can be considered the management of temporary, activity-specific data.

The following types of state conditions and data can exist:

- active and passive states
- stateful and stateless conditions
- context, session, and business state data
- context data and context rules

Each of these is explained individually in the *Types of State* section later in this chapter. Also note that throughout this chapter state data is associated with the color orange (Figure 11.3) to highlight its transfer to and from the service.

Figure 11.3

Service and repository symbols are primarily used to illustrate how state data (orange) can transition through various temporary containers at runtime.

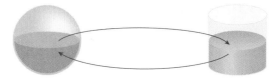

Origins of State Management

State information is required to do just about anything meaningful with software programs because data about an activity is fundamental to runtime processing.

Older, two-tier client-server solutions made state management a natural part of the primary solution components. The client user-interface would often retain large amounts of activity-specific data in memory for extended periods (Figure 11.4). This was not considered a problem because each client program was deployed on a dedicated computer, intended for use by a single user.

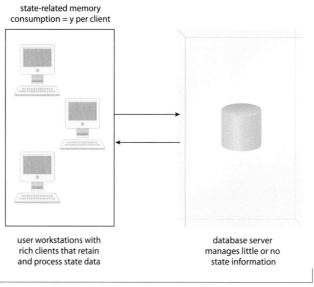

state-related memory
consumption = y per client

user workstations with
rich clients that retain
and process state data

database server
manages little or no
state information

two-tier Application A

Figure 11.4

Typical one-sided division of state management responsibilities in a typical two-tier client-server architecture.

In traditional distributed computing models, application processing logic shifted from the client workstation to the middle tier. As a result, a server-side program was now required to manage interaction with multiple client programs, each with their own individual state information processing requirements (Figure 11.5).

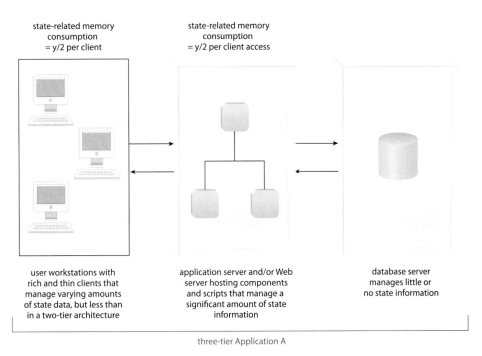

state-related memory
consumption
= y/2 per client

state-related memory
consumption
= y/2 per client access

| user workstations with rich and thin clients that manage varying amounts of state data, but less than in a two-tier architecture | application server and/or Web server hosting components and scripts that manage a significant amount of state information | database server manages little or no state information |

three-tier Application A

Figure 11.5

Note that the "y/2" value is arbitrary. In most contemporary Web-based solutions, the clients are relatively thin (browser-based), requiring the server-side components to manage a higher percentage of state data.

When actively processing or retaining state information, a program is constantly consuming a base amount of memory and CPU cycles. A server-side program accessed concurrently by multiple clients can rapidly and significantly increase this amount (Figure 11.6).

Because runtime usage scenarios are not always predictable and because hardware budgets are not always flexible, the risk of a concurrently accessed server-side program becoming a performance bottleneck is very real. Although state data processing requirements are not always the primary cause of system memory consumption, they contribute significantly.

In response to this problem, variations of distributed architectures were formed to alleviate components from state management responsibilities by providing *state delegation* and *state deferral* options. A common architectural extension that supported state deferral was centered around alternative state storage. A dedicated database (or a set of dedicated tables within an existing database) could be used by components to write and then later retrieve state data (Figure 11.7).

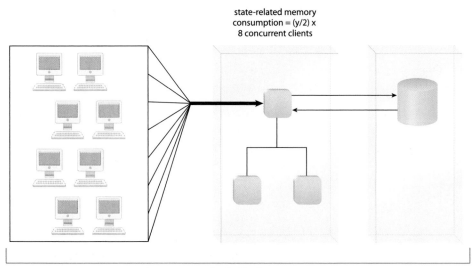

state-related memory
consumption = (y/2) x
8 concurrent clients

Application A

Figure 11.6

Multiple clients concurrently accessing the same application component. Some enterprise solutions have
thousands of clients that can raise concurrent access numbers into the hundreds.

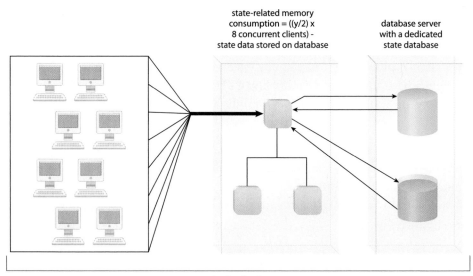

state-related memory
consumption = ((y/2) x
8 concurrent clients) -
state data stored on database

database server
with a dedicated
state database

Application A

Figure 11.7

A separate database positioned as a state management deferral extension of the architecture (the orange area represents state data). Note that databases utilized in this role are often located on the application server alongside
components.

Often these databases were physically located on the same application server as the components (as opposed to a separate database server) to reduce the performance impact caused by remote data access. In-memory databases were also used to further optimize data access by avoiding disk access. (The use of databases for state deferral is documented in more detail in the *Measuring Service Statelessness* section.)

To date, a variety of state management approaches have been developed. Middleware, for example, has become a popular state processing deferral option. It establishes a central, self-sufficient, and intentionally stateful part of the infrastructure that can be leveraged by other solutions within the enterprise.

Deferral vs. Delegation

The temporary relocation of state information is referred to as state deferral because the intention is usually to retrieve the information at some later point. We are therefore postponing (deferring) the responsibility of managing the state data. To accomplish state management deferral we temporarily delegate this responsibility to another part of the architecture (such as a database). Therefore, we achieve state management deferral through temporary and periodic state management delegation.

Note that in this book the processes of state management delegation and deferral are collectively referred to as state deferral.

SUMMARY OF KEY POINTS

- State data is information primarily associated with a current activity, and state management represents the processing of this information.

- Past technology architectures have shifted the responsibility of state management throughout client and server tiers.

- Architectural state deferral extensions can be employed to temporarily alleviate programs from the burden of state management in order to increase overall scalability.

11.2 Profiling this Principle

As was established in the previous section, components that were part of traditional distributed solutions needed to deal with concurrent invocation scenarios and the subsequent requirements to manage multiple types and values of state data from different clients.

Because of the emphasis service-orientation places on reuse, state management becomes a greater concern. A typical service not only exists as a program created to interact with multiple client requests in relation to the automation of a specific business task, it needs to be capable of serving high volumes of client interactions in support of multiple (and potentially increasing) amounts of business tasks (Figure 11.8).

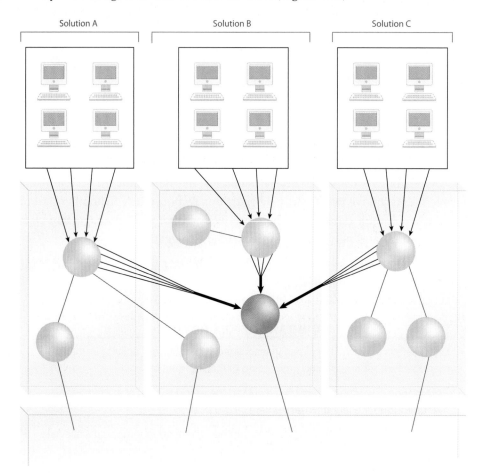

Figure 11.8

Multiple clients from multiple business processes subjecting the same service to a range of state processing requirements.

Therefore, the focus on streamlining the management of state information within the architecture is increased to the extent that we now have a principle dedicated to this aspect of service design.

Furthermore, as with other parts of service-orientation, the actual implementation of this principle is not as much on a service level, but on an individual capability level. The implications of this are explored in Table 11.1 and in subsequent sections.

Principle Profile	
Short Definition	*"Services minimize statefulness."*
Long Definition	*"Services minimize resource consumption by deferring the management of state information when necessary."*
Goals	• To increase service scalability. • To support the design of agnostic service logic and improve the potential for service reuse.
Design Characteristics	What makes this somewhat of a unique principle is the fact that it is promoting a condition of the service that is temporary in nature. Depending on the service model and state deferral approach used, different types of design characteristics can be implemented. Some examples include: • Highly business process-agnostic logic so that the service is not designed to retain state information for any specific parent business process. • Less constrained service contracts so as to allow for the receipt and transmission of a wider range of state data at runtime. • Increased amounts of interpretative programming routines capable of parsing a range of state information delivered by messages and responding to a range of corresponding action requests.
Implementation Requirements	Although state deferral can reduce the overall consumption of memory and system resources, services designed with statelessness considerations can also introduce some performance demands associated with the runtime retrieval and interpretation of deferred state data. Here is a short checklist of common requirements that can be used to assess the support of stateless service designs by vendor technologies and target deployment locations:

- The runtime environment should allow for a service to transition from an idle state to an active processing state in a highly efficient manner.

- Enterprise-level or high-performance XML parsers and hardware accelerators (and SOAP processors) should be provided to allow services implemented as Web services to more efficiently parse larger message payloads with less performance constraints.

- The use of attachments may need to be supported by Web services to allow for messages to include bodies of payload data that do not undergo interface-level validation or translation to local formats.

The nature of the implementation support required by the average stateless service in an environment will depend on the state deferral approach used within the service-oriented architecture.

| **Web Service Region of Influence** | Building a service to maximize the stateless condition affects the service contract design but can also directly influence how service logic is designed, right down to the individual programming routines and even the core algorithms that lie beneath each service capability. |

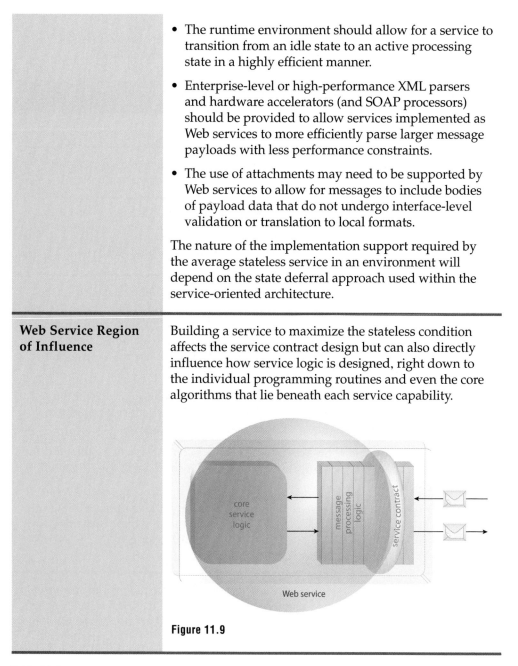

Figure 11.9

Table 11.1
A profile for the Service Statelessness principle.

SUMMARY OF KEY POINTS

- The Service Statelessness principle emphasizes the need to reduce or eliminate system resource consumption due to unnecessary state management processing.

- The primary objective of this design principle is to maximize service scalability, especially within agnostic services more likely to be reused and recomposed.

11.3 Types of State

There are different state values and different types of state information. While state management is a common part of just about any program and platform, the manner in which state types and data are described and labeled can vary (Figure 11.10). Let's therefore cover some fundamentals to establish terminology referenced throughout this chapter.

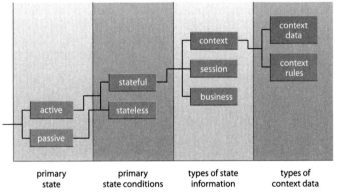

Figure 11.10

Most services transition through all of these states and conditions and are required to work with at least some form of session or context information.

Active and Passive

As established in the *State Management in Abstract* section earlier, a software program can transition through different states in its lifetime. The simple example in that section described two basic states a car was capable of having: in motion and stationary. A software program—or in this case a service—can also have two comparable, primary states:

- active
- passive

The first represents the service being invoked or executed and therefore entering an active state. The latter refers to the period during which the service is not in use and therefore exists in a passive or "non-active" state.

Stateless and Stateful

During the design stage of a service, we are very interested in what will happen when the service is active. We are so interested, in fact, that we have additional states to represent specific types of active conditions. In relation to our discussion of state management, there are two primary conditions:

- stateless
- stateful

These terms are used to identify the active or runtime condition of a service as it relates to the processing required to carry out a specific task. When automating a particular task, the service is required to process data specific to that task. We can refer to this information as *state* data.

A service can be active but may not be engaged in the processing of state data. In this idle condition, the service is considered to be *stateless*. As you may have guessed, a service that is actively processing or retaining state data is classified as being *stateful*.

A classic example of statelessness is the use of the HTTP protocol. When a browser requests a Web page from a Web server, the Web server responds by delivering the content and then returning to a stateless condition wherein it retains no further memory of the browser or the request (unless programmed otherwise).

Session and Context Data

The data a service processes when it is stateful can also vary. Many terms have been used to classify different types of state data, but we'll settle on the following:

- session data
- context data
- business data

Session data typically represents information associated with retaining a connection made between a program and its client program (or client user). This connection may or may not be an actual physical connection.

For example, if you access a Web site with your browser, it may be programmed to establish a unique session identifier to correlate future interaction with the browser and other parts of the site. This value is then passed between the browser and the Web site with each subsequent exchange. Similarly, correspondence between a Web service and its consumer can be kept in synch through the use of correlation identifiers that are passed within SOAP headers. In both cases, the identifier is a type of state information we'll refer to as session data.

Listing #1

```
<Header>
  <x:CorrelationID xmlns:x="http://..." mustUnderstand="1">
    2342357892-JDJ903KD
  </x:CorrelationID>
</Header>
```

Listing #2

```
<Header>
  <wsa:MessageID>
    uuid:22009893-774qy4
  </wsa:MessageID>
</Header>
```

Example 11.1

A correlation identifier can exist as a custom SOAP header as shown in Listing #1. Correlation information has also been standardized by some WS-* specifications, most notably WS-Addressing. Listing #2 displays a SOAP header containing a WS-Addressing correlation construct.

In service compositions, the execution of a business task can take the shape of a runtime activity that spans multiple services. In this case, the state information that is passed between them (if any) goes beyond session-type information in that it pertains to more than just keeping track of the session. This type of activity-specific information is what we refer to as *context data*.

Associated with context data is the actual logic used to process it. Usually this logic is tied to the workflow rules that govern the processing of the activity. We therefore make a further distinction between context data and *context rules*.

```
<Header>
  <wsc:CoordinationContext>
    <wsu:Identifier>
      http://www.soabooks.com/ids/process/23532
    </wsu:Identifier>
```

```
      <wsu:Expires>
         2010-04-23T24:00:00.000
      </wsu:Expires>
      <wsc:CoordinationType>
         http://schemas.xmlsoap.org/ws/2003/09/wsat
      </wsc:CoordinationType>
      ...
   </wsc:CoordinationContext>
</Header>
```

Example 11.2

The WS-Coordination specification provides a context management framework that can represent context data and context rules in standardized SOAP headers. In this example, the `CoordinationType` element establishes that WS-AtomicTransaction protocols (rules) are in use.

Finally, *business data* represents information that is relevant to the business task currently executing. This typically refers to persistent data retrieved from a repository. The classic example is a set of data records returned by a database query. It may be required to store this information in memory for data sharing or future reference purposes within the lifespan of a service activity.

Unlike the other forms of state information that have been covered, business data is typically transported within the SOAP body as part of the message payload. It therefore is not data that actually represents or expresses the state of the service or the activity; however, the need for it to be temporarily persisted by the service can require that the service remain stateful.

There are other forms of state information you will encounter or perhaps even create yourself when designing services. The types described in this section are common to most service processing requirements.

NOTE

Another Web service specification associated with state management is WS-ResourceTransfer (WS-RT), which has evolved from related efforts, including WS-ResourceLifetime, WS-ResourceProperties, and the WS-Resource Framework. These specifications classify state data as WS-Resources (or resource properties) that are formally represented by standardized element constructs.

For more information about WS-Addressing, WS-Coordination, and WS-AtomicTransaction, visit **www.ws-standards.com**. To view any of the referenced Web services specifications (including WS-RT), see **www.soaspecs.com**.

11.4 Measuring Service Statelessness

Using the state types and data just established, we can define common categories to measure the level of a service capability's statelessness during its participation in a runtime activity. It is then the collective levels of the capabilities that determine the extent of a service's overall statelessness (Figure 11.11).

Figure 11.11

As with most service-orientation design characteristics, measures of statelessness can exist at different levels within different service capabilities.

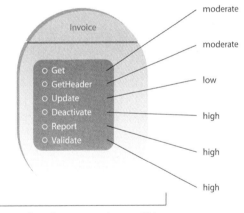

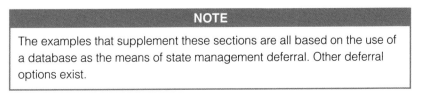

Provided here is a set of categories that can be used to label a service or any one of its capabilities in order to communicate its level of statelessness.

NOTE

The examples that supplement these sections are all based on the use of a database as the means of state management deferral. Other deferral options exist.

Non-Deferred State Management (low-to-no statelessness)

The service capability encapsulates solution logic that is embedded with a significant amount of activity-specific details, including context rules and session management routines. This type of logic will often cause the service to remain active and stateful for continuous periods that may span the execution time of an activity. Even when acting as a composition member, this type of service may need to remain active for the duration of its participation in the overall activity (Figure 11.12).

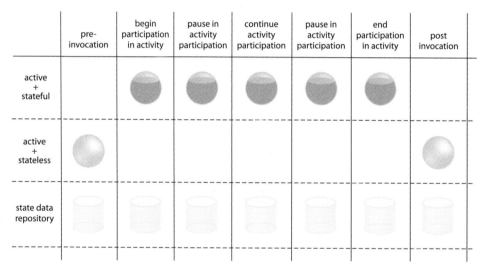

Figure 11.12

A service with non-deferred state management remains stateful throughout the course of its involvement within a service activity.

Services delivered in support of a specific business process are often designed this way by default when service-orientation is not a significant influence or when the nature of the service is intentionally process-specific (as with task services). Though the increased amount of state management processing can inhibit scalability, the benefit to this form of design is that the service does not require an external state deferral extension. As a result, the service does not form a direct dependency on its surrounding architecture.

Partially Deferred Memory (reduced statefulness)

A service capability can be designed to defer state data without having to switch between stateless and stateful conditions. When a service is expected to receive significant quantities of state data at runtime, it can be designed to off-load portions of this data during periods where the data is not required. The service continues to stay active while still retaining some of the state data (Figure 11.13).

Typically the type of state information deferred by the service is business data, such as large record sets returned from database queries or context data representing an accumulation of activity-specific details. State data more commonly retained includes some forms of context rules and session information.

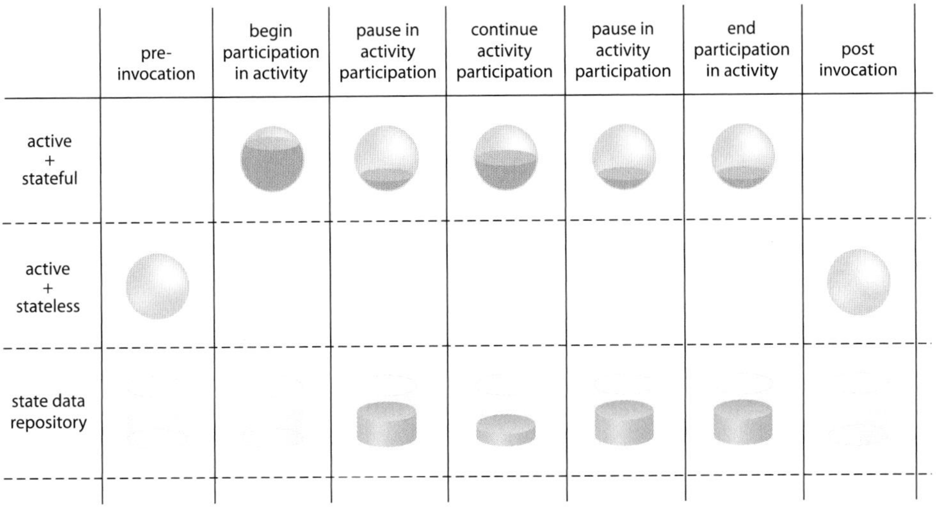

	pre-invocation	begin participation in activity	pause in activity participation	continue activity participation	pause in activity participation	end participation in activity	post invocation
active + stateful		●	●	●	●	●	
active + stateless	●						●
state data repository			▬	▬	▬	▬	

Figure 11.13
With the ability to off-load some of its state data, a service with partially deferred state management remains active and stateful but consumes less memory due to the decreased quantity of state data it retains.

This approach reduces overall memory consumption for each activity a service instance is required to process.

Partial Architectural State Management Deferral (moderate statelessness)

During longer running activities, there are often extended periods during which a participating service runs idle. If state management options exist, these are the most obvious places to use them. Although the service will be transitioned into stateless modes during these gaps of inactivity, the service is not designed to take advantage of every possible opportunity to become stateless (Figure 11.14).

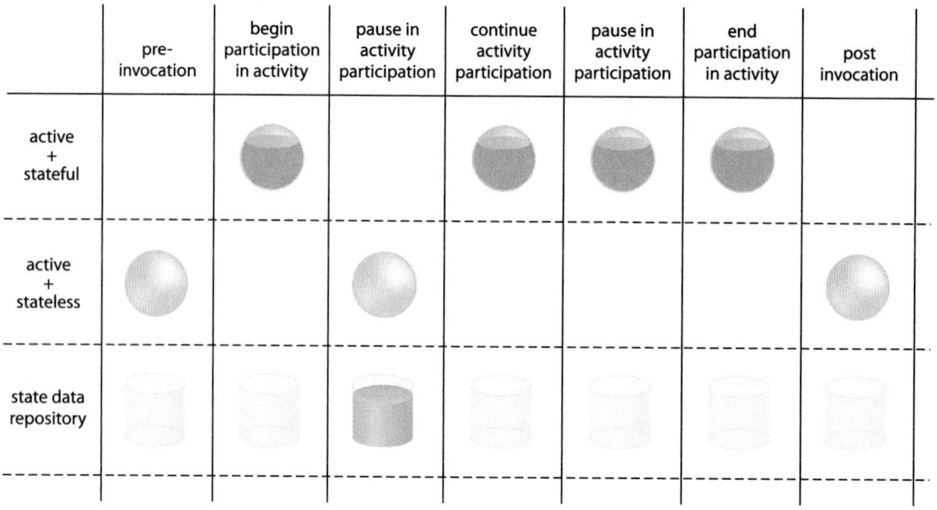

	pre-invocation	begin participation in activity	pause in activity participation	continue activity participation	pause in activity participation	end participation in activity	post invocation
active + stateful		●		●	●	●	
active + stateless	●		●				●
state data repository			◗				

Figure 11.14

This service, based on a different form of partial state deferral, is able to transition into a stateless mode at certain times.

Full Architectural State Management Deferral (high statelessness)

The service capabilities are designed to maximize any reasonable opportunity to become stateless (Figure 11.15). Furthermore, the option to off-load state information (primarily context and business data) while stateful whenever possible is also leveraged.

Internally Deferred State Management (high statelessness)

As with the non-deferred level, no architectural state deferral option is used. Instead, the service benefits from an implementation that has achieved the absolute isolation level of pure autonomy, which provides it with its own, internal state deferral option. This is commonly implemented via a dedicated database that the service can use to store and retrieve temporary activity data in order to maximize its existence in a stateless condition. As a result, this form of stateless service design would be visually illustrated the same as the full architectural option shown in Figure 11.15.

NOTE
Several architectural design patterns exist to provide established state management deferral extensions for services.

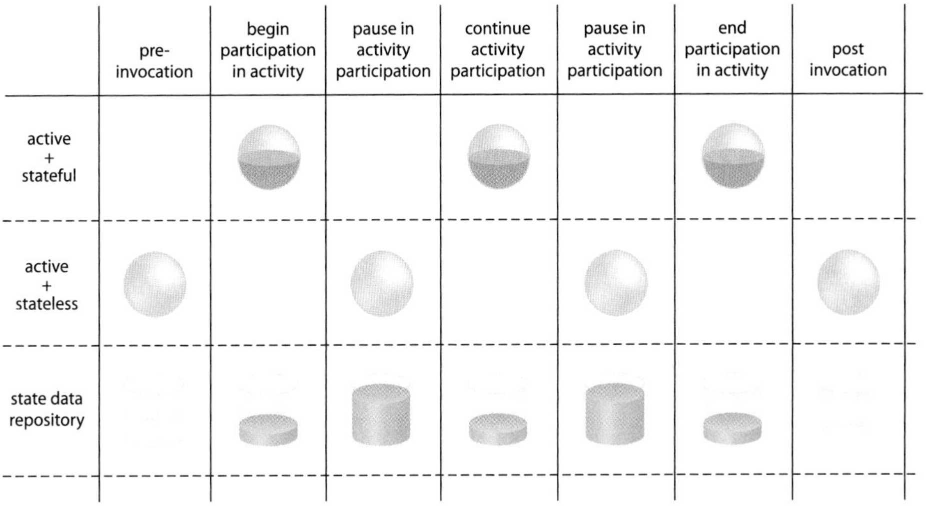

	pre-invocation	begin participation in activity	pause in activity participation	continue activity participation	pause in activity participation	end participation in activity	post invocation
active + stateful		●		●		●	
active + stateless	●		●		●		●
state data repository		▬	■	▬	■	▬	

Figure 11.15

The service with fully deferred state management maximizes its opportunities to exist in a stateless condition. Even when stateful, it defers state data when possible.

SUMMARY OF KEY POINTS

- Various measures of statelessness can be attained, most of which rely on the existence of architectural state management deferral extensions.

- Each capability within a service can have a different level of statelessness.

11.5 Statelessness and Service Design

This section raises considerations for incorporating stateless design characteristics into services.

Messaging as a State Deferral Option

In addition to database-centric state deferral options, it is important to understand how messaging, as a part of the overall architecture, can also be positioned in support of stateless service design.

Messages as a Source of State Information

Generic design considerations advocated by the Service Reusability principle and the reduction in validation constraints promoted by the Service Abstraction principle can significantly reduce the amount of activity-specific logic embedded within services. This effectively makes agnostic services more "activity dumb" and places the responsibility of supplying services with activity context data and rules on the message layer. Although in this role messages can be seen as a state deferral option, they can also increase performance overhead by requiring that services carry out the additional processing needed to parse, process, and interpret commands, rules, and instructions at runtime.

Furthermore, messages can be custom-designed to carry business state data throughout a service activity, thereby further alleviating services from state management responsibilities. Whether or not this is a wise design decision often comes down to the quantity of the data itself. If implemented, business data can be carried within custom SOAP headers, SOAP attachments, or as part of the SOAP body itself.

Although it can also be viewed as a form of external state deferral that requires the service to couple itself to its surrounding architecture, it is important to note that when using Web services, services form dependencies on an *industry-standard* communications framework, as opposed to a custom, enterprise-specific architecture.

FOR EXAMPLE

A business process within a mid-sized airline company was automated by a composition of services in which stateless design was emphasized. One of the agnostic services participating in the composition provided a code lookup capability that, based upon input selection criteria, would return a specific list of airport codes.

These codes were required by all of the other participating services. Once retrieved by the utility lookup service capability, the codes were placed in a custom SOAP header that accompanied all messages exchanged throughout the remaining service activity. Although every service in the composition needed to retrieve and process the codes, no one service was ever required to retain the code list in memory. This helped reduce the duration by which several services in the composition needed to remain stateful.

Service Statelessness and Service Instances

As much as we may emphasize the preference for services to reside in a stateless condition, they will always need to be stateful at some point in time—and often for extended periods.

While actively stateful, multiple instances of the same service can (and often do) concurrently exist, each involved in its own service activity. When a pool of service instances exists, service consumers need to be able to identify and communicate with specific instances within that pool.

The WS-Addressing specification provides a set of SOAP headers called Endpoint References that establish an industry standard syntax for defining service instance-specific identifiers (Example 11.3).

```
<Header>
  ...
  <wsa:From>
    <wsa:Address>
      http://...
    </wsa:Address>
    <wsa:ReferenceProperties>
      <app:id>
        unn:K342e553ds
      </app:id>
    </wsa:ReferenceProperties>
    <wsa:ReferenceParameters>
      <app:sesno>
        35268456
      </app:sesno>
    </wsa:ReferenceParameters>
  </wsa:From>
  <wsa:MessageID>
    uuid:243234234-43gf433
  </wsa:MessageID>
  ...
</Header>
```

Example 11.3

The WS-Addressing header from Example 11.1 accompanied by endpoint reference constructs that identify the service instance that transmitted the message.

Even though service instance identification relates more to how a service exists in a stateful condition, it is an important aspect of service design to understand when applying this principle to Web services.

As explored in the *Measuring Service Statelessness* section of this chapter, a service may shift between stateful and stateless conditions multiple times in the course of a single service activity. Depending on the invocation approach and technology used to create and define service instances, the instance identifiers may actually be recreated each time the service transitions from stateless to stateful. This may be undesirable as it can introduce some complexity into the overall management of the service activity, especially if the instance identifiers themselves comprise a form of state data.

Service Statelessness and Granularity

When services are required to receive and process ranges of state data at runtime, the granularity of their corresponding contracts can certainly be affected. Specifically, data and constraint granularity may need to be reduced to allow for larger amounts of data and ranges of values to be received.

Unlike other design principles that tend to affect the definition of message body contents, Service Statelessness can influence the granularity of both custom message header and body structures. However, it really does come down to the nature of the state information itself. As established earlier in the *Types of State* section, state data may be expressed by standardized WS-* specifications, which establish predefined element constraints.

Service Statelessness and Service Models

Unlike some other principles where we can safely claim that it is prudent to pursue the principle to whatever extent feasible, regardless of the nature of the service, statelessness is a quality that needs to be evaluated separately for each service model.

Entity Services

Because entity services are responsible for processing business logic, they will always participate in the automation of business processes. These processes may already be represented by the scope of a capability's logic, or they will be larger, parent processes that compose the entity service capability as one of several composition members. Alternatively, the entity service itself may need to compose other services to carry out its capabilities.

All of these scenarios emphasize the importance of standardizing state management across capabilities within an entity service and, to whatever extent feasible, across all entity services in an inventory. These conventions need to extend to the data representation of business and context information (and rules) delivered via messages to ensure consistent interoperability.

Utility Services

Utility services are sometimes intentionally designed to violate this principle. For example, a design pattern exists that advocates the creation of a set of utility services as stateful system resources responsible for managing state data on behalf of other services.

Essentially, the cross-cutting functionality provided by these types of utility services is state management itself. They therefore become stateful extensions of the infrastructure so that statelessness can be more easily realized in the rest of the service inventory.

Task Services

Because task-centric services have a functional scope centered around a business process, they are deliberately designed to encapsulate context rules. How they manage context data, though, can vary.

Task services are often positioned as composition controllers, and for significantly sized compositions, there may very well be a need for them to defer context data in order to alternate between stateful and stateless conditions. However, for smaller tasks, performance across composition members may be efficient enugh to allow for the task service to remain stateful and maintain context and session data for the duration of the activity.

Orchestrated Task Services

Unlike other service models, orchestrated task services are fully expected to remain stateful. The nature of orchestration technology is to manage an activity during its entire lifespan. If the duration of process inactivity exceeds a certain timeout period, state data is stored in a database until the point at which it needs to be revived.

How Service Statelessness Affects Other Principles

Provided here are brief explorations of how statelessness in services can influence and support other service-orientation design principles (Figure 11.16).

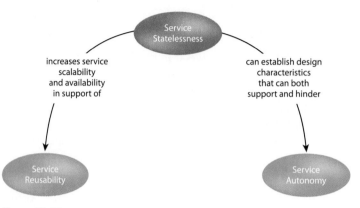

Figure 11.16

Service Statelessness exists primarily to increase scalability in support of the widespread reuse of services, but its implementation is closely tied to a service's autonomy level.

Service Statelessness and Service Reusability

If we look back at the goals listed in Table 11.1, we can see how prominently reuse has driven the need for this design principle.

Let's revisit these items to clearly illustrate the connection:

- Decreasing activity-specific logic makes a service more agnostic (and agnostic services are more reusable).

- Increasing the scalability and availability of services allows them to be reused by more service consumers in more service compositions.

Service Statelessness and Service Autonomy

Statelessness and autonomy go hand-in-hand in service design. When properly applied, each supports the goals of the other, and both ultimately support the fundamental goals of service-oriented computing.

As established in Chapter 10, autonomy is the measure by which a service has independent control over its environment. Because the nature of state information is typically specific to a given activity or business process, by shifting state management and processing responsibilities outside of the service boundary, the chances of service logic having to form dependencies on larger business tasks are reduced. This makes the service more self-sufficient and positions it as a standalone part of a technical environment, thereby directly increasing its overall autonomy.

The flipside to this benefit is the fact that state management deferral options provided by the surrounding architecture can require that the service form a direct dependency outside of its boundary. This type of external implementation coupling can actually compromise a service's overall autonomy, as explained in the upcoming *Risks Associated with Service Statelessness* section. See also the *Service Autonomy and Service Statelessness* section in Chapter 10 for an explanation of how increased levels of autonomy support stateless service design.

SUMMARY OF KEY POINTS

- A messaging framework can act as an architectural state management deferral extension by allowing state data to be placed and carried with individual messages.

- Stateless design is a consideration of special importance to services that act as composition controllers.

11.6 Risks Associated with Service Statelessness

We've been focusing on the benefits of increasing a service's stateless condition. However, this is a principle that must be applied with care and sound judgment. The following sections highlight some of the more common pitfalls of stateless service design.

Dependency on the Architecture

Keeping the management of state information within the self-contained boundary of a service is often a safe approach to building reliable service logic. Even from a governance perspective, it can be easier to maintain and evolve a service that has full control over its own state processing.

When we choose to move the responsibility of state management outside of a service boundary, we then need to design the service logic to work with however the overall architecture has been designed to manage state. In other words, we need to create a dependency between the service design and an external state deferral option. While there are clear benefits to deferring state, the resulting dependencies need to be carefully assessed, especially from a long-term evolutionary perspective.

BEST PRACTICE

Architectural state deferral extensions are ideally standardized across an enterprise or, at minimum, across a service inventory. This usually requires establishing a formal architectural design standard and settling on a reliable and flexible state deferral design that can accommodate a wide range of service requirements. Standardizing this type of extension protects the inventory from potentially disruptive changes that can invalidate numerous services.

Increased Runtime Performance Demands

Deferring state management allows a service to remain stateless for longer periods of time. This increases a service's availability but does not necessarily increase its runtime performance. In fact, the runtime processing that may be required for state data to be retrieved or interpreted and then acted upon by the service can introduce layers of performance overhead in addition to the actual processing of the message contents. Performance assessment is therefore an important part of designing state deferral extensions as well as the services that use them.

Also note that complex context rules or large bodies of state information can impose unreasonable processing requirements and may demand that the service not use a particular type of state deferral approach.

Underestimating Delivery Effort

Almost every one of the service-orientation principles introduces new considerations and design requirements that will increase the cost and effort to deliver solution logic. Service Statelessness is no exception.

The fact that activity-specific data will need to be received, interpreted, processed, and deferred at runtime requires the service's underlying solution logic to contain sophisticated algorithms and routines. This results in not just extra design considerations, but also additional programming and testing efforts to ensure the service is capable of dealing with a range of usage scenarios plus a range of activity data.

A common risk associated with stateless service design is underestimating the actual effort required to achieve a flexible and generic level of statelessness. This is especially relevant to agnostic services that may need to remain stateless and activity-neutral to retain a high reuse potential.

SUMMARY OF KEY POINTS

- When delivering services that rely on architectural state management deferral extensions, these services become dependent on that part of the architecture (which may compromise their autonomy).

- By increasing statelessness, services are often required to perform more run-time processing.

11.7 CASE STUDY EXAMPLE

Preliminary tests of the Web services being developed for the Cutit Lab Project process indicate no immediate concerns in relation to excessive statefulness of any given service. Therefore, the need to introduce a state deferral extension to the planned architecture is initially considered unnecessary.

However, prior to moving the services into production, they are subjected to a formal testing cycle during which stress and volume tests are performed. Service operations are required to process ranges of input and output data far beyond the sample data used in the developer's lab.

The results indicate that the Simulate operation of the Formulas service can take minutes to carry out the calculation-heavy processing required to generate the simulations report when specific types of base formulas are applied. The underlying formula's database is already optimized and dedicated, and outside of investing in very expensive infrastructure upgrades that would increase the server's overall processing power, no options for performance improvement are identified.

This new bottleneck in the process workflow changes the expectations of the overall process execution. No longer can the Run Lab Project service guarantee that its Start operation will be completed in real time. Instead, some conditions are defined during which the longer response times will need to be accepted (all of which are documented as part of the revised service SLA).

Based on these revelations, Cutit architects decide to revisit the state management issue. They know now that there will be times when the Run Lab Project service will need to wait for extended periods for the completion of the Formulas service's

Simulate operation. So the question is raised: "Do we want the Run Lab Project service to remain stateful during these periods?"

It is fortunate for Cutit that the types of input values that will trigger the longer calculation periods are known in advance. This allows architects to map out separate real-time and long-running service activity scenarios. It also enables them to design the affected services in such a manner that state management deferral is only carried out when required (based on the input data in use).

Solution Architecture with State Management Deferral

Prior to having to invoke the Formulas service's Simulate operation, the Run Lab Project service will already have composed several operations from both the Formulas and the Materials services. The generation of the simulation report is one of the final steps in the business process.

Therefore, by the time the Simulate operation comes into the picture, a significant amount of session, context, and business state data will have been collected into memory, including entire inventory item and base formula document records. Keeping all of this information locked up in memory for any period of time exceeding three seconds is considered unacceptable primarily because it may compromise system resources that are needed for other programs and services located on the same physical server.

As a result, it is confirmed that some form of state deferral extension will be required for the Run Lab Project service. After some discussion, Cutit architects decide to install a dedicated state database on the server. Furthermore, the Run Lab Project service logic will be modified as follows:

Step 1

While carrying out all of the prior processing to automate the Lab Project business process, the Run Lab Project service will have collected and placed various types of state data into memory (Figure 11.17).

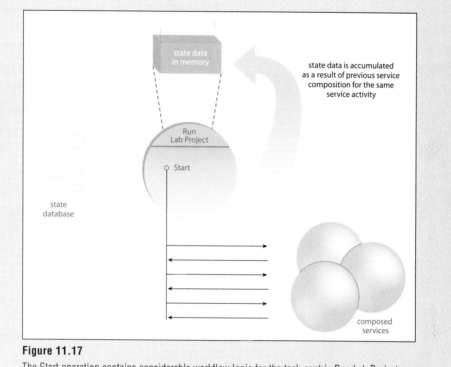

Figure 11.17

The Start operation contains considerable workflow logic for the task-centric Run Lab Project service, resulting in a build-up of activity-specific state data.

Step 2

When ready to call the Formulas service's Simulate operation, the Run Lab Project service retrieves the numeric category code of base formulas to be used as input values. (The code is stored in the predefined `category` element in the Base Formula document.) It then calls the Simulate operation of the Formulas service by transmitting a request message containing the required input values (Figure 11.18).

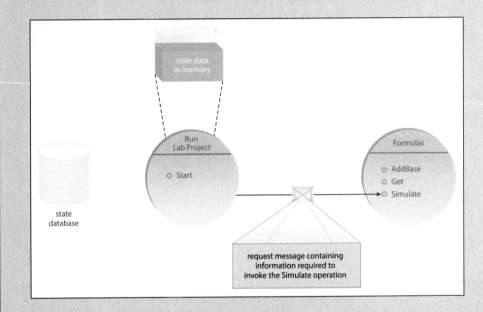

Figure 11.18

The criteria required for the Run Lab Project's Start operation logic (used to determine whether or not it will need to eventually utilize the state deferral database) is accessible before it even invokes the Formulas service.

Step 3

If the category code for both base formula documents was equal to or higher than "9," then a long-running operation execution time is expected. In this case, the Start operation initiates a separate routine that moves all of the state data currently in memory into the state database (Figure 11.19).

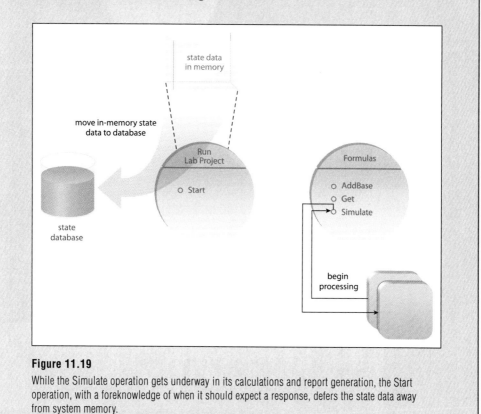

Figure 11.19

While the Simulate operation gets underway in its calculations and report generation, the Start operation, with a foreknowledge of when it should expect a response, defers the state data away from system memory.

Step 4

The Run Lab Project service stays active while waiting for a response from the Formulas service. However, its memory consumption is minimal because all state data was stored to disk within the state database (Figure 11.20).

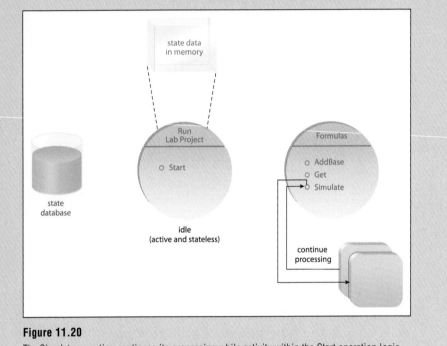

Figure 11.20
The Simulate operation continues its processing while activity within the Start operation logic has ceased.

Step 5

Finally, a response message is transmitted by the Simulate operation (Figure 11.21).

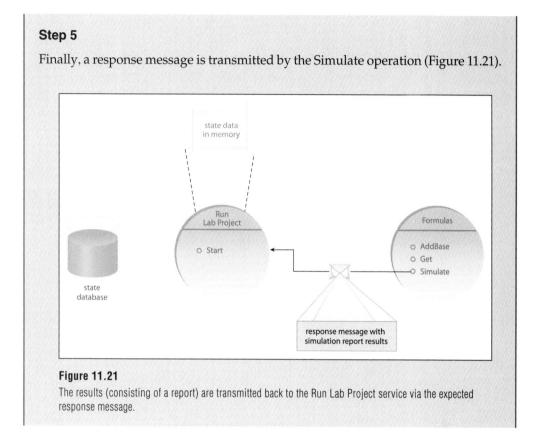

Figure 11.21

The results (consisting of a report) are transmitted back to the Run Lab Project service via the expected response message.

Step 6

As originally established in the case study background provided at the end of Chapter 5, a separate compensation process can be triggered if errors are returned in the report. Upon receiving a failed report in the response message, the Start operation is back in action. It resumes processing by moving the state data back into its memory space. Meanwhile, the Formulas service is in an idle state waiting for its next invocation (Figure 11.22).

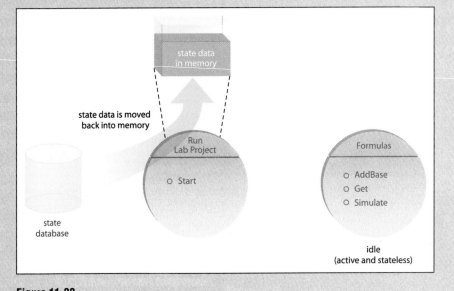

Figure 11.22
The state data is transferred once again in preparation for the upcoming composition processing.

Step 7

The Start operation continues processing the next set of workflow sequences by composing additional services for which the relocated state data will be required (Figure 11.23).

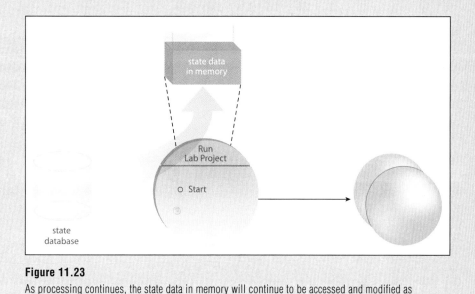

Figure 11.23

As processing continues, the state data in memory will continue to be accessed and modified as required.

This architecture would qualify the service as having attained a moderate level of statelessness. Not every opportunity to minimize statefulness was utilized, but a partial state management deferral architecture was designed to alleviate the primary identified state data-related burden.

Chapter 12

Service Discoverability (Interpretability and Communication)

It can be easily argued that the design principle service-orientation should be credited with popularizing the most is that of Service Discoverability. In this chapter we explore the innovative concepts behind service discovery (Figure 12.1) and the associated service discoverability and interpretability design characteristics.

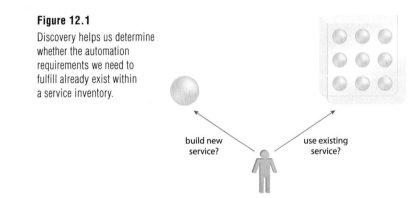

Figure 12.1

Discovery helps us determine whether the automation requirements we need to fulfill already exist within a service inventory.

build new service?

use existing service?

12.1 Discoverability Explained

Although the term "discovery" brings to mind the need for something to be effectively searched for and located, the concept of discovery as implemented within an enterprise actually implies a great deal more.

Discovery requires:

- a means of consistently communicating information about resources (meta information) that we want to make available for discovery

- meta information to be accurately defined by those who understand the underlying resource the best

- meta information to be clearly documented by those who have the appropriate communication skills

- meta information to be centrally stored and maintained in a consistent format

- us to enable access to meta information to those who we want to make the resources available for discovery

- the meta information to be effectively searched in response to criteria-driven queries

- the meta information to be clearly understood by those who will review the results of discovery queries

When we embark on a discovery process, we need to have a good understanding of what it is we're looking for in order to establish a set of selection criteria. Although there can be several reasons for wanting to discover a resource, the most common question that we look to have answered is: *"Does the functionality I need already exist, or do I need to build it?"*

To come up with an effective answer, we need information about the resources already available. Types of meta information that have proven to be repeatedly useful are:

- the purpose of a resource

- the capabilities of a resource

- the limitations of resource capabilities

To evaluate available resources, we can apply selection criteria to this meta information. If we cannot find an appropriate resource, we may either decide to use a less effective one that already exists, or we may decide to build a new resource that we know will fulfill our requirements (which may entail extending an existing resource).

This is a critical decision point for which an enterprise needs to be prepared. The quality of meta information we define, the manner in which we make this information available, and how well we implement discovery as a whole all collectively determine whether that one decision is carried out properly. If the meta information made available is inadequate or not easily accessible, there is the constant risk that it will be misunderstood or not even viewed at all.

When this happens, two detrimental actions usually follow:

1. Users lose out on the opportunity to reuse an existing, available resource and end up building their own.

2. A new resource is delivered with functionally that overlaps with the existing (undiscovered) resource, introducing redundancy into the enterprise.

When these consequences occur repeatedly, goals associated with achieving reuse and normalization are severely undermined, and the overall enterprise architecture becomes bloated and convoluted.

All of this can be avoided by understanding discovery and planting the information we know will be searched for later on in advance.

Discovery and Interpretation, Discoverability and Interpretability in Abstract

The concepts behind discovery are quite straight-forward. From an architectural perspective, it is often desirable for individual units of solution logic to be easily located. The process of searching for and finding solution logic within a specified environment is referred to as *discovery*.

A key aspect of discovery is that you may or may not have been aware of the logic's existence before you discovered it. By discovering that something you want to build already exists, you avoid creating redundant logic. By discovering that something you want to build does not yet exist, you can safely define the scope of your development effort.

Discovery is often classified as an extension of infrastructure and therefore associated with enterprise architecture. For something within the enterprise to be discoverable, it needs to be equipped with meta information that will allow it to be included within the scope of discovery searches. An architectural component that can adequately be discovered is considered to have a measure of *discoverability* (Figure 12.2).

Figure 12.2

A simplified example of common discoverability meta data—a standardized expression of a service's purpose and capabilities.

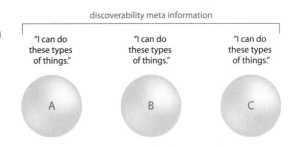

discoverability meta information

"I can do these types of things."   "I can do these types of things."   "I can do these types of things."

A   B   C

Discoverability information is essentially a combination of the content in a service contract and meta data in the corresponding registry record.

Most discovery processes and technologies are currently geared toward humans. It is the system designers and developers who are required to work with or build new pieces of the enterprise that are most in need of a means of locating what already exists (Figure 12.3).

Figure 12.3
The human discovery process essentially consists of querying and filtering.

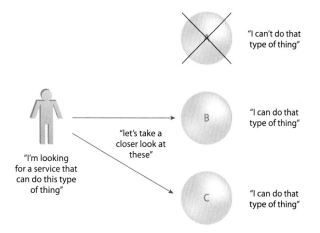

Once located by a human, it is important that the purpose and capabilities of the architectural component be clearly understood. This level of clarity or "communications quality" is referred to as *interpretability* (Figure 12.4).

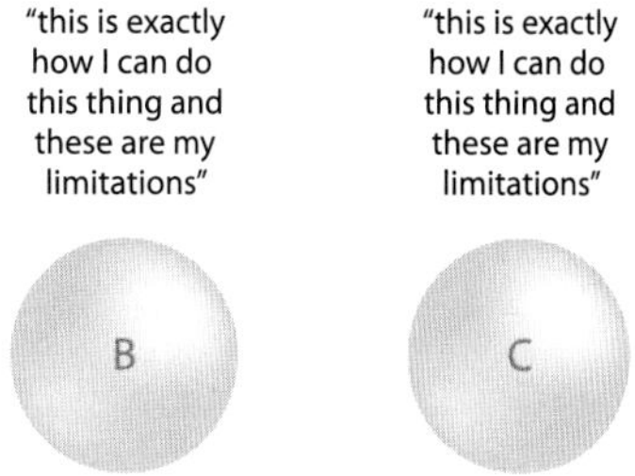

Figure 12.4
The communications quality of service meta data represents the extent to which the design characteristic of interpretability is implemented.

"this is exactly how I can do this thing and these are my limitations"

B

"this is exactly how I can do this thing and these are my limitations"

C

The steps involved by a human to evaluate the query results of a discovery process and to then choose a service as being capable of fulfilling desired automation requirements is part of the *interpretation* process (Figure 12.5).

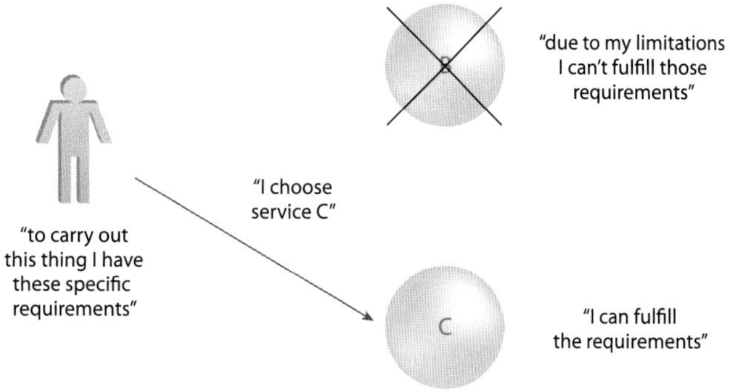

Figure 12.5
The interpretation process follows the discovery process and consists of assessment and, ultimately, selection.

"due to my limitations I can't fulfill those requirements"

"I choose service C"

"to carry out this thing I have these specific requirements"

C

"I can fulfill the requirements"

The primary motivation behind implementing discoverability and interpretability design characteristics is in support of establishing structured discovery and interpretation processes based on the use of a *service registry*. When an organization positions a service registry as a central part of its infrastructure, it establishes a formal enterprise mechanism for enabling on-demand location, retrieval, and interpretation of service meta data (Figure 12.6).

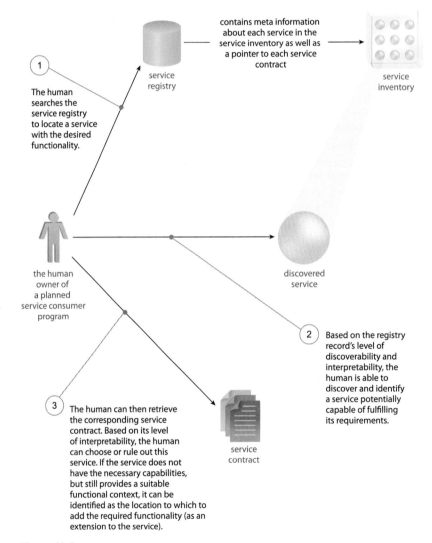

Figure 12.6
Discovery and interpretation in action.

> **NOTE**
>
> Some platforms make a distinction between a service registry and a service repository. For example, the term "repository" may be used at design-time to refer to the database of service profile records, whereas the term "registry" may be more associated with runtime usage. In this book we only use the term "service registry," regardless of whether it is discussed within the context of a runtime scenario.

Origins of Discovery

Although some organizations have achieved a measure of success in establishing reusable components, a formal process for discovery of these resources has not been common. The concept of incorporating discovery as a primary consideration within a technology architecture is therefore relatively new within the span of IT history.

Centralized discovery mechanisms were primarily put into place in support of reuse initiatives. Projects centered around the delivery of shared objects or components required a means of communicating the availability of these resources to other parts of the enterprise. Various types of discovery extensions were used, ranging from LDAP directories to Excel spreadsheets. Often the catalog of shared components was simply described on a publicly accessible Web page as part of the overall corporate intranet.

The advent of UDDI as part of the first-generation Web services platform brought the formalization of discovery into the spotlight. Although it was not widely adopted, its release came just before the mainstream emergence of SOA.

In fact, it was the existence of a discovery mechanism that primarily distinguished SOA from previous distributed architecture models. Even though this model (Figure 12.7) represents an early incarnation of SOA that has long been surpassed, it is still an important part of service-oriented computing history and highlights just how fundamental discoverability is.

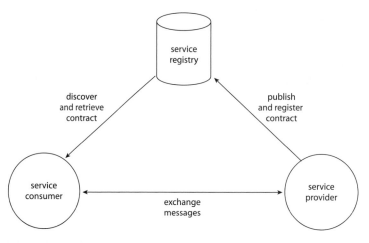

Figure 12.7

The original architectural representation of SOA positioned the existence of a discovery component (the service registry) as one of three primary parts of what distinguished a service-oriented architecture.

SUMMARY OF KEY POINTS

- Discovery is the process of discovering a service and interpretation is the process of understanding its purpose and capabilities.

- Discoverability and interpretability are measures of a service's ability to support discovery and interpretation processes.

12.2 Profiling this Principle

Discoverability and interpretability represent two closely related service design characteristics that are directly associated with this principle, as described in Table 12.1. Although you could split them into separate principles, they are generally represented collectively by Service Discoverability.

Principle Profile	
Short Definition	*"Services are discoverable."*
Long Definition	*"Services are supplemented with communicative meta data by which they can be effectively discovered and interpreted."*
Goals	• Services are positioned as highly discoverable resources within the enterprise. • The purpose and capabilities of each service are clearly expressed so that they can be interpreted by humans and software programs. Achieving these goals requires foresight and a solid understanding of the nature of the service itself. Depending on the type of service model being designed, realizing this principle may require both business and technical expertise.
Design Characteristics	• Service contracts are equipped with appropriate meta data that will be correctly referenced when discovery queries are issued. • Service contracts are further outfitted with additional meta information that clearly communicates their purpose and capabilities to humans. • If a service registry exists, registry records are populated with the same attention to meta information as just described. • If a service registry does not exist, service profile documents are authored to supplement the service contract and to form the basis for future registry records. (See Chapter 15 for more details about service profiles.)
Implementation Requirements	• The existence of design standards that govern the meta information used to make service contracts discoverable and interpretable, as well as guidelines for how and when service contracts should be further supplemented with annotations.

- The existence of design standards that establish a consistent means of recording service meta information outside of the contract. This information is either collected in a supplemental document in preparation for a service registry, or it is placed in the registry itself.

You may have noticed the absence of a service registry on the list of implementation requirements. As previously established, the goal of this principle is to implement design characteristics within the service, not within the architecture.

Web Service Region of Influence

Even though we ultimately want a discovery mechanism in place, it is also ideal for service contracts to be independently discoverable and interpretable. From a Web service perspective, this principle is focused solely on the service contract documents.

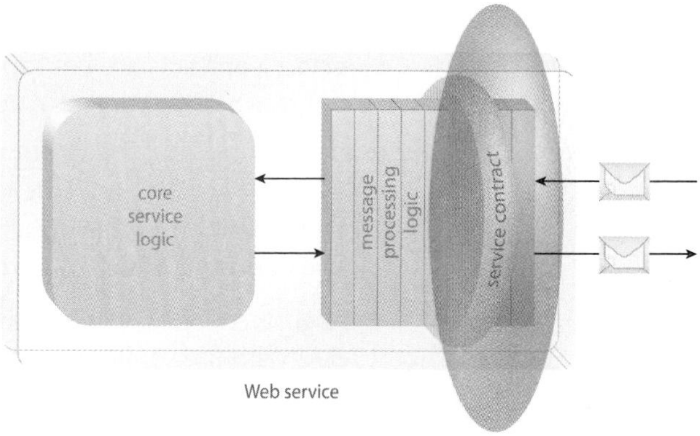

Web service

Figure 12.8

Table 12.1

A profile for the Service Discoverability principle.

SUMMARY OF KEY POINTS

- The Service Discoverability principle encompasses both discoverability and interpretability design characteristics.

- The key goal of this principle is to improve the communications quality of service meta data.

12.3 Types of Discovery and Discoverability Meta Information

There are some key terms that help us distinguish different discovery methods and meta information types most commonly used to enhance discoverability and interpretability.

Design-Time and Runtime Discovery

By far the most common form of discovery is carried out by humans. Those responsible for building service consumer programs or assembling service compositions require the ability to search a service inventory during the design phase.

As a result, we refer to the manual process of discovery by humans as *design-time discovery*. Figure 12.9 illustrates how design-time discovery requires the existence of a central discovery mechanism, most commonly a service registry. Both mediums of discoverability meta information discussed so far (service registry records and contracts) are searched for and assessed as humans carry out the discovery and interpretation processes described previously in the *Discovery and Interpretation, Discoverability and Interpretability in Abstract* section.

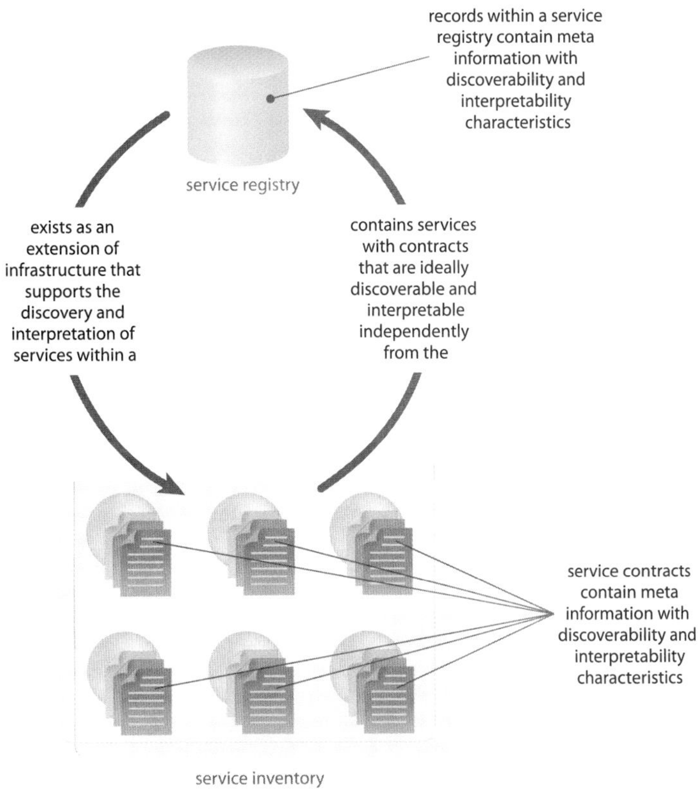

Figure 12.9

The relationship between a service registry and a service inventory as they collectively enable design-time discovery within an enterprise.

records within a service registry contain meta information with discoverability and interpretability characteristics

service registry

exists as an extension of infrastructure that supports the discovery and interpretation of services within a

contains services with contracts that are ideally discoverable and interpretable independently from the

service contracts contain meta information with discoverability and interpretability characteristics

service inventory

Common discovery technologies, such as UDDI (Example 12.1), provide programmatic interfaces into service registry repositories. This enables us to build programs and services capable of issuing dynamic discovery queries. The result is an automated process called *runtime discovery*.

```
<discoveryURLs>
  <discoveryURL useType="businessEntity">
    http://www.soabooks.com?businesskey=kv04292j-sf0f93msl
  </discoveryURL>
</discoveryURLs>
```

Example 12.1
The UDDI `discoveryURL` construct establishing the address of an XML document that can describe a business and associated services.

While this may imply the ability for a service to automatically initiate a discovery process and then locate and even consume the discovered service at runtime, it will require further technology innovations before it becomes part of the mainstream SOA landscape.

One could argue that the front-end tools used by humans to issue queries against service registries carry out runtime discovery because they make use of the registry APIs. However, this term is usually used in reference to discovery-related functionality carried out by services as part of an overall composition or solution.

One runtime technology that is somewhat associated with the discovery of Web services is that of meta data exchange. Through the implementation of the WS-Metadata-Exchange specification, a service consumer is capable of programmatically requesting the most current technical service contract documents from a service (Example 12.2). This automated form of contract access and retrieval has several uses, including runtime version checking.

```
<Envelope ...>
  <Header>
    ...
    <wsa:MessageID>
      uuid:4906496704
    </wsa:MessageID>
  </Header>
  <Body>
```

```
  <wsx:GetMetadata>
    <wsx:Dialect>
      http://www.w3.org/2001/XMLSchema
    </wsx:Dialect>
  </wsx:GetMetadata>
  </Body>
</Envelope>
```

Example 12.2

A SOAP message containing a GetMetadata construct that is requesting the service contract's XML schema. Note the use of the WS-Addressing `MessageID` element we established in Chapter 11.

NOTE

To learn more about UDDI and WS-MetadataExchange, see
`www.ws-standards.com` and `www.soaspecs.com`.

Discoverability Meta Information

When defining what meta information to add or augment in support of service discovery, we need look no further than the four types of meta data we defined earlier in the *Types of Meta Abstraction* section of Chapter 8. As shown in Figure 12.10, to support our goal of attaining enhanced discoverability and interpretability, we need to focus on the functional and quality of service meta information types.

Figure 12.10

Two of the four types of meta information established in Chapter 8 are relevant to discoverability.

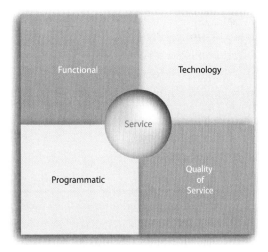

Functional Meta Data

Functional meta data represents the most fundamental measure of discoverability a service is expected to attain. By applying the Standardized Service Contract principle, we are guaranteed a level of consistency as to how the purpose and capabilities of services are expressed through the technical service contract. By extending this concept to further apply standardization to the actual registry records, we ensure that a service can be located and understood, based on how its meta information is documented.

Functional discoverability often comes down to the clarity and appropriateness with which services and capabilities are labeled. Services that do not possess standardized contracts are often not considered to have attained functional discoverability on an independent basis. In fact, these types of services may not have any significant level of discoverability.

Furthermore, services that *only* achieve this level of discoverability will usually need to be interpreted by technical professionals who can derive the capabilities of individual capabilities by studying the specified data exchange requirements.

Quality of Service Meta Data

After we have located one or more services we are interested in using, there is a process of assessment and filtering that can be completed in order to choose the most suitable service for our purposes and to ensure that it will be able to fulfill the expected runtime requirements.

Quality of service meta data encompasses behavioral characteristics, operational thresholds, and policies, all of which are associated with the service's runtime existence. Several of these details can be added to the service registry, in which case discovery searches with relatively sophisticated criteria can be issued.

Either way, the availability of quality of service meta information can significantly aid human interpretability.

SUMMARY OF KEY POINTS

- Both design-time and runtime variations of the discovery process exist; however, design-time discovery is more common.

- Of the four meta abstraction types established in Chapter 8, functional and quality of service meta data are relevant to this principle.

12.4 Measuring Service Discoverability

Provided in the following sections are some suggested guidelines for assessing and labeling the extent of a service's discoverability and interpretability.

Fundamental Levels

We can establish some baseline measures using the following simple checklist:

1. Has functional meta information been documented in plain English?

2. If yes, has functional meta information been clearly expressed as part of the service contract for discoverability purposes?

3. Has quality of service information been documented in non-technical English?

4. Has quality of service meta information been clearly expressed as part of the service contract or a formal SLA?

5. Has a service profile document or (if a service registry exists) the corresponding service registry record been created?

6. Does the service profile/registry record contain all relevant functional meta information?

7. Does the service profile/registry record contain all relevant quality of service meta information?

8. Have business subject matter experts contributed to the definition of business-centric discoverability meta information?

9. Has all discoverability meta documentation been subjected to standards and conventions to ensure consistency?

10. Has all discoverability meta documentation been reviewed and refined by a communications expert?

Simple labels can be used to represent fundamental levels that indicate that this principle has been applied to certain meaningful extents. For example, a level of "negligible discoverability content" or just "none" could be assigned if you answered "yes" to two or fewer of these questions. A level of "partial discoverability content" could be used when seven out of ten of the items were addressed, and a level of "complete discoverability content" could represent the completion of this checklist.

> **NOTE**
>
> Even if no quality of service information exists, simply having researched and assessed that fact qualifies as a "yes" answer to questions 3, 4, and 7.

What these simple levels communicate is only that the necessary discoverability meta information was put in place and that interpretability has been taken into account. Because they do not communicate the quality of this information, these levels may not be an indication of a service's *actual* discoverability.

Custom Rating System

The quality of the meta data used to establish significant levels of discoverability (and interpretability) within a given service depends on how well that information expresses the functional and quality of service details of the service and how well those details relate to and tie in with the service's surrounding enterprise environment.

For example, if a standardized vocabulary is in place, then the appropriate values would need to have been applied in order for keyword searches to be an effective means of discovery.

Therefore, measuring the actual discoverability of a service requires:

- a thorough understanding of the service's functional context and capabilities

- first-hand knowledge of the service's surrounding environment, including the standard discovery platform in use

With this information on hand, a custom rating system can be put in place to label estimated Service Discoverability effectiveness. (For more information about using standard service profiles and vocabularies, see Chapter 15.)

12.5 Discoverability and Service Design

Even though discoverability represents a broad design characteristic that originally helped define both SOA and service-orientation, it is often one of the most neglected areas of service design. Based on what we've learned about discoverability and interpretability so far, let's take a closer look at how incorporating these design characteristics can influence the overall service design.

Service Discoverability and Service Modeling

Applying this principle effectively requires documenting a consistent collection of relevant meta information from the beginning of the service delivery process. The service modeling sub-process of service-oriented analysis requires that business and technology experts collaborate to conceptualize service candidates. It is during this preliminary process that a great deal of useful meta information can be harnessed, specifically for business services.

Business subject matter experts will understand the meaning behind business service candidates and will likely also be able to communicate behavioral details in relation to business rules. Documenting this intelligence while it is readily accessible is a key part of completing the service modeling process.

Later, when the actual service contract is formed as part of the service-oriented design process, options are explored for physically attaching and formalizing available meta information (Figure 12.11).

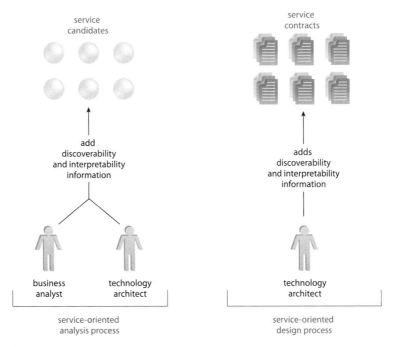

Figure 12.11

Discoverability is one of the few principles that is actively applied during both the service-oriented analysis and design stages.

Service Discoverability and Granularity

Unless certain security or privacy considerations need to be taken into account, Service Discoverability represents the one principle that does not tend to have a direct effect on any level of service granularity. When applying this principle, the focus is on supplementing the service contract with additional meta data used for communication and identification purposes. Although we may add content to the actual service contract, it is usually in the form of annotations that describe what has already been defined as the technical service contract.

Service Discoverability and Policy Assertions

While discoverability details can be incorporated into WSDL and XML schema definitions via human-readable annotations, there are several creative ways a service can be made more discoverable and interpretable through the use of optional or ignorable policy assertions.

Previous chapters have already discussed WS-Policy features, such as the `wsp:optional` and `wsp:ignorable` attributes, policy alternatives, and policy parameters, all of which can be used to present various preferences and compliance options to service consumer designers.

While these extensions increase the flexibility with which consumer programs can utilize a service, they can also be used to simply provide hints about a service's underlying logic, behavior, and even limitations. Although these hints can express both functional and quality of service type meta data, they are generally only legible to those technical professionals that actually understand the WS-Policy language and also have knowledge of any proprietary assertion vocabularies that may be in use.

Service Discoverability and Service Models

All services, regardless of service model, should be discoverable. Even though discoverability clearly plays a larger role in the effective utilization of agnostic services, it is important to be able to locate and understand *any* member of a service inventory.

How Service Discoverability Affects Other Principles

The design considerations raised by this principle directly shape and extend a service's meta data. Therefore, this principle can affect others that rely on or influence meta information (Figure 12.12).

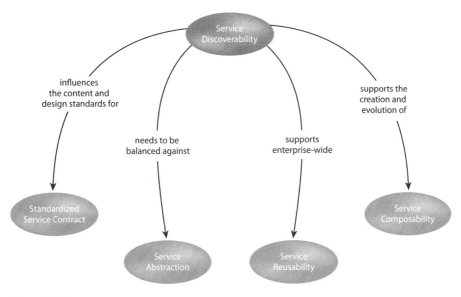

Figure 12.12

The application of this principle infuses a service-oriented enterprise with clarity and communication, which is why it can support and affect other parts of service-orientation.

Service Discoverability and Standardized Service Contract

Clearly, to make a service more easily discoverable and interpretable affects what is published in the service contract. In fact, Service Discoverability can directly influence the definition of functional expression design standards that are a common result of applying the Standardized Service Contract principle. In some cases, this principle may even be responsible for entirely new naming conventions in support of enhanced functional expression.

Service Discoverability and Service Abstraction

While the principle of Service Abstraction encourages us to reduce the amount of information published in a contract, Service Discoverability asks us to publish more. Therefore, a balance is required to ensure that we do not over-document the service contract with discoverability-related meta information. While much of the information is geared toward supplemental discovery queries and human interpretation, there is always the danger of publishing details about the service that may have negative repercussions down the road.

Once we have achieved the appropriate balance of discoverability and abstraction, the discoverability of the subsequently implemented service will be based on the meta information that is published (not abstracted).

Service Discoverability and Service Reusability

One could state that the primary purpose of emphasizing Service Discoverability is to support Service Reusability. Therefore, when pursuing the application of this principle, we need to remain cognizant of the ultimate impact effective Service Discoverability will have on realizing reuse (and consequently attaining many of the strategic goals associated with an enterprise-wide SOA initiative).

Having stated all of that, does the application of Service Discoverability in any way actually affect the application of the Service Reusability principle? In fact it does, primarily in relation to the service contract. When expressing reusable functionality, we are encouraged to apply discoverability-related design standards to ensure that the purpose and capabilities of the service are as clearly expressed as possible through the actual technical contract.

Service Discoverability and Service Composability

As further explored in Chapter 13, this principle establishes a key success factor in carrying through effective *design-time* composition processes. When modeling service compositions, it is imperative that potential composition members be easily located and identified so as to avoid the inadvertent creation of redundant service logic.

Furthermore, as compositions evolve in response to changes in parent business processes or in pursuit of increasing overall business requirements fulfillment, it is essential to be able to effectively survey an enterprise in search of new services and capabilities that were added since the original version of a composition was created.

SUMMARY OF KEY POINTS

- Service Discoverability is one of the three principles applied during analysis and design stages.
- Documenting discoverability information can be an important part of service modeling, especially for business services.
- Although this principle advocates publishing more meta information, its application is moderated by Service Abstraction considerations.
- Service Discoverability directly supports Service Reusability because highly discoverable services have the best chance of being repeatedly reused.

12.6 Risks Associated with Service Discoverability

The pitfalls associated with this principle are especially difficult to gauge because an improper application of discoverability will not tend to reveal itself until long *after* the service has been deployed.

Post-Implementation Application of Discoverability

Applying this principle after a service has been deployed can compromise the quality of its discovery-related meta information. It is natural for those originally involved in the service modeling and design processes to lose touch with the details and subtleties of the service when asked to document its meta information months after its original definition—or perhaps someone other than those who built the service is asked to provide this information instead. Either way, the quality of discoverability and interpretability meta data will usually suffer.

Those involved with the design of a service are best suited to providing the initial draft of discovery-related documentation. These individuals will have the most intimate knowledge of what the service is capable of and for what usages it is more or less suitable. Therefore, it is considered a best practice to have the meta information added at design-time, prior to the initial release of the service.

This also relates to the supplemental annotations that are sometimes required to further clarify complex parts of the service contract. Those who initially design these parts are generally the most qualified to define their purpose and meaning.

Application of this Principle by Non-Communicative Resources

Often the definition of service contracts is left to the same team responsible for building the service itself. As explained in the previous section, this is generally desirable. However, while these individuals may be the most qualified, they may not be skilled communicators.

Even though services will often need to be discovered by individuals with the same level of technical expertise as those who delivered them, it should not be assumed that this will always be the case. Services need to be discoverable by a variety of IT professionals, including project managers, departmental managers, business analysts, and perhaps even external contractors that may be unfamiliar with internal discoverability-related design conventions.

SUMMARY OF KEY POINTS

- It is inadvisable to apply this principle after a service has been implemented because discoverability and interpretability details are bound to be lost.

- When discoverability information is only documented by business or technical professionals, it may be inadequate for use by other project team members.

12.7 CASE STUDY EXAMPLE

Cutit is just in the process of delivering its first set of services in support of the Lab Project business process. Therefore, it has not yet implemented a central service registry, nor has it even assessed potential registry products in the marketplace.

Cutit analysts and architects are fully aware of the fact that eventually they will reach a point where their service inventory will have grown sufficiently to warrant this important part of their SOA infrastructure. In the meantime, though, their immediate services are equipped with no real discoverability meta information. Outside of technical Web service contracts, those who will need to asses these services will have little to go by.

Service Profiles (Functional Meta Information)

It is decided that architects will produce an official profile document for each service. These documents will be posted on the local intranet alongside SLAs and links that point to the corresponding service WSDL, XML schema, and WS-Policy definitions. (See Chapter 15 for more information about service profile documents.)

The service profiles need to be structured in a standardized manner so that all organize meta information the same way. One of the primary purposes of the profiles is to form the basis for service registry records that will later need to be created once a service registry product is in place. Therefore, the Cutit team researches and takes into account common types of registry record values when determining the profile format.

They eventually settle on the following list of meta data fields:

- Service Name

- Purpose - Short Description

- Purpose - Detailed Description

- Service Model

- Capabilities

- Owner Contact Information

- Status

Furthermore, the following meta data for service capabilities is documented separately so that each can be individually assessed:

- Operation Name

- Purpose - Short Description

- Purpose - Detailed Description

- Status

The initial set of published documents is greeted with mixed reviews. While developers have no problem learning about the services, others have difficulty deciphering the many technical references in the descriptions.

For example:

- Project managers interested in surveying these new services as potentially reusable assets for their upcoming projects can't make heads or tails of the purpose descriptions because they are simply too technical.

- Business analysts who have been made aware of the fact that they will be involved in service-oriented analysis and service modeling projects in the near future study the new services because they sound like resources that tie into processes they will need to document. However, outside of making some assumptions based on the service and capability names, they are also at a loss as to what the services actually do.

- Even external contractors (including other architects) are a bit confused primarily because the profiles have been written from the perspective of those who are already intimately familiar with the surrounding architecture and technologies. Individuals new to this environment are not provided enough information to understand all of the profile content.

Subsequent complaints and meetings result in an acknowledgement that the initial drafts of the profiles are not adequate. They are removed from the intranet, and a second version for each service is planned. Only this time, the original business analysts and business subject matter experts are also asked to contribute.

Together with the architects they produce a set of refined service profiles with a number of improvements:

- The profiles document both business and technology aspects of each service in plain English.

- These profiles are further supplemented with keywords from a recently created taxonomy vocabulary. These keyword values are intended to establish the basis for future discovery query criteria.

- To round things off, a technical writer is brought in to copyedit each profile document. This ensures consistency in terminology and writing style across profiles.

Table 12.2 shows a sample profile produced by the Cutit team for the Materials service.

Name: Materials

Purpose (short): Provides common capabilities associated with the processing of externally purchased and internally developed lab materials.

Purpose (detailed): Materials is a Web service with a functional scope that corresponds to the Lab Materials business entity. This service provides capabilities specifically associated with the processing of materials-related information and functions. Note that some materials are purchased, whereas others are developed internally. Different data structures are used to represent purchased and developed material records, which is why separate Get operations are provided.

Service Model: Entity

Taxonomy Keywords: lab, materials, ingredients, orders, reservations

Custodian: Enterprise Architecture Group (E-mail: ...)

Status: in development (scheduled for release Nov. 12)

Version: 1.0

Name: GetDeveloped	Purpose: Retrieves a complete record for an internally developed lab materials item. Taxonomy Keywords: lab, materials, ingredients Status: in development
Name: GetPurchased	Purpose: Retrieves a complete record for an externally purchased lab materials item. Taxonomy Keywords: lab, materials, ingredients Status: in development
Name: ReportStock-Levels	Purpose: Reports the current in-stock quantity of an internally developed or an externally purchased item. Taxonomy Keywords: lab, materials, ingredients Status: in development

Table 12.2
The revised profile for the Materials service.

The team agrees that ultimately Owner and Version fields will be required for individual capabilities as well. For now, these fields are added but left blank.

Related Quality of Service Meta Information

A preliminary SLA is also put together for the Materials service consisting of the following meta data:

- service availability

- guaranteed response times for individual capabilities

- range of allowable input and output values

- expiry date of the service or any one of its capabilities

- fault condition response processes

- usage requirements and policies

This SLA will exist as a separate document that is considered an official extension of the Materials service contract. The meta data collected in the preceding profile is intended to complement the SLA and improve the communications quality of the service contract by providing descriptive information specifically for discoverability and interpretability purposes.

Chapter 13

Service Composability
(Composition Member Design
and Complex Compositions)

A s much as reuse is considered a core part of service-orientation, its successful realization has a great deal to do with effective and repeated aggregation. Service composition therefore lies very much at the heart of SOA and represents design characteristics and runtime dynamics that form the basis of this principle (Figure 13.1).

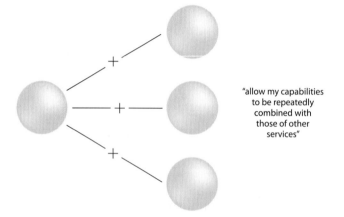

"allow my capabilities to be repeatedly combined with those of other services"

Figure 13.1

Assembling capabilities from different sources to solve a larger problem is the foundation of distributed computing. This principle introduces new design considerations that ensure that services are able to participate in multiple compositions to solve multiple larger problems.

13.1 Composition Explained

Software composition is nothing new. Many past programs and systems have been comprised of files and components shaped together to form some type of runtime aggregate. Understanding what constitutes software composition and how it has been applied in the past will help us better appreciate the level of sophistication to which service-orientation aims to take this concept.

Composition in Abstract

If something is decomposed, it can be recomposed. In fact, composition is usually the reason something is decomposed in the first place. We break a larger thing apart because we see potential benefit in being able to do things with the individual pieces that we would not have the freedom to do were they to exist as just a whole (Figure 13.2).

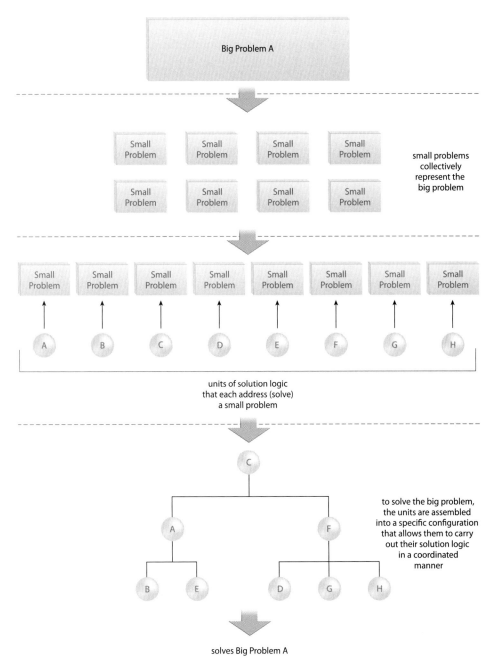

Figure 13.2

The separation of concerns theory encourages us to break down a larger problem into multiple smaller problems (concerns). This gives us the opportunity to build corresponding pieces of solution logic, each of which solves a small problem (addresses an individual concern). These capabilities are part of units that are assembled into a composition through which they are coordinated to collectively solve the large problem.

Applying this approach establishes an environment where solution logic exists as composable units. As a result, there is the constant opportunity to recompose the same solution logic in order to solve new problems (Figure 13.3).

Figure 13.3

The same units originally created to solve Big Problem A are recomposed to collectively solve a different problem.

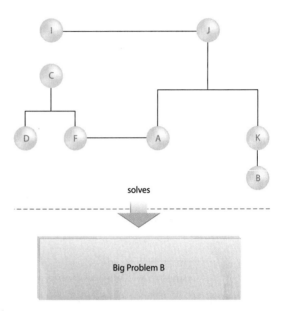

When we apply this rationale to the world of automation, the implications become pretty clear. Why build one large program that can only perform a fixed set of functions, when we can decompose that program into smaller programs that can be combined in creative ways to provide a variety of functions for different purposes? This is the basis of the separation of concerns theory discussed in Chapter 4.

Origins of Composition

Composition was a key design innovation in the evolution of IT. It became a common part of custom solution architecture but also was fundamental to the design of commercial software products and especially operating systems.

The advent of the dynamic link library (DLL) popularized composition in that it made the physical separation of reusable units of logic highly accessible by implementing these units as generic library files with public technical interfaces. Instead of the notorious monolithic executable, a program could now be decomposed into numerous dll files and a much smaller executable (Figure 13.4). This then allowed the dynamic link libraries to be used by other programs, each represented by their own executable file.

Figure 13.4

Multiple executable files accessing reusable dynamic link libraries. This architecture is reminiscent of the relationship between task and agnostic services.

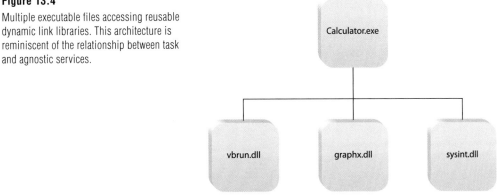

Object-oriented design approaches supported and further formalized the notion of decomposition and recomposition. Programming logic was essentially separated into classes that provided methods that could be subsequently composed into an aggregate (Figure 13.5).

Figure 13.5

A simple object hierarchy in which an aggregate object composes others.

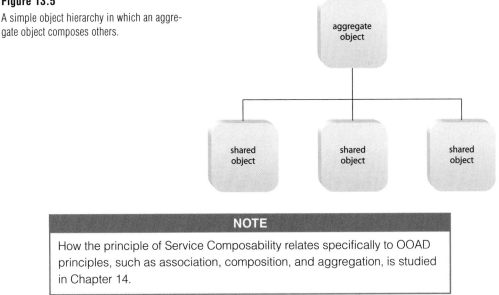

> **NOTE**
>
> How the principle of Service Composability relates specifically to OOAD principles, such as association, composition, and aggregation, is studied in Chapter 14.

Much like object-orientation, service-orientation provides a design platform whereby logic is decomposed and recomposed (Figure 13.6). Unlike past design paradigms, though, service-orientation places different expectations on the ability for services to be composed. These unique requirements will be discussed throughout this chapter.

Figure 13.6

A service-oriented composition equivalent to
past composition variations.

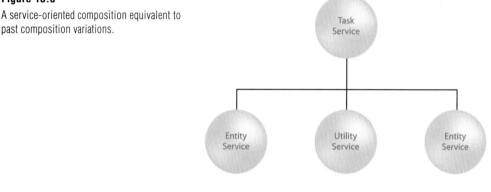

SUMMARY OF KEY POINTS

- The concept of composition is a fundamental part of software design in that we can benefit from the decomposition of solution logic so that it can be recomposed into new configurations to solve a variety of problems.

- Various forms of composition have existed in the past, ranging from the assembly of simple programming libraries to the more formal approaches defined by object-orientation.

13.2 Profiling this Principle

As we explore later in the *How Service Composability Affects Other Principles* section, this is a principle that is pretty much related to and supported by every other part of the service-orientation paradigm. In fact, several other principles exist primarily in support of service composition.

A question one could raise then is: "If all other principles collectively shape a service in support of composition, then why is a separate principle dedicated to service composition required?"

Each of the other principles establishes specific design characteristics individually. As illustrated early on in the *Principles that Implement vs. Principles that Regulate* section of Chapter 5, Service Composability is intended to ensure that the design characteristics collectively required for the service to support effective composition are sufficiently implemented.

Note that the upcoming profile in Table 13.1 makes reference to two terms ("composition member" and "designated controller") that are defined in the subsequent *Composition Concepts and Terminology* section.

Principle Profile	
Short Definition	*"Services are composable."*
Long Definition	*"Services are effective composition participants, regardless of the size and complexity of the composition."*
Goals	When discussing the goals of Service Composability, pretty much all of the goals of Service Reusability apply. This is because service composition often turns out to be a form of service reuse. In fact, you may recall that one of the objectives we listed for the Service Reusability principle was to enable wide-scale service composition.
	However, above and beyond simply attaining reuse, service composition provides the medium through which we can achieve what is often classified as the ultimate goal of service-oriented computing. By establishing an enterprise comprised of solution logic represented by an inventory of highly reusable services, we provide the means for a large extent of future business automation requirements to be fulfilled through…you guessed it: service composition.
Design Characteristics for Composition Member Capabilities	Ideally, every service capability (especially those providing reusable logic) is considered a potential composition member. This essentially means that the design characteristics already established by the Service Reusability principle are equally relevant to building effective composition members.
	Additionally, there are two further characteristics emphasized by this principle:
	• The service needs to possess a highly efficient execution environment. More so than being able to manage concurrency, the efficiency with which composition members perform their individual processing should be highly tuned.
	• The service contract needs to be flexible so that it can facilitate different types of data exchange requirements for similar functions. This typically relates to the ability of the contract to exchange the same type of data at different levels of granularity.

The manner in which these qualities go beyond mere reuse has to do primarily with the service being capable of optimizing its runtime processing responsibilities in support of multiple, simultaneous compositions.

Design Characteristics for Composition Controller Capabilities

Composition members will often also need to act as controllers or sub-controllers within different composition configurations. However, services designed as designated controllers are generally alleviated from many of the high-performance demands placed on composition members.

These types of services therefore have their own set of design characteristics:

• The logic encapsulated by a designated controller will almost always be limited to a single business task. Typically, the task service model is used, resulting in the common characteristics of that model being applied to this type of service.

• While designated controllers may be reusable, service reuse is not usually a primary design consideration. Therefore, the design characteristics fostered by Service Reusability are considered and applied where appropriate, but with less of the usual rigor applied to agnostic services.

• Statelessness is not always as strictly emphasized on designated controllers as with composition members. Depending on the state deferral options available by the surrounding architecture, designated controllers may sometimes need to be designed to remain fully stateful while the underlying composition members carry out their respective parts of the overall task.

Of course, any capability acting as a controller can become a member of a larger composition, which brings the previously listed composition member design characteristics into account as well.

Implementation Requirements	As demanding as service reuse is on runtime deployment requirements, it pales in comparison to service composition. As a result, hosting runtime environments need to be as scalable and reliable as possible. This typically translates into the need for dedicated, clustered servers with fail-over and the availability of mature runtime service technology.
	Services implemented as Web services often require standardized implementations of several key WS-* extensions, including those associated with security, reliable messaging, activity management, and cross-service transactions.
Web Service Region of Influence for Composition Members	Many of the design considerations introduced by this principle have to do with the optimization and tuning of the service architecture in support of effective and efficient composition participation.
	The potential scope of this principle can essentially encompass all parts of a service acting as a composition member primarily because composition builds on reuse and other design characteristics established by supporting principles.
	Figure 13.7

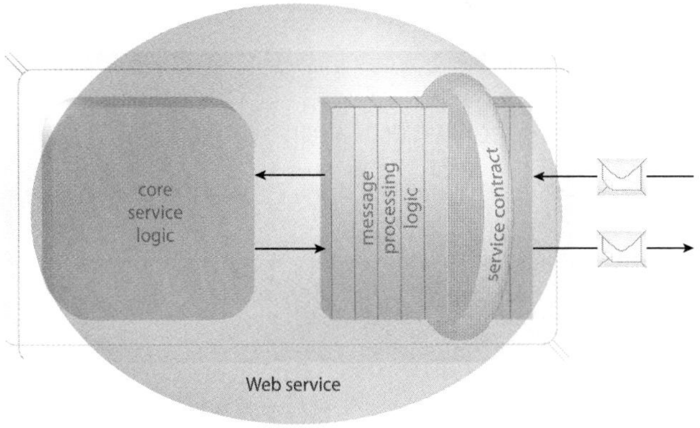

Web Service Region of Influence for Designated Controllers	In the case of a designated controller, the focus of this principle is primarily on the core service logic.
	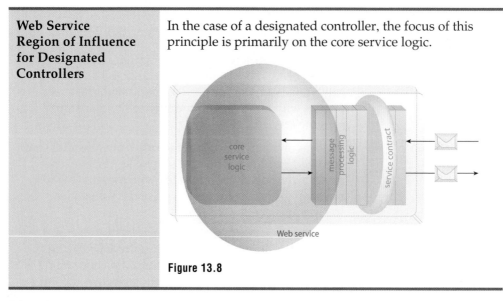
	Figure 13.8

Table 13.1

A profile for the Service Composability principle.

SUMMARY OF KEY POINTS

- Service Composability is closely associated with Service Reusability because composition can be seen as a form of reuse.

- A key emphasis of this principle is to ensure that services are designed to participate as effective members of multiple compositions, even when immediate composition requirements do not exist.

- The application of this principle can affect just about any part of a service architecture.

13.3 Composition Concepts and Terminology

Compositions introduce new terms and concepts that need to be properly incorporated into actual composition design specifications. This next set of sections describes the following terms and discusses related concepts:

- Composition
- Composition Instance

- Composition Member
- Composition Controller
- Composition Sub-Controller
- Composition Member Capability
- Composition Controller Capability
- Designated Controller
- Collective Composability
- Service Activity
- Point-to-Point
- Primitive Composition
- Complex Composition
- Composition Initiator

Compositions and Composition Instances

A service composition is typically associated with the automation of a business process. When defining the workflow logic of this process, various decision points are created to determine the flow of data and action in response to runtime variables and conditions. Therefore, it can be helpful to distinguish between a *static business process definition* (comprised of workflow logic) and a *business process instance* that represents what parts of the workflow logic actually occurred at runtime.

Similarly, service *compositions* are defined at design-time when required inter-capability interactions are mapped out to accommodate various scenarios in support of the business process workflow logic. A service *composition instance* represents what actually happens when an occurrence of the workflow logic is carried out by a series of service instances at runtime.

> **NOTE**
>
> Although this section makes a distinction between a business process and a business process instance and a composition and a composition instance, this distinction is not made elsewhere in the book. For simplicity's sake, the term "service composition" is used to refer to both a static composition definition and a composition instance unless otherwise qualified.

Composition Members and Controllers

When taking part in compositions, services can fulfill different roles depending on how they are positioned within the overall composition configuration. As a *composition controller*, the service is located at the head of a composition hierarchy. This occurs when the service capability that is being executed contains and carries out logic that invokes capabilities in other services (Figure 13.9).

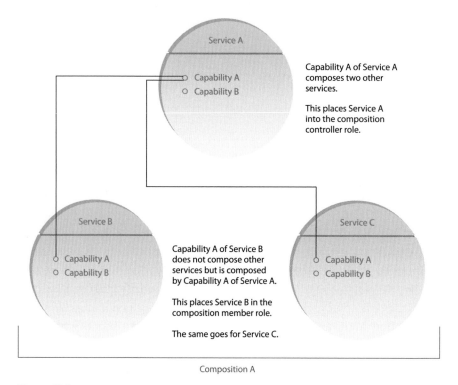

Figure 13.9
Services assume composition roles based on how their individual capabilities participate within the composition.

A *composition member*, on the other hand, represents a service being composed by another. Again, as shown in Figure 13.9, it is the fact that the service's capability is being invoked by another service that places the service into this role.

A composition member may compose other composition members, which can, in turn, compose others as well (Figure 13.10). Composition members that compose other services can be further qualified as *sub-controllers*.

This terminology is important especially when working with business services. As described in the *Service Composition and Service Models* section, the controller role can just as easily be assumed by an entity service as it can by a task service. However, it is less common for a task service to be a sub-controller than it is for an entity service.

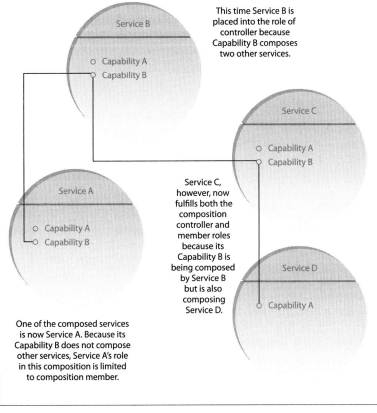

Composition B

Figure 13.10

The same services from Composition A are reutilized as participants in a new composition. New capabilities are now involved, which changes service composition roles.

Service Compositions are Actually Service Capability Compositions

The composition controller and member labels are used to represent roles services assume, depending on their position within a given service activity. It is important to continually remind ourselves that it is actually the individual service capabilities that are responsible for placing services into these roles.

Therefore, the capabilities themselves can be further qualified, as follows:

- *composition controller capability* (or just *controller capability*)

- *composition member capability*

When using these role classifications, it is also helpful to acknowledge that they may be temporary for services, but more likely permanent for capabilities. For example, if three of six capabilities within a service encapsulate logic that composes other services, then the service will only be classified a controller when one of those three capabilities is invoked. However, each of these three capabilities will always be controller capabilities for as long as they compose other services.

Regardless of the controller designation, this principle emphasizes the need for all service logic to be composable, which means that all six of the service's capabilities will ideally have been designed to carry out their capabilities as an effective part of larger compositions.

Designated Controllers

Services, in their entirety, can also be designed as *designated controllers*, which limits them to the controller role only. The classic example of a designated controller is a task service with just one capability used to kick off the automation of a business process which will involve the composition of multiple other services.

Collective Composability

Depending on the extent to which the Service Abstraction principle is applied to a reusable service, when we incorporate one of its capabilities into a new composition, we may not be aware of the fact that it is acting as a composition controller. We will therefore place the same expectations on that service capability in terms of performance, reliability, and overall quality of service, as we would on any other.

However, underneath the covers, it is the collective measure of composability of all members involved in a composition that ultimately determines the quality of service offered by the controller of the composition. Furthermore, because Service Composability is comprised of and directly supported by other principles, it is their application that collectively determines the overall quality of a composition. For example, the individual levels of capability autonomy for each composition member can be combined to represent the levels of autonomy of a composition's controller capability, as illustrated in Figure 13.11.

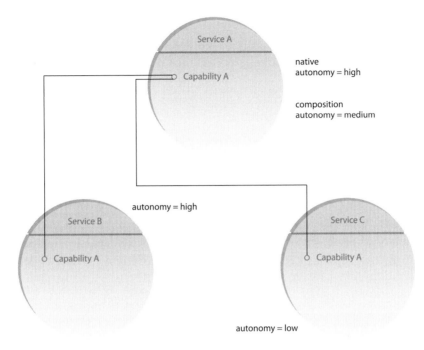

Figure 13.11

Even though Capability A's native autonomy is high, its overall autonomy (the autonomy of the composition it encapsulates) is lower due to the fact that the autonomy level of one of its composed service capabilities is low.

You can take this a step further and even equate the effectiveness of composition members with the success of SOA as a whole. As discussed shortly, the advent of the complex service composition is considered a key factor to leveraging the investment that goes into assembling an effective service inventory.

> **NOTE**
>
> A related architectural consideration is the concept of "composition autonomy," as referenced later in the *Service Composability and Composition Autonomy* section.

Service Compositions and Web Services

Fulfilling the roles of composition controller and member may seem straight forward at first glance. When we think of implementing a service as a Web service, it is evident that a Web service can easily be called by others, and its underlying solution logic can easily be designed to call other Web services.

Web services indeed establish a level of native composability, which is one of the reasons they provide such a suitable means of building SOA. However, the mere ability to compose and be composed does not guarantee that a Web service will end up being sufficiently effective in these roles. It is only through the application of this and other supporting principles that a service can be fully prepared for the demands that come with sophisticated compositions.

Service Activities

Before we can model a composition, we have to establish a means of mapping the flow of data and processing through a composed environment. To accomplish this, we need to define a *service activity*—the mapping of an inter-service message path. A service activity is intentionally limited to representing interaction *between* services only. A service activity does not represent what occurs within the underlying service logic.

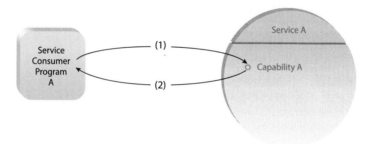

Figure 13.12

An example of a primitive service activity. The consumer program interacts with Capability A of Service A to carry out a simple point-to-point data exchange.

There are *primitive* and *complex* service activities, as illustrated in Figures 13.12 and 13.13. Depending on the level of Service Abstraction applied to a given controller capability, what may appear to be a primitive service activity may actually be a complex service activity.

For example, Capability A in Figure 13.12 may be abstracting the complex composition illustrated in Figure 13.13. The implications of "hidden compositions" is further discussed in the *Service Composability and Service Abstraction* section.

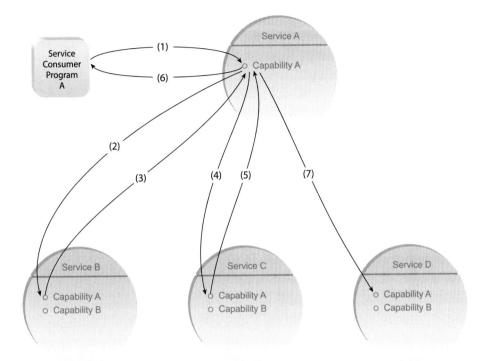

Figure 13.13

A complex service activity spanning a service composition. The numbered arrows represent the activity sequence.

Composition Initiators

The scope of a service composition does not always map to the corresponding service activity. We qualify a collection of services as being part of a composition through association with a well-defined business process. In other words, the functional scope of a service composition is determined by the business process it automates.

A service activity can (and often does) exceed this scope. If we draw a boundary around a set of coordinated services that collectively execute a business task, we usually end up with a composition controller and several composition members. A runtime component that exists outside of this boundary is usually represented by the service consumer program responsible for invoking the composition controller in order to kick off the service composition.

In this case, the service activity spans beyond the composition to include the program responsible for initiating the composition logic. When carrying out this role, the program can be referred to as the *composition initiator*.

A composition controller is therefore the service at the head of a composition and the one that typically embodies the parent functional context and scope by encapsulating the required business process logic. A composition initiator is generally not a composition controller; instead, it is a program that exists outside of the composition but fulfills this role by initiating the composition logic. In the previously displayed Figure 13.13, the composition initiator would be Service Consumer A, whereas the composition controller is Service A.

NOTE
A service consumer can assume the roles of both composition initiator and composition controller if it exists as a program that contains the range of required composition logic but does not make itself available as a service. However, it is often desirable to reserve the "controller" label for programs to which service-orientation has been applied.

FOR EXAMPLE
A claims assessment business process in an insurance company was comprised of numerous steps including the validation of submitted claims data and the lookup of corresponding client account data (including historic information). The process logic was encapsulated by the Assess operation of the Claim entity Web service and was carried out as follows:

1. An instance of the process was initiated by a legacy Web application responsible for collecting the claim submission from the end-user.

2. This application invoked the Assess operation of the Claim Web service.

3. The Assess operation logic subsequently invoked the Validate operation of the ClaimRules Web service to apply appropriate validation rules.

4. The Assess operation then invoked the Get and GetHistory operations of the Customer Web service to retrieve the required client account and background data.

5. Upon a successful assessment, the Assess operation logic updated the status of the claim record in a local database and then also called the Update operation of the Customer service to insert a reference to the new claim in the client account record.

Within this scenario, the following composition-related roles occurred:

- The legacy Web application that invoked the Claim service acted as the *composition initiator*.

- The Claim service acted as the *composition controller,* and its Assess operation can be classified as the *composition controller capability.*

- The ClaimRules and Customer services acted as *composition members.*

- The ClaimRules service's Validate operation and the Customer service's Get, GetHistory, and Update operations can all be classified as *composition member capabilities.*

- The scope of the *service composition instance* consisted of the interaction between the Claim, ClaimRules, and Customer services.

- The scope of the *service activity* encompassed the service composition instance but also included interaction between the Claim composition controller service and the legacy application that acted as composition initiator.

Although this process was often carried out on its own, it was eventually also positioned as a sub-process for a larger, expanded Client and Claims Setup (CCS) business process that allowed a customer to create a new account and submit one or more claims at the same time.

For this new process, a separate CCS task Web service was created, which encapsulated the parent business process logic. This task service invoked the Claim Web service's Assess operation once for every claim submitted. In this expanded scenario, the CCS service assumed the role of *composition controller,* and the Claim service acted as both a *sub-controller* and a *composition member.*

Point-to-Point Data Exchanges and Compositions

Continuing our discussion of composition scope, it is worthwhile establishing what extent of service activity constitutes a minimal service composition.

A simple interaction between a single service and its consumer can be referred to as a *point-to-point* exchange (a term that clearly originated from the world of integration architecture). Because this model (or architecture) is limited to a primitive service activity between two endpoints, we do not consider it a service composition.

The minimum scope of a service composition must encompass a complex service activity that spans two services plus the composition initiator. In other words, a consumer program that interacts with a service that does not invoke any other services is an example of the point-to-point model. In a scenario where the consumer program interacts with a service that invokes one or more additional services, a service composition is represented by all activity participants, excluding the composition initiator.

Although in relation to the Service Composability principle we are primarily interested in models that combine multiple services into actual compositions, it's important to acknowledge that the point-to-point model represents the vast majority of past service implementations, especially for services built as Web services. Many Web services have been positioned as endpoints or wrappers for legacy environments and therefore had no need to compose other services. They were simply being utilized to support a specific integration channel.

Types of Compositions

Having established the point-to-point model, let's introduce two additional terms to categorize two common types of service compositions. The minimal composition configuration we just described is often implemented during the early stages of a service inventory when few actual composable services are available. Service activities tend to be modest in size and complexity. We therefore label the more simple configurations as *primitive compositions*.

A common example of a primitive composition is a set of Web services consisting of the initial sender, one or two intermediary services, and an ultimate receiver. The intermediaries may perform supplementary processing, such as routing or perhaps content filtering. Overall, though, the service activity is relatively straight-forward and often limited to the utilization of first-generation Web services technologies and the processing of one document or one set of parameter data.

More sophisticated composition configurations and requirements are needed to automate larger and more demanding business processes. For these situations, we build *complex service compositions*, which are explained and further defined in the following section.

SUMMARY OF KEY POINTS

- Depending on the nature of the composition in which a service is participating, the service and its capabilities can assume composition controller and/or composition member roles.

- Services can be designated controllers if warranted by their underlying logic and their position within the service inventory.

- Service activities represent the message exchanges between services, not the activity that occurs within service boundaries.

- Composition initiators are programs that trigger a composition but reside outside of the composition boundary.

- To constitute a composition requires at least two services, one of which is then invoked by a composition initiator. A point-to-point model represents the scenario when only the initiator and one service are involved.

- Primitive compositions represent simple message exchanges across two or more services.

13.4 The Complex Service Composition

As we establish and add to a growing service inventory, we begin to witness the gradual dissolution of the traditional application and the concept of integration (as described in *The Service Composition* section of Chapter 4). More and more we move toward an environment where a significant extent of the automation required for a given business process is achieved by drawing from a reserve of agnostic services.

> **NOTE**
>
> The following stages document the accumulation and reuse of agnostic services only. Each indicated development project may also need to deliver non-agnostic task services in order to fulfill all automation requirements and establish the needed parent composition logic.

Stages in the Evolution of a Service Inventory

There are three fundamental phases that enterprises tend to transition through as their service inventory evolves and grows. The further an organization progresses through these stages, the closer it gets to a point at which it can begin to realize effective complex service compositions.

Stage 1: Initial Service Delivery Projects

The first set of agnostic services is produced by projects primarily in support of immediate solution requirements. However, if design standards in support of service-orientation are followed, each service is positioned as a member of the service inventory with the intention of future reuse and composition (Figure 13.14).

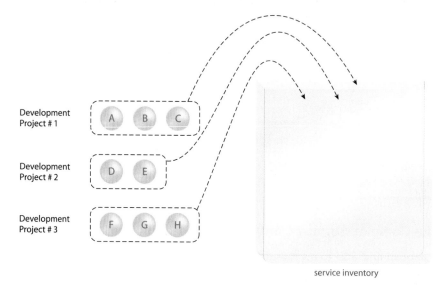

Figure 13.14

The service inventory is born, as the initial projects begin to deliver standardized services.

In this stage there may be some compositions required to immediately automate high priority business processes, but they may be modest in nature and complexity. Furthermore, wrapper services may be relatively common, representing legacy environments that limit the composition's ability to fully implement key service-orientation design characteristics.

Stage 2: Hybrid Applications and a Growing Service Inventory

As service-orientation begins to spread across an enterprise (or one of its domains), the existence of actual service compositions becomes increasingly commonplace. The more a service inventory grows, the more potential composition members we have to choose from. However, with the service inventory still incomplete, some automation requirements are fulfilled using hybrid architectures that borrow from traditional solution environments and supplement them with services (Figure 13.15).

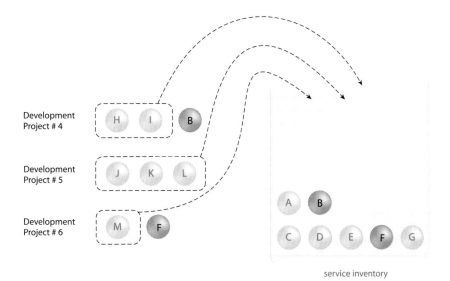

service inventory

Figure 13.15

The quantity of services increases as do the options for service compositions. But, the service inventory is still incomplete. (Red colored symbols represent existing agnostic services being reused as part of new compositions.)

Stage 3: A Service Inventory is Established

When the majority of planned agnostic services have actually been delivered, the overall service inventory offers a rich choice of composition members (Figure 13.16). Even complex business processes can now be automated by composing services together into sophisticated configurations.

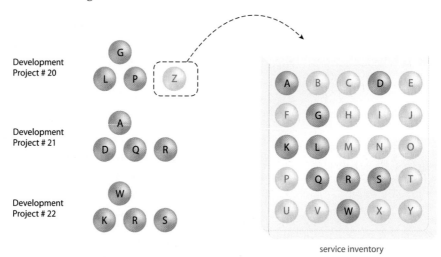

Figure 13.16

The evolution of a service inventory is relatively complete. As the inventory grows, so does the complexity potential of the average service composition.

Defining the Complex Service Composition

It is at Stage 2 that we begin to see the *complex service composition* as a core and consistent part of the solution landscape. By the time we near Stage 3, composed solutions become an unavoidable fact of life. What then separates a complex composition from others? Let's revisit this term and list some of its distinguishing characteristics.

A complex service composition implemented with Web services:

- will generally utilize some form of context or transaction management system
- will make extensive use of SOAP headers
- will have comprehensive exception handling features
- will need to facilitate multiple runtime scenarios
- will increase governance requirements
- is more likely to be composed by a task service than an entity service capability

The first item on this list represents a crucial ingredient for complex compositions. The fact that vendor Web services platforms have historically not provided sufficient industry-level support for these requirements is one of the primary reasons advanced composition has been inhibited in the past.

Preparing for the Complex Service Composition

Building a service-oriented architecture in support of complex service compositions is often not a high priority for organizations that are just getting into the design and delivery of services. The realization of a large service inventory is so far down the road that worrying about the existence of sophisticated composition configurations seems premature.

One of the primary goals of several service-orientation principles is to establish specific design characteristics within services that equip them for a planned target state. This avoids one of the biggest impacts organizations face as they move their environments closer to a standardized service-oriented architecture: retrofitting.

The principle of Service Composability is no exception. Its purpose is to emphasize service composition participation within services that may not need to be involved with compositions for quite some time. Successfully applying this principle now positions each service as a truly reusable part of the enterprise in support of the demands that will come with the arrival of the complex service composition.

SUMMARY OF KEY POINTS

- Complex service compositions emerge out of maturing service inventories.

- Compositions are qualified as "complex" when they meet certain requirements, most of which are associated with the delivery of sophisticated solution logic via aggregated services.

- The Service Composability principle prepares services for immediate and eventual participation in complex compositions.

13.5 Measuring Service Composability and Composition Effectiveness Potential

As with most of the other principles, Service Composability represents design characteristics that are achieved to a particular measure. With this principle in particular, that
measure is highly dependent on the extent to which related principles have also been
applied (Figure 13.17).

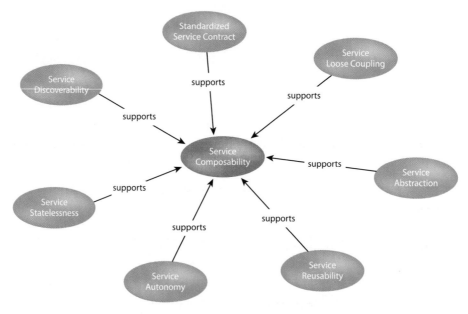

Figure 13.17

All of the other principles in the service-orientation paradigm end up (directly or indirectly) contributing to the
extent of composability attainable by a service. However, we are about to explore how these principles affect
different states of the composition.

Because composability can become a critical success factor for a service inventory, we
will take the time to more closely study the importance and collective influences other
principles have. This will allow us to gauge the level of a service's real-world composability within the context of service-orientation.

Evolutionary Cycle States of a Composition

A service composition is typically tied to the automation of a particular business process
or task. Therefore, even though it may be comprised of multiple reusable services that
are also allocated to other compositions, each composition configuration can be consid-

ered the equivalent of a traditional application (which is why they are sometimes referred to as "composite applications").

As such, it is subject to similar but still distinct lifecycle phases. We are interested in these phases at this point because they represent different states of existence for the service composition. In order to measure the potential impact resulting from the application of our remaining service-orientation principles, we need to study how they can affect each one of these states.

The three lifecycle phases we'll be concentrating on are:

- *Design Phase*—The stage at which composition members are chosen and the service composition configuration is first designed.

- *Runtime (Implementation) Phase*—The stage at which the composition is operational and active.

- *Governance Phase*—Essentially, the long-term evolution of the service composition is considered here, including potential recomposition of its member services.

The next three sections explore the extent to which other design principles support these three stages.

> **NOTE**
>
> The next two sections are comprised of six tables that address a range of assessment-related issues, questions, and criteria. This information is provided for the detailed evaluation and measuring of service compositions and the composability levels of individual services. If you are reading this chapter for the first time and you don't require this amount of detail at this point, feel free to skip ahead to the *Composition and Service Design* section.

Composition Design Assessment

The following table provides a rating for each service-orientation design principle as it relates to the design process of a service composition. This allows us to roughly measure the significance of individual design characteristics that may support the design of complex service compositions (Table 13.2).

Composition Assessment Chart / Impact on Design Process		
Design Principle	**Relation**	**Common Level of Importance**
Standardized Service Contract	Increases standardization of the composition member service contracts and reduces the necessity for intra-composition message transformation. Increased standardization can greatly decrease the complexity of composition designs.	High
Service Loose Coupling	Reducing dependency requirements allows a service to become part of more types of compositions, which can provide more design-time options.	Medium
Service Abstraction	Increased information hiding reduces awareness of what lies beneath a composition controller. This can simplify the design of service compositions as long as the involved composition controllers (and sub-controllers) are fully trusted.	Medium
Service Reusability	The more reusable the logic provided by a service, the more opportunities it will have to participate in compositions.	High
Service Autonomy	Service-level autonomy reduces the functional overlap across services, which further enhances the quality of composition designs by establishing normalization across composition members.	Medium

Composition Assessment Chart / Impact on Design Process (continued)		
Design Principle	**Relation**	**Common Level of Importance**
Service Statelessness	The reduction of state management responsibilities affects the design of services in that they become more generic and dependent on external context management extensions. From a design perspective, this can stream-line compositions if all services utilize the same state management exten-sions. Conversely, it can increase the complexity of the service composition if some services require different state management facilities than others.	Low
Service Discoverability	With an increased awareness of poten-tial candidates for service composition members, the opportunity to leverage whatever the existing service inven-tory has to offer is maximized. There-fore, the discoverability of services can greatly benefit the composition design process.	High

Table 13.2
How the application of other service-orientation design principles can impact the design process of service compositions.

Composition Runtime Assessment

Perhaps the most critical measure of success for a service composition is the extent to which it fulfills runtime performance and reliability expectations. Because the composition is comprised of numerous services, its runtime success is judged by the collective effectiveness of its composition members. As a starting point it is therefore valuable to identify and understand which of the service-orientation principles contribute design characteristics that directly impact the composition's overall runtime performance (Table 13.3).

Composition Assessment Chart / Impact on Runtime Performance		
Design Principle	**Relation**	**Common Level of Importance**
Standardized Service Contract	By reducing or even eliminating data transformation requirements, the use of standardized service contracts by composition members and controllers can dramatically enhance the runtime performance of service compositions.	High
Service Loose Coupling	Actual runtime composition performance and behavior can be improved through any form of reduced external coupling.	Medium
Service Abstraction	Whether the underlying details of a service composition member are hidden at runtime has no direct bearing on the composition's overall performance. Hiding the composition details of a controller service may, in fact, increase the likelihood of the service being shared by more consumers, potentially leading to increased usage demands.	Low
Service Reusability	A reusable service will likely need to facilitate multiple service consumers. If the service implementation environment is not fully prepared, this could also hinder its performance as part of any one service composition.	Medium
Service Autonomy	The extent of control a service exercises over its underlying execution environment has a direct bearing on its effectiveness as a member of a service composition, primarily in relation to runtime performance and reliability.	High

Composition Assessment Chart / Impact on Runtime Performance (continued)		
Design Principle	**Relation**	**Common Level of Importance**
Service Statelessness	Maximizing the duration at which a service remains in a stateless condition increases the service's overall availability and accessibility. This contributes to the reliability of the service composition, as well as the predictability of its behavior.	High
Service Discoverability	After a service composition has been implemented, discoverability is of little consequence to its runtime performance. In fact, composition members that remain discoverable can very well be reused by other compositions, which could begin competing for their resources.	Low

Table 13.3

How the application of other service-orientation design principles can support the runtime performance of service compositions.

Composition Governance Assessment

Finally, it is also very valuable to know how the long-term management of the composition's evolution can potentially be influenced or impacted by specific design characteristics of its composition members (Table 13.4).

Composition Assessment Chart / Impact on Governance		
Design Principle	**Relation**	**Common Level of Importance**
Standardized Service Contract	Evolving a composition to allow for the removal or addition of composition members (or the reconfiguration of existing composition members) is all facilitated by the usage of standardized service contracts. Without compliance to design standards, disparate contract designs can increase composition complexity and the resulting effort required to overcome contract disparity.	High
Service Loose Coupling	By requiring fewer dependencies between services, loosely coupled relationships make changing a service composition easier than if more dependencies between the services existed or were required.	Medium
Service Abstraction	By enforcing information hiding upon each service composition member, the composition itself is shielded from changes that may occur within individual member service boundaries. Therefore, limiting the utilization of services to only what is published in concise service contracts (and without assumptions based on a knowledge of underlying details) increases the longevity potential for service compositions.	High
Service Reusability	Even though highly reusable services may continue to challenge the stability of a service composition due to competing service consumers (as described in Table 13.2), the fact that their capabilities are designed to be generic in nature allows for them to more easily accommodate recomposition requirements.	Low

Composition Assessment Chart / Impact on Governance (continued)		
Design Principle	**Relation**	**Common Level of Importance**
Service Autonomy	Higher levels of autonomy provide increased flexibility for services to be recomposed. Therefore, this principle can improve the overall governance of the composition design.	Medium
Service Statelessness	State management does not usually have a direct influence on the evolution of the composition. However, it could aid recomposition requirements because the reduction of state management processing makes service logic more generic and therefore more process agnostic.	Low
Service Discoverability	One manner in which discoverability in general can aid the governance of an existing service composition is that it can provide the constant opportunity for alternative composition members to be located. The newly discovered composition members could potentially replace or supplement members of an existing composition.	Medium

Table 13.4

How the application of other service-orientation design principles can support the long-term governance of service compositions.

Measuring Composability

So far this chapter has documented how service-orientation principles support different service composition lifecycle stages. The focus has therefore been on service compositions as a whole, not on the composability potential of individual services or their capabilities. Service-level composability is what this principle is primarily about, but to determine a meaningful measure of composability requires the previously established, holistic perspective of the composition.

As explained early on, Service Composability is a principle that shapes and positions the application of others for a greater goal. Therefore, to assess the potential a service has of achieving this goal requires that the implemented levels of other principles be individually evaluated (on a service capability level) and then collectively evaluated (on a composition level).

This form of assessment can be carried out in three steps, each corresponding to one of the previously described composition lifecycle stages:

- *Composition Design*—To what extent can the service capability be effectively composed?

- *Composition Runtime*—To what extent will the service capability fulfill its role within the composition?

- *Composition Governance*—To what extent can the service capability accommodate composition changes subsequent to deployment?

This type of evaluation process is not centered around a specific service composition instance or definition. The objective is to assess a service's overall potential to support any of the three composition stages.

Provided next in Tables 13.5, 13.6, and 13.7, is a set of checklists that raise questions to help determine the different forms of composability potential. These tables correspond to the previous Composition Assessment Charts (the "Common Levels of Importance" established for each corresponding principle are repeated here for reference purposes).

NOTE

All of the questions provided in the following assessment questionnaires are intentionally worded so that a positive answer is always "yes." This allows for a more simplified preliminary evaluation.

Service Capability Checklist / Support for Composition Design	
Assessment Question	**Common Level of Importance**
Standardized Service Contract *Are the input and output messages required by the capability standardized with those used by other services (for the same information sets) within the same inventory?* If they are, then this service capability will not require that transformation layers be designed in order for it to be incorporated within the composition.	High
Service Loose Coupling *Does the capability avoid high levels of implementation, technology, contract-to-logic, and functional coupling?* Each of these forms of negative coupling can introduce design complexities and inflexibilities that can inhibit the overall composition.	Medium
Service Abstraction *For all of the meta information the service capability abstracts, does it provide a clear expression of important quality of service characteristics?* As long as the appropriate guarantees are made, the service capability can be pulled into compositions while continuing to abstract underlying implementation details (which may include further composition logic).	Medium
Service Reusability *Was the service capability designed for high reusability?* Service capabilities with targeted or complete measures of reusability are more likely to be immediately useful to composition designs.	High
Service Autonomy *Was the capability designed as part of a service that was normalized in relation to others in the same service inventory, and does it have a reasonable level of service logic autonomy?* Composing capabilities from services that have service contract autonomy and do not impose severe runtime autonomy constraints immediately eases the design of compositions.	Medium

Service Capability Checklist / Support for Composition Design (continued)	
Assessment Question	**Common Level of Importance**
Service Statelessness *Does the capability utilize a state management deferral method that is consistent with other services in the same inventory?* If it doesn't, service activity processing requirements need to be assessed in order to understand how any potential incompatibilities in relation to state data transfer may impact the composition.	Low
Service Discoverability *Is the service equipped with all of the necessary meta data required for it to be easily located and understood by composition designers?* Design characteristics that communicate both pros and cons in relation to any of the previously listed issues in this table can help composition designers assess whether the service's capabilities are suitable for planned composition configurations.	High

Table 13.5

This is a questionnaire-style checklist for the assessment of a service capability's potential to be composed at design-time. The assessment questions correspond to the assessment issues listed in Table 13.2.

Service Capability Checklist / Support for Runtime Composition Participation	
Assessment Question	**Common Level of Importance**
Standardized Service Contract *Does the service capability avoid runtime transformation requirements?* Although this is a repeat of the corresponding design-time question, the difference here is the imposition of runtime performance overhead resulting from transformation layers that need to be invoked to translate between disparate message data models.	High
Service Loose Coupling *Does the service capability avoid dependencies on any external implementation resources that are shared by other parts of the enterprise?* Depending on who is assessing the capability and how much of the underlying details have been abstracted, it may be possible to determine if implementation coupling will introduce unpredictable runtime behavior. Alternatively, this information may be documented in the accompanying SLA.	Medium
Service Abstraction *If underlying implementation details are hidden or protected, are all capability runtime characteristics relevant to composition involvement documented as part of a policy, profile, or SLA?* As long as the composition owner can reliably design the composition to accommodate known service capability constraints and as long as all other reliability guarantees are fulfilled when the capability is active as part of the deployed composition, then abstraction should not be a concern.	Low
Service Reusability *Is the service capability being moderately reused by other service consumer programs or compositions?* Depending on whether this statistical data is revealed, a composition designer can assess whether the capability can also handle involvement in the new composition. Alternatively, if the service owner guarantees runtime performance and predictability due to a strong hosting environment, then concurrent usage should be addressed.	Medium

Service Capability Checklist / Support for Runtime Composition Participation (continued)	
Assessment Question	**Common Level of Importance**
Service Autonomy *Does the service capability have adequate control over its execution at runtime?* This is often a critical piece of information that services will publish within an SLA or policy. Providing the autonomy level enables the composition designer to determine whether the capability could compromise the performance or reliability of the composition as a whole and whether reducing isolation levels of individual capabilities may actually be required to increase the autonomy of the composition as a whole (in which case redundant service implementations may need to be explored). Part of this determination is also the service's role within the composition (if it is part of sequential process logic execution, this concern is amplified).	High
Service Statelessness *Does the service capability maintain an acceptable level of statelessness at runtime?* Knowing whether the service architecture implements a meaningful level of state management deferral allows the composition designer to assess whether the service capability will be able to handle some of the activity data it will encounter in that particular composition configuration.	High
Service Discoverability *Will service discoverability be in any way limited subsequent to implementation as part of this composition?* The answer to this question is almost always "no," which may be a consideration that needs to be factored in, especially for new services with high reuse potential that has not yet been tapped. However, it is generally the service owner's responsibility to ensure that while the service is discoverable, it will not be overused so as to jeopardize its existing consumers.	Low

Table 13.6

This is a questionnaire-style checklist for the assessment of a service capability's potential to participate within a composition at runtime. The assessment questions correspond to the assessment issues listed in Table 13.3.

Service Capability Checklist / Support for Composition Governance	
Assessment Question	**Common Level of Importance**
Standardized Service Contract *Will the service capability avoid introducing transformation requirements if it needs to be recomposed?* This raises the same issue as in the previous two checklists. If transformation requirements come with using the capability, then changing its position within the overall composition will impose additional effort.	High
Service Loose Coupling *Does the capability avoid coupling to external parts of the enterprise, such as shared resources or parent business processes?* If yes, then the range of opportunities to reutilize the capability within the scope of the composition will be increased.	Medium
Service Abstraction *Is meta information about the capability protected by high levels of information hiding and access control measures?* If this is the case, then the chances of the composition designer creating prohibitive dependencies between the capability and the overall composition are reduced. This benefits both the composition and service owners in the long-term as each is less dependent on the other if either implementation needs to be changed.	High
Service Reusability *Is the service contract highly generic, and does the service provide high levels of reusability?* If it does, it can potentially benefit composition governance in that there may be additional ways to incorporate the service as the composition changes (perhaps there are two or three similar capabilities that give the composition designer a choice of how to process a particular document).	Low

Service Capability Checklist / Support for Composition Governance (continued)	
Assessment Question	**Common Level of Importance**
Service Autonomy *Is the service logic normalized, and is the service implementation relatively isolated?* If the answer is "yes" to both of these questions, the composition owner will have more flexibility as to how any service capabilities can be repositioned or utilized differently within revised composition configurations.	Medium
Service Statelessness *Do implemented state management deferral extensions increase parent process independence of the service and enable the capability to process more generic state data?* Should this be the case, then some gain in terms of recomposing service capabilities may be attainable.	Low
Service Discoverability *Is service capability meta data easily discoverable and interpretable?* This governance consideration is not about a service capability's relationship to an existing composition. Instead, it is associated with the composition owner's ability to locate (discover) new service capabilities in addition to or in replacement of any existing service capabilities the composition already uses. Typically, this consideration is in preparation for when the service inventory evolves and grows subsequent to the initial composition implementation.	Medium

Table 13.7

This is a questionnaire-style checklist for the assessment of a service capability's potential to accommodate the governance of a composition. The assessment questions correspond to the assessment issues listed in Table 13.4.

Why No Levels?

Concrete assessment levels cannot be provided for this principle because beyond the generic issues raised by the preceding checklists, there are several other major factors that need to be taken into account, all of which will be specific to each enterprise environment.

These include:

- Features and capabilities of development platforms and technologies used to build services and support parts of the service-oriented architecture.

- Runtime capacity and capabilities and environment-specific factors, such as existing integration architectures and security policies.

- Governance technology platforms and processes, as well as policies and overall strategic goals.

Any one of these factors can shift the levels of importance that were established in the previous assessment tables. Furthermore, they can also raise new issues and criteria for determining the actual composability potential of a service for any of the composition stages.

However, the assessment charts and checklists that have been provided establish a solid starting point for performing a thorough, service capability-level measurement of composability. It is recommended that you take the time to customize these generic lists so that they best incorporate your unique requirements and environmental characteristics.

SUMMARY OF KEY POINTS

- There are three stages within the lifecycle of a service composition that can be individually assessed: design-time, runtime, and post-implementation governance.

- To measure the effectiveness of a service composition requires the evaluation of individual and collective controller and composition services.

- Because Service Composability is determined by the collective application of other service-orientation principles, a good indicator to assessing the composition stages is an understanding of how individual principles support them.

13.6 Composition and Service Design

These next sections address additional service design issues associated with the Service Composability principle and service composition in general.

Service Composability and Granularity

As we know, Service Composability relies on the collective and balanced application of all other principles. Those principles that already influence the granularity of services and capabilities do so in full support of realizing the potential for service capabilities to be repeatedly composed.

Therefore, as part of applying this principle, each capability needs to be assessed individually to ensure that the application of other principles has resulted in the granularity levels that are suitable for the service to act as an effective composition member.

In support of this assessment, it can be helpful to be aware of fundamental metrics and tendencies when associated with granularity within services across a service inventory:

- *Service Granularity*—If more granular services exist within a service inventory, more services will need to be invoked in an average composition.

- *Capability Granularity*—If services are comprised of more granular capabilities, more capabilities will need to be composed in an average composition.

- *Data Granularity*—Coarse data granularity tends to result in more data being transmitted throughout an average runtime composition instance.

- *Constraint Granularity*—Fine constraint granularity results in more validation logic being executed by the service contract layer with each data exchange within an average service composition.

Service Composability and Service Models

We mentioned earlier how the most likely candidates to fulfill the designated composition controller role are services based on the task service model. While this may be true, it is important to always take the possibility into account that any service capability could, one day, be called upon to act as a composition member as part of a larger service aggregate (Figure 13.18).

The services most likely to contain capabilities that act as dedicated composition members with limited service controller requirements are based on the utility model. Often utility services interface directly with a variety of proprietary resources that are part of the native enterprise environment, and therefore further service composition may not be required.

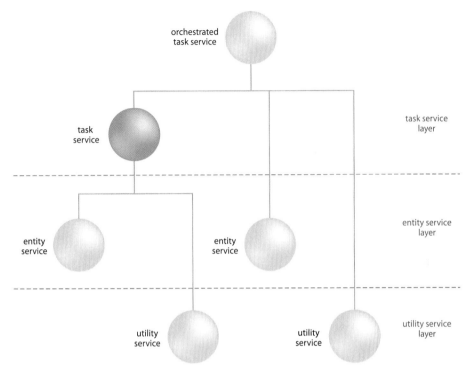

Figure 13.18

A task service positioned as a composition member and sub-controller within a complex composition spearheaded by a parent orchestrated task service.

Entity services can easily contain capabilities that are themselves highly composed as well as controllers of elaborate compositions. However, not all entity services need to be composed by task or orchestrated task services; sometimes, a business task can be fulfilled wholly by an entity service capability simply because the provided agnostic logic addressed all of the business requirements (Figure 13.19).

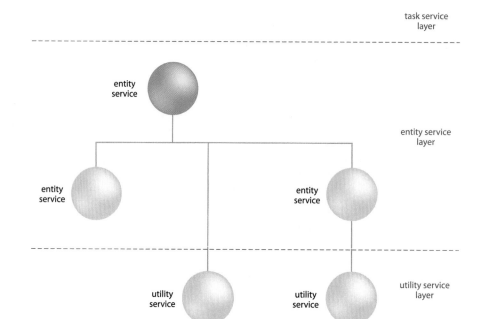

Figure 13.19
An entity service assuming the controller role at the head of a complete composition.

Service Composability and Composition Autonomy

A design option that can be applied to increase the autonomy of a set of composed services is to isolate the composition itself. This will typically require redundant implementations of agnostic composition members, but it can be an effective means of overcoming some of the autonomy concerns associated with complex service compositions.

Composition autonomy can be applied to all or a subset of the participating composition members. Sometimes a nucleus of service capabilities collectively providing a mission critical piece of functionality is identified as being suitable for increased composition autonomy through isolation.

Because the Service Composability design principle is focused on the design of individual services, it does not specifically address the concerns of compositions as a whole. These issues are instead tackled by separate architectural design patterns.

Service Composability and Orchestration

Orchestration represents the process by which various resources within an enterprise can be coordinated to carry out a body of business process logic. Orchestration technology is most commonly associated with a central activity management platform that also provides features common to traditional EAI middleware, such as data and technology transformation and transaction management.

New generation variations of these platforms have emerged with native support for hosting, invoking, and composing services built as Web services. The foremost technology used to express Web services composition logic is based on the Web Services Business Process Execution Language (WS-BPEL).

Incorporating orchestration into a Web services-based SOA provides the option of establishing a parent layer that abstracts business process logic and assumes the responsibility of carrying out numerous complex service compositions. Because WS-BPEL process definitions can themselves be encapsulated by services, this layer will typically host a series of *orchestrated* task services. (See Example 13.1 for a sample of WS-BPEL markup code.)

```
<sequence name="main">
  <invoke name="Step1"
    partnerLink="Invoice"
    portType="inv:InvoiceInterface"
    operation="GetTotals"
    inputVariable="RequestMsg"
    outputVariable="ResponseMsg"
  />
  <switch name="TotalCheck">
    <case condition="getVariableData
      ('ResponseMsg',
       'ResponseParameter',
       '/inv2:InvoiceResponseType/Total') &gt;
       getVariableData('input',
       'payload',
       '/po:POType/TotalBilled')">
      <throw
        xmlns="http://schemas.xmlsoap.org/ws/2003/..."
        name="ValidationFailed"
        faultName="InvoiceTotalFailed"/>
    </case>
  </switch>
  ...
</sequence>
```

Example 13.1

A fragment of a WS-BPEL process definition with some decision logic. The Invoice service is invoked (composed), and the Total value is then extracted from its response message. This value is subsequently used as criteria for a switch/case decision construct (which is a lot like a case/else statement in procedural programming).

Although orchestration layers tend to represent the parent business process logic at the top of composition hierarchies, they are not limited to this role. From a Service Composability perspective, each capability within a service may be required to compose other service capabilities in addition to being composed itself. For example, a Web service operation invoked by a parent WS-BPEL process may encapsulate and execute its own WS-BPEL process logic.

This represents just one example of the types of design considerations that can be raised during the application of this principle within SOA implementations built around orchestration platforms.

> **NOTE**
>
> `www.ws-standards.com` provides a basic WS-BPEL tutorial, and the corresponding specification documents can be further viewed at `www.soaspecs.com`. More detailed examples of building WS-BPEL process definitions and a step-by-step description of service-oriented business process design are provided in the book *Service-Oriented Architecture: Concepts, Technology, and Design*.

How Service Composability Affects Other Principles

Having previously studied the impact other service-orientation principles have on the different composition stages, it's time now to concentrate on the flipside by studying how the application of this principle influences others (Figure 13.20).

Service Composability and Standardized Service Contract

As indicated by the high level of importance assigned to the Standard Service Contract principle in relation to composition design, runtime execution, and governance (Tables 13.2, 13.3, and 13.4 respectively), the application of the Service Composability emphasizes the need for consistent contract standardization. In fact, considerations raised by the Service Composability principle can shape overarching contract design standards in support of requirements specific to compositions (especially complex compositions).

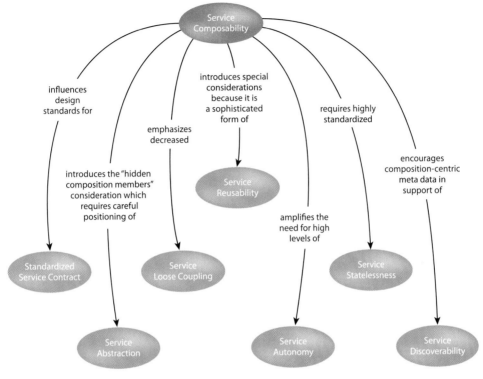

Figure 13.20
Service Composability can shape the application of all other principles.

Service Composability and Service Loose Coupling

To maximize the potential for services to be composed requires that their implementations be as flexible and self-contained as possible. Obviously, Service Autonomy is a prime consideration here (as discussed shortly). However, the dependencies a service brings with it can establish fundamental constraints that directly affect its attainable level of composability, as explained in the *Service Loose Coupling and Service Composability* section of Chapter 7. Service Composability strongly emphasizes the reduction of the negative coupling types described in this chapter.

Service Composability and Service Abstraction

As you may have gathered from the *Measuring Service Composability and Composition Effectiveness Potential* section, these two principles have an interesting relationship. When designing a complex service composition, it is natural to want to establish a complete perspective of all the services involved in carrying out the parent business task.

However, if we are to hide information about what underlies one or some of the composition members, then even the most complex of compositions may appear to be little more than a point-to-point exchange.

This introduces the concept of *hidden composition members*, a likely occurrence in modern SOA implementations, especially when the Service Abstraction principle is firmly applied. We essentially end up with most of a composition becoming an invisible part of an environment (Figure 13.21).

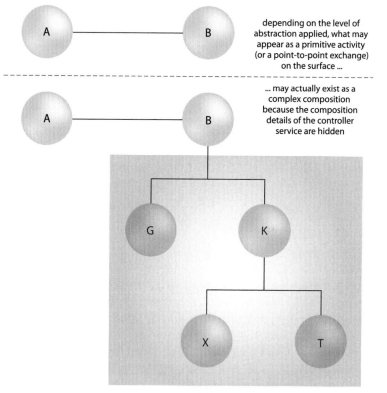

depending on the level of abstraction applied, what may appear as a primitive activity (or a point-to-point exchange) on the surface ...

... may actually exist as a complex composition because the composition details of the controller service are hidden

hidden composition members

Figure 13.21

When abstraction is applied to the extent that complex compositions are hidden, the requirement for those compositions to perform efficiently and reliably is greatly amplified. In return, the composition owner gains greater control over how to evolve the composition configuration.

When mixing Service Abstraction and Service Composability considerations, it can be difficult to determine how much information should be hidden. The answer usually lies in the level of confidence a service owner has in the service's ability to fulfill the promises made by its contract.

Service Composability and Service Reusability

When a mature service inventory has been established, service composition becomes the most common form of reuse. Still, though, it is worth noting that these two principles, and the design characteristics each promotes, can theoretically exist independently from each other.

Let's explore why:

Can a service be reusable and not composable?—Yes, because we don't consider a point-to-point service activity as representing a "real" composition. Therefore, any service that has multiple service consumers and participates in point-to-point activities limited to two services is not really a composition member or controller, but still can be considered a reusable service. Even though it exists as a distributed piece of logic and can therefore still be technically composed, the fact that it was never designed with composability in mind limits its potential to be an effective (and reliable) part of multiple, larger compositions.

Can a service be composable and not reusable?—Yes, because services can be delivered for one specific composition only, where each service has a high level of service-to-consumer coupling (as explained in the *Contract-to-Functional Coupling* section of Chapter 7). However, because we expect composable services to be capable of acting as members of compositions that don't yet exist at the time of their implementation, we expect them to demonstrate some meaningful extent of reusability—should it be required.

Service Composability and Service Autonomy

The relationship between these two principles is integral. As explained in Chapter 10, a controller service is required to sacrifice its autonomy when composing others. Therefore, the controller's actual autonomy can become equivalent to the combined measures of autonomy of all involved service composition members.

A high (and preferably exclusive) level of control over the logic encapsulated by a service is a key design characteristic that makes for an effective composition member. However, as previously discussed in the *Service Composability and Composition Autonomy* section, it may sometimes be necessary to increase the collective autonomy of a group of composition members.

This increased emphasis on pursuing high levels of runtime execution control highlights the reality that the lower levels of autonomy commonly associated with wrapper services representing legacy environments may very well make these types of services unsuitable for complex compositions.

Service Composability and Service Statelessness

As with Service Autonomy, the Service Statelessness principle establishes design characteristics in full support of complex service compositions. Minimizing the state management responsibilities of every composition member can lead to a leaner, more optimized overall execution of composition instances.

To repeatedly assemble effective service compositions from the same inventory requires that services share state data in a consistent and efficient manner. State deferral options (especially those based on the use of messages) therefore need to be highly standardized to avoid having to resort to the runtime transformation or conversion of state data.

Service Composability and Service Discoverability

A primary issue addressed by joining these two principles is in identifying the controller service capability of a composition as being responsible for expressing the collective scope of the composition logic it encapsulates to whatever extent the Service Abstraction principle permits.

If Service Abstraction is not rigidly applied, then the details of the underlying composition may intentionally be made available. However, this composition, as represented by the controller service, will need to be discovered in the first place. This amplifies the significance of accurately defining meta information for discovery and interpretation purposes.

Additionally, it can be helpful to make information associated with a service capability's composability levels available. This better enables those responsible for designing service compositions to evaluate potential composition members.

SUMMARY OF KEY POINTS

- Service Composability shapes the application of all other principles to ensure that they collectively contribute to a service's ability to participate in a composition.

- Standardized Service Contract and Service Reusability, as well as Service Loose Coupling and Service Autonomy, are among the key principles that need to be kept aligned in support of this principle.

13.7 Risks Associated with Service Composition

Building services to be composable introduces little risk, but once those services actually need to be assembled into significantly sized compositions, that's when formal risk assessment becomes a very good idea. In this section we highlight some of the common issues associated with service compositions in general.

Composition Members as Single Points of Failure

Many of the challenges that come with building composed solution logic are similar to those documented as part of the Service Reusability principle. A service composition will typically be comprised of numerous reusable services, each of which may be utilized in different compositions as part of different business process scenarios.

Therefore, the risks associated with these composition members existing as single points of failure may be amplified to whatever extent an organization comes to depend on complex compositions that share the same service implementations.

Composition Members as Performance Bottlenecks

Perhaps the number one concern associated with larger service compositions is runtime performance. The latency of a controller service encapsulating a composition of multiple additional services will still be measured against other services representing a great deal less logic.

As a result, the importance of response times of individual composition members becomes paramount because the overall performance of the controller service will typically be determined by the execution times of all its active composition member services.

> **NOTE**
>
> Several design patterns address the risks described in this section by advocating the use of redundant implementations, clustering, and designs that strategically combine stateless and autonomous designs.

> **BEST PRACTICE**
>
> It is extremely important to be aware of performance limitations inherent to the infrastructure within which composition members will be hosted. In fact it is considered a best practice to invest in formal stress and volume tests prior to delivering services so as to collect statistics that accurately measure the performance boundaries of a given environment.

These statistics subsequently become the basis for design standards that introduce constraints that may need to limit the size of service compositions based on a formula that takes the quantity of composition members and the message volume and sizes into account.

Governance Rigidity of "Over-Reuse" in Compositions

Let's imagine a future state in which an enterprise is automated almost entirely by an array of complex service compositions. The average agnostic composition member is involved in six or seven different compositions, each automating its own unique business task.

As much as service-orientation is aimed at achieving a high level of reusability, it is also concerned with establishing an environment that is highly agile—adaptive and responsive to change. In an enterprise where so many services are being reused by different types of compositions, altering these services becomes very difficult. One design change to an existing service's logic or contract can affect a number of compositions and jeopardize the tasks they automate.

Although there are design patterns that can alleviate this situation, often an organization decides that contracts simply won't change. They get extended, if required, but the nature of the logic that has been established and is being actively and repeatedly used becomes untouchable.

When services are designed with a great deal of care and insight, the longevity of their contracts is maximized. However, in the absence of the effort or expertise required to do so (or if completely unforeseen changes hit an organization), sometimes implemented services will end up representing outdated logic.

In this case, traditional governance and evolution approaches might not apply. Instead, we may need to resort to service versioning, which opens the door to a whole new aspect of SOA governance.

SUMMARY OF KEY POINTS

- The traditional risks and issues surrounding service reuse are amplified with service composition.

- Reliability, performance, and governance concerns all need to be planned for in support of proliferating complex compositions across an enterprise.

13.8 CASE STUDY EXAMPLE

Because the services created so far were designed specifically in support of the Lab Project business process, the Cutit team is not too concerned with their ability to assemble the composition to be encapsulated by the Run Lab Project task service.

However, there is a realization that they should think beyond this initial service delivery project. Each of the agnostic services that had been developed will be positioned as potentially reusable enterprise resources within the planned service inventory. Furthermore, it is well known how difficult it will be to make fundamental changes after they are deployed and in use.

Therefore, the Cutit team members agree that an assessment of the services' overall composability potential would be wise. Following an analysis, a report is delivered that documents the results. Provided here is the design-time checklist portion of the report as it was completed for the GetPurchased operation of the Materials service (as per the checklist established in Table 13.5).

1. *Are the input and output messages required by the capability standardized with those used by other services (for the same information sets) within the same inventory?*

   Yes, keeping in mind that the service inventory does not yet have that many services. As explained in the case study example in Chapter 6, the Materials service is intentionally designed to adhere to enterprise data representation standards.

2. *Does the capability avoid high levels of implementation, technology, contract-to-logic, and functional coupling?*

   Yes, as described in Chapter 7, the GetPurchased operation is standardized and therefore has a high level of logic-to-contract coupling. This alleviates consumer services from having to concern themselves with the proprietary details of the actual materials item data format required by the legacy inventory control system that is encapsulated by the underlying Inventory service (which is composed by the GetPurchased operation).

3. *For all of the meta information the service capability abstracts, does it provide a clear expression of important quality of service characteristics?*

Yes, as documented in Table 8.2 in the Chapter 8 case study example, quality of service meta information was published in an SLA to supplement the functional meta information in the service contract.

4. *Was the service capability designed for high reusability?*

Yes, as briefly mentioned at the beginning of the Chapter 9 case study example, the Materials service as a whole underwent the same process that was documented for the Inventory service in relation to maximizing its reusability potential.

5. *Was the capability designed as part of a service that was normalized in relation to others in the same service inventory, and does it have a reasonable level of service logic autonomy?*

Yes, because the service was modeled in accordance with a preliminary service inventory blueprint, steps were taken to ensure its functional boundary did not overlap with those of other services. Additionally, as illustrated in Figure 10.13 at the end of the Chapter 10 case study example, the GetPurchased operation's functional autonomy was further improved by increasing the autonomy level of the Inventory service's GetItem operation (which is composed by GetPurchased).

6. *Does the capability utilize a state management deferral method that is consistent with other services in the same inventory?*

The GetPurchased operation is not equipped with any form of state management deferral. Its SLA guarantees a constant real-time response for the retrieval of materials records. (Incidentally, these records end up forming part of the state data that is processed via the state management deferral architecture used by the Run Lab Project service's Start operation, as described in the case study example in Chapter 11.)

7. *Is the service equipped with all of the necessary meta data required for it to be easily located and understood by composition designers?*

Yes, the service profile established in the Chapter 12 case study example provides well-defined functional meta information within a standardized format that is further supplemented with quality of service meta data.

Essentially, this process helps Cutit validate that the application of other principles was successful, not just on an individual basis, but in support of future composability requirements as well. Figure 13.22 shows the final composition configuration, concluding this part of the Cutit Saws case study.

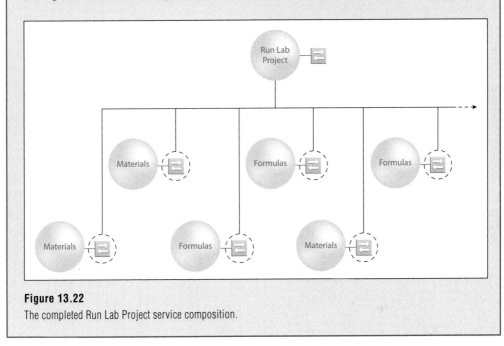

Figure 13.22
The completed Run Lab Project service composition.

Part III

Supplemental

Service-Orientation and Object-Orientation: A Comparison of Principles and Concepts

Chapter 4 established that one of the primary influences of service-orientation was the well established object-oriented design paradigm. There is much common ground between these two design philosophies. In fact, if it weren't for the innovative design principles and patterns formalized by object-orientation, the service-oriented architectural model and the Web services framework would not exist as they do today.

The following chapter explores this historical relationship by providing a comparative study. It is worth noting that this comparison of service-orientation and object-orientation is _not_ comprehensive. A thorough study would require a detailed analysis that takes numerous perspectives into account and would therefore likely deserve a book of its own. This chapter simply provides a comparison of concepts and principles (as well as underlying goals). The main purpose of this chapter is as an educational supplement to Part II of this book. It is primarily intended for those already familiar with object-orientation and now interested in understanding service-orientation.

As a result, this chapter does not explain object-oriented design in detail. If you are unfamiliar with object-orientation, you would benefit from reading an introductory tutorial prior to studying the upcoming sections. Also note that in this chapter the terms "object-oriented analysis and design" (OOAD) and "object-orientation" are used interchangeably.

NOTE

It is very important to keep in mind that object-orientation and service-orientation are complementary design paradigms that can be successfully used separately and together. Even though this chapter contrasts concepts and principles, the intention is not to state that one design approach needs to be chosen over the other. As previously mentioned, this comparison is provided for educational purposes only so that service-orientation can be more clearly understood by those with an OOAD background.

14.1 A Tale of Two Design Paradigms

Object-oriented analysis and design was responsible for popularizing the vision of building streamlined applications comprised of reusable, flexible software. Further supported by the sophisticated processes and conventions of the unified modeling language

(UML) and a set of classic design patterns that changed the face of distributed application design, object-orientation evolved into a well-rounded and mature design framework.

OOAD originally grew out of a need to bring order to unstructured development processes that had resulted in various problems, including the creation of the notorious spaghetti code. It drew from best practices that emerged from procedural programming approaches and combined these with a design philosophy that aimed to shape software into units that more closely mirrored the real world.

Object-orientation aspires to maximize the fulfillment of business requirements throughout the lifespan of an application, including its post-deployment upgrades and extensions. It provides numerous rules and guidelines that govern the careful separation of application logic and data into objects that can be individually maintained to help minimize the impact of change on the application as a whole.

Many of the UML conventions and documentation techniques further provide a comprehensive means of expressing customer requirements and predictable runtime application behavior. Collectively, families of UML diagrams and specifications combined with established principles and practices help designers ensure that applications are built to be both robust and flexible. Also on the agenda for object-oriented applications is the fostering of reusable code. Key techniques, such as inheritance and polymorphism (discussed in the upcoming *A Comparison of Principles* section), are positioned to allow different software programs to benefit from logic already created for others.

As established in the *A Comparison of Goals* section, service-orientation shares many of the same goals as OOAD. It seeks to establish a flexible design framework that allows for the agile accommodation of ever-changing business requirements. Much like OOAD, service-orientation is very concerned with minimizing the impact of change upon software programs already deployed and in use. Principles such as Service Loose Coupling and Service Composability, for example, address long-term governance requirements so as to allow implemented services to continue to evolve in tandem with the business.

A common distinction between the two design paradigms is one of scope (Figure 14.1). While object-orientation never explicitly limits the extent to which its principles can be applied, in real-world environments, they have commonly been realized within single applications or collections of related applications. When reuse was attained, it was often at the utility level resulting in libraries of "common components" shared by custom-developed applications.

Figure 14.1

Historically, object-orientation has been applied to segments of the enterprise. Service-orientation aims to harmonize a larger amount of the enterprise or, ideally, the enterprise as a whole.

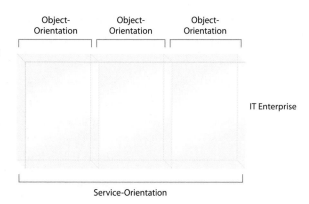

Additionally, several of the object-oriented design principles and patterns were developed during a time when the majority of IT enterprises were building componentized or distributed applications using RPC technology. The reuse potential of any given object was typically limited to the boundary of the RPC platform. In larger environments comprised of various technology platforms, an RPC implementation therefore represented a specific architectural zone. To enable connectivity with other zones required bridging or integration technologies. The increased demand for cross-application and cross-platform connectivity led to the emergence of EAI (which, incidentally, is another major influence on service-orientation).

Although they have many roots in object-orientation, SOA and service-orientation owe their current mainstream status to the emergence and successful adoption of the Web services framework. Even though the feature-set provided by the first generation Web services platform was primitive at best, it established the potential to break through proprietary application and platform boundaries so as to inspire visions of true, cross-enterprise inter-connectivity and federation.

The architectural model that underlies SOA and the principles behind service-orientation were all developed in support of this vision. As a result, they have a great deal of synergy with the maturing second-generation Web services platform. Figure 14.2 illustrates how OO, EAI, and Web services, along with BPM, comprise the major influences of service-orientation.

Within service-orientation, solution logic designed as services is intentionally positioned as enterprise resources and sometimes even enterprise-*wide* resources. This enterprise-centric perspective is one of the main reasons that only a subset of object-orientation principles was carried over into service-orientation (as explained in the *A Comparison of Principles* section).

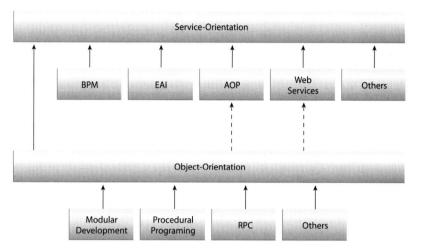

Figure 14.2

While object-orientation evolved out of approaches that included procedural programming, service-orientation builds upon the object-oriented design paradigm and, together with additional
influences, establishes a distinct paradigm of its own.

SUMMARY OF KEY POINTS

- Much of service-orientation owes its existence to the concepts, principles, and patterns that originated from object-orientation.

- Service-orientation has several influences other than object-orientation, includ-ing BPM, EAI, and Web services.

- The increased scope of service-orientation together with additional influences explains why some of the original object-orientation principles are not part of service-orientation.

14.2 A Comparison of Goals

Before comparing concepts and principles, it is important that we establish the fundamental objectives behind each of these design approaches. Chapter 3 described the
strategic goals associated with service-oriented computing, several of which are in direct
alignment with the original goals of object-orientation. Some, however, differ in that
they are specific to service-orientation's enterprise-centric scope.

This section specifically explores the following common OOAD goals and discusses
how they compare and relate to service-orientation principles and goals:

- Increased Business Requirements Fulfillment

- Increased Robustness

- Increased Extensibility

- Increased Flexibility

- Increased Reusability and Productivity

To better understand how service-orientation relates to and supports these particular object-orientation goals (Figure 14.3), we need to take a closer look at each.

Figure 14.3

Service-orientation inherits all of the primary OOAD goals (inner circle) but further increases their scope and adds others (outer circle).

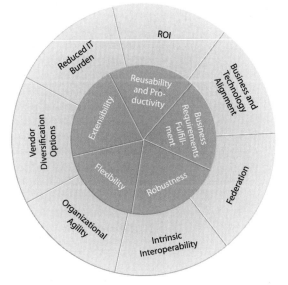

Increased Business Requirements Fulfillment

Through specialized analysis and design techniques (that include business-centric deliverables such as use cases), OOAD advocates the design and development of applications more capable of meeting specific business needs.

Increased business requirements fulfillment is also a priority for service-orientation and a primary design consideration for all of its principles. Many of the design characteristics fostered by these principles are geared toward enabling a design-time process that allows for the creation of sophisticated composition configurations in response to a range of envisioned business requirements.

Strategic service-orientation goals, such as "increased vendor diversity options," are intended to establish an environment that empowers an organization to continuously leverage technology innovation in support of maximizing the fulfillment potential of business requirements. Furthermore, OOAD's emphasis on partitioning solution logic into units that more closely resemble real-world objects is in alignment with the "increased business and technology domain alignment" goal, which aims to incorporate real-world representation at domain and enterprise levels.

Increased Robustness

Object-oriented solutions can be delivered to withstand a range of exception conditions because of extra design considerations applied to the various parts (objects) that comprise the solution and due to the use of formal design-time deliverables, such as activity, sequence, and state diagrams, that map out potential runtime usage scenarios.

Increased robustness is a goal of service-orientation from both short-term implementation and long-term governance perspectives. Service compositions are expected to work as required in their immediate deployment but are also designed to remain robust as their individual members are repurposed in support of fulfilling different business requirements as part of different compositions.

Service Autonomy and Service Statelessness represent two key principles dedicated to ensuring services are reliable and scalable during their runtime existence while concurrently supporting the automation of multiple solutions.

Increased Extensibility

Once implemented and in use, an object-oriented solution's functional scope can be increased without requiring significant redevelopment by leveraging the componentized nature of its application design.

Several service-orientation principles aim to establish the freedom for service compositions to be extended or recomposed in response to an increase in business requirements scope. The fact that functional contexts are carefully modeled and defined for each service allows for individual service contracts to be cleanly extended with new capabilities and without disruption to existing consumer programs.

The goals of "increased federation" and "increased intrinsic interoperability" aim to harmonize an enterprise in which solutions comprised of service compositions can be modified and extended through the incorporation of new service capabilities with minimal impact (due to the native compatibility established by standardization in support of intrinsic interoperability).

Increased Flexibility

After an object-oriented solution is deployed, it can be further evolved and enhanced with minimal disruption to its users through the targeted application of key design techniques, such as encapsulation, abstraction, and inheritance.

Enabling an organization to freely govern and evolve a service is a prime concern of the Service Loose Coupling and Service Abstraction principles, both of which protect an enterprise from the proliferation of unhealthy dependencies. This establishes an environment in which individual service capabilities can be refactored and enhanced as required.

The flexibility to augment services individually carries over to an increased flexibility to evolve a service inventory and the underlying service-oriented architecture itself. Flexibility, in fact, is at the heart of the "increased organizational agility" goal.

Increased Reusability and Productivity

Object-oriented solution logic can be designed for reuse, thereby lowering the subsequent effort to build applications that require the same type of logic. The Service Reusability principle clearly corresponds to this goal, but it is worth mentioning that all of the other service-orientation design principles are also positioned to fully support the widespread realization of reusable service logic.

As a result, reusability, as part of SOA, becomes more of an expected, secondary design characteristic than an actual objective. The goal of "increased ROI" is closely associated with the successful application of this principle.

SUMMARY OF KEY POINTS

- Five of the common goals of OOAD are increased business requirements fulfillment, increased robustness, increased extensibility, increased flexibility, and increased reusability and productivity.

- Service-orientation supports all of these goals, only it does so with a broadened, enterprise-centric emphasis on long-term governance and strategic benefit.

- While the realization of object-orientation goals is primarily associated with the use of component-based and RPC-based technology platforms, the attainment of service-orientation goals is more commonly related to the use of the Web services framework.

14.3 A Comparison of Fundamental Concepts

Conceptually, object-orientation and service-orientation have similarities, but they are not the same. This section establishes the terms and definitions used by each design approach in relation to both common and differential concepts.

> **NOTE**
>
> The examples in the upcoming sections use UML conventions. Various approaches have emerged for applying UML to the design of XML schemas and Web services. The focus of this chapter is not on how to adapt UML conventions to express XML schema or WSDL definition structures. Unless otherwise indicated, this comparison is specifically about fundamental service-orientation and object-orientation, which naturally raises issues as to how UML relates to services (regardless of their implementation).

Classes and Objects

Object-orientation provides a means of organizing solution logic into *classes* (Figure 14.4) that essentially act as containers for definitions of related behaviors and properties.

A runtime instance of a class is an *object* (much like a runtime instance of a service is a service instance). Therefore, a class can be seen as a design template from which various objects are spawned, each with their own unique runtime state and data.

A class is comparable to but not equivalent to a technical service contract. A class can define a combination of public access and private implementation details, whereas a service contract only expresses public information. In this regard, a service contract more closely resembles an interface implemented by a class (as explained in the *Interfaces* section).

Figure 14.4

The class symbol (left) and the chorded circle symbol (right) both establish a container and a functional context associated with invoice-related functionality.

Methods and Attributes

Object-oriented classes define *methods* and *attributes* so as to associate behavior and data with objects. Behaviors represent functionality the class is capable of carrying out. Each behavior is expressed and described by an individual method definition. Methods are sometimes also referred to as operations; however, the term operation has now become more synonymous with the use of Web services.

Class properties represent a form of predefined state data associated with the class and are expressed through the definition of attributes. Attributes can also be referred to as variables.

Methods and attributes can be declared as private or public to the class. It has become a best practice to only allow the public access or modification of attributes via public methods (further qualified as "accessor methods").

Services express behaviors as capabilities in abstract. A capability is the equivalent of a method if a service is implemented as a component and an operation if the service is deployed as a Web service. A Web service contract cannot define private operations.

Due to the emphasis on statelessness, service contracts are discouraged from defining attributes, as shown in Figure 14.5.

Figure 14.5

The class symbol (left) expresses an attribute and a method, whereas the service symbol (right) only defines a capability.

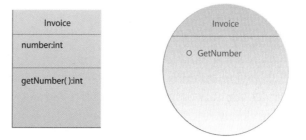

Messages

Communication between the invoker of an object and the object whose method is invoked is carried out through the exchange of *messages*. This is an abstract term used as part of the OOAD vocabulary and therefore does not imply how a message is physically comprised in the real world.

Because object-orientation is typically applied to components that rely on non-industry standard (often RPC-based) communication protocols, messages are most commonly expressed as binary units of communication that are exchanged synchronously. The contents of a message depend on the data type of the input or output values defined as part of the method and the supporting technical platform. RPC platforms support a variety of data types including those that can represent objects themselves.

Messages used by services implemented as Web services typically manifest themselves as text-based units of communication that can be exchanged synchronously or asynchronously. In this context, they are messages in a more traditional sense (as used by e-mail systems or messaging-oriented middleware).

The input and output values of Web service operations are represented by messages that are usually structured by XML schema complex types. They can have document-centric complex type hierarchies comprised of numerous values, each with a different data type. This is why the base chorded circle symbol expresses service contracts without specifying data types.

Object methods are frequently designed to exchange fine-grained parameter data. This is because the connection they establish with other objects (whether local or remote) is generally persistent. Once in place, data exchange is efficient.

Web services commonly rely on the stateless HTTP protocol to exchange messages. Because they do not have the benefit of a persistent, stateful connection, operations often need to be designed to exchange document-centric messages; messages comprised of larger amounts of data, such as entire business documents. As discussed in the preceding chapters, almost every service-orientation principle can impact the size of service messages by influencing capability, data, and validation granularity.

Figure 14.6 illustrates how the design of a class can be affected differently when shaped by object-oriented and service-oriented principles and further contrasts this with a typical service contract. Note the differences in method and operation granularity across these three samples; service-oriented design encourages the addition of coarse-grained capabilities that are more message-centric and support the exchange of XML documents. This affects both the granularity of capabilities as well as the choice of data type.

NOTE

The last section in this chapter provides guidelines for designing service-oriented classes in case you need to model services using the UML class notation.

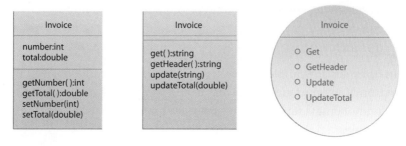

Figure 14.6

An object-oriented class (left), a service-oriented class (middle), and a service contract (right). Note that the attributes omitted by the middle class are public.

Interfaces

Collections of related methods can be defined (but not implemented) within *interfaces* (Figure 14.7). A class can then be designed to implement an interface, thereby establishing a formal endpoint into the logic encapsulated by the class. In this role, the interface can abstract additional details about the class from the outside world.

Service-orientation is focused on both the definition of the service contract and its underlying solution logic. A service contract on its own is comparable to an implemented class interface in that it provides the official entry point for publicly available service functionality while also abstracting underlying service details.

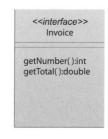

Unlike a class that exposes its attributes and methods (with or without the use of an interface) as an embedded extension of itself, a service contract exists as a physically decoupled architectural component when implemented as a Web service.

Figure 14.7

An Invoice interface expressing two methods.

A Web service contract can be viewed as a potentially sophisticated form of technical interface in that it is capable of expressing a range of logic, including data exchange requirements, validation rules, and even semantic policies in addition to implementation details, such as ports and bindings.

The WSDL definition used to express a Web service contract contains a `portType` element construct that formally establishes the Web service operations. In this regard, a Web service `portType` is a lot like an object-oriented interface (in fact, the `portType` element is renamed `interface` in WSDL version 2.0). Note that a WSDL definition can contain multiple `portType` constructs, much the same way as a class can implement multiple interfaces.

A service that exists as a Web service may or may not encapsulate object-oriented logic. If it does, then service-orientation design principles can affect the manner in which classes are designed, as explored in the *A Comparison of Principles* section.

SUMMARY OF KEY POINTS

- Implemented interfaces are most comparable to service contracts.
- Service-orientation can affect the definition of Web service operations and object methods and attributes.
- Message format and granularity are highly influenced by service-orientation.

14.4 A Comparison of Design Principles

The object-orientation design paradigm is comprised of a rich set of fundamental and supplemental design principles that structure and organize object logic within and across classes. Several of these principles have been carried over into service-orientation to varying extents, while others have been omitted entirely.

This section discusses how service-orientation relates to each of the following object-oriented design principles:

- Encapsulation
- Inheritance
- Generalization and Specialization
- Abstraction
- Polymorphism
- Open-Closed Principle (OCP)
- Don't Repeat Yourself (DRY)
- Single Responsibility Principle (SRP)
- Delegation
- Association

- Composition

- Aggregation

By understanding the relationship between object-oriented and service-oriented design, we can identify several specific origins of individual service-orientation principles. More importantly, though, we can establish how specifically services are designed differently from objects.

Encapsulation

To encapsulate means to enclose something in a container. Within object-orientation, *encapsulation* is associated with information hiding. It is a principle that states that an object should only be accessed via a public interface and that its implementation should remain hidden from other objects. The object is the container.

The object-orientation encapsulation principle is comparable to the service-orientation Service Abstraction principle, which is also concerned with the deliberate hiding of information (Figure 14.8).

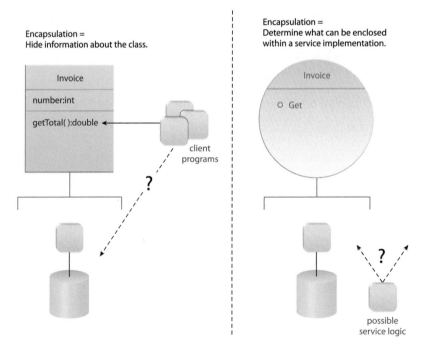

Figure 14.8
Although both revolve around the same meaning behind encapsulation, each design paradigm uses the term somewhat differently.

Services still encapsulate logic and implementations, just as objects do (because, like objects, services are containers). However, within service-orientation, the term "encapsulation" is used more so to refer to *what* is being enclosed within (encapsulated by) the container. In fact, service encapsulation is related to a fundamental SOA design pattern that is applied to determine what logic is and is not suitable as part of a given service.

Inheritance

A primary means by which object-orientation aims to achieve code reuse is by organizing logic into classes and then establishing relationships between these classes. Various types of relationships can exist, the most formal of which is *inheritance*.

Two classes can form a parent-child relationship, where the child class is automatically assigned (inherits) the methods and attributes of the parent class. When two classes are associated in this manner, the parent class is referred to as the *super-class* of the child class, and the child class is the *sub-class* of the parent class. A sub-class can do anything the super-class can do, plus it can be further extended with unique functionality (through a process called *specialization*).

The concrete bond formed between a super-class and its sub-class is often labeled as an "is-a" relationship because whatever the sub-class exits as is an implementation of what is defined in the super-class. This relationship is expressed using a white, triangular arrow head, as shown in Figure 14.9.

Due to the emphasis on individual service autonomy and reduced inter-service coupling, inheritance between services is generally discouraged within service-orientation. And because services do not formally implement each other, they are not required to establish "is-a" relationships.

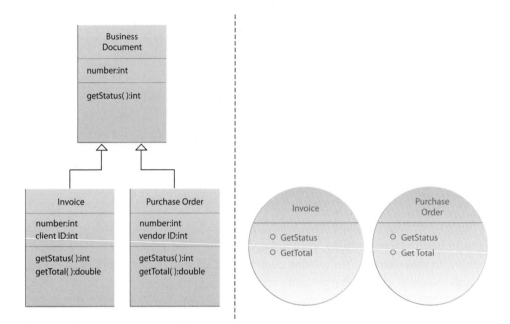

Figure 14.9

With inheritance, sub-classes (bottom left) representing specific types of business documents can implement an abstract super-class (top left) to inherit a common method and attribute. Entity services (right) representing business documents may share similar capabilities, but none are inherited.

NOTE
In some circles it has become an OOAD convention to not repeat inherited attribute and method names in sub-classes because their existence can be assumed via the expressed inheritance relationship. Inherited attributes and methods are intentionally displayed in all examples in this chapter to more clearly establish a comparison with corresponding service definitions.
It is also worth noting that interface inheritance is possible within Web services, as of version 2.0 of the WSDL specification via the `interface` element's `extends` attribute. See **www.soaspecs.com** to read up on this feature as explained in the W3C WSDL 2.0 primer document.

Generalization and Specialization

A well-designed, top-level super-class (also referred to as the *abstract class* or *base class*) expresses a highly generic interface with broad applicability. This allows for the definition of a range of sub-classes.

Generalization is achieved when a parent super-class is defined. Because sub-classes implement distinct (specialized) variations of a super-class, their definition is referred to as *specialization*. Generalization is another way of saying a class has a "is-a-kind-of" relationship with another class, whereas specialization represents the previously described "is-a" relationship.

There are concepts similar to generalization and specialization within service-orientation; only because inheritance is not supported, they exist differently (Figure 14.10). Within the context of service design, generalization and specialization relate directly to granularity. The more specialized a service, the greater the extent of its service-level granularity.

Determining the right degree of specialization for each service is a critical decision point and one that establishes a service's functional context and concrete boundary. However, there are opportunities to adjust the level of a service's specialization during its post-implementation lifespan. Through the use of service design patterns, for example, an existing coarse-grained (more generalized) service can be decomposed into finer-grained (more specialized) services for functional and practical reasons, but not as a result of inheritance.

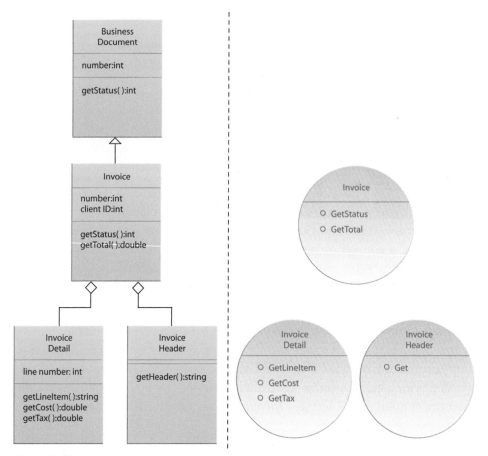

Figure 14.10

The three-level hierarchy (left) includes the Invoice class, which is a specialization of the generalized Business Document class, and the Invoice Detail and Invoice Header classes, which are aggregates of the Invoice class. Technically, the Invoice Detail and Invoice Header classes are not considered specialized because they are not based on "is-a" relationships. Alternatively, because the Invoice Detail and Invoice Header services (right) have a higher level of service granularity than the Invoice service, they can be considered more specialized (but not in a traditional OOAD sense). (Note the use of the diamond symbol to indicate an aggregated relationship. This is explained further in the upcoming *Aggregation* section.)

NOTE

The aforementioned base or abstract classes defined through the creation of generalized classes are not actually implemented in the real world in that instances or objects are not generated from these classes. Instead, they exist to establish inheritance structures and specialized sub-classes. In service-orientation the use of an abstract class is voluntary, as explained in the *Guidelines for Designing Service-Oriented Classes* section at the end of this chapter.

Abstraction

Another information hiding-related principle in object-orientation is that of abstraction. Specifically, the purpose of abstraction is to create a simplified class that hides the complexity of the underlying implementation and exposes only the most necessary (abstract) methods and attributes. Abstraction can be applied to support inheritance for the definition of abstract classes that are not implemented but instead form the parent super-class from which numerous specialized sub-classes can be defined and implemented.

Conceptually, object-oriented abstraction is similar to Service Abstraction in that both principles ultimately intend to streamline public information about underlying solution logic and implementation details (Figure 14.11). However, because service-orientation does not support inheritance, there is no corresponding notion of an abstract class.

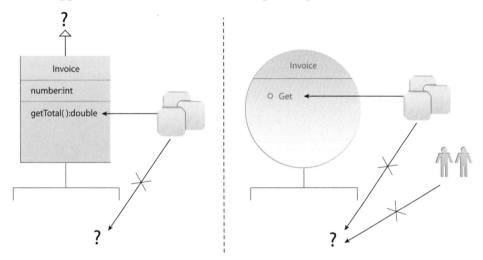

Figure 14.11

While object-oriented abstraction (left) is primarily concerned with hiding complexity (in this case, the underlying implementation) from other consumer programs, Service Abstraction (right) also limits human access and awareness of underlying service details.

Polymorphism

When multiple object-oriented sub-classes inherit and retain a method from a super-class, you can end up with multiple classes that have identically named methods. Even though the method definitions are the same, the implementation will vary across the sub-classes because each sub-class is specialized in a distinct manner. Therefore, the same message sent to any one of these sub-classes will have different results based on the variance of the sub-class implementations. This is known as *polymorphism*.

Because inheritance does not exist in service-orientation, this form of polymorphism is also not applied to individual services (Figure 14.12). The closest thing to polymorphism that can be realized in support of service-orientation is the consistent functional expression of service contracts, as per the Standardized Service Contract principle. This typically results in similar or identically named capabilities across numerous services. (The consistent use of standardized, verb-based, CRUD-style operations within entity services is an example of this.)

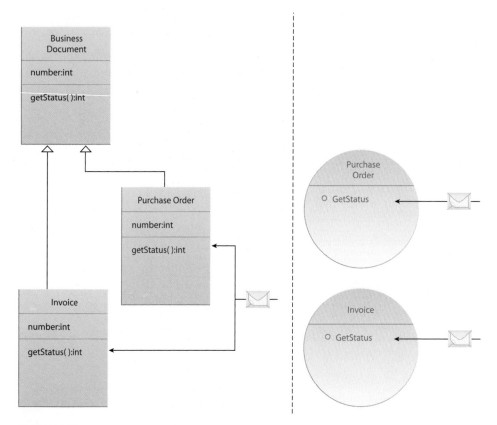

Figure 14.12

The specialized sub-classes (left) that inherited the getStatus method are each capable of processing the same input message. The Purchase Order and Invoice services (right), on the other hand, express GetStatus capabilities that each require their own specific input message.

This level of interface consistency is the result of naming conventions applied to the contract designs. There is no expectation that identically named capabilities of different services support the same messages. Therefore, this would not qualify as true polymorphism.

Open-Closed Principle (OCP)

This basic design principle states that classes should allow (be open to) extension but disallow (be closed to) modification of what has already been implemented. This is a key design requirement that helps protect reusable functionality upon which multiple client programs have already formed dependencies. It is fully applicable to service contracts and is required when applying the Service Reusability principle in order to minimize subsequent governance burden (Figure 14.13).

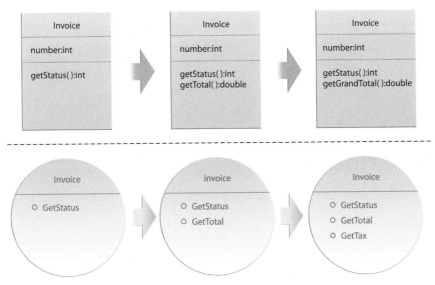

Figure 14.13
The class on the top right violates this principle by renaming (not overriding) an already implemented method, whereas each of the services on the bottom comply with this principle by only extending the service contract.

Don't Repeat Yourself (DRY)

By avoiding redundant code, objects can be more effectively reused, and wasted development effort can be minimized. This principle simply states that if reusable logic exists, it should be separated so that it can be made available for reuse. The rationale behind this principle forms the basis of the Service Normalization pattern and the use of agnostic service models (Figure 14.14). By avoiding functional overlap we furthermore avoid redundancy across service designs in support of the Logic Centralization pattern.

Figure 14.14

The class and the service on the left are each further decomposed so as to extract reusable logic into a separate agnostic functional context represented by the class and service on the bottom right.

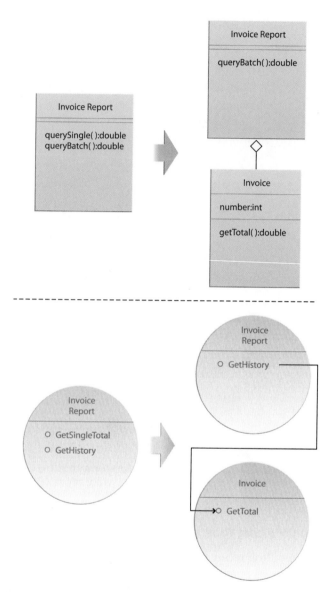

Single Responsibility Principle (SRP)

Object-oriented units of solution logic designs are ideally centered around a single overall purpose. The *single responsibility principle* encourages us to limit their functional scope to this purpose so that they are only required to change if that one purpose changes.

In service-orientation, this corresponds to the consistent use of service models that establish distinct functional service contexts (Figure 14.15). An entity service, for example, can be dedicated to processing associated with a business entity. Similarly, a task service's sole purpose is the automation of a specific business process.

Figure 14.15

The coarse-grained, dual-purpose Client Account class and service (left) are each decomposed into two groups of behaviors that represent two distinct, single-purpose functional contexts (right).

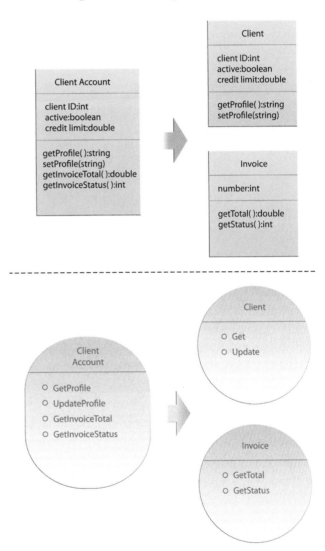

The single responsibility principle is closely related to the notion of *cohesion*. A class or service has increased cohesion when it defines (and sticks to) a specific functional context. This establishes it as a container for a group of highly related methods or capabilities. Alternatively, a class or service with low cohesion is one that violates this principle by defining a functional context that encompasses multiple purposes.

Note that cohesion and service granularity don't always go hand-in-hand. A service can have a coarse level of service granularity and still be highly cohesive. However, because the functional scope of services that facilitate numerous purposes or responsibilities naturally tends to result in lower (broader) granularity, services with low cohesion are usually more coarsely grained.

NOTE

Previous chapters have made reference to positioning services as multi-purpose enterprise resources in support of the Service Reusability principle. In this context, the term "multi-purpose" refers to the utilization of a single service (or any one of its capabilities) within multiple usage scenarios. The service itself retains a specific functional context and boundary and therefore can be said to have a single responsibility.

Delegation

This simple principle states that if an object requires logic that already exists in another object, then it should give (*delegate*) the responsibility of carrying out that logic to the other object instead of carrying it out itself. The key condition of applying this principle is that the behavior of the object to which the responsibility is being delegated not be required to change.

Consistent use of this fundamental design consideration fully supports Service Reusability and the realization of widespread Logic Centralization (Figure 14.16). In fact, delegation directly corresponds to the fundamental service design patterns that require the invocation and reuse of logic external to a service's functional context so as to preserve the integrity of this context. In service-orientation, the rationale behind this principle is what drives the need for service composition.

Figure 14.16

Instead of carrying out the retrieval of a range of invoice data on its own, the Client class delegates the responsibility by invoking a corresponding Invoice class. The Client service's GetOwing capability does the same by invoking the Invoice service's GetUnpaid capability.

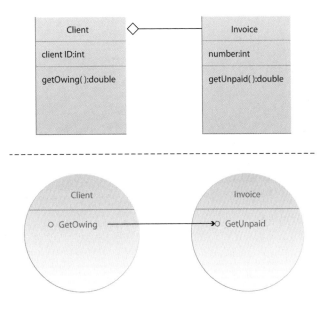

Association

In OOAD, an *association* between two classes represents a relationship. Relationships are required to carry out delegation so that objects can invoke and communicate with each other at runtime. There are different types of associations, the simplest of which establishes a "uses-a" relationship that allows one class to exchange messages with another. The two classes can be unrelated and independent; one just uses functionality the other has to offer.

Other, more formal types of associations define different types of relationships. Aggregation and composition, for example, create "has-a" relationships between classes that have ownership implications (as explained in the upcoming sections).

Service interaction is very similar to the former type of association in that services only need to be able to use each other's capabilities without ownership-related limitations. This is why service interaction is typically identified using the same (or similar) arrowhead used to express object-oriented association relationships (Figure 14.17).

Figure 14.17

The Client class has an association with the Purchase Order class (top) similar to how the Client service relates to the Purchase Order service (bottom).

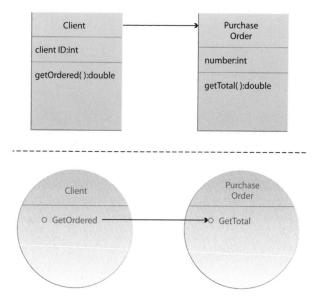

Composition

The concept of composition in object-orientation and service-orientation is similar but, as with encapsulation, the term is used differently. In OOAD *composition* refers to a form of association that establishes an ownership structure between classes. A parent class is composed of others and therefore creates "has-a" relationships with other classes.

Furthermore, composed objects have a lifespan associated with the parent object, meaning that they are destroyed when the parent object ceases to exist. Composition relationships are identified with lines that end with a black diamond shape attached to the class responsible for initiating the composition (Figure 14.18).

In service-orientation, the term "composition" refers to an assembly or aggregate of services with no predefined ownership structure. Therefore, the rules associated with OOAD composition do not apply. Services are free to invoke capabilities within other services, and the composition controller service instance responsible for initiating the composition does not need to remain active for as long as any of the composition member service instances. This level of freedom is important to fully realize the potential of Service Composability.

Figure 14.18

The Client class composes a related Account class, which is implemented by one of three sub-classes depending on the nature of the account (top). In this case, the Account interface is owned by the Client class and cannot exist without it. The Account service, on the other hand, is simply invoked by the Client service with no ownership implications (bottom).

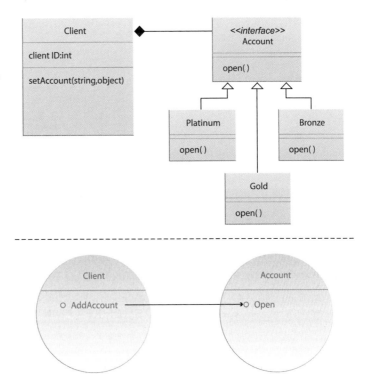

Aggregation

The object-orientation principle of aggregation is similar to that of composition, but different rules apply to the relationships between participating objects. Classes with an aggregation association still establish an ownership structure based on a "has-a" relationship. However, the lifespan of the object that initiates an aggregation does not need to equal the lifespan of the other participating objects. In other words, the class being aggregated is allowed to exist independently outside of the parent (container) class acting as the aggregator. Aggregation relationships are distinguished by a line with a white diamond touching the class that is aggregating others.

As with composition, aggregation does not apply to service-orientation because it is still based on a "has-a" ownership structure. As mentioned in the *Association* section, service interaction most closely resembles a "uses-a" relationship (Figure 14.19).

Figure 14.19

The Client class aggregates the Invoice class (top) because Clients have invoices, and invoices can exist independently from clients. However, the Client service invokes the Invoice service (bottom) as it would any other service.

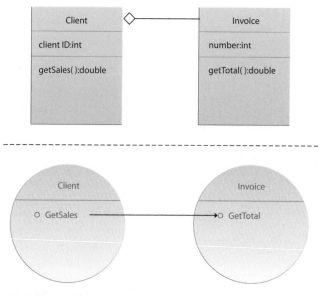

SUMMARY OF KEY POINTS

- The underlying concepts behind several principles are similar in object-orientation and service-orientation. However, the meanings associated with some of the terms can vary.

- Many of the differences between OOAD principles and service-orientation design principles relate to the fact that inheritance is not supported within service-orientation.

- Many of the similarities between OOAD and service-orientation principles can be traced back to their common goals.

14.5 Guidelines for Designing Service-Oriented Classes

To conclude this study, it is worth framing service-orientation design considerations within the context of OOAD conventions and class design.

The remaining sections provide a set of guidelines for designing service-oriented classes. These guidelines can be helpful should you be required to model services using the UML class notation.

Implement Class Interfaces

Classes positioned as services should always implement interfaces so that an official public contract is expressed separately from additional class details that may need to remain hidden. This directly supports the Standardized Service Contract, Service Loose Coupling, and Service Abstraction principles.

Limit Class Access to Interfaces

This guideline is essentially a translation of the Contract Centralization pattern and the consumer-to-contract coupling type defined by the Service Loose Coupling principle. This positive form of coupling protects the underlying class implementation details the same way it prevents negative forms of coupling within services that exist as Web services.

Do Not Define Public Attributes in Interfaces

This already exists as a best practice in OOAD, but it is worth repeating here in support of service-orientation. The Service Statelessness principle encourages services to exist as solution units capable of reverting to a stateless condition whenever appropriate. Removing attributes from the public interface forces all communication through methods (be they accessor methods or otherwise) and therefore places the control of how state is managed within the service (which is exactly where we want it).

Use Inheritance with Care

Inter-service inheritance is not formally advocated by service-orientation in support of realizing the independence and freedom we seek to establish in every service via the Service Loose Coupling, Service Autonomy, and Service Composability principles.

Intra-service inheritance (the application of inheritance to classes encapsulated by the service) can be applied to strengthen the structure of intra-service logic, as required. However, there needs to be a constant awareness that coarse-grained services may need to be decomposed into finer-grained (more specialized) services at some point.

As per the corresponding service design patterns, we can prepare for service decomposition by how we design a service's contract and logic. Service logic comprised of components tightly bound through inheritance structures will be more difficult to decompose into physically separate services than if the underlying class structures are less inter-dependent.

Avoid Cross-Service "has-a" Relationships

Service compositions require the freedom to allow composition members to act independently from the parent controller, even if that means they remain active after the controller instance is destroyed. Furthermore, services can't be limited to some form of pre-determined ownership hierarchy; as per the Service Composability principle, a service ideally needs to be able to compose or be composed by any other service within a given inventory.

Unless there is a need for strict rules around the association of object lifespans to parent objects, "uses-a" associations are a more "service-friendly" means of composing classes than composition or aggregation.

Use Abstract Classes for Modeling, Not Design

As explained in the *Generalization and Specialization* section, the use of abstract classes within service-orientation is not required. Because no formal inheritance relationships are defined, no base or abstract service is needed for other services to be designed.

However, the use of abstract classes can be helpful during the service-oriented analysis phase (especially for those familiar with OOAD). Abstract classes can be informally defined as the base or root of collections of related classes so as to ensure consistency in the definition of service candidate functional contexts and service capability candidates. As such, their use can be incorporated into a customized variation of the service modeling process.

Use Façade Classes

Façades have not been discussed in this chapter because they technically represent an OO design pattern (as opposed to a design principle). The book *SOA: Design Patterns* covers the OO Façade pattern and discusses how it ties into service-orientation. However, it is worth mentioning here that from a service design perspective, creating façade classes is a very important and common technique (also referred to as the Service Façade pattern) for structuring components as standalone services or as part of service-oriented Web services.

SUMMARY OF KEY POINTS

- Service-oriented classes can be designed by applying service-orientation design principles and regulating the use of certain object-orientation design principles.

- The established best practice of using interfaces within OOAD is carried over as a key guideline when designing service-oriented classes.

- The use of inheritance within service-oriented class designs needs to be carefully gauged so as not to lead to ownership structures that may inhibit the evolution of services and service inventories.

NOTE

This chapter has established some fundamental comparisons limited to principles and concepts only. There is more to be explored, especially in the areas of design patterns. *SOA: Design Patterns* includes a comparative analysis of SOA and OO design patterns that reveals further commonality and differences between service-orientation and object-orientation.

Chapter 15

Supporting Practices

Each of the following recommended practices can be considered an additional "best practice" in its own right in that each provides a proven approach or consideration in support of applying service-orientation design principles.

The practices associated with vocabularies and roles in particular raise issues that can be addressed during SOA planning stages in preparation for subsequent service analysis and design projects.

15.1 Service Profiles

When collecting discoverability-related meta information, it is helpful to use a standardized template or form that ensures the same type of data is documented for each service. This can be especially useful during the early analysis stages, when service candidates are just being conceptualized as part of the service modeling process. The document used to record details about a service is the *service profile*.

Figure 15.1 illustrates how the service profile emerges from the initial analysis phases, but can then continue to accompany a service as it progresses through subsequent design, delivery, and governance stages. A service profile can very much become a living document that is owned and maintained by service custodians.

Once a service is finally deployed, some organizations transpose the contents of the service profile to the service registry, whereas others choose to keep the service profile as a separate document (in which case the service's registry record may include a pointer to the location of the profile document).

Figure 15.1

A service profile initially acts as a repository of meta information when a service is first conceptualized during early analysis stages and then provides valuable details for design and delivery-related documents used during later lifecycle phases.

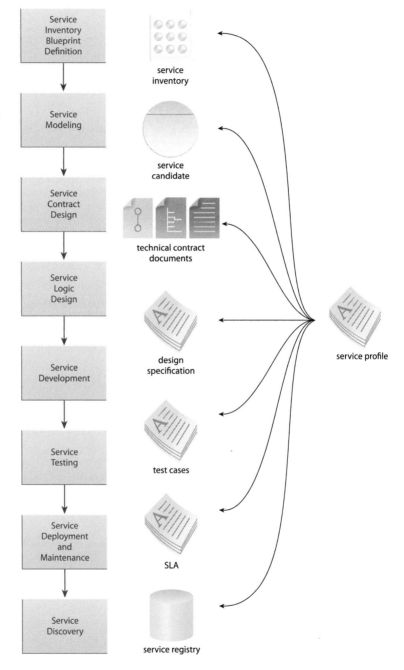

Service-Level Profile Structure

There is no one official profile format for the service profile. However, with an understanding of how services typically evolve throughout project delivery lifecycles, the following baseline fields are recommended: -

- *Service Name*

- *Purpose Description (Short)* - A concise, one sentence description of the service context and purpose.

- *Purpose Description (Detailed)* - A full explanation of the service context and its functional boundary with as many details as necessary.

- *Service Model* - Entity, Utility, Task, Orchestrated Task, or a custom variation.

- *QoS Requirements* - This field captures various anticipated quality of service requirements, characteristics, or limitations that affect the service as a whole. Examples include security, performance, availability, and transaction requirements (each of which could easily justify its own field in the profile).

- *Capabilities* - The profile should document capabilities that exist and are in development, as well as those that are only planned and tentatively defined. Color coding is often useful to make these distinctions as is the use of the capability "status" field (described shortly).

- *Keywords* - This field can contain one or more keywords ideally taken from an official service inventory-level taxonomy or vocabulary. Service profile keywords should correspond to the keywords used by a service registry.

- *Version* - The version number of the service currently being documented is noted here. Depending on the version control system in use, version numbers may only be applicable to service capabilities.

- *Status* - The development status of the service (or service version) is expressed in this field using standard terms identifying a project lifecycle stage, such as "analysis," "contract design," "development," or "production." If the service is not in production, it can be helpful to include an estimated delivery date.

- *Custodian* - Details on how to reach the official service custodian or owner, as well as others that contributed to this documentation.

Capability Profile Structure

Because a service acts as a container for a collection of capabilities, additional "sub-profiles" need to be established to represent each individual capability separately, as follows:

- *Capability Name*

- *Purpose Description* - A concise explanation of the capability's overall purpose and functional context (similar to the short service description).

- *Logic Description* - A step-by-step description of the logic carried out by the capability. This can be supplemented with algorithms, workflow diagrams, or even entire business process definitions, depending on what stage the capability definition is at.

- *Input/Output* - These two fields provide definitions of a capability's allowable input and/or output value(s) and associated constraints. It can be helpful to describe these in plain English during the service modeling phase. The details established here can make reference to existing schema types.

- *Composition Role* - The execution of capability logic can place a service into various temporary runtime roles, depending on its position within service composition configurations. This field can be filled out with a description of the capability's role, or it can simply contain a term used to identify predefined roles, such as those introduced in Chapter 13.

- *Composition Member Capabilities* - A list of services (and specifically their capabilities) composed by the capability logic. This provides a convenient cross-reference to other service capabilities on which the current capability has formed dependencies. Ideally, identified composition member capabilities are mapped to the portions of the business process logic (documented in the *Logic Description* field) so that delegated logic is clearly indicated.

- *QoS Requirements* - As with the corresponding field in the service-level profile structure, this field is dedicated to collecting quality of service details. However, the information documented here pertains specifically to the service capability, which means it may need to be derived from or correlated with the service-level quality of service details in some cases.

- *Keywords* - Often the same keywords that apply to the service can be carried over to the capability. But it is not uncommon for additional keywords to be added to individual capabilities so as to better classify their purpose. Keywords for services and capabilities should originate from the same parent vocabulary.

- *Version* - Depending on the versioning system in place, capabilities themselves may be versioned with a number, or new capability versions may be added with the version number appended to the capability name.

- *Status* - The same lifecycle identifiers used for services can be applied to the status of individual capabilities. However, this field can also be used to earmark capabilities that were identified during the modeling stage but for which no specific delivery date exists.

- *Custodian* - More often than not, the custodian of the service will be the custodian (or one of the custodians) of the related capabilities. However, when multiple business and technology experts collaborate on a given service, some are only there to assist with the definition of one service capability (or a subset of service capabilities). In this case separate custodians may need to be associated with individual capabilities.

Additional Considerations

Customizing Service Profiles

What we've established so far is fundamental profile documentation. Organizations are encouraged to customize and extend this to whatever extent required. Each of the principles covered prior to this chapter provided the option of identifying additional types of meta information, primarily associated with the extent to which principle characteristics were implemented.

Therefore, when documenting a service at various lifecycle stages, its profile can be further appended with levels, such as those summarized in Table 15.3 in the upcoming *Vocabularies* section.

Service Profiles and Service Registries

Much of the information assembled into service profiles will form the basis for service registry records. Depending on whether a service registry exists within an organization at the time the profile is being defined, it is advisable to become familiar with the registry product's record format. This will allow you to better align the service profile template with how the profile information may need to be represented within the service registry.

Service Profiles and Policies

While the WSDL and XML schema definitions will often naturally emerge from existing data models, design standards, and the interoperability requirements documented as part of the service-oriented analysis phase, policy definition is not always as straight forward. Much of the information collected in the service profile document (especially as part of the QoS fields) can form the basis for policies.

It is up to those that shape the full service contract (which, as originally illustrated in Figure 6.2, is comprised of technical and non-technical documents) to decide whether a given policy should be expressed via a technical syntax, such as the WS-Policy language, whether it is better represented within an SLA, or whether it should be part of the service contract at all.

Of course another important piece of information that needs to be kept within service profiles is any *existing* policies that are identified as pertaining to the service or any one of its capabilities. An additional field dedicated to providing a link to relevant (technical or non-technical) policies may be warranted within enterprises that have several centralized policies already in use.

Service Profiles and Service Catalogs

The structure of a service profile is ideally standardized so that different project teams consistently document the services they deliver. As more service profiles are created, they can be assembled into a *service catalog*. A service catalog is essentially a documentation of the services within a service inventory (much the same way a product catalog may describe the inventory of items a company has in its warehouse).

If an organization is creating multiple domain service inventories, each with its own design standards and governance processes, then service profile structures may vary. Therefore, a separate service catalog is generally created for each service inventory.

SUMMARY OF KEY POINTS

- As services move from concept to candidate to physical design, it is important to consistently document them using standardized service profiles.

- The use of service profiles is most effective when combined with a standardized vocabulary or taxonomy.

- Service profile documents can be compiled into an inventory-specific service catalog.

15.2 Vocabularies

When services are delivered by various project teams, the need for consistency in how service characteristics, contexts, keywords, and other forms of meta information are labeled and classified is paramount. If different teams use different conventions, it can jeopardize the potential for services to be repeatedly composed and can further burden the governance of service inventories.

In relation to service-orientation design principles, the following vocabularies are relevant and should always be standardized:

* Service-Oriented Computing Terms

* Service Classification Terms

* Design Principle and Characteristic Types, Categories, Labels

* Design Principle Application Levels

* Service Profile Keywords

The next set of sections revisits some of the terms, labels, and categories described in earlier chapters to provide an overview of the vocabularies established in this book. Each of these vocabularies can be further customized and extended for specific enterprise environments. The key is to do so consistently and make the official vocabularies widely available to all relevant project team members.

Service-Oriented Computing Terms

The following set of terms represents the fundamental taxonomy that establishes the core elements and parts of a typical service-oriented computing platform:

* Service-Oriented Architecture

* Service-Orientation Design Paradigm

* Service-Orientation Design Principles

* Service-Oriented Solution Logic

* Service

* Service Model

* Service Composition

* Service Inventory

* Service Inventory Blueprint

These terms are defined and described in Chapters 3 and 4.

Service Classification Terms

Table 15.1 lists the core service models referenced throughout this book and also provides alternative industry terms. (Service models were first introduced in Chapter 3.)

Service Model	Classification	Alternative Terms	Corresponding Service Abstraction Layer
Entity Service	Business, Agnostic	Entity-Centric Business Service Business Entity Services	Entity Service Layer
Utility Service	Non-Business, Agnostic	Application Service Infrastructure Service Technology Service	Utility Service Layer
Task Service	Business, Non-Agnostic	Task-Centric Business Service Business Process Service	Task Service Layer
Orchestrated Task Service	Business, Non-Agnostic	Process Service Business Process Service Orchestration Service	Parent Business Process Layer Orchestration Layer

Table 15.1

The terms used to represent these fundamental service models also carry over to how the corresponding service abstraction layers are labeled.

Types and Associated Terms

Various terms were established in Chapters 5 through 13. Some defined types of design characteristics, whereas others provided categories of relevant information, as listed in Table 15.2.

Design Principle	Types
All	Service Granularity Capability Granularity Data Granularity Constraint Granularity
Standardized Service Contract	Functional Service Expression Standardization Data Representation Standardization (or Data Model Standardization)
Service Loose Coupling	Logic-to-Contract Coupling Contract-to-Logic Coupling Contract-to-Technology Coupling Contract-to-Implementation Coupling Contract-to-Functional Coupling Consumer-to-Implementation Coupling Consumer-to-Contract Coupling
Service Abstraction	Technology Information Abstraction Functional Abstraction Programmatic Logic Abstraction Quality of Service Abstraction
Service Reusability	n/a
Service Autonomy	Runtime Autonomy Design-Time Autonomy
Service Statelessness	Active and Passive (Primary States) Stateful and Stateless (Primary State Conditions) Context, Session, and Business (State Information Types) Context Data and Context Rules (Context Data Types)
Service Discoverability	Design-Time Discovery Runtime Discovery Functional Meta Data Quality of Service Meta Data

Design Principle	Types
Service Composability	Primitive Composition Complex Composition Service Activities Composition Controller Composition Sub-Controller Designated Controller Composition Member Composition Initiator Composition Instance Composition Member Capability Point-to-Point

Table 15.2

Collections of related terms used to classify various types of characteristics and information. (Note that the granularity types listed in the first row were introduced in Chapter 5.)

Design Principle Application Levels

Several of the chapters in this book provided suggested labels to communicate to what extent a principle was applied to a service capability or to the service as a whole. Table 15.3 summarizes these levels.

Design Principle	Levels
Standardized Service Contract	Levels Dependent on Design Standards
Service Loose Coupling	Non-Centralized Consumer Coupling Centralized Consumer Coupling (plus numeric rating)
Service Abstraction	Detailed Contract Abstraction Concise Contract Abstraction Optimized Contract Abstraction Mixed Detailed Contract Abstraction Open Access Controlled Access No Access
Service Reusability	Tactical Reusability Targeted Reusability Complete Reusability

Design Principle	Levels
Service Autonomy	Service Contract Autonomy Shared Autonomy Service Logic Autonomy Pure Autonomy
Service Statelessness	Non-Deferred State Management Partially Deferred Memory Partial Architectural State Management Deferral Full Architectural State Management Deferral Internally Deferred State Management
Service Discoverability	Custom Rating System
Service Composability	Custom Rating System (for composition design, composition runtime, and composition governance stages)

Table 15.3

Some design principles provide specific, measurable application levels, while others provide suggested rating systems that depend on environment-specific factors.

SUMMARY OF KEY POINTS

- Establishing a standard vocabulary of terms used for classification and communication purposes can streamline the delivery of services.

- This book provides numerous terms and classifications that can be further extended or customized.

- Vocabularies are ideally distributed to and used by all project team members.

15.3 Organizational Roles

As explained in Chapter 4, applying service-orientation design principles on a broad basis changes the complexion of an IT enterprise. Organizational structures and project delivery lifecycles and processes are affected and subjected to changes, as are ownership and governance responsibilities and priorities.

Changes on an organizational level result in changes to those who work within the organization.

Traditional IT positions are impacted as the need for new roles emerges in response to the distinct requirements associated with the delivery, deployment, and maintenance of services, service inventories, and service-oriented technology architecture implementations (Figure 15.2). It is important to gain an understanding of these new roles as early on in the delivery lifecycle as possible so that project teams are fully prepared.

Provided in this section are descriptions for the following set of common roles:

- Service Analyst
- Service Architect
- Service Custodian
- Schema Custodian
- Policy Custodian
- Service Registry Custodian
- Technical Communications Specialist
- Enterprise Architect
- Enterprise Design Standards Custodian (and Auditor)

Note that this list is limited to roles associated specifically with the application of service-orientation design principles as they relate to the aforementioned deliverables and delivery stages.

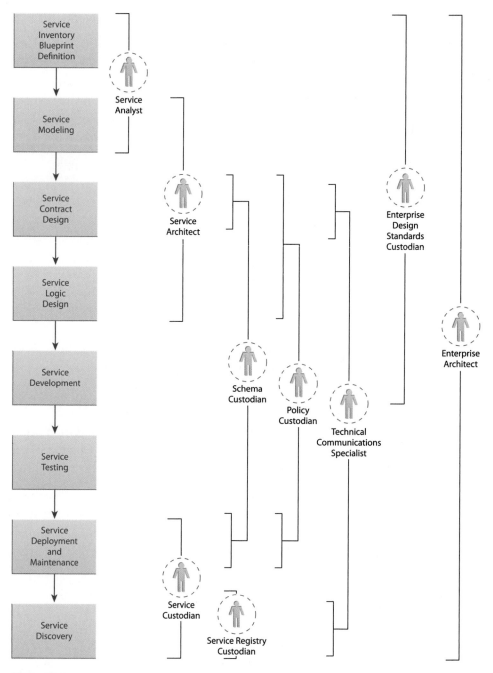

Figure 15.2

Common roles associated with service-orientation can be required in various stages of a typical service delivery lifecycle.

Service Analyst

This role requires expertise in the definition of service candidates, service capability candidates, and service composition candidates. A service analyst is therefore proficient in all aspects of the service-oriented analysis process, including the delivery of service candidates through the service modeling process.

The service analyst role can be assumed by architects and business analysts that participate in a project's service-oriented analysis phase. Alternatively, it can form the basis of a team leader role within this process, essentially a specialist in service-oriented analysis that coordinates and leads architects and business analysts throughout all process steps. The latter variation can be very effective in larger enterprise environments where every iteration through a business process can require the participation of different business and technology subject matter experts.

Principles most associated with this role: Service Reusability, Service Autonomy, Service Discoverability

Service Architect

The service architect is primarily concentrated on the physical design of services. Therefore, this role is more associated with the service-oriented design process and the various service model-specific service design processes an organization may be using.

Service architects are enlisted when an organization is ready to proceed to the design and development stages of an SOA initiative. They essentially use the service candidate definitions as a starting point, apply related design standards and conventions, and deliver service contract and logic designs.

The actual development of the contract and logic may be carried out by development teams. However, service architects proficient with contract technologies may assume the responsibility of delivering the technical contracts themselves. Furthermore, service architects may be required to contribute to service design standards as well.

Depending on the scope of a service delivery project, the same individual may be able to assume both service analyst and service architect roles.

Principles most associated with this role: All

Service Custodian

A service custodian owns the governance responsibilities of one or more specific services. These duties do not just revolve around the extension and expansion and maintenance of service logic, but also include having to protect the integrity of the service context and its associated functional boundary. Therefore, a service custodian can take ownership of a service as early as when its context is defined (and verified) during the service-oriented analysis stage.

Service custodians are important to the evolution of agnostic services. Their involvement ensures that no one project team inadvertently skews the design of an agnostic service in favor of their requirements. They are furthermore responsible for hiding non-essential information about service designs from the outside world (as per the access control levels established by the Service Abstraction principle). As a result, service custodians often require a good amount of authority.

Note that depending on how service details are documented, a service custodian may author, own, and maintain a service's corresponding profile document.

Principles most associated with this role: All

Schema Custodian

Originally established in the book *Service-Oriented Architecture: A Field Guide to Integrating XML and Web Services,* this role is still very much required for the governance of environments where services are delivered as Web services. The flexibility provided by the Web services framework to allow a data representation architecture (comprised of XML schemas) to be created and standardized independently from the service layer enables schemas to be separately defined and maintained. Ideally, this role is assumed by data analysts or other types of specialists with an intimate knowledge of an organization's information architecture.

The need for XML schema language expertise is a key prerequisite of this role. Not only are schema custodians often called upon to deliver new standardized XML schemas, they are also responsible for augmenting or extending schemas in response to changing business requirements (which also leads to the need to manage schema versions).

In support of realizing service-orientation, schema custodians ensure that service contract schemas are properly positioned as standardized and centralized parts of service inventories. Schema custodians may even own design standards pertaining to data representation.

Principles most associated with this role: Standardized Service Contract, Service Loose Coupling, Service Abstraction

Policy Custodian

Although this role can be assumed by the same person acting as the Schema Custodian, it is not uncommon for different individuals (or even different groups) to be responsible for defining and maintaining policy assertions for Web service contracts. Often these technical policy expressions are tied to existing security polices, in which case their need may not actually be identified until later in the project delivery lifecycle when the actual service logic is being designed. Other forms of policies, such as those that express a proprietary assertion syntax to represent specific business rules and policies, may be defined and owned by a combination of technical and business professionals.

Because service polices can be tied to existing corporate policies, they may be subject to more change than other parts of the service contract. Therefore, their initial definition is important to avoid embedding too much potentially volatile policy logic in the service contract. Similarly, their subsequent governance is also important to ensure they are kept in alignment with the actual polices they may have been derived from.

Overall, policy management can turn into a significant responsibility that can involve subject matter experts representing various IT departments. The document *Guidelines for Policy Assertion Authors* is a useful resource published by the W3C as a supplement to the WS-Policy specification (see www.soaspecs.com).

Principles most associated with this role: Standardized Service Contract, Service Loose Coupling, Service Abstraction (Note that other design principles can be affected when policies are used to express details about a service's underlying logic and behavior.)

Service Registry Custodian

Once a service registry is introduced into an enterprise, it will need to be religiously administered by one or more qualified individuals. If the content in the registry is ever allowed to go stale or somehow becomes inaccurate, the registry itself loses significance as a central part of the SOA infrastructure.

The service registry custodian is tasked with the overall administration of one or more private service registries. This goes beyond the installation and maintenance of the registry product, it encompasses the constant responsibility of ensuring a high quality of registry record content, which ties directly into how discoverability-related meta information is defined and recorded for individual services.

Although service registry custodians will typically not author discoverability content themselves, they will often own standards or conventions that dictate the nature of meta data used to populate service registry profile records.

Principles most associated with this role: Standardized Service Contract, Service Discoverability

Technical Communications Specialist

As explained in Chapter 12, the communications quality of service meta information can often be questionable. Although technically and business-wise accurate, comments, annotations, and general information within the service profile document can lack the clarity required for discovery and interpretation by a broader audience.

A technical communications specialist is usually someone with a background in technical writing who is enlisted to refine initial drafts of service profiles and associated meta data. The responsibility of this individual is to express discoverability information in plain English, using standard vocabularies so that a range of project team members can effectively query and understand service contracts and associated profiles.

Principles most associated with this role: Service Discoverability

Enterprise Architect

Although this is not a new role by any means, it represents a position that is greatly emphasized by the cross-application (cross-silo) scope of service inventory delivery projects.

Technology architects with an enterprise perspective are expected to:

- author or contribute to enterprise design standards
- become involved in service delivery projects to ensure that agnostic services are properly positioned
- assess service runtime usage and determine required infrastructure
- evaluate security concerns of individual service capabilities
- help define and perhaps even own service inventory blueprints

As discussed in the *Governance Concerns* section of Chapter 9, the demand for enterprise-centric resources can dramatically increase in service-oriented environments. This may very well require that existing enterprise architecture groups be expanded.

In larger organizations there may also be the need for *enterprise domain architects*—a variation of this role that specializes in a particular segment of the overall enterprise. These architects would then be focused on the definition and governance of domain-specific service inventories.

Principles most associated with this role: All

Enterprise Design Standards Custodian (and Auditor)

As explained in the *Using Design Principles* section of Chapter 5, it is beneficial to derive design standards from service-orientation design principles so that the principles are consistently realized across all services.

Furthermore, as enterprise architecture groups grow in response to the changes incurred by an SOA transition, design standards can be authored by multiple experts, each contributing conventions associated with a particular aspect of service design (such as security, performance, transactions, etc.).

To ensure that design standards are kept in alignment and used wherever appropriate, it may very well be necessary to establish an official custodian. This individual would be responsible for the evolution of the design standards but also for their enforcement. Therefore, this role often involves performing audits of proposed service or service-oriented solution designs.

The authority required to carry out auditing responsibilities can sometimes raise concerns within IT environments not accustomed to such formal use of design standards. Therefore, this role can sometimes be more successfully established within the boundaries of a specific enterprise domain, where a given set of standards applies only to a specific domain service inventory, not the enterprise as a whole.

Principles most associated with this role: All

NOTE

This list does not represent all possible roles associated with an SOA transition initiative. A title dedicated to SOA Governance is planned for the *Prentice Hall Service-Oriented Computing Series from Thomas Erl* in which organizational roles will be comprehensively explored and defined and also associated with appropriate governance processes.

SUMMARY OF KEY POINTS

- Service-orientation brings with it a shift toward an enterprise-centric perspective when it comes to delivering solution logic.

- Various new roles can be defined in support of applying service-orientation principles in analysis, design, and governance capacities.

Chapter 16

Mapping Service-Orientation Principles to Strategic Goals

There is no better way to conclude this book than by leveraging everything that's been covered so far to establish concrete links between service-orientation design principles and the strategic goals and benefits of service-oriented computing and SOA.

Figure 16.1 lists the eight principles covered in Part II along with the primary goals first established in Chapter 3. The following sections represent these goals individually, and each contains a table that summarizes the relationship between a goal and related principles.

Although this information is supplied here for reference purposes, an understanding of these relationships helps provide further insight into the strategic significance of service-orientation.

16.1 Principles that Increase Intrinsic Interoperability

As was first established in Chapter 4, interoperability is a fundamental design characteristic fostered by all of the service-orientation design principles. Table 16.1 revisits this discussion by describing each principle's contribution to increasing the extent of intrinsic service interoperability.

Increased Inherent Interoperability	
Principle	**Relationship**
Standardized Service Contract	The fact that service contracts are consistently standardized guarantees a baseline measure of interoperability because of a natural compatibility between data models defined in technical service contracts.
Service Loose Coupling	Reducing the amount of required service coupling fosters interoperability by making individual services less dependent on each other and therefore more open to sharing data with different service consumers.

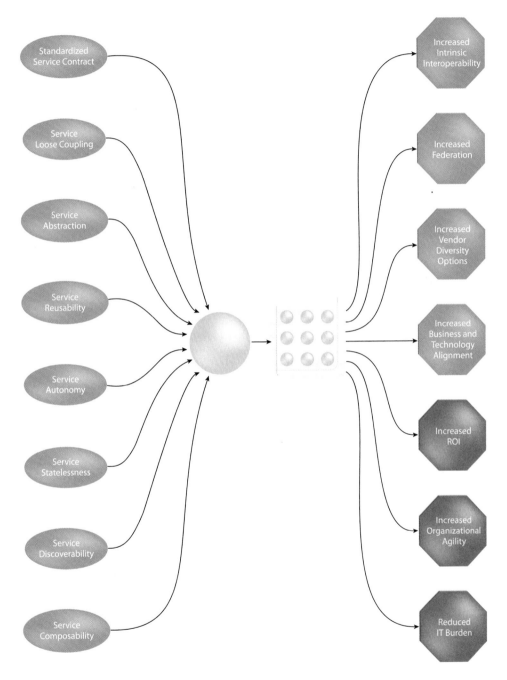

Figure 16.1

It can be helpful to understand how exactly service-orientation principles contribute to strategic service-oriented computing goals and benefits. This chapter explores these relationships.

Increased Inherent Interoperability	
Principle	**Relationship**
Service Abstraction	This principle results in the abstraction of service details, thereby limiting interoperation to the service contract. This increases a service's long-term interoperability potential by allowing its underlying logic to evolve more independently.
Service Reusability	Service Reusability considerations naturally increase interoperability as they outfit services with design characteristics geared for repeated usage by numerous service consumers (with which reusable services will need to effectively interoperate).
Service Autonomy	By increasing a service's individual autonomy it establishes itself as a more reliable enterprise resource with predictable runtime behavior. This, in turn, increases its attainable level of interoperability.
Service Statelessness	Through an emphasis on stateless design, the availability and scalability of services increase, allowing them to interoperate more frequently and reliably.
Service Discoverability	To enable interoperability between a service consumer and a service, the appropriate service must first be located. Therefore, application of the Service Discoverability principle increases the chances for a service to maximize its interoperability potential.
Service Composability	For services to be repeatedly composable, they must be highly interoperable. Therefore, shaping each service into an effective composition member increases its native ability to interoperate with others.

Table 16.1

How design principles foster specific design characteristics that can help increase native interoperability between services.

16.2 Principles that Increase Federation

Regardless of what lies beneath a given service, it is ideal to establish a highly federated service inventory where all proprietary and potentially disparate implementation details are blanketed with a standardized, harmonized service contract layer. Table 16.2 highlights the core three design principles that foster such an environment.

Increased Federation	
Principle	**Relationship**
Standardized Service Contract	By requiring the constant use of design standards that standardize the functional expression and data representation of service contracts, service inventories are guaranteed to infuse an enterprise with increased harmonization and federation.
Service Loose Coupling	A key objective of federation is to unify disparate environments while preserving their respective self-governance. By minimizing negative forms of coupling, this principle effectively increases the independence of each service implementation while supporting the overall goal of attaining federated interoperability between services.
Service Abstraction	Although the service contract layer of a service inventory needs to be federated, the underlying service implementations do not. To avoid issues that can lead to inventory governance challenges (and perhaps jeopardize the extent of attainable federation), this principle hides and protects information beyond the service contracts.

Table 16.2
How design principles can help increase the extent of achievable federation.

16.3 Principles that Increase Vendor Diversification Options

Positioning a service-oriented architecture to be vendor-agnostic enables an organization to leverage multiple vendor products and technologies, as required. Table 16.3 explains how select design principles help position services to fully leverage a vendor-neutral architecture.

Increased Vendor Diversification Options	
Principle	**Relationship**
Standardized Service Contract	By applying design standards to the service contract, we can avoid embedded characteristics that may be proprietary to an underlying vendor platform. Repeatedly doing so establishes a decoupled layer of service endpoints with no ties to vendor technology.
Service Loose Coupling	Any form of coupling by the service contract to proprietary or vendor-specific details is discouraged by this principle so as to alleviate service consumers from having to form negative dependencies. Therefore, Service Loose Coupling further reinforces the creation of a vendor-neutral service contract layer.
Service Abstraction	By shielding the outside world from service implementation details, vendor technology used to develop and host services is also hidden. This provides the greatest opportunity for future vendor diversification as individual service implementations can be upgraded or replaced with different vendor technologies, as required.
Service Autonomy	The more autonomous a service implementation is, the more control we have over how it can be evolved. Therefore, highly autonomous services provide the greatest amount of freedom for diversifying vendor technologies and products.

Table 16.3

How design principles can help increase available vendor diversification options.

16.4 Principles that Increase Business and Technology Domain Alignment

When we discuss the alignment of business and technology from a service-orientation perspective, we are mainly focused on the service-oriented analysis process. During this stage, business and technology experts collaborate to define conceptual service candidates.

In terms of synchronizing business logic through the encapsulation and expression of the physical services that will eventually be based on these candidates, we are primarily concerned with business services (based on task and entity service models). Table 16.4 focuses on how five particular principles support the alignment of business and technology, three of which are commonly associated with the service modeling process.

Increased Alignment of Business and Technology Domains	
Principle	**Relationship**
Standardized Service Contract	Service contracts are standardized via a custom design process that is based on the completion of a preceding analysis process during which services are jointly conceptualized by business and technology experts. This enables contracts to be shaped in accordance with well-defined and validated business service contexts that were created with the intention of unifying business and technology domains.
Service Reusability	Each of these three principles is taken into consideration during the service modeling sub-process of the service-oriented analysis process. Their application results in refined service candidates and service candidate capabilities. When applied to the definition of services with a business-centric context, each aids in the alignment between real-world business logic and the technology resources that will be used to express and implement this logic.
Service Autonomy	
Service Discoverability	
Service Composability	The fundamental ability to assemble services into endless composition configurations enables an organization to continually adjust its existing automation environments in response to and in support of changing business requirements. This provides the ultimate potential for enterprise technology resources to be consistently positioned in alignment with business requirements and directions.

Table 16.4

How design principles can support the continuous alignment of business and technology domains.

16.5 Principles that Increase ROI

All eight design principles support the potential for services to provide repeated financial returns. As explained in Table 16.5, an emphasis on ROI highlights the objective of service-orientation to maximize service reuse and recomposition capacity.

Increased ROI	
Principle	**Relationship**
Standardized Service Contract	When services are implemented with standardized contracts, they are naturally compatible and can therefore be repeatedly repurposed to help solve a range of business problems.
Service Loose Coupling	By ensuring that service consumers minimize service dependencies and avoid negative forms of service coupling, service owners are free to evolve services by changing or replacing their implementations. This allows services to be scaled and refactored in support of maximizing business requirements fulfillment for a range of consumers.
Service Abstraction	When services are treated more like black boxes, they can be governed with a greater degree of independence. As a result, service logic and implementation can be optimized and evolved to continually facilitate repeated reuse and recomposition.
Service Reusability	By applying commercial design considerations, agnostic services are turned into self-contained software units providing needed functionality in such a way that it can be repeatedly reused to automate different business processes.
Service Autonomy	Services with increased autonomy have the freedom to carry out their logic in a reliable and predictable manner. This establishes them as dependable enterprise resources that can be repeatedly leveraged for different purposes.

Increased ROI	
Principle	**Relationship**
Service Statelessness	To maximize the return on the investment of services requires that reuse and recomposition opportunities be leveraged wherever possible. By decreasing the periods during which services remain stateful, their scalability can be increased, thereby raising usage (and reuse) thresholds.
Service Discoverability	For agnostic services to be successfully reused, project teams need to be able to easily locate and understand their respective capabilities. The application of this principle minimizes risks associated with the miscommunication and misinterpretation of services.
Service Composability	Because services are specifically designed to act as effective composition members, all opportunities to enlist them into increasingly large and complex compositions can be explored. The more compositions a service can participate in, the more it will provide repeated value.

Table 16.5
How design principles can help increase the return on investment of services.

16.6 Principles that Increase Organizational Agility

As with other strategic goals, attaining a state of increased organizational responsiveness is a goal collectively achieved by applying all principles to a meaningful extent together with the various technology adoption and organizational changes required to fully support the delivered services in the long term. Table 16.6 describes how each principle plays its part to help increase business agility on an organizational level.

Increased Organizational Agility	
Principle	**Relationship**
Standardized Service Contract	Standardized service contracts overcome data representation disparity (which avoids data transformation requirements), as well as functional expression disparity (which improves design-time service utilization). These benefits allow for services to be more easily connected and composed, resulting in more efficient and effective business requirements fulfillment.
Service Loose Coupling	By freeing service consumers from having to couple to underlying service implementations, organizations have the freedom to evolve these implementations in response to changing business requirements. Due to the decoupling of the service contract from the implementation, changes can be accommodated more efficiently and with minimal impact on the rest of the enterprise.
Service Abstraction	The deliberate hiding of service implementation details leads to an environment where only service contracts and associated registry profile records officially describe the service. This further supports the autonomy with which service implementations can be augmented or even replaced in response to changing business requirements.
Service Reusability	With the increased emphasis on delivering reusable service capabilities, services are positioned as multi-purpose enterprise resources. As a result, more of the logic that already exists in reusable services can be re-leveraged to accommodate new or changing business requirements. This can dramatically reduce the scope of a development project, thereby also reducing the time and effort (and expense) of automating new business processes and fulfilling new business requirements.

Increased Organizational Agility	
Principle	**Relationship**
Service Autonomy	The gain in reliability and predictability resulting from increased levels of service autonomy directly supports the constant option to efficiently recompose and reposition services in response to changing business requirements.
Service Statelessness	Utilizing services to support a wide range of reuse and composition requirements can introduce high scalability demands. By minimizing a stateful condition, usage thresholds are increased, thereby making services more available for concurrent usage in support of repeated composition to efficiently accommodate business change.
Service Discoverability	By improving the communications quality of services, any and all opportunities to leverage their capabilities can be realized to accommodate existing and changing business requirements.
Service Composability	Ensuring that service capabilities are delivered as effective composition members guarantees that services will be able to participate in a wide variety of complex compositions and complex business processes. Ultimately, the ability to effectively compose and recompose services establishes the fundamental mechanics required for a service-oriented enterprise to efficiently respond to change.

Table 16.6
How design principles can help increase organizational agility.

16.7 Principles that Reduce the Overall Burden of IT

How service-orientation can contribute to the ultimate state of a streamlined IT enterprise is explored in Table 16.7.

Reduced IT Burden	
Principle	**Relationship**
Standardized Service Contract	By ensuring that services are naturally compatible and can be effectively reused and recomposed with minimal complexity (and minimal data transformation), this principle supports the reduction of logic redundancy and an increase in project delivery efficiency.
Service Loose Coupling Service Abstraction	The extent of service governance freedom attained by these two principles directly supports the ability to evolve service implementation environments without significantly impacting the rest of the enterprise (thereby avoiding traditional burdens associated with integration and platform replacement projects).
Service Reusability	By centralizing reusable services, logic redundancy can be dramatically reduced. When applied to significant portions of an enterprise, this effectively decreases the quantity of solution logic that needs to be hosted, governed, and maintained. As a result, the physical size of an IT enterprise can shrink, along with the effort and budget required to operate it.
Service Autonomy	The increased reliability achieved by autonomous services allows for them to be more effectively reused and recomposed, thereby supporting the goal of eliminating unnecessary redundant logic. Furthermore, the notion of a normalized service inventory is reinforced by autonomy-related design considerations.
Service Statelessness	Similarly, the increased scalability achieved by services designed to maximize statelessness allows for them to be more effectively reused and recomposed, thereby reducing infrastructure requirements and the need for red undant implementations.

Reduced IT Burden	
Principle	**Relationship**
Service Discoverability	By increasing the communications quality of service contracts and profiles, the cost and effort to discover and properly utilize reusable services is reduced. Because the risk of misinterpreting or not locating services is correspondingly decreased, the costs and complications that come with introducing unnecessary redundant logic into the enterprise are reduced.
Service Composability	Finally, through the fundamental ability to repeatedly compose services into new composition configurations, an unprecedented amount of reuse opportunities can be fulfilled. This principle essentially preserves the normalized service inventory perspective, thereby supporting the ultimate goal of streamlining IT as a whole.

Table 16.7

How design principles can help reduce the size and operational burden of an IT department.

Part IV

Appendices

Appendix A

Case Study Conclusion

The original goals set by the Cutit Saws organization related mostly to their desire to expand the company without having to repeatedly endure the constraints and efforts of extending their integrated custom application environment. Cutit was essentially concerned that if they did not improve the overall responsiveness of their organization, they would miss out on upcoming business opportunities. Growing the business over the next few years is especially important because of their plans to eventually make the company available for sale.

Cutit chose to invest in an SOA initiative to address these and other strategic issues. The initial project proceeded with a modest scope comprised of a high-level service inventory blueprint and the delivery of a small set of services. These services were built specifically in support of the Lab Project business process, which represents a key part of their R&D department.

During the design phase of this project, services were shaped according to service-orientation design principles, as documented at the end of each chapter in Part II.

This approach had the following overall results:

- Four Web services were delivered as part of a coordinated service composition that is automating the Lab Project business process as expected.

- Three of the four Web services are entity services offering operations that are agnostic to the Lab Project process and therefore provide functionality that can be reused in support of additional business processes.

- The four Web services collectively establish the beginning of a service inventory. Each expresses a federated service contract that abstracts its underlying implementation, thereby giving Cutit the freedom to evolve the services individually in the future.

- The effort and cost of delivering these services exceeded the amounts normally allocated for an equivalent quantity of solution logic during past delivery projects. These numbers were further increased when combined with the time and money spent on the up-front analysis required to define a high-level service inventory blueprint. Cutit justified this initial overhead as an investment required to work toward the more agile and cost-effective enterprise environment they are seeking to establish.

By participating in the hands-on design of service-oriented solution logic, the Cutit team gained real-world experience that will prove valuable for subsequent service delivery projects. Overall, this first step toward realizing a standardized service inventory and architecture has established an important foundation that future projects can continue to build on.

Note that this storyline continues in the book *SOA: Design Patterns* where Cutit Saws becomes one of three organizations for which case study examples are provided.

Appendix B

Process Descriptions

This appendix contains illustrations and brief descriptions of processes associated with the analysis, design, and overall delivery of services. This information is provided here for reference purposes only. Most of the process steps are described in detail and further supplemented with case study and contract code examples in the book *Service-Oriented Architecture: Concepts, Technology, and Design*. Note that this content is regularly updated and refined as part of a mainstream SOA methodology. Earlier print runs of *Service-Oriented Architecture: Concepts, Technology, and Design* contain variations of these processes.

Also if you haven't already, it is recommended that you read through the brief process introductions provided in the *Service-Oriented Analysis and Service Modeling* and *Service-Oriented Design* sections located in Chapter 3.

B.1 Delivery Processes

Bottom-Up vs. Top-Down

There are several project delivery approaches that can be employed to build services. The bottom-up strategy, for example, is tactically focused in that it makes the fulfillment of immediate business requirements a priority and the prime objective of the project. On the other side of the spectrum is the top-down strategy, which advocates the completion of an inventory analysis prior to the physical design, development, and delivery of services.

As shown in Figure B.1, each approach has its own benefits and consequences. While the bottom-up strategy avoids the extra cost, effort, and time required to deliver services via a top-down approach, it ends up imposing increased governance burden as bottom-up delivered services tend to have shorter lifespans and require more frequent maintenance, refactoring, and versioning.

The top-down strategy demands more of an initial investment because it introduces an up-front analysis stage focused on the creation of the service inventory blueprint. Service candidates are individually defined as part of this blueprint so as to ensure that subsequent service designs will be highly normalized, standardized, and aligned.

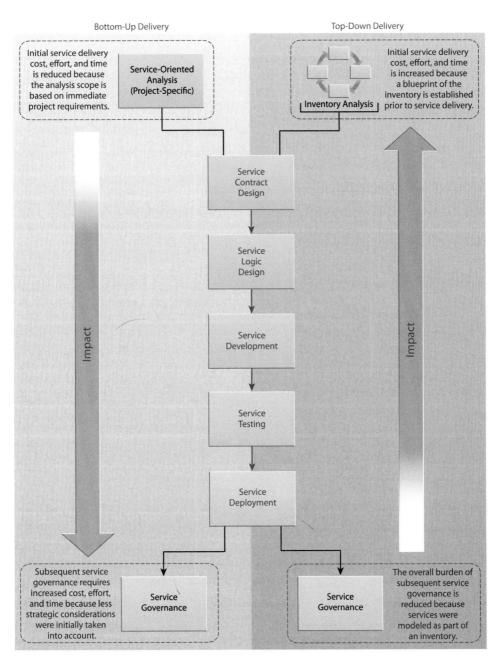

Figure B.1
A comparison of bottom-up and top-down delivery strategies.

The Inventory Analysis Cycle

Figure B.2 illustrates how the inventory analysis part of the top-down delivery process is comprised of an iterative cycle during which the inventory blueprint is incrementally defined as a result of repeated iterations. The following sections describe each step in this cycle.

Define Enterprise Business Models

Many of the services that will eventually be modeled and designed will be business services responsible for accurately encapsulating and expressing business logic. Therefore, a key input for this process is a comprehensive, up-to-date set of business models and specifications (such as business process definitions, business entity models, logical data models, etc.). The amount of business documentation required is determined by the scope of the planned service inventory.

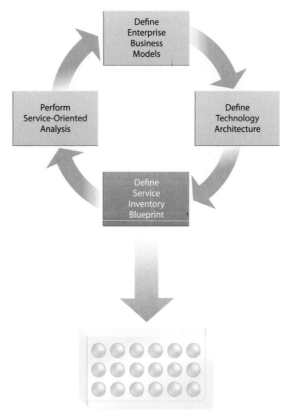

Figure B.2

Common process steps for the inventory analysis. Iterations through this cycle result in the definition and population of a service inventory blueprint.

Define Technology Architecture

An initial technology architecture platform is required to understand any features or constraints that could affect the definition of service candidates. As iterations through the analysis steps are completed, there is opportunity to refine the planned technology architecture to whatever extent feasible in response to the evolving complexion of the service inventory blueprint.

Define Service Inventory Blueprint

During the first iteration, the blueprint needs to be established with predefined service models and a physical service inventory boundary. Subsequently, as the service-oriented analysis process is carried out for each business process definition, service candidates are produced and begin populating the inventory blueprint.

Perform Service-Oriented Analysis

This process is explained in the upcoming *Service-Oriented Analysis Process* section.

Inventory Analysis and Service-Oriented Design

As shown in Figure B.3, service-oriented design represents a separate process that is initiated at whatever point an organization is ready to proceed to the physical design of service contracts. This step is explained in the *Service-Oriented Design Processes* section in this appendix.

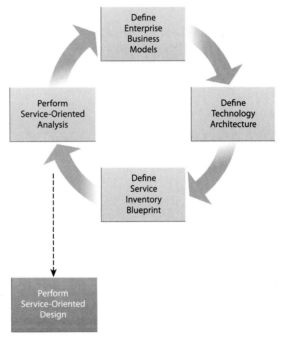

Choosing a Delivery Strategy

To realize the strategic goals associated with service-oriented computing, carrying out a meaningful extent of top-down delivery is generally required. This does not necessarily mean that *all* possible up-front analysis be completed prior to service delivery.

Top-down requirements need to be weighed against an organization's tactical priorities. While some can define a comprehensive inventory blueprint in advance, others may only be able to create a high-level service blueprint before heading into the service design phase. Yet another approach is to carry out a full inventory analysis but reduce the scope and size of the planned inventory.

Figure B.3

The service-oriented design process is carried out when the organization has decided it is time to begin creating physical service contract designs.

Alternative processes can also be considered, such as the meet-in-the-middle strategy (also known as *agile delivery*). This approach allows for an on-going analysis and definition of a service inventory blueprint, while high-priority services are delivered in advance. At a later point, after the analysis efforts have sufficiently progressed, services that have been previously deployed are revisited. If necessary, they are then redeveloped and brought in alignment with the revised blueprint.

Choosing a delivery approach is a critical decision point because it represents a decision an organization will usually need to live with for quite some time.

B.2 Service-Oriented Analysis Process

A separate analysis is dedicated to each business process definition associated with a given service inventory. For the full definition of a service inventory blueprint, a complete top-down delivery process is carried out, comprised of numerous iterations through service-oriented analysis process steps.

Figure B.4 and the following sections explain how service-oriented analysis actually represents a parent process consisting of two information gathering steps and then a third step represented by the service modeling sub-process.

Define Analysis Scope

During this step business analysts are asked to clearly establish the boundary of the analysis. Most commonly, there is a ratio of one analysis process to one business process definition. However, business processes can be complex or multi-layered (containing nested processes) and may or may not already be representing portions of business logic already analyzed during a previous iteration of the service inventory analysis cycle. Therefore, this step may also require identifying portions of a given business process for which service modeling is not required.

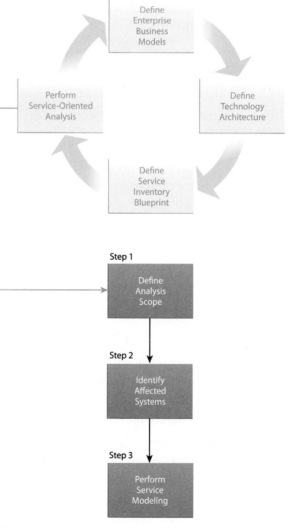

Figure B.4
A high-level service-oriented analysis process.

Identify Affected Systems

It is helpful to have an understanding of what existing parts of the enterprise will be affected by the scope of the planned business process analysis. Especially relevant are legacy systems that may later raise service encapsulation and autonomy challenges. These types of constraints can directly impact the partitioning of logic into services and the ultimate granularity at which service candidates are defined.

Perform Service Modeling

This step represents the service modeling process, as explained in the following section.

B.3 Service Modeling Process

Service modeling is the process of conceptualizing services and capabilities prior to their actual physical definition and development. Because nothing concrete is defined during this stage, we qualify the results of carrying out this process with the term "candidate." Service modeling essentially identifies service capability candidates that are grouped into service candidates that are subsequently assembled into service composition candidates.

The iterative nature of the aforementioned inventory analysis allows for service candidates to be repeatedly revised and refined prior to the creation of corresponding services.

The service modeling steps displayed in Figure B.5 are too detailed to describe individually in this appendix. In a nutshell, a business process definition is decomposed (Step 1) into its most detailed representation, resulting in a series of granular actions. Those suitable for service encapsulation become potential service capability candidates (Step 2).

The service logic of each capability candidate is assessed in terms of whether it is specific or agnostic to the current business process. Agnostic capability candidates are grouped into agnostic service candidates usually based on entity and utility service models (Step 3), whereas non-agnostic capability candidates are placed into a task service candidate with a functional scope usually equivalent to the business process (Step 4).

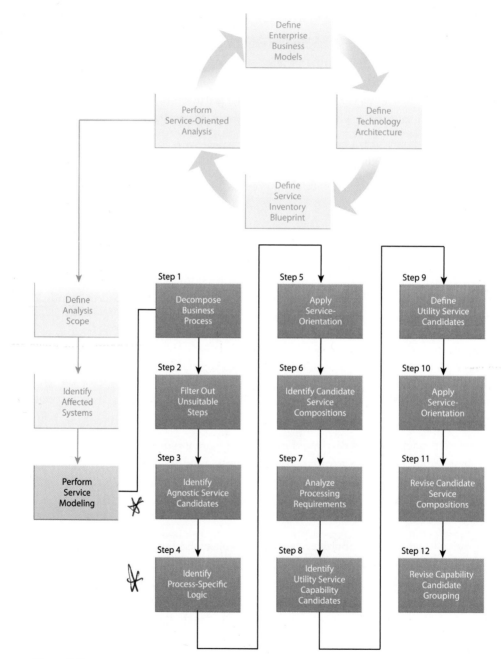

Figure B.5

A common service modeling process.

During subsequent iterations of this process, the chances of identifying already defined capability candidates increase. Therefore, a separate discovery step (not shown) is added to ensure that no redundant capability or service candidates are introduced into the blueprint. Also select service-orientation principles are applied to shape modeled service candidates in preparation for their eventual designs (Step 5).

The following three service-orientation principles are typically applied during the service modeling process:

- Service Reusability

- Service Autonomy

- Service Discoverability

How these principles relate to this process is explained in the *[Principle Name] and Service Modeling* section within the corresponding chapters (9, 10, and 12).

After the initial set of service candidates is established, a candidate composition is assembled and subjected to possible runtime scenarios (Step 6). Subsequently, each of the identified service capability candidates is further studied to explore any additional processing requirements that may be needed to carry out its functionality. This kicks off the second half of the service modeling process (Steps 7–12) during which additional utility service capability candidates are generally defined. The process ends with an extended composition candidate modeling step and a final revision of all capability and service candidate definitions created so far.

B.4 Service-Oriented Design Processes

All of the effort put into the analysis and service modeling processes results in a collection of service candidates that establishes the starting point for service design. Every candidate definition can be used as input for a service-oriented design process. A different process exists for each of the four primary service models, but all are shaped and structured around the application of service-orientation design principles. Unlike the service modeling process where only a subset of the principles come into play, all eight principles are fully applied during service design.

Design Processes and Service Models

As shown in Figure B.6, there is a suggested sequence in which services can be designed, based on their respective service models. Entity services have the most independence because they derive their functional context from predefined business entities. Prior service modeling efforts will have ideally established refined and balanced entity service candidates with appropriate levels of service and capability granularity.

Utility services are typically designed next. Even though they don't have the benefit of pre-defined functional contexts and are therefore more difficult to create, they still can be delivered independently due to the fact that they typically encapsulate agnostic functionality.

A further benefit to designing and even delivering entity and utility services first is that they can be tested independently as generic, reusable resources. When task-centric services are delivered thereafter, they can immediately be designed to bind to the agnostic service contracts to finalize the required composition logic.

This sequence is only suggested and not required. There may be circumstances during which it makes more sense to change the order in which services are designed or to design and deliver a group of services simultaneously.

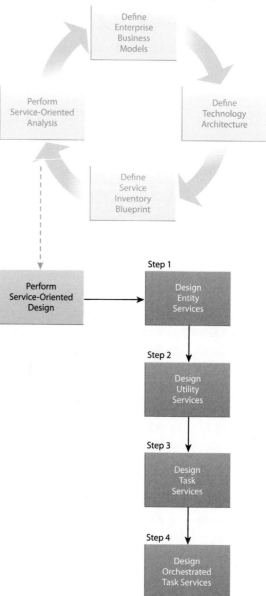

Figure B.6
Common service-oriented design processes.

The individual service design processes are too detailed to be included in this appendix. Many design considerations are taken into account, shaping a service contract in support of standards, principles, and practical constraints.

When building services as Web services, these processes essentially advocate defining the required XML schema complex types first to ensure consistency with other service contracts that may be using the same set of standardized schemas. An abstract WSDL definition is then built around the complex types and further adjusted and optimized by the application of service-orientation principles and design standards.

For agnostic services, these processes raise special considerations associated with the extension of planned service logic in support of increased reusability potential. Finally, other services required to carry out the defined Web service operations are also identified, as per previously modeled composition candidates.

Each service model has unique design requirements, which is why each deserves its own design process. Task-centric service design processes have less emphasis on exploring reusability and are more concentrated on the service's role as parent controller. Design processes for orchestrated task services tend to be distinct in that they generally require the design of service-oriented business processes which, in the Web services world, usually involves the creation of WS-BPEL process definitions.

Service Design Processes and Service-Orientation

The design of services is carried out in two specific phases. The service contract design process represents the first stage during which the technical contract is created, standardized, and finalized. This stage may involve the delivery of a series of contracts or just one, depending on the scope of the service delivery project and the overall methodology being used. At some point thereafter, the actual service logic is designed and then developed in support of the contract. Figure B.7 illustrates this simple but important sequence and also reminds us that service-orientation applies to both stages of service design.

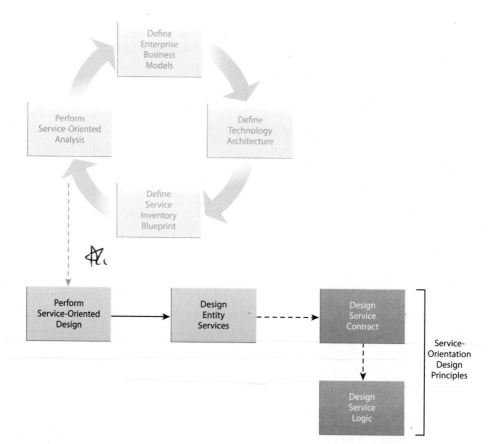

Figure B.7

An example of how the design of an entity service is partitioned into contract and logic design stages, both of which are shaped by service-orientation design principles.

NOTE
All of the processes described in this appendix are generic and should be considered starting points only. Analysis and design processes will almost always require further customization in order for them to be successfully incorporated within an organization's existing delivery processes and methodologies.

Appendix C

Principles and Patterns Cross-Reference

S OA: *Design Patterns* is a book dedicated to providing a set of service and architectural design pattern catalogs and languages. Because it was written together with *SOA: Principles of Service Design*, there was an opportunity to provide references to a modest subset of its pattern collection within several of the preceding chapters.

For quick reference purposes, Table C.1 provides an alphabetical list of referenced patterns, along with pointers as to where they are described. Note that a bold entry represents a section that introduces a design pattern by providing a brief description.

Design Pattern	Referenced
Contract Centralization	**Chapter 7, *Standardized Service Coupling and Contract Centralization***
	Chapter 7, *Consumer-to-Contract Coupling*
	Chapter 7, *Measuring Consumer Coupling*
	Chapter 7, *Service Loose Coupling and Service Design*
	Chapter 8, *Profiling this Principle (For Example section)*
	Chapter 9, *Logic Centralization and Contract Centralization*
Contract Denormalization	Chapter 6, *How Standardized Service Contract Design Affects Other Principles*
	Chapter 7, *Service Loose Coupling and Service Granularity*
	Chapter 8, *Multi-Consumer Coupling Requirements*
	Chapter 9, *Service Reusability and Service Granularity*
	Chapter 10, *Service Contract Autonomy (services with normalized contracts)*
	Chapter 10, *Service Autonomy and Service Granularity*

Design Pattern	Referenced
Domain Inventory	Chapter 6, *Standardization of Service Data Representation* Chapter 9, *Challenges to Achieving Logic Centralization*
Logic Centralization	Chapter 7, *Service Consumer Coupling Types* **Chapter 9, Standardized Service Reuse and Logic Centralization** Chapter 9, *Service Reusability and Service Modeling* Chapter 9, *How Service Reusability Affects Other Principles* Chapter 9, *Cultural Concerns* Chapter 9, *Governance Concerns* Chapter 10, *Service Contract Autonomy (services with normalized contracts)*
Schema Centralization	**Chapter 6, Standardization of Service Data Representation** Chapter 6, *Case Study Example*
Service Façade	Chapter 7, Limitations of Logic-to-Contract Coupling **Chapter 14, Guidelines for Designing Service-Oriented Classes**
Service Normalization	Chapter 9, *Understanding Logic Centralization* **Chapter 10, Service Contract Autonomy (services with normalized contracts)**
Validation Abstraction	Chapter 6, *Standardization and Service Granularity* Chapter 7, *Consumer-to-Contract Coupling* Chapter 8, *Service Abstraction and Service Granularity*

Table C.1
The primary patterns referenced in this book and pointers as to where these references are located.

SOA: Design Patterns is a title available as part of the *Prentice Hall Service-Oriented Computing Series from Thomas Erl*. See www.soabooks.com for more information.

Additional Resources

Following is a list of resource Web sites that provide supplementary content for books in this series. If you'd like to be automatically notified of new book releases, new supplementary content for this title, or key changes to these Web sites, send a blank e-mail to `notify@soabooks.com`.

`www.soabooks.com`

The official site of the *Prentice Hall Service-Oriented Computing Series from Thomas Erl*. Numerous resources are provided, including sample chapters from available books and updates and corrections.

`www.soamag.com`

This site is the home of *The SOA Magazine*, a monthly publication officially associated with this book series. This magazine is dedicated to publishing specialized articles, case studies, and papers that explore various aspects of service-oriented computing.

`www.soaglossary.com`

A master glossary for all books in the *Prentice Hall Service-Oriented Computing Series by Thomas Erl* is hosted by this site. SOAGlossary.com is expected to steadily grow as new titles are developed and released.

`www.soaspecs.com`

This Web site establishes a convenient central portal to industry standards and specifications covered or referenced by titles in this book series.

`www.soaposters.com`	If you are interested in ordering reference posters for books in this series, visit this site for a preview and further details.
`www.ws-standards.com`	A series of concise tutorials about various first- and second-generation Web services technologies is provided at this site. It can be beneficial to read these introductory articles prior to studying the actual Web services specification.
`www.xmlenterprise.com`	A set of short tutorials focused on XML and XML-related technologies. If you are unfamiliar with XML, it is recommended you read through these articles prior to learning about Web services.

About the Author

Thomas Erl is the world's top-selling SOA author, the Series Editor of the *Prentice Hall Service-Oriented Computing Series from Thomas Erl*, and Editor of *The SOA Magazine*.

With over 70,000 copies in print, his first two books, *Service-Oriented Architecture: A Field Guide to Integrating XML and Web Services* and *Service-Oriented Architecture: Concepts, Technology, and Design* have become international bestsellers and have been translated into several languages. Books by Thomas Erl have been formally reviewed and endorsed by senior members of major software organizations, including IBM, Sun, Microsoft, Oracle, BEA, HP, SAP, Google, and Intel.

Thomas is also the founder of SOA Systems Inc. (www.soasystems.com), a company specializing in SOA training and strategic consulting services with a vendor-agnostic focus. Through his work with standards organizations and independent research efforts, Thomas has made significant contributions to the SOA industry, most notably in the areas of service-orientation and SOA methodology.

Thomas is a speaker and instructor for private and public events, and has delivered many workshops and keynote speeches. He has also developed an industry-recognized SOA training and certification program. For more information, see www.soaschool.com and www.soatraining.com.

Papers and articles written by Thomas have been published in numerous industry trade magazines and Web sites, and he has delivered Webcasts and interviews for many publications, including the *Wall Street Journal*.

For more information, visit www.thomaserl.com.

About the Photographs

Matching photos to chapters has become an interesting process for me and one of the few occasions during which I get to marry art with technology. The front cover photo and the photos used throughout the divider pages in this book display more examples of modern architecture when compared to previous titles. The primary reason for this was because they better express the "feel" of this book due to its emphasis on the application of modern service engineering design techniques.

I took these photos during visits to Tallinn, Bangkok, Hong Kong, Singapore, Vienna, Chicago, Washington, and Salt Lake City.

Index

BOOKS ONLINE
ENABLED

THIS BOOK IS SAFARI ENABLED

INCLUDES FREE 45-DAY ACCESS TO THE ONLINE EDITION

The Safari® Enabled icon on the cover of your favorite technology book means the book is available through Safari Bookshelf. When you buy this book, you get free access to the online edition for 45 days.

Safari Bookshelf is an electronic reference library that lets you easily search thousands of technical books, find code samples, download chapters, and access technical information whenever and wherever you need it.

TO GAIN 45-DAY SAFARI ENABLED ACCESS TO THIS BOOK:

● Go to **http://www.prenhallprofessional.com/safarienabled**

● Complete the brief registration form

● Enter the coupon code found in the front of this book on the "Copyright" page

PRENTICE HALL

If you have difficulty registering on Safari Bookshelf or accessing the online edition, please e-mail customer-service@safaribooksonline.com.

SOA Training & Certification

Content from this book and other series titles has been incorporated into an industry-recognized SOA training and certification program developed by author Thomas Erl and provided by SOA Systems Inc. This program is comprised of a collection of courses, seminars, and workshop labs that can be taken with or without formal testing and certification.

Available certification designations include:
• Certified SOA Consultant
• Certified SOA Analyst
• Certified SOA Architect

Program content and testing requirements are reviewed by a committee consisting of members from major SOA organizations and academic institutions. All courses are revised on a quarterly basis to stay in alignment with industry developments.

For more information visit www.soaschool.com and www.soatraining.com.

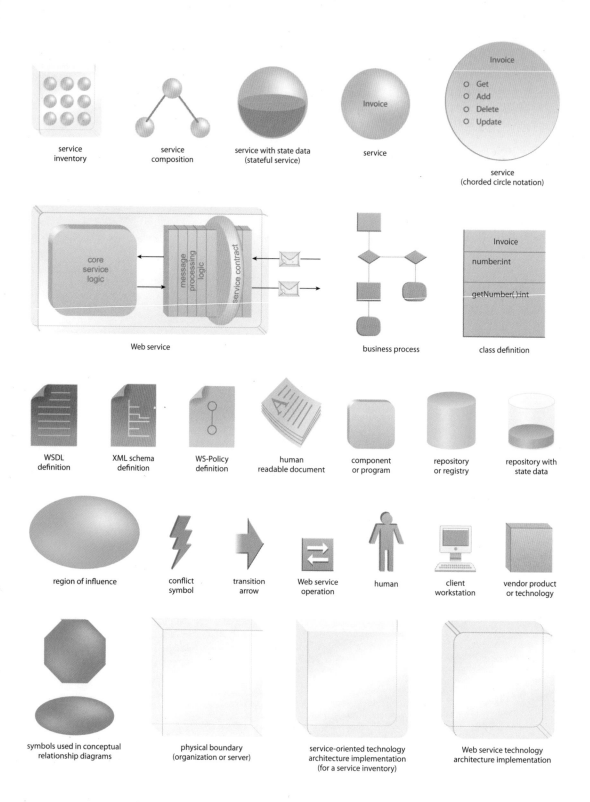

service
inventory

service
composition

service with state data
(stateful service)

service

Invoice

○ Get
○ Add
○ Delete
○ Update

service
(chorded circle notation)

core
service
logic

message
processing
logic

Service contract

Web service

business process

Invoice

number:int

getNumber( ):int

class definition

WSDL
definition

XML schema
definition

WS-Policy
definition

human
readable document

component
or program

repository
or registry

repository with
state data

region of influence

conflict
symbol

transition
arrow

Web service
operation

human

client
workstation

vendor product
or technology

symbols used in conceptual
relationship diagrams

physical boundary
(organization or server)

service-oriented technology
architecture implementation
(for a service inventory)

Web service technology
architecture implementation